THE VITAL PAST

THE VITAL PAST

Writings on the Uses of History

EDITED BY STEPHEN VAUGHN

THE UNIVERSITY OF GEORGIA PRESS Athens

© 1985 by the University of Georgia Press
Athens, Georgia 30602
All rights reserved

Designed by Kathi L. Dailey
Set in 10 on 13 Linotron Trump Medieval
with Weiss display

The paper in this book meets the guidelines for
permanence and durability of the Committee on
Production Guidelines for Book Longevity of the
Council on Library Resources.

Printed in the United States of America

89 88 87 86 85   5 4 3 2 1

Library of Congress Cataloging in Publication Data

Main entry under title:

The Vital past.

Includes index.
1. History—Philosophy—Addresses, essays, lectures.
2. History—Study and teaching—Addresses, essays,
lectures.   I. Vaughn, Stephen, 1947–
D16.8.V52   1985   901   84-16204
ISBN 0-8203-0753-X
ISBN 0-8203-0754-8 (pbk.)

CONTENTS

Contents | vii

PREFACE

*T*hree factors led to this book. The first was the curiosity that most people have about their profession. To have been an historian in the 1970s, when teaching and research positions were virtually nonexistent, required more than passing interest in the subject. Second, my curiosity coincided with working for the Organization of American Historians. In the late 1970s under Richard S. Kirkendall, then executive secretary, the OAH sought to reverse the decline of history teaching in the public schools. To many people it was unclear why this decline had occurred. Finally, in 1981 I began teaching history in the School of Journalism and Mass Communication at the University of Wisconsin and there confronted different problems. Journalism by its nature is preoccupied with the present. Yesterday's newspaper is "old news." How to convince people who were, or would be, working in the media that events decades or even centuries ago were relevant to their endeavors was at once challenging and stimulating.

The selections in this volume help explain the value of history. All, of course, postdate the Industrial Revolution, which unleashed forces that transformed the world and made the present age appear radically different from what went before. Most of these essays were written in the nuclear era. The substantial number of works defending history since the middle of our century suggests that historians have not been unmindful of the changes of their own time.

Undoubtedly writings do not appear in this book that others might have chosen. I have used notes throughout to suggest additional readings. This volume does not deal with methodology per se, nor is it directed to other historians, although many surely will enjoy rereading some of the selections. Rather, the book seeks to reach a wider audience, one that may be skeptical about studying the past and uncertain of what history has to offer a rapidly changing world. Invariably the shortcomings of this work reflect my own limited expertise as evidenced by the lack of selections from such areas as the Soviet Union, China, and Africa. A range of writers nevertheless appears, and no conscious effort has been made to limit selections by ideology, politics, nationality, race, or sex.

The object has been to stimulate, to give insight into the excitement and worth of the past. Selections organize around the heads of "History and the Individual" and "History and Society," with sub-heads under each theme. The reader will discover, however, that few essays fit neatly under any one heading and that most cut across several themes. That some themes are repetitive suggests that there is common ground among historians on the value of their craft.

Most of the selections have been shortened, and footnotes have been eliminated except where they point to further readings on the uses of history. Readers are encouraged to look at the writings in their original form.

I wish to thank many friends who read and commented on all or parts of the volume: James L. Baughman, Maurice Baxter, Allan Bogue, Richard Maxwell Brown, William Cohen, Carl Degler, Rufus Fears, Robert H. Ferrell, Lawrence de Graaf, Paul Holbo, Suellen Hoy, Robert Kelley, Richard S. Kirkendall, Gerda Lerner, Forrest McDonald, Jack McLeod, Harold L. Nelson, Boyd C. Shafer, MaryAnn Yodelis Smith, Lester Stephens, Beverly M. Vaughn, Charles Weeks, Robert W. Wiebe, and Allan Winkler. I owe a special thank you to Mary Kuusisto, Susan Dewane, and Virginia Trapino for typing.

A grant from the University of Wisconsin made possible the final revision of this work. I am also especially grateful to my colleagues in Madison for their unfailing interest, support, and encouragement.

Finally, thanks go to the many presses and journals that permitted reprinting.

ACKNOWLEDGMENTS

The editor and the publisher gratefully acknowledge the publications in which the essays in this book first appeared.

Carl L. Becker, "Everyman His Own Historian," *American Historical Review* 37, no. 2 (January 1932): 221–36.

Herbert Butterfield, "The Dangers of History," in *History and Human Relations* (London: Collins, 1951).

Henry Steele Commager, "The Nature of History," in *The Nature and the Study of History* (Columbus, Ohio: Charles E. Merrill, 1965).

Donald M. Dozer, "History as Force," *Pacific Historical Review* 34, no. 4 (November 1965): 375–95. © 1965 by The Pacific Coast Branch, American Historical Association. Reprinted by permission of The Branch.

G. R. Elton, "Putting the Past Before Us," review of *The Teaching of History*, by Dennis Gunning, *Times Literary Supplement*, September 8, 1978.

David Hackett Fischer, *Historians' Fallacies: Toward a Logic of Historical Thought* (New York: Harper and Row, 1970). Copyright © 1970 by David Hackett Fischer. Abridged selection (pp. 307–18) reprinted by permission of Harper and Row, Publishers, Inc.

John Hope Franklin, "The Historian and Public Policy," *The History Teacher* 11, no. 3 (May 1978): 377–91. © 1978 by the University of Chicago. Reprinted by permission of the author.

W. B. Gallie, "The Uses and Abuses of History," in *Philosophy and the Historical Understanding* (New York: Schocken Books, 1964).

Colin B. Goodykoontz, "The Founding Fathers and Clio," *Pacific Historical Review* 23, no. 2 (May 1954): 111–21, 123. © 1954 by The Pacific Coast Branch, American Historical Association. Reprinted by permission of The Branch.

Otis L. Graham, Jr., "The Uses and Misuses of History: Roles in

Policymaking," *The Public Historian* 5, no. 2 (Spring 1983): 5–19. © 1983 by The Regents of the University of California. Reprinted by permission of The Regents and the author.

Carl G. Gustavson, "A Most Dangerous Product: History," in *The Mansion of History* (New York: McGraw-Hill, 1976).

Harold J. Hanham, "History," *Harvard University Handbook for Undergraduates*, Spring 1972, 70–72.

Philip D. Jordan, "The Usefulness of Useless Knowledge," *The Historian* 22, no. 3 (May 1960): 237–49.

Michael Kammen, "On Knowing the Past," *New York Times*, February 6, 1979, A17. © 1979 by The New York Times Company. Reprinted by permission.

George F. Kennan, "The Experience of Writing History," *Virginia Quarterly Review* 36, no. 2 (Spring 1960): 205–14. Reprinted by permission.

George O. Kent, "Clio the Tyrant: Historical Analogies and the Meaning of History," *The Historian* 32, no. 1 (November 1969): 99–106.

David S. Landes and Charles Tilly, "What Is History?" in *History as Social Science*, ed. Landes and Tilly (Englewood Cliffs, N.J.: Prentice-Hall, 1971).

Gordon Leff, "The Past and the New," *The Listener* 10 (April 1969): 485–87. Reprinted by permission of the author.

Gerda Lerner, "The Necessity of History and the Professional Historian," *Journal of American History* 69, no. 1 (June 1982): 7–20.

Allan J. Lichtman and Valerie French, "Past and Present: History and Contemporary Analysis," in *Historians and the Living Past: The Theory and Practice of Historical Study*, ed. Lichtman and French (Arlington Heights, Ill.: AHM, 1978), 1–2, 3–13. Reprinted by permission of the publisher, Harlan Davidson, Inc.

Henri-Irénée Marrou, "The Usefulness of History," in *The Meaning of History*, trans. Robert J. Olsen (Baltimore: Helicon, 1966).

Allan Nevins, "A Proud Word for History," in *The Gateway to History*, rev. ed. (Chicago: Quadrangle Books, 1963). Reprinted by permission of The Trustees of Columbia University in the City of New York.

Harold Perkin, "The Uses of History," in *History: An Outline for the Intending Student*, ed. Perkin (London: Routledge and Kegan Paul, 1970).

David Pratt, "The Functions of Teaching History," *The History Teacher* 7, no. 3 (May 1974): 410–25.

Arthur M. Schlesinger, Jr., "The Inscrutability of History," *Encounter* 27 (November 1966): 10–17. Reprinted by permission of the author.

Boyd C. Shafer, "History, Not Art, Not Science, but History: Meanings and Uses of History," *Pacific Historical Review* 29, no. 2 (May 1960): 159–70. © 1960 by The Pacific Coast Branch, American Historical Association. Reprinted by permission of The Branch and the author.

Lester D. Stephens, "The Uses of History" and "Lessons, Analogies, and Prediction," in *Probing the Past: A Guide to the Study and Teaching of History* (Boston: Allyn and Bacon, 1974). Reprinted by permission of the author.

David F. Trask, "A Reflection on Historians and Policymakers," *The History Teacher* 11, no. 2 (February 1978): 219–26.

George Macaulay Trevelyan, "Clio, a Muse," in *Clio, a Muse, and Other Essays Literary and Pedestrian* (New York: Longmans, Green, 1914).

Barbara W. Tuchman, "Is History a Guide to the Future?" in *Practicing History: Selected Essays* (New York: Alfred A. Knopf, 1981).

Frederick Jackson Turner, "The Significance of History," in *The Early Writings of Frederick Jackson Turner, with a List of All His Works*, comp. Everett E. Edwards (Madison: University of Wisconsin Press, 1938).

Stephen Vaughn, "History: Is It Relevant?" *Social Studies* 74, no. 2 (March–April 1983): 56–61.

Howard Zinn, "What Is Radical History?" in *The Politics of History* (Boston: Beacon Press, 1970). Copyright © 1970 by Howard Zinn. Reprinted by permission of Beacon Press and the author.

THE VITAL PAST

INTRODUCTION

History: Is It Relevant?

Stephen Vaughn

How valuable is history for our generation? This book attempts to answer that question and in so doing to provide a rationale for studying the past. On the surface this undertaking is not as easy as it once might have been, for there is a widespread belief that history may no longer be relevant to modern life. We live, after all, in an age that appears radically different from the world that came before us. Nuclear weapons, genetic engineering, jet transportation, space travel, a communications revolution (need one mention more?) have transformed our planet. We have more information about the world at our disposal than ever before, and that information grows daily at a staggering rate. Scientific knowledge doubles, we are told, in less than a decade, and thousands of books are published each year in the English language alone. Truly, our age is like no other.

But ours is not the first generation to consider itself unique and to believe that its problems are of greater significance than those of earlier times. Hear the historian Polybius, more than a century before Christ: "For in all the vast variety of disorder, struggles, changes, which the power of this deity introduces into human life, we shall find none equal to . . . none worthy to be compared for their importance with those events which have happened in the present age."[1]

Nor is our generation apparently the first to manifest skepticism about the past. There have always been people who doubted the value of history. Everyone knows that the French Encyclopedist Voltaire declared history "but a pack of tricks we play on the dead." The poet Carl Sandburg called the past "a bucket of ashes." The automobile maker Henry Ford asserted that "history is bunk." Friedrich Nietzsche, the German philosopher, argued that history overwhelmed weak minds, burdened the human spirit, and hindered freedom; and the French writer Paul Valéry suggested that the past filled people's heads with "false memories" and encouraged "either a delirium of grandeur or a delusion of persecution." Forces always seem at work undermining an appreciation of history. Some of these forces are peculiarly American; others no doubt exist in virtually all industrial and postindustrial societies.

Americans especially have put a premium on becoming rather than being. A part of their history appears to have been a repudiation of the past. For many people the American Revolution meant freedom from both the Old World and colonial history and suggested that the nation's promise lay in the present and future. "The earth belongs always to the living generation," Thomas Jefferson reminded James Madison, and "the dead have neither powers nor rights over it." Throughout the nineteenth century, history frequently seemed a hindrance to a practical-minded, problem-solving people. "The dogmas of the quiet past are inadequate to the stormy present," Abraham Lincoln lamented during the Civil War. "As our case is new, so we must think anew, and act anew." Later, near the end of the century, the novelist William Dean Howells beheld "no past for us; there is only a future."

How do we account for these unhistorical attitudes? In the cases of Ford and Jefferson such remarks may not reflect their real opinions about history.[2] But taken as a whole these statements do say something. They reflect sentiments that many people share about the past. For some, history is truly what George Macaulay Trevelyan called the "black night of the utterly forgotten." No simple explanations account for why this should be, but one thinks of the absence of a strong conservative tradition, the frontier with its emphasis on rugged individualism, the belief expressed by Ralph Waldo Emerson and others that Nature and personal experience made tradition irrelevant, and the appearance of millions of immigrants from diverse backgrounds lacking a shared history. Other developments, many of which are not confined to the United States, have influenced think-

ing about history. The growth of cities, of industry, and of technology—all have dramatically changed our world. They have transformed the natural landscape, substituting an artificial environment. The city with its fevered activity, its ever-changing landmarks, may nullify the past. Life here has been called "a kind of
prolonged today" symbolized by the daily newspaper. More than one
observer has commented on the rejection of history or at least alienation from the past in much of the modern art and architecture of
urban areas. So drastic has been this break from earlier times, this
"great mutation," as one president of the American Historical Association called it, that some fear it has made the connection between
the recent and distant pasts impossible, inflicting a form of historical amnesia on present-day mankind.[3]

But more than physical changes have been involved. People in industrial, urban societies frequently think of time in a manner that
obscures the past. Attention is focused on the present, which is
thought to be progressing toward a brighter future. Change is believed to be not only inevitable but desirable. Indeed, industry and
technology have accelerated change, and it is this incessant change,
coupled with economic abundance, which leads each generation to
reject predecessors and see the past, in the words of the late historian Richard Hofstadter, as "despicably impractical and uninventive,
simply and solely as something to be surmounted." In twentieth-
century, consumer-oriented society with its perhaps planned ob-
solescence, it is not surprising that the past too would be rejected as
utterly out of date.[4]

Rapid accumulation of scientific knowledge contributes to the belief that each decade is an improvement, and this has given a false
sense of security in regard to the past. Consider the application of
science to medicine. So many seemingly miraculous discoveries
have been made that the medical practice of only a half century ago
now appears primitive. So too have numerous other fields been
touched, if not transformed, by the discoveries of our day. Such may
partially account for why people adopt a linear view of the past
which traces "history as a progression of mankind, leading ever up-
ward, until we reach the apex of the human experience—the present. We, for our time, are the finished product." The present thus
appears to be the most important part of history.[5]

In another way developments in science may affect attitudes toward the past. We know that theories in one field of knowledge are often applied, or misapplied, to other fields. Charles Darwin's theory of evolution changed politics and economics in the late nineteenth and twentieth centuries. It also altered thinking about history. People increasingly saw "reality as an ongoing process," and "a similar consciousness of the relationship between past, present, and future" developed, writes the intellectual historian Stow Persons. Lost in this change was "any sense of an authoritative past. . . . The past and the future radiate out from the present . . . and both are increasingly obscure as they recede from the present."[6]

The revolution in physics begun by Albert Einstein and others may be no less important. Sir Isaac Newton's physics had major influence on seventeenth- and eighteenth-century philosophy and religion. Einstein's theory of relativity helped overturn Newton's universe and suggested a new way of viewing time. Relativity, according to John Marcus, "denied the idea of a universally definitive sequence of objective time," and the hope "of arriving at any ultimate temporal order." History's meaning was limited "to the particular perspective of a period." The past was therefore prevented from "playing a transcendent role."[7]

Much twentieth-century thought says that historical experience is meaningless, that life is purposeless, operating only according to the laws of probability and chance. The great wars of this century with their unprecedented destruction have helped to foster such ideas. A sizable body of twentieth-century literature reflects despair and alienation from history.[8] Certain strains of existentialism, so popular after World War II, stress existing in the present and doubt whether anything can be learned from the past. We hear novelist Albert Camus saying through one of his characters, "I've always been far too much absorbed in the present moment, or the immediate future, to think back." We learn from Jean Paul Sartre that "the present is what exists and all that is not present does not exist. The past does not exist." There has also been substantial twentieth-century thinking that questions, even denies, the idea of progress. If it is true that faith in progress has waned, this fact may have implications for study of the past; the historian E. H. Carr has written that "a society which has lost belief in its capacity to progress in the future will quickly cease to concern itself with its progress in the past."[9]

Finally, other recent developments have brought a decline in historical consciousness. The post–World War II baby boom, television, sophisticated mass advertising, and affluence have been important. A youth culture has emerged and with it a new conception of time. Instead of looking to the future, the "now" generation sees a never-ending present. The past for it is simply irrelevant. How do we account for this culture? Television with its swift reversals of time, what Marshall McLuhan called "total involvement in all-inclusive *nowness*," has been important; advertising that emphasizes things new and dwells in "a one-day world" has surely been a significant factor; and affluence that allowed youth to delay the workplace and prolong adolescence has undoubtedly been significant. Small wonder that history pales for students, especially when they are confronted with untalented, poorly trained, or overly specialized teachers.[10]

These explanations help to account, at least in part, for the past's seeming irrelevance. Why, then, in the face of these realities should we bother to spend any time with history at all?

The answer to that question lies in the realization that regardless of how new or different our world may appear, the study of the past continues to offer many things. On a personal level, history influences us every day in a multitude of ways, as selections by Carl Becker and Carl Gustavson make clear. Reading about history should expand experience and increase the likelihood that we will act wisely. Historical study should make us less egocentric, revealing how other humans have confronted similar problems in other times. History can develop values as well as self-knowledge and a sense of identity. Moreover, the process of studying the past can enrich our lives and prepare us for many endeavors. As it expands our reservoir of experience, it enhances freedom, stimulates creative imagination, and lifts bonds of time and place, thus suggesting to us larger possibilities for action. On a societal level, history assists us to become more effective participants in the surrounding world by enabling us to escape short-range perspectives and to understand better the origins of the present. It can inspire and aid in the creation of a more intelligent future. It can also serve those who would make sound public policy, and it provides an antidote to the misuses of the past by policymakers and others.

Each of us constantly draws from the past. Becker maintained that everyone is his or her own historian, because everyone calls on past experience, however narrow or personal. The question is not whether we will use history to guide actions in the present and future but whether we will use it wisely.

We should not assume that history is merely a book of recipes to be consulted. That risks grave error and may well lead us to miss a major advantage of historical study. It is the *process* of entering into the past, making a segment of it for a time into our present, that is often as important as the information we learn. It is the process rather than the result of studying history which sometimes is most valuable. If we rearrange the past when we write or speak about it, so too does the study of earlier times change us. Transformation results when we place ourselves in the position of other people in bygone times. Historical study can pull us away from self-centeredness and make us more aware of the likely results of our actions, a necessary first step in the development of maturity and wisdom. Just as living in a different culture can give insight into one's own society, so immersing oneself in a different time period (preferably a different century from one's own) helps one transcend assumptions common to our age, to rise above what Reinhold Niebuhr called the "flux of temporal events." In this sense, the study of the past for its own sake is valuable.[11]

The past can be a source of values, self-understanding, and identification. Let us consider values. Many issues confronting human beings are perennial. Does God exist and, if so, what is His character? What is the nature of the universe? What is the nature of humankind? In what kind of society should men and women live? To turn the matter in a slightly different way, the historian Ralph H. Gabriel once said that two of the most important questions a person can ask are, "What is my relationship to the enveloping universe and what is my relation to the society of which I am a part?" With such questions serious thought begins and how we answer such queries can influence behavior. Why should not history help with answers? These questions have been pondered by every generation.[12]

Early in life nearly everyone confronts the reality of one's own mortality. Who has not wondered if men are divinely created with the potential for eternal life, or if Shakespeare was right that life is but a dream rounded by an endless sleep, "a walking shadow, a poor player that struts and frets his hour upon the stage and then is heard no more"? My own first efforts to grapple with such questions led me to consider the writings of Plato, St. Augustine, Kant, and others. The result was an essay on absolute truth; the *process* of writing was a revelation. History came alive. In studying how others wrestled with the very questions that troubled me, I was, to use Trevelyan's words, made aware of "the quasi-miraculous fact that once on this earth . . . walked men and women, as actual as we are today, thinking their own thoughts, swayed by their own passions but now all gone, one generation vanishing after another, gone as utterly as we ourselves shall shortly be gone like ghosts at cockcrow." I realized that I was not the first person to ask such questions. The conclusions I reached, which I recognized were hardly final, differed from those held by any one individual I had read and yet they owed something to each of these figures. In such fashion I attempted to build on the past, and in so doing I tore down barriers of time and mortality, and thus enlarged my consciousness beyond my own generation.

The past is not the only source from which we can draw values. We need not necessarily agree with Polybius that knowledge of past events affords "the best instruction for the regulation of good conduct of human life." But we should acknowledge that history has long provided human beings with inspiration, models of behavior, and sources of self-understanding. In his *History of Rome*, Titus Livius observed that in the past one sees "examples of every possible type" and "from these you may select for yourself . . . what to imitate, and also what . . . to avoid."[13] From history we may learn the best of what has been thought, said, and done. An inexhaustible store of role models waits to be discovered in the past. While we may find examples of frailty and depravity, we may also find courage and humanity.

The past can also help to reveal our limitations and potential and thereby give us a better understanding of ourselves and a richer insight into our fellow humans. "Knowing yourself means knowing what you can do," the philosopher of history R. G. Collingwood wrote, "and since nobody knows what he can do until he tries, the only clue to what man can do is what man has done. The value of history, then, is that it teaches us what man has done and thus what man is."[14] Faith in history may have declined, but in this turbulent era when values are in disarray, if not decay, the past offers a compass by which we may fix our course.

Historical study can enhance personal freedom. We owe much of our identity to our personal histories, which we call memory, the Dutch historian G. J. Renier reminds us, and without it we cannot make decisions, improve the quality of our lives, or perhaps even survive. History is society's memory, and a society that has forgotten its past is condemned to confusion just as certainly as the amnesiac. Study of history extends both personal and collective memories and expands knowledge. One will find a wealth of ideas, a treasure house to inspire imagination and to spark creativity. The greater our remembered experience, the better will be our sense of orientation, the more fertile our creative imaginations, the greater the likelihood that we will make wise decisions as we confront the present and future. History does not guarantee wisdom but does make us aware of larger possibilities for action. Just as practice makes a musician or athlete better able to perform, so study of history makes us better prepared to confront the crises of modern life. History can teach self-discipline, and the skills one acquires from its study prepare us for many activities. In lifting bonds of time and place, in freeing us from the tyranny of the present, history gives greater freedom and becomes an instrument enhancing liberty. Of all learned endeavors, the study of the past can be the most exciting, humanizing, broadening—and hence the most liberating.[15]

History is also valuable to society. Knowledge of the past can make people more effective and enlightened participants in the world around them. It is difficult to name a social, political, or economic problem—or an effort to solve such a problem—not shaped by history. Questions about war and peace, race relations, the distribution of wealth, the place of government, the fate of the environment, and the role of the sexes, to mention but a few such matters, have been confronted before. While such problems rarely if ever recur in the same fashion, they do afford opportunity for us to learn from earlier mistakes and to build on previous successes. "The deeper [our] foundations . . . in the past," Karl Jaspers declared, "the more outstanding [our] participation in the present."[16]

The past can speak to the present, not in a superficial way but in a manner that will enable us to decide what is important. "Piety to the past is not for its own sake nor for the sake of the past," John Dewey said, "but for the sake of a present so secure and enriched, that it will create a better future." While the antiquarian tries to bring back the past for its own sake, Frederick Jackson Turner believed "the historian strives to show the present to itself by revealing its origin from the past." History does not need to be written or read with an eye to the present to be valuable, but some of the very best historical writers seek understanding of contemporary events.[17]

Explaining the present in terms of its origins can be important but it is not easy—the road is lined with pitfalls. One such pitfall is reading present-day values into the past. Much of what passes for popular and "relevant" history is often little more than present-day interests imposed on the past. The historian Herbert Butterfield warned that the writer who is too eager to please his own age may steal from it one of the most important results of historical study, "namely the advantage of an escape from merely contemporary views and short-range perspectives."[18]

In a fashion all history is influenced to some extent by the present and projections of the future. This fact helps explain why each generation writes its history anew.[19] A distinction must be drawn between the writer who merely reads the present into the past or who manipulates the past to support some group or course of action already agreed upon in the present, and the author concerned about present problems who looks to history to see what light it can shed. When the latter path is followed and an honest effort views the past on its own terms, history can give us a better sense of orientation. Letting present-day concerns overly intrude into the past can only limit history's usefulness to a free society. Too often the past becomes merely a "grab bag from which to snatch footnotes for a priori opinion," the diplomatic historian William A. Williams reminds us. "The historical experience" should not be "one of staying in the present and looking back." Rather it should be "one of going back into the past and returning to the present with a wider and more intense consciousness of the restrictions of our former outlook."[20]

The past is too important and dangerous to be ignored or taken for granted. Mankind has always used it to give life a sense of meaning and destiny, to justify institutions, to sanctify morality, to validate social relations, to guess the future. Regardless of how severe the break between recent and distant times has been, the past is alive in every society and influences the way we think and act. Frequently myth is more powerful than truth in guiding our actions; what we believe to have happened is more important than what did happen. Most people in some degree are captives of assumptions or myths about the past, and there are individuals and groups who can manipulate misconceptions for their own ends. "The more literate and sophisticated the society becomes," the British historian J. H. Plumb observed, "the more complex and powerful become the uses to which the past is put." History can "be made to serve every conceivable theory or temperamental peculiarity," Pieter Geyl noted. George Orwell wrote in *1984* that "who controls the past controls the future." We might therefore agree with Butterfield that we should study earlier times "precisely because so much bad history exists in the world already." Just as historical investigation can free us from the bonds of the present, so can it help us escape the tyranny resulting from superficial knowledge of the past.[21]

Thus, historical study can serve as an antidote to the misuse of history by our leaders, and it can save us from being victimized by analogies. Policymakers and other officials are often influenced by what they believe to be the "lessons of the past."[22] It is important that they learn to use history with intelligence and wisdom. Our sense of the future is closely bound to our sense of history, and it is difficult to plan for the future without reference to historical trends, without making analogies with the past.

Indeed, the historical analogy is one of the most powerful devices of persuasion, its logic seemingly inescapable. Policymakers seldom use history systematically. Instead they employ the past in a haphazard manner, usually drawing analogies from the limited experience of one or two generations.

A little knowledge is dangerous, and the more superficial our view of history the easier it becomes for some people to draw lessons from the past. Policies that affect millions of lives are often predicated on ill-conceived assumptions about history. When we become too eager to transpose the recent past onto current events, when we formulate analogies on limited experience we risk becoming entrapped by our misconceptions. "Our knowledge," Philip D. Jordan reminded us, is "a torch of smokey pine that lights the pathway but one step ahead."[23]

The past provides no simple answer for the present. We must be on guard against anyone who claims that it does. We do not have to believe Santayana when he said that those who fail to remember the past are doomed to repeat it. Still, those who do not remember are in jeopardy of suffering at the hands of those who say they do.

References

1. *The General History of Polybius*, vol. 1, trans. Hampton (Oxford, 1823), bk. 1, chap. 1, p. 5.

2. See, for example, the selections in this volume by Michael Kammen, Allan Nevins, and Carl G. Gustavson. For a discussion of Thomas Jefferson's ambivalent attitude toward history see Marcus Cunliffe, "Thomas Jefferson and the Dangers of the Past," *Wilson Quarterly* 6 (Winter 1982): 96–107. On Jefferson and others see Michael Kammen, *A Season of Youth: The American Revolution and the Historical Imagination* (New York: Alfred A. Knopf, 1978), 4–11.

3. First quotation, Page Smith, *The Historian and History* (New York: Alfred A. Knopf, 1964), 235. See also pp. 240–41. Second quotation, Carl Bridenbaugh, "The Great Mutation," *American Historical Review* 68 (January 1963): 316. See also John T. Marcus, *Heaven, Hell and History: A Survey of Man's Faith in History from Antiquity to the Present* (New York: Macmillan, 1967), 243–44. Also on the modern press and notions of time see Daniel J. Czitrom, *Media and the American Mind: From Morse to McLuhan* (Chapel Hill: University of North Carolina Press, 1982), 154, 158–59, 162. See too Harold A. Innis, *Changing Concepts of Time* (Toronto: University of Toronto Press, 1952), 15, 108.

4. Hazel Hertzberg, "The Teaching of History," in *The Past Before Us: Contemporary Historical Writing in the United States*, ed. Michael Kammen (Ithaca, N.Y.: Cornell University Press, 1980), 492; for quotation, Richard Hofstadter, *Anti-intellectualism in American Life* (New York: Random House, Vintage Books, 1962), 238; and Gilman M. Ostrander, *America in the First Machine Age, 1890–1940* (New York: Harper and Row, 1970), 227.

5. Kenneth Hilton, "Some Practical Classroom Remedies for Parochialism of the Present," *Social Studies* 69 (July–August 1978): 163.

6. Stow Persons, "Darwinism and American Culture," in *Intellectual History in America: From Darwin to Niebuhr*, ed. Cushing Strout, 2 vols. (New York: Harper and Row, 1968), 2:7, 8.

7. See Marcus, *Heaven, Hell and History*, 233, 235.

8. Warren Susman argued that particularly since the end of World War II one sees in major intellectual trends "a fundamentally anti-historical view of the world." Writing in 1964, he said that "many of our newer literary

vogues . . . are deliberately wedded to the present moment alone. . . . Our leading movements in painting, especially abstract expressionism and 'pop' art, offer the most immediate kind of experience, more clearly divorced from any sense of history than any other movement in painting since the Renaissance." See Warren I. Susman, "History and the American Intellectual: Uses of a Usable Past," *American Quarterly* 16 (Summer 1964): 263, 261.

9. Marcus, *Heaven, Hell and History*, 239–42; Hertzberg, "The Teaching of History," 489–90; Herbert London, "The Relevance of 'Irrelevance': History as a Functional Discipline," *NYU Education Quarterly* 11 (1971): 9–15. First quotation, Albert Camus, *The Stranger*, trans. Stuart Gilbert (New York: Alfred A. Knopf, 1946), 127; second quotation, Jean Paul Sartre, *Nausea*, trans. Robert Baldick (1938; reprint, Harmondsworth, U.K.: Penguin, 1965), 139; third quotation, E. H. Carr, *What Is History?* (London: Macmillan, 1961), 127. See also Oron J. Hale, "The Dignity of History in Times of War," *Journal of Modern History* 15 (March 1943): 5–6.

10. Hertzberg, "The Teaching of History," 493; quotations from Marshall McLuhan, *Understanding Media: The Extensions of Man* (New York: McGraw-Hill, 1964), 335, and Wyndham Lewis, *Time and Western Man* (London: Chatto and Windus, 1927), 28.

Some writers have blamed overspecialized courses and teachers for the decline of history at the undergraduate level. See Warren L. Hickman, "The Erosion of History," *Social Education* 43 (January 1979): 18–22. See also William H. McNeill, "Studying the Sweep of the Human Adventure," *Chronicle of Higher Education*, January 30, 1978, 32. On the decline of the traditional history curriculum see William H. McNeill, "World History in the Schools," in *New Movements in the Study and Teaching of History*, ed. Martin Ballard (Bloomington: Indiana University Press, 1970), esp. 20–21.

11. See James Turner, "Recovering the Uses of History," *Yale Review* 70 (January 1981): 224; Pardon E. Tillinghast, *The Specious Past: Historians and Others* (Reading, Mass.: Addison-Wesley, 1972), 48–49; quotation, Reinhold Niebuhr, *Faith and History* (New York: Scribner's, 1949), 18.

12. A commendable effort to write history in this fashion is Franklin L. Baumer's *Modern European Thought: Continuity and Change in Ideas, 1600–1950* (New York: Macmillan, 1977). See also Ralph H. Gabriel, "Ideas in History," *History of Education Journal* 10, nos. 1–4 (1959): 8.

13. First quotation, *The General History of Polybius*, vol. 1, bk. 1, chap. 1, p. 1; second quotation, Titus Livius, *The History of Rome*, trans. Canon Roberts (New York: n.p., n.d.), 1:2. Northrop Frye's words in justifying the study of literature are also relevant to history. Reading literature (and history) makes us "soon realize that there's a difference between the world you're living in and the world you want to live in. . . . In other words, liter-

ature [and history] not only leads us toward the regaining of identity, but it also separates this state from its opposite, the world we don't like and want to get away from." Northrop Frye, *The Educated Imagination* (Bloomington: Indiana University Press, 1964), 19, 55.

14. R. G. Collingwood, *The Idea of History* (1946; reprint, New York: Oxford University Press, Galaxy Books, 1962), 10.

15. See R. G. Renier, *History: Its Purpose and Method* (London: George Allen and Unwin, 1950), 13, 24; Carl Becker to Henry Johnson, December 1922, in *"What Is the Good of History?": Selected Letters of Carl L. Becker*, ed. Michael Kammen (Ithaca, N.Y.: Cornell University Press, 1973), 86; Turner, "Recovering the Uses of History," 225–26; Paul Oskar Kristeller, "The Philosophical Significance of the History of Thought," *Journal of the History of Ideas* 7 (June 1946): 362; Myron A. Marty, "Teaching History as a Liberating Art," in *New Directions in Community Colleges: Merging the Humanities*, ed. Leslie Koltai (San Francisco: Jossey-Bass, 1975), 32–33; Bridenbaugh, "The Great Mutation," 326.

16. Karl Jaspers, *The Origin and Goal of History* (New Haven, Conn.: Yale University Press, 1953), 271.

17. First quotation, John Dewey, *Human Nature and Conduct: An Introduction to Social Psychology* (New York: Holt, 1922), 21; second quotation, Frederick Jackson Turner, "The Significance of History," in *The Early Writings of Frederick Jackson Turner, with a List of All His Works*, comp. Everett E. Edwards (Madison: University of Wisconsin Press, 1938), 53. For the view that history should not necessarily be written to explain contemporary events, that the study of the distant past can be valuable in enhancing our perspective, see Charles E. Nowell, "Has the Past a Place in History?" *Journal of Modern History* 24 (December 1952): 331–40. A. G. Little said that the historian's most worthwhile task is not "to trace back the institutions and ways of thought which have survived, as though we were at the end and climax of history. It is at least as important to retrieve the treasures that have been dropped on the way and lost, which, if restored, would enrich our civilization." Quoted in Geoffrey Barraclough, *History in a Changing World* (Norman: University of Oklahoma Press, n.d.), 6.

18. Herbert Butterfield, *History and Human Relations* (London: Collins, 1951), 164.

19. Students are sometimes puzzled as to why interpretations of history change and why historians alter their views about the past. One effort to explain this matter is Carl N. Degler, "Why Historians Change Their Minds," *Pacific Historical Review* 45 (May 1976): 167–84.

20. William Appleman Williams, *History as a Way of Learning: Articles, Excerpts, and Essays* (New York: New View Points, 1973), 7, 8.

21. The past is manipulated in a multitude of ways in any society, as

Carol Kammen and Michael Kammen have shown. Chauvinism, which sometimes takes the form of national, sectional, state, ethnic, or local pride, works to censor the past. The imperatives of group solidarity or survival often lead to the manipulation of the past, as do the requirements of advertising and public relations. Using the past to validate or justify a present desire, or to satisfy some psychological or personal need, also distorts history. See Carol Kammen and Michael Kammen, "The Uses and Abuses of the Past: A Bifocal Perspective," *Minnesota History* 48 (Spring 1982): 3–12. For quotations see J. H. Plumb, *The Death of the Past* (Boston: Houghton Mifflin, 1970), 11; Pieter Geyl, *The Use and Abuse of History* (New Haven, Conn.: Yale University Press, 1955), 75; George Orwell, *Nineteen Eighty-Four: A Novel* (New York: Harcourt, Brace, 1949), 251; and Butterfield, *History and Human Relations*, 171.

22. An important work examining how policymakers use and misuse history—often unconsciously—is Ernest May's *"Lessons" of the Past: The Use and Misuse of History in American Foreign Policy* (New York: Oxford University Press, 1973).

23. Philip D. Jordan, "The Usefulness of Useless Knowledge," *The Historian* 22 (May 1960): 249.

HISTORY AND
THE INDIVIDUAL

History and
the Expansion of Experience

No matter what one may think about the formal study of the past, everyone uses history on a daily basis. Our present actions depend heavily on our remembering past experiences. Few writers have ever made this point more clearly than did the historian Carl Becker.[1] "The chief value of history," Becker said, "is that it is an extension of the personal memory, and an extension which masses of people can share."[2] There are two histories, he argued: "the actual series of events that once occurred; and the ideal series that we affirm and hold in memory." The first is unchanging, but the second is incomplete and changes constantly as our knowledge increases. As a result, Becker believed that "of all the creatures man alone has a specious present that may be deliberately and purposely enlarged and diversified and enriched." The study of the past artificially extends our social memory and personal experience. It allows us to understand what we are doing in view of what has already happened and what we hope to accomplish.

References

1. Another fine work which makes this point is J. H. Hexter's *The History Primer* (New York: Basic Books, 1971), esp. 19–53. See also Thomas P. Weinland and Arthur D. Roberts, "Clio at the Crossroads," *Social Studies* 69 (January–February 1978): 35.

2. Carl Becker to Henry Johnson, December 1922, in *"What Is the Good of History?": Selected Letters of Carl L. Becker,* ed. Michael Kammen (Ithaca, N.Y.: Cornell University Press, 1973), 86.

Everyman His Own Historian

Carl L. Becker

Although Carl Becker (1873–1945) primarily taught European history with a special emphasis on the eighteenth century and the French Revolution, most of his scholarly writing dealt with American history. His books include *The Eve of the Revolution* (1918), *The United States, An Experiment in Democracy* (1920), *The Declaration of Independence* (1922), *Modern History* (1931), and *Modern Democracy* (1941). Becker was president of the American Historical Association, and the following essay was his presidential address delivered at Minneapolis in 1931. It was first published in the *American Historical Review* (January 1932).

Once upon a time, long long ago, I learned how to reduce a fraction to its lowest terms. Whether I could still perform that operation is uncertain; but the discipline involved in early training had its uses, since it taught me that in order to understand the essential nature of anything it is well to strip it of all superficial and irrelevant accretions—in short, to reduce it to its lowest terms. That operation I now venture, with some apprehension and all due apologies, to perform on the subject of history.

I ought first of all to explain that when I use the term history I mean knowledge of history. No doubt throughout all past time there actually occurred a series of events which, whether we know what it was or not, constitutes history in some ultimate sense. Nevertheless, much the greater part of these events we can know nothing about, not even that they occurred; many of them we can know only imperfectly; and even the few events that we think we know for sure we can never be absolutely certain of, since we can never revive them, never observe or test them directly. The event itself once occurred, but as an actual event it has disappeared; so that in dealing with it the only objective reality we can observe or test is some material trace which the event has left—usually a written document. With these traces of vanished events, these documents, we must be content since they are all we have; from them we infer what the event was, we affirm that it is a fact that the event was so and so. We do not say "Lincoln is assassinated," we say "it is a fact that Lincoln was assassinated." The event *was*, but is no longer; it is only the affirmed fact about the event that *is*, that persists, and will persist until we discover that our affirmation is wrong or inadequate. Let us then admit that there are two histories: the actual series of events that once occurred; and the ideal series that we affirm and hold in memory. The first is absolute and unchanged—it was what it was whatever we do or say about it; the second is relative, always changing in response to the increase or refinement of knowledge. The two series correspond more or less, it is our aim to make the correspondence as exact as possible; but the actual series of events exists for us only in terms of the ideal series which we affirm and hold in memory. This is why I am forced to identify history with knowledge of history. For all practical purposes history is, for us and for the time being, what we know it to be.

It is history in this sense that I wish to reduce to its lowest terms. In order to do that I need a very simple definition. I once read that "History is the knowledge of events that have occurred in the past." That is a simple definition, but not simple enough. It contains three words that require examination. The first is knowledge. Knowledge is a formidable word. I always think of knowledge as something that is stored up in the *Encyclopaedia Britannica* or the *Summa Theologica*; something difficult to acquire, something at all events that I have not. Resenting a definition that denies me the title of historian, I therefore ask what is most essential to knowledge. Well, memory, I should think (and I mean memory in the broad sense, the memory of events inferred as well as the memory of events observed); other things are necessary too, but memory is fundamental: without memory no knowledge. So our definition becomes, "History is the memory of events that have occurred in the past." But events—the word carries an implication of something grand, like the taking of the Bastille or the Spanish-American War. An occurrence need not be spectacular to be an event. If I drive a motor car down the crooked streets of Ithaca, that is an event—something done; if the traffic cop bawls me out, that is an event—something said; if I have evil thoughts of him for so doing, that is an event—something thought. In truth anything done, said, or thought is an event, important or not as may turn out. But since we do not ordinarily speak without thinking, at least in some rudimentary way, and since the psychologists tell us that we cannot think without speaking, or at least not without having anticipatory vibrations in the larynx, we may well combine thought events and speech events under one term; and so our definition becomes, "History is the memory of things said and done in the past." But the past—the word is both misleading and unnecessary: misleading, because the past, used in connection with history, seems to imply the distant past, as if history ceased before we were born; unnecessary, because after all everything said or done is already in the past as soon as it is said or done. Therefore I will omit that word, and our definition becomes, "History is the memory of things said and done." This is a definition that reduces history to its lowest terms, and yet includes everything that is essential to understanding what it really is.

If the essence of history is the memory of things said and done, then it is obvious that every normal person, Mr. Everyman, knows some history. Of course we do what we can to conceal this invidious truth. Assuming a professional manner, we say that so and so knows no history, when we mean no more than that he failed to pass the examinations set for a higher degree; and simple-minded persons, undergraduates and others, taken in by academic classifications of knowledge, think they know no history because they have never taken a course in history in college, or have never read Gibbon's *Decline and Fall of the Roman Empire.* No doubt the academic convention has its uses, but it is one of the superficial accretions that must be stripped off if we would understand history reduced to its lowest terms. Mr. Everyman, as well as you and I, remembers things said and done, and must do so at every waking moment. Suppose Mr. Everyman to have awakened this morning unable to remember anything said or done. He would be a lost soul indeed. This has happened, this sudden loss of all historical knowledge. But normally it does not happen. Normally the memory of Mr. Everyman, when he awakens in the morning, reaches out into the country of the past and of distant places and instantaneously recreates his little world of endeavor, pulls together as it were things said and done in his yesterdays, and coordinates them with his present perceptions and with things to be said and done in his tomorrows. Without this historical knowledge, this memory of things said and done, his today would be aimless and his tomorrow without significance.

Since we are concerned with history in its lowest terms, we will suppose that Mr. Everyman is not a professor of history, but just an ordinary citizen without excess knowledge. Not having a lecture to prepare, his memory of things said and done, when he awakened this morning, presumably did not drag into consciousness any events connected with the Liman von Sanders mission or the Pseudo-Isidorian Decretals; it presumably dragged into consciousness an image of things said and done yesterday in the office, the highly significant fact that General Motors had dropped three points, a conference arranged for ten o'clock in the morning, a promise to play nine holes at four-thirty in the afternoon, and other historical events of similar import. Mr. Everyman knows more history than this, but at the moment of awakening this is sufficient: memory of things said and done, history functioning, at seven-thirty in the morning, in its very lowest terms, has effectively oriented Mr. Everyman in his little world of endeavor.

Yet not quite effectively after all perhaps; for unaided memory is notoriously fickle; and it may happen that Mr. Everyman, as he drinks his coffee, is uneasily aware of something said or done that he fails now to recall. A common enough occurrence, as we all know to our sorrow—this remembering, not the historical event, but only that there was an event which we ought to remember but cannot. This is Mr. Everyman's difficulty, a bit of history lies dead and inert in the sources, unable to do any work for Mr. Everyman because his memory refuses to bring it alive in consciousness. What then does Mr. Everyman do? He does what any historian would do: he does a bit of historical research in the sources. From his little Private Record Office (I mean his vest pocket) he takes a book in MS., volume XXXV it may be, and turns to page 23, and there he reads: "December 29, pay Smith's coal bill, 20 tons, $1017.20." Instantaneously a series of historical events comes to life in Mr. Everyman's mind. He has an image of himself ordering twenty tons of coal from

Smith last summer, of Smith's wagons driving up to his house, and of the precious coal sliding dustily through the cellar window. Historical events, these are, not so important as the forging of the Isidorian Decretals, but still important to Mr. Everyman: historical events which he was not present to observe, but which, by an artificial extension of memory, he can form a clear picture of, because he has done a little original research in the manuscripts preserved in his Private Record Office.

The picture Mr. Everyman forms of Smith's wagons delivering the coal at his house is a picture of things said and done in the past. But it does not stand alone, it is not a pure antiquarian image to be enjoyed for its own sake; on the contrary, it is associated with a picture of things to be said and done in the future; so that throughout the day Mr. Everyman intermittently holds in mind, together with a picture of Smith's coal wagons, a picture of himself going at four o'clock in the afternoon to Smith's office in order to pay his bill. At four o'clock Mr. Everyman is accordingly at Smith's office. "I wish to pay that coal bill," he says. Smith looks dubious and disappointed, takes down a ledger (or a filing case), does a bit of original research in his Private Record Office, and announces: "You don't owe me any money, Mr. Everyman. You ordered the coal here all right, but I didn't have the kind you wanted, and so turned the order over to Brown. It was Brown delivered your coal: he's the man you owe." Whereupon Mr. Everyman goes to Brown's office; and Brown takes down a ledger, does a bit of original research in his Private Record Office, which happily confirms the researches of Smith; and Mr. Everyman pays his bill, and in the evening, after returning from the Country Club, makes a further search in another collection of documents, where, sure enough, he finds a bill from Brown, properly drawn, for twenty tons of stove coal, $1017.20. The research is now completed. Since his mind rests satisfied, Mr. Everyman has found the explanation of the series of events that concerned him.

Mr. Everyman would be astonished to learn that he is an historian, yet it is obvious, isn't it, that he has performed all the essential operations involved in historical research. Needing or wanting to do something (which happened to be, not to deliver a lecture or write a book, but to pay a bill; and this is what misleads him and us as to what he is really doing) the first step was to recall things said and done. Unaided memory proving inadequate, a further step was essential—the examination of certain documents in order to discover the necessary but as yet unknown facts. Unhappily the documents were found to give conflicting reports, so that a critical comparison of the texts had to be instituted in order to eliminate error. All this having been satisfactorily accomplished, Mr. Everyman is ready for the final operation—the formation in his mind, by an artificial extension of memory, of a picture, a definitive picture let us hope, of a selected series of historical events—of himself ordering coal from Smith, of Smith turning the order over to Brown, and of Brown delivering the coal at his house. In the light of this picture Mr. Everyman could, and did, pay his bill. If Mr. Everyman had undertaken these researches in order to write a book instead of to pay a bill, no one would think of denying that he was an historian.

II

I HAVE TRIED to reduce history to its lowest terms, first by defining it as the memory of things said and done, second by showing concretely how the memory of things said and done is essential to the performance of the simplest acts of daily life. I wish now to note the more general implications of Mr. Everyman's activities. In the realm of affairs Mr. Everyman has been paying his coal bill; in the realm of consciousness he has been doing that fundamental thing which enables man alone to have, properly speaking, a history: he has been re-enforcing and enriching his immediate perceptions to the end that he may live in a world of semblance more spacious and satisfying than is to be found within the narrow confines of the fleeting present moment.

We are apt to think of the past as dead, the future as nonexistent, the present alone as real; and prematurely wise or disillusioned counselors have urged us to burn always with "a hard, gemlike flame" in order to give "the highest quality to the moments as they pass, and simply for those moments' sake." This no doubt is what the glowworm does; but I think that man, who alone is properly aware that the present moment passes, can for that very reason make no good use of the present moment simply for its own sake. Strictly speaking, the present doesn't exist for us, or is at best no more than an infinitesimal point in time, gone before we can note it as present. Nevertheless, we must have a present; and so we create one by robbing the past, by holding on to the most recent events and pretending that they all belong to our immediate perceptions. If, for example, I raise my arm, the total event is a series of occurrences of which the first are past before the last have taken place; and yet you perceive it as a single movement executed in one present instant. This telescoping of successive events into a single instant philosophers call the "specious present." Doubtless they would assign rather narrow limits to the specious present; but I will willfully make a free use of it, and say that we can extend the specious present as much as we like. In common speech we do so: we speak of the "present hour," the "present year," the "present generation." Perhaps all living creatures have a specious present; but man has this superiority, as Pascal says, that he is aware of himself and the universe, can as it were hold himself at arm's length and with some measure of objectivity watch himself and his fellows functioning in the world during a brief span of allotted years. Of all the creatures, man alone has a specious present that may be deliberately and purposefully enlarged and diversified and enriched.

The extent to which the specious present may thus be enlarged and enriched will depend upon knowledge, the artificial extension of memory, the memory of things said and done in the past and distant places. But not upon knowledge alone; rather upon knowledge directed by purpose. The specious present is an unstable pattern of thought, incessantly changing in response to our immediate perceptions and the purposes that arise therefrom. At any given moment each one of us (professional historian no less than Mr. Everyman) weaves into this unstable pattern such actual or artificial memories as may be necessary to orient us in our little world of endeavor. But to be oriented in our little world of endeavor we must be prepared for what is coming to us (the payment of a coal bill, the delivery of a presidential address, the establishment of a League of Nations, or whatever); and to be prepared for what is coming to us it is necessary, not only to recall certain past events, but to anticipate (note I do not say predict) the future. Thus from the specious present, which always includes more or less of the past, the future refuses to be excluded; and the more of the past we drag into the specious present, the more an hypothetical, patterned future is likely to crowd into it also. Which comes first, which is cause and which effect, whether our memories construct a pattern of past events at the behest of our desires and hopes, or whether our desires and hopes spring from a pattern of past events imposed upon us by experience and knowledge, I shall not attempt to say. What I suspect is that memory of past and anticipation of future events work together, go hand in hand as it were in a friendly way, without disputing over priority and leadership.

At all events they go together, so that in a very real sense it is impossible to divorce history from life: Mr. Everyman cannot do what he needs or desires to do without recalling past events; he cannot recall past events without in some subtle fashion relating them to what he needs or desires to do. This is the natural function of history, of history reduced to its lowest terms, of history conceived as the memory of things said and done: memory of things said and done (whether in our immediate yesterdays or in the long past of mankind), running hand in hand with the anticipation of things to be said and done, enables us, each to the extent of his knowledge and imagination, to be intelligent, to push back the narrow confines of the fleeting present moment so that what we are doing may be judged in the light of what we have done and what we hope to do. In this sense all *living* history, as Croce says, is contemporaneous: in so far as we think the past (and otherwise the past, however fully related in documents, is nothing to us) it becomes an integral and living part of our present world of semblance.

It must then be obvious that living history, the ideal series of events that we affirm and hold in memory, since it is so intimately associated with what we are doing and with what we hope to do, cannot be precisely the same for all at any given time, or the same for one generation as for another. History in this sense cannot be reduced to a verifiable set of statistics or formulated in terms of universally valid mathematical formulas. It is rather an imaginative creation, a personal possession which each one of us, Mr. Everyman, fashions out of his individual experience, adapts to his practical or emotional needs, and adorns as well as may be to suit his aesthetic tastes. In thus creating his own history, there are, nevertheless, limits which Mr. Everyman may not overstep without incurring penalties. The limits are set by his fellows. If Mr. Everyman lived quite alone in an unconditioned world he would be free to affirm and hold in memory any ideal series of events that struck his fancy, and thus create a world of semblance quite in accord with the heart's desire. Unfortunately, Mr. Everyman has to live in a world of Browns and

Smiths; a sad experience, which has taught him the expediency of recalling certain events with much exactness. In all the immediately practical affairs of life Mr. Everyman is a good historian, as expert, in conducting the researches necessary for paying his coal bill, as need be. His expertness comes partly from long practice, but chiefly from the circumstance that his researches are prescribed and guided by very definite and practical objects which concern him intimately. The problem of what documents to consult, what facts to select, troubles Mr. Everyman not at all. Since he is not writing a book on "Some Aspects of the Coal Industry Objectively Considered," it does not occur to him to collect all the facts and let them speak for themselves. Wishing merely to pay his coal bill, he selects only such facts as may be relevant; and not wishing to pay it twice, he is sufficiently aware, without ever having read Bernheim's *Lehrbuch*, that the relevant facts must be clearly established by the testimony of independent witnesses not self-deceived. He does not know, or need to know, that his personal interest in the performance is a disturbing bias which will prevent him from learning the whole truth or arriving at ultimate causes. Mr. Everyman does not wish to learn the whole truth or to arrive at ultimate causes. He wishes to pay his coal bill. That is to say, he wishes to adjust himself to a practical situation, and on that low pragmatic level he is a good historian precisely because he is not disinterested: he will solve his problems, if he does solve them, by virtue of his intelligence and not by virtue of his indifference.

Nevertheless, Mr. Everyman does not live by bread alone; and on all proper occasions his memory of things said and done, easily enlarging his specious present beyond the narrow circle of daily affairs, will, must inevitably, in mere compensation for the intolerable dullness and vexation of the fleeting present moment, fashion for him a more spacious world than that of the immediately practical. He can readily recall the days of his youth, the places he has lived in, the ventures he has made, the adventures he has had—all the crowded events of a lifetime; and beyond and around this central pattern of personally experienced events, there will be embroidered a more dimly seen pattern of artificial memories, memories of things reputed to have been said and done in past times which he has not known, in distant places which he has not seen. This outer pattern of remembered events that encloses and completes the central pattern of his personal experience, Mr. Everyman has woven, he could not tell you how, out of the most diverse threads of information, picked up in the most casual way, from the most unrelated sources—from things learned at home and in school, from knowledge gained in business or profession, from newspapers glanced at, from books (yes, even history books) read or heard of, from remembered scraps of newsreels or educational films or *ex cathedra* utterances of presidents and kings, from fifteen-minute discourses on the history of civilization broadcast by the courtesy (it may be) of Pepsodent, the Bulova Watch Company, or the Shepard Stores in Boston. Daily and hourly, from a thousand unnoted sources, there is lodged in Mr. Everyman's mind a mass of unrelated and related information and misinformation, of impressions and images, out of which he somehow manages, undeliberately for the most part, to fashion a history, a patterned picture of remembered things said and done in past times and distant places. It is not possible, it is not essential, that this picture should be complete or completely true: it is essential that it should be useful to Mr. Everyman; and that it may be useful to him he will hold in memory, of all the things he might hold in memory, those things only which can be related with some reasonable degree of relevance and harmony to his idea of himself and of what he is doing in the world and what he hopes to do.

In constructing this more remote and far-flung pattern of remembered things, Mr. Everyman works with something of the freedom of a creative artist; the history which he imaginatively recreates as an artificial extension of his personal experience will inevitably be an engaging blend of fact and fancy, a mythical adaptation of that which actually happened. In part it will be true, in part false; as a whole perhaps neither true nor false, but only the most convenient form of error. Not that Mr. Everyman wishes or intends to deceive himself or others. Mr. Everyman has a wholesome respect for cold, hard facts, never suspecting how malleable they are, how easy it is to coax and cajole them; but he necessarily takes the facts as they come to him, and is enamored of those that seem best suited to his interests or promise most in the way of emotional satisfaction. The exact truth of remembered events he has in any case no time, and no need, to curiously question or meticulously verify. No doubt he can, if he be an American, call up an image of the signing of the Declaration of Independence in 1776 as readily as he can call up an image of

Smith's coal wagons creaking up the hill last summer. He suspects the one image no more than the other; but the signing of the Declaration, touching not his practical interests, calls for no careful historical research on his part. He may perhaps, without knowing why, affirm and hold in memory that the Declaration was signed by the members of the Continental Congress on the fourth of July. It is a vivid and sufficient image which Mr. Everyman may hold to the end of his days without incurring penalties. Neither Brown nor Smith has any interest in setting him right; nor will any court ever send him a summons for failing to recall that the Declaration, "being engrossed and compared at the table, was signed by the members" on the second of August. As an actual event, the signing of the Declaration was what it was; as a remembered event it will be, for Mr. Everyman, what Mr. Everyman contrives to make it: will have for him significance and magic, much or little or none at all, as it fits well or ill into his little world of interests and aspirations and emotional comforts.

III

WHAT THEN OF US, historians by profession? What have we to do with Mr. Everyman, or he with us? More, I venture to believe, than we are apt to think. For each of us is Mr. Everyman too. Each of us is subject to the limitations of time and place; and for each of us, no less than for the Browns and Smiths of the world, the pattern of remembered things said and done will be woven, safeguard the process how we may, at the behest of circumstance and purpose.

True it is that although each of us is Mr. Everyman, each is something more than his own historian. Mr. Everyman, being but an informal historian, is under no bond to remember what is irrelevant to his personal affairs. But we are historians by profession. Our profession, less intimately bound up with the practical activities, is to be directly concerned with the ideal series of events that is only of casual or occasional import to others; it is our business in life to be ever preoccupied with that far-flung pattern of artificial memories that encloses and completes the central pattern of individual experience. We are Mr. Everybody's historian as well as our own, since our histories serve the double purpose, which written histories have always served, of keeping alive the recollection of memorable men and events. We are thus of that ancient and honorable company of wise men of the tribe, of bards and story-tellers and minstrels, of sooth-sayers and priests, to whom in successive ages has been entrusted the keeping of the useful myths. Let not the harmless, necessary word "myth" put us out of countenance. In the history of history a myth is a once valid but now discarded version of the human story, as our now valid versions will in due course be relegated to the category of discarded myths. With out predecessors, the bards and story-tellers and priests, we have therefore this in common: that it is our function, as it was theirs, not to create, but to preserve and perpetuate the social tradition; to harmonize, as well as ignorance and prejudice permit, the actual and the remembered series of events; to enlarge and enrich the specious present common to us all to the end that "society" (the tribe, the nation, or all mankind) may judge of what it is doing in the light of what it has done and what it hopes to do.

History as the artificial extension of the social memory (and I willingly concede that there are other appropriate ways of apprehending human experience) is an art of long standing, necessarily so since it springs instinctively from the impulse to enlarge the range of immediate experience; and however camouflaged by the disfiguring jargon of science, it is still in essence what it has always been. History in this sense is story, in aim always a true story; a story that employs all the devices of literary art (statement and generalization, narration and description, comparison and comment and analogy) to present the succession of events in the life of man, and from the succession of events thus presented to derive a satisfactory meaning. The history written by historians, like the history informally fashioned by Mr. Everyman, is thus a convenient blend of truth and fancy, of what we commonly distinguished as "fact" and "interpretation." In primitive times, when tradition is orally transmitted, bards and story-tellers frankly embroider or improvise the facts to heighten the dramatic import of the story. With the use of written records, history, gradually differentiated from fiction, is understood as the story of events that actually occurred; and with the increase and refinement of knowledge the historian recognizes that his first duty is to be sure of his facts, let their meaning be what it may. Nevertheless, in every age history is taken to be a story of actual events from which a significant meaning may be derived; and in every age the illusion is that the present version is valid because the related facts are true, whereas former versions are invalid because based upon inaccurate or inadequate facts.

Never was this conviction more impressively displayed than in our own time—that age of erudition in which we live, or from which we are perhaps just emerging. Finding the course of history littered with the *debris* of exploded philosophies, the historians of the last century, unwilling to be forever duped, turned away (as they fondly hoped) from "interpretation" to the rigorous examination of the factual event, just as it occurred. Perfecting the technique of investigation, they laboriously collected and edited the sources of information, and with incredible persistence and ingenuity ran illusive error to earth, letting the significance of the Middle Ages wait until it was certainly known "whether Charles the Fat was at Ingelheim or Lustnau on July 1, 887," shedding their "life-blood," in many a hard fought battle, "for the sublime truths of Sac and Soc." I have no quarrel with this so great concern and with hoti's business. One of the first duties of man is not to be duped, to be aware of his world; and to derive the significance of human experience from events that never occurred is surely an enterprise of doubtful value. To establish the facts is always in order, and is indeed the first duty of the historian; but to suppose that the facts, once established in all their fullness, will "speak for themselves" is an illusion. It was perhaps peculiarly the illusion of those historians of the last century who found some special magic in the word "scientific." The scientific historian, it seems, was one who set forth the facts without injecting any extraneous meaning into them. He was the objective man whom Neitzsche described—"a mirror: accustomed to prostration before something that wants to be known, . . . he waits until something comes, and then expands himself sensitively, so that even the light footsteps and gliding past of spiritual things may not be lost in his surface and film [*Beyond Good and Evil*, 140]. "It is not I who speak, but history which speaks through me," was Fustel's reproof to applauding students. "If a certain philosophy emerges from this scientific history, it must be permitted to emerge naturally, of its own accord, all but independently of the will of the historian" [quoted in *English Historical Review* 5]. Thus the scientific historian deliberately renounced philosophy only to submit to it without being aware. His philosophy was just this, that by not taking thought a cubit would be added to his stature. With no other preconception than the will to know, the historian would reflect in his surface and film the "order of events throughout past times in all places"; so that, in the fullness of time, when innumerable patient expert scholars, by "exhausting the sources," should have reflected without refracting the truth of all the facts, the definitive and impregnable meaning of human experience would emerge of its own accord to enlighten and emancipate mankind. Hoping to find something without looking for it, expecting to obtain final answers to life's riddle by resolutely refusing to ask questions—it was surely the most romantic species of realism yet invented, the oddest attempt ever made to get something for nothing!

That mood is passing. The fullness of time is not yet, over-much learning proves a weariness to the flesh, and a younger generation that knows not Von Ranke is eager to believe that Fustel's counsel, if one of perfection, is equally one of futility. Even the most disinterested historian has at least one preconception, which is the fixed idea that he has none. The facts of history are already set forth, implicitly, in the sources; and the historian who could restate without reshaping them would, by submerging and suffocating the mind in diffuse existence, accomplish the superfluous task of depriving human experience of all significance. Left to themselves, the facts do not speak; left to themselves they do not exist, not really, since for all practical purposes there is no fact until some one affirms it. The least the historian can do with any historical fact is to select and affirm it. To select and affirm even the simplest complex of facts is to give them a certain place in a certain pattern of ideas, and this alone is sufficient to give them a special meaning. However "hard" or "cold" they may be, historical facts are after all not material substances which, like bricks or scantlings, possess definite shape and clear, persistent outline. To set forth historical facts is not comparable to dumping a barrow of bricks. A brick retains its form and pressure wherever placed; but the form and substance of historical facts, having a negotiable existence only in literary discourse, vary with the words employed to convey them. Since history is not part of the external material world, but an imaginative reconstruction of vanished events, its form and substance are inseparable: in the realm of literary discourse substance, being an idea, *is* form; and form, conveying the idea, *is* substance. It is thus not the undiscriminated fact, but the perceiving mind of the historian that speaks: the special meaning which the facts are made to convey emerges from the substance-form which the historian employs to recreate imaginatively a series of events not present to perception.

In constructing this substance-form of vanished events, the historian, like Mr. Everyman, like the bards and story-tellers of an earlier time, will be conditioned by the specious present in which alone he can be aware of his world. Being neither omniscient nor omnipresent, the historian is not the same person always and everywhere; and for him, as for Mr. Everyman, the form and significance of remembered events, like the extension and velocity of physical objects, will vary with the time and place of the observer. After fifty years we can clearly see that it was not history which spoke through Fustel, but Fustel who spoke through history. We see less clearly perhaps that the voice of Fustel was the voice, amplified and freed from static as one may say, of Mr. Everyman; what the admiring students applauded on that famous occasion was neither history nor Fustel, but a deftly colored pattern of selected events which Fustel fashioned, all the more skillfully for not being aware of doing so, in the service of Mr. Everyman's emotional needs—the emotional satisfaction, so essential to Frenchmen at that time, of perceiving that French institutions were not of German origin. And so it must always be. Played upon by all the diverse, unnoted influences of his own time, the historian will elicit history out of documents by the same principle, however more consciously and expertly applied, that Mr. Everyman employs to breed legends out of remembered episodes and oral tradition.

Berate him as we will for not reading our books, Mr. Everyman is stronger than we are, and sooner or later we must adapt our knowledge to his necessities. Otherwise he will leave us to our own devices, leave us it may be to cultivate a species of dry professional arrogance growing out of the thin soil of antiquarian research. Such research, valuable not in itself but for some ulterior purpose, will be of little import except in so far as it is transmuted into common knowledge. The history that lies inert in unread books does no work in the world. The history that does work in the world, the history that influences the course of history, is living history, that pattern of remembered events, whether true or false, that enlarges and enriches the collective specious present, the specious present of Mr. Everyman. This is why the history of history is a record of the "new history" that in every age rises to confound and supplant the old. It should be a relief to us to renounce omniscience, to recognize that every generation, our own included, will, must inevitably, understand the past and anticipate the future in the light of its own restricted experience, must inevitably play on the dead whatever tricks it finds necessary for its own peace of mind. The appropriate trick for any age is not a malicious invention designed to take anyone in, but an unconscious and necessary effort on the part of "society" to understand what it is doing in the light of what it has done and what it hopes to do. We, historians by profession, share in this necessary effort. But we do not impose our version of the human story on Mr. Everyman; in the end it is rather Mr. Everyman who imposes his version on us—compelling us, in an age of political revolution, to see that history is past politics, in an age of social stress and conflict to search for the economic interpretation. If we remain too long recalcitrant Mr. Everyman will ignore us, shelving our recondite works behind glass doors rarely opened. Our proper function is not to repeat the past but to make use of it, to correct and rationalize for common use Mr. Everyman's mythological adaptation of what actually happened. We are surely under bond to be as honest and as intelligent as human frailty permits; but the secret of our success in the long run is in conforming to the temper of Mr. Everyman, which we seem to guide only because we are so sure, eventually, to follow it.

Neither the value nor the dignity of history need suffer by regarding it as a foreshortened and incomplete representation of the reality that once was, an unstable pattern of remembered things redesigned and newly colored to suit the convenience of those who make use of it. Nor need our labors be the less highly prized because our task is limited, our contributions of incidental and temporary significance. History is an indispensable even though not the highest form of intellectual endeavor, since it makes, as Santayana says, a gift of "great interests . . . to the heart. A barbarian is no less subject to the past than is the civic man who knows what the past is and means to be loyal to it; but the barbarian, for want of a transpersonal memory, crawls among superstitions which he cannot understand or revoke and among people whom he may hate or love, but whom he can never think of raising to a higher plane, to the level of a purer happiness. The whole dignity of human endeavor is thus bound up with historic issues, and as conscience needs to be controlled by experience if it is to become rational, so personal experience itself needs to be enlarged ideally if the failures and success it reports are to touch impersonal interests" [*The Life of Reason*, 5:68].

I do not present this view of history as one that is stable and must prevail. Whatever validity it may claim, it is certain, on its own premises, to be supplanted; for its premises, imposed upon us by the climate of opinion in which we live and think, predispose us to regard all things, and all principles of things, as no more than "inconstant modes or fashions," as but the "concurrence, renewed from moment to moment, of forces parting sooner or later on their way." It is the limitation of the genetic approach to human experience that it must be content to transform problems since it can never solve them. However accurately we may determine the "facts" of history, the facts themselves and our interpretations of them, and our interpretation of our own interpretations, will be seen in a different perspective or a less vivid light as mankind moves into the unknown future. Regarded historically, as a process of becoming, man and his world can obviously be understood only tentatively, since it is by definition something still in the making, something as yet unfinished. Unfortunately for the "permanent contribution" and the universally valid philosophy, time passes; time, the enemy of man as the Greeks thought; tomorrow and tomorrow and tomorrow creeps in this petty pace, and all our yesterdays diminish and grow dim: so that, in the lengthening perspective of the centuries, even the most striking events (the Declaration of Independence, the French Revolution, the Great War itself; like the Diet of Worms before them, like the signing of the Magna Carta and the coronation of Charlemagne and the crossing of the Rubicon and the battle of Marathon) must inevitably, for posterity, fade away into pale replicas of the original picture, for each succeeding generation losing, as they recede into a more distant past, some significance that once was noted in them, some quality of enchantment that once was theirs.

History, Maturity, and Wisdom

Although the study of history is frequently criticized for being impractical, knowledge of the past is useful for mental growth and the development of perspective. The process of studying the past is sometimes as important as the information gained.[1] The English historian J. H. Hexter argued that "history is not necessarily and not always directly concerned with explanation even in the broadest tolerable sense of that term. A quite legitimate concern of many historical accounts is . . . to confront the readers with a human situation and to enhance their awareness of it." History can offer us "a measure of that ability to know and understand what it is like to be another" which is necessary to achieving maturity.[2]

Arguing along similar lines, G. R. Elton explains that study of the past breaks down self-centeredness and makes us more aware of the consequences of our actions. Even if we grant that history is not a "practical" subject, there is often great value in considering "impractical" or "useless" knowledge, and Philip D. Jordan proposes that the past should be studied as though "it has no bearing on anything beyond itself." Both Jordan and Michael Kammen suggest that through the study of history we gain a more discriminating memory and with that surely come clearer thinking and better judgment.

All of this is but another way of saying that in addition to promoting maturity, history can be important to the development of wisdom. The Czechoslovakian-born historian of nationalism Hans Kohn maintained that "history, rightly studied, can sharpen man's critical insight into human relationships and personality. . . . Historical perspective may help in the rejection of both the utopias of enthusiasm and the utopias of despair in regarding the present as not too bad and in expecting not too much from the future. . . . Past mistakes can be avoided, and new ways can be found."[3] Gordon Leff takes a similar stand in his essay, stating that "history is indispensable to understanding what is indispensable to men," and Harold J. Hanham reminds us that the original purpose of having students study the past was the "inculcation of wisdom." Harold Perkin further develops the above ideas when he says that "it is not *what* is studied but *how* it is studied that matters." History is useful "to everyone who has to deal with human beings in complex situations." It provides "understanding of the world around us and the people in it." Incidentally, both Hanham and Perkin perceptively point out that training in history prepares one for many different fields of endeavor.

References

1. This point is also made by James Turner in "Recovering the Uses of History," *Yale Review* 70 (January 1981): 224. In addition, see Pardon E. Tillinghast, *The Specious Past: Historians and Others* (Reading, Mass.: Addison-Wesley, 1972), 48.

2. Hexter's work does not appear in this volume, but see his *The History Primer* (New York: Basic Books, 1971), 207, 215.

3. See Hans Kohn, "A Historian's Creed for Our Time," *South Atlantic Quarterly* 52 (July 1953): 343, 347.

Putting the Past Before Us

G. R. Elton

G. R. Elton (b. 1921) is a specialist in British history who has taught at
the University of Glasgow, Cambridge University, and Clare College.
He has written extensively on the Tudor period, and his books include
*The Tudor Revolution in Government: Administrative Changes in the
Reign of Henry VIII* (1953), *The Practice of History* (1967), *The Future of
the Past: An Inaugural Lecture* (1968), and *The Body of the Whole
Realm: Parliament and Representation in Medieval and Tudor En-
gland* (1969). "Putting the Past Before Us" first appeared in the *Times
Literary Supplement* (September 8, 1978).

*W*hy should children be taught history? What part should history play in the education provided by the schools? Much
depends on what one supposes education is for: I would pro-
pose that its overwhelming purpose lies in preparing the adolescent
for adult status. This certainly involves the acquisition both of
knowledge and of techniques of thinking, but that is far from being
enough.

Among the characteristics which most notably differentiate the
adolescent from the fully grown personality two stand out. The adolescent's primary problem lies with himself, with his or her recent
discovery of the self and the consequent search for a personal
identity. All of a sudden the sole meaning of the world seems to lie
in the existence of this one visible entity—the self. Self-centeredness—referring all experience to oneself (sometimes called existentialism)—is the natural state of man between the dependence of
childhood and the emergence of whatever finished product there
may be; even the famous idealism of youth is usually little more
than uninformed self-righteousness and the inability to conceive of
a set of circumstances and attitudes different from one's own. There

is nothing much wrong with this, provided the condition is transitory; growing up means outgrowing this phase. Second, adolescence of necessity lacks experience, especially the experience of consequences; the so-called rashness of youth—the taking of risks both sensible and senseless—usually reflects an inability to foresee the results of action.

For both these inescapable obstacles to growing up, a study of history can provide exceptionally useful, because exceptionally accessible, remedies. Even a superficial acquaintance with the existence, through millennia of time, of numberless human beings helps to correct the normal adolescent inclination to relate the world to oneself instead of relating oneself to the world; if growing up means coming to terms with the fact that everybody has to live in company, and that in that company he or she will not be the sole focus of interest, understanding about other people in other times and places powerfully assists by putting the uniqueness of one's personal experience into proper perspective. The effect is much improved if it becomes clear that the world in which one lives and with which one is familiar is not the only world that can exist or has existed; the variety of cultures and societies discoverable even in a mere 5,000 years of documented history acts as a powerful antidote to the conviction that all problems can be solved by the prejudices and preconceptions that seem so much like eternal verities to the newly self-conscious adolescent. Secondly, history, demonstrating at every turn the consequences of action, can begin to bring home the fact that one's self affects future events and the fates of others in ways that need thinking about—that merely doing what one wants, or what one thinks right, can lead to results which even the doer will come to regard as highly regrettable.

Thus history teaches those adjustments and insights which help the adolescent to become adult, surely a worthy service in the education of youth. But if it is to teach those lessons, real thought has to be given to the kind of history that is brought before the adolescent. Here, unfortunately, the fashion of the day undermines the virtues of the subject. If it is to help by showing up the variety of human experience, it is a mistake to concentrate on that historical society and situation which is nearest to the student's own world: no history is less adapted to the purpose than that of the past 200 years. Its very familiarity merely buttresses the adolescent conviction that the only world that can be, or should be, is his own. If that is so, he can either settle comfortably into a self-centered existence or adopt the even less adult way of rejecting the existing world for an imaginary one, often supposed by ignorance to have existed in the past. The history of Utopian or Golden Age dreamers provides plenty of evidence for what such enduringly adolescent attitudes may do in the real world.

Nor does it help that schoolteachers have heard about the inadvisability of ascribing historical events to individuals, to great men or men less than great. If it were true (as it is often taught) that man's fate is ruled by impersonal forces, the lessons of cause-and-effect, of the responsibility of action, would easily be lost. Working historians help themselves with such shorthand notions, and some of them come to believe in the reality of such abstractions; they do not necessarily come to harm. But the areas of operation at present—and often rightly—preferred by working historians are by no means automatically the right areas to put before the growing child, nor should he or she be treated as though he or she were merely half-developed practitioners of the real enterprise. There are ways of looking at the past appropriate to the child, the adolescent, the university student, the professional historian, and none of them is altogether like any of the rest.

Least of all should the history taught in schools be a mere pale replica of that which preoccupies the research scholar. Instead it should seek to stir the imagination into grasping the long passage of time, the vast numbers and varieties of human beings, the differences as well as the samenesses throughout the aeons, so that a real interest in the past may become a first preparation for coming to terms with the real, the adult, world. Since that sort of semi-emotional understanding is also basic to an advanced historical understanding—since no one can be a historian merely by intellectual labour and without a deep-rooted feeling for people in their own time and on their own terms—this kind of history is also important to that small minority of adolescents who become historians; but their needs are not a primary concern. The primary concern is to help children grow up, becoming better, more thoughtful, more tolerant human beings.

Nothing is lost and much is gained by postponing the details of historical science until a proper imaginative and other-people centered grasp of the immensity of mankind's experience has been established. . . .

. . . I would wish to use [imagination] in order to call up the unfamiliar and not immediately present. Very recent history or the study of, say, a village site is supposed to make history real: but what they make real is only the same old thing, and the whole virtue of diversity, the awe of difference, are lost. I would rather have children hear of pharaohs and Assyrians, of Incas and life under the Han dynasty, than of industrial revolutions or Tudor monarchs. Once they grasp that there have been strange, yes and wondrous, things as real as the experience they meet day by day, they are halfway to growing up.

And secondly I would not wish to concentrate so much on the techniques of thinking—conceptualization and analysis—which can do good only after the reality of the matter so treated has been firmly grasped. I know that I am asking, among many things, that examination syllabi should be changed and that teachers should acquire a taste for the autonomy of the past instead of the relevance of the present. But I am encouraged to think that I may not be wholly wrong when I look at the common effect of current historical study in the schools. Teaching there is nowadays often enthusiastic and committed (in various ways), and it has moved a long way from the deadening effects of memorizing stuff meaningless to the child (the clauses of the Second Reform Act—remember?). Nevertheless, it still lacks the one commitment that really matters—the commitment to the real, ever-present, ever-vanished past. History should be taught because it is history, not because it can be an instrument in intellectual—or worse, political—instruction. Far too many children still emerge with a conviction that history is dull, and they do so because it gets built round concepts, not people. Even those whose interest survives—through natural aptitude, good fortune, exceptional teaching, but rarely through "doing projects"—have little sense of the reality of the past, which to them involves, not knowing about mankind and its fate, but the solving of intellectual puzzles. The clouds trailed by Piaget, Bruner, and Bloom still hide the sun.*

---

*Jean Piaget, Jerome Bruner, and Benjamin S. Bloom have written on educational theory. See, for example, Jean Piaget, *The Child's Conception of the World* (New York: Harcourt, Brace, 1929); Jerome Bruner, *The Process of Education* (Cambridge, Mass.: Harvard University Press, 1960); and Benjamin Samuel Bloom, *All Our Children Learning: A Primer* (New York: McGraw-Hill, 1981).

The Usefulness
of Useless Knowledge

Philip D. Jordan

Philip D. Jordan (b. 1903) taught at Long Island University, Miami University, and the University of Minnesota. He specialized in medicine and public health as well as frontier law in nineteenth-century America, and his writings included *The National Road* (1948) and *Frontier Law and Order* (1970). "The Usefulness of Useless Knowledge" was originally published in *The Historian* (May 1960).

*T*he text for this article is taken from the first chapter of the gospel according to Bertrand Russell. Found on page forty-eight of his essay on how to read and understand history it reads: "The State, when it educates you, has the public object of supplying you with useful knowledge."[1] If, perchance, the source of this text seems unorthodox—which, indeed, it is—I can provide the faithful with another. In the second verse of the fifteenth chapter of the Book of Job is written: "Should a wise man utter vain knowledge, and fill his belly with the east wind?"

Historians will recognize that each of these quoted texts is an historical source. Although one is more ancient than the other, there is no standard of criticism which validly maintains that an older source is truer and the more to be depended upon. Values do not necessarily grow better with age the way fine whiskey does. Each of these texts appears in type and so presumably must be of more than ordinary significance, for in this country that which is printed is considered more reliable than that which is not printed. This judgment is the reason why teachers can silence doubting Thomases by spreading wide a textbook and proclaiming, "It says so right here."

This is an excellent classroom device, for at one and the same time it stifles curiosity in the student, relieves the instructor from the intellectual exertion of really meeting the challenge of doubt and skepticism, and makes the printing press a sort of contemporary Delphic oracle.

The textbook, a sort of outward manifestation of an inward disgrace, is symbolic of the emphasis placed upon the cult of usefulness and practicality which has grown with the years until now the cult is a mystic order whose priests hold that history must perform a truly utilitarian service to society. The teaching of history, it is argued, helps the child to be a better citizen; history helps to develop character and integrity in young Americans and aids the young person to become an informed citizen.

In short, the current feeling is that history, if it is to justify itself, must *do* something, and this something must be beneficial to society. History becomes, to quote Exodus, a balm of Gilead, "an oil of holy ointment, an ointment compounded after the art of the apothecary." To change the figure of speech: history is a tool which man can be taught to use in order to help him solve his problems. This itch to set Clio to doing something practical is not localized—it manifests itself among both professionals and laymen.

I can understand, by calling upon all my tolerance, the almost fierce demand for practicality made by non-scholars who want their children trained and equipped as they quaintly say "to meet life." But, even drawing upon all my patience, I cannot comprehend the teacher who emphasizes or recognizes only the useful or the utilitarian value of history. Perhaps I may relate the saga told of a youthful delegate to a convention of the National Council for the Social Studies, who stuck in the tar pit of usefulness. He too, like knights of old, conceived that history and the social sciences were embarked upon a noble mission of secular salvation. This young Don Quixote, whose lance was shattered before he smote the windmill, is alleged to have said:

> I spoke in the discussion period to the effect that our major task [the task of the social scientists] should be to make social science more scientific and not to desert social science for chemistry and physics. . . . I thought that the major task that faced us in social science was determining which aspects of scientific methods which had proven successful in biology or astronomy or physics could be used in the study of human society.

If history is included among the social sciences, then this ardent young missionary would have history bend more and more to the scientific method to the end that more might be learned of human society. In a sense this earnest young man was only repeating Francis Bacon, who once said that the natural scientist must "put Nature to the question." The only difficulty is that the historian is under no obligation to make up his mind about anything in any stated time period. History, despite what J. B. Bury wrote, is not a science. Indeed, it is doubtful whether history belongs in the same category as political science, sociology, anthropology, or geography.

Familiarity, as Arnold Toynbee has said, is the opiate of imagination; but unfamiliarity, I submit, may be the opiate of reason. Both the advocate of history as a utilitarian subject and the delegate who endorsed scientific methods seemed to be quite unaware that they were sponsoring a theory of progress enunciated by scholars of the Enlightenment. Among these, of course, were Turgot, who looked forward to a future perfection, and Condorcet, whose stimulating *Sketch of the Historical Progress of Mankind* pictured a coming era of sublime social perfection. If belief in providence was replaced by belief in progress, then most certainly progress became identified with the useful, the utilitarian, the materialistic. From here it is only one short step to a devastating conclusion: anything which is useful is socially good and desirable. To be of worth, history must be utilitarian. It must make good citizens, must train for social responsibility, must enable the indoctrinated to help solve man's problems. Useful knowledge is set against useless knowledge. The former has value; the latter is silly and wasteful.

No one can reasonably object to a technique or concept merely because it is useful. But this is not the point. The real question is, Can any one object to an idea or a body of knowledge just because it is useless?

Is it not possible that throughout the long history of mankind useless, impractical ideas and methods have in some magical and mysterious fashion exerted a more useful influence than might be supposed? Always there is a difference between the philosophy of a beginning and the credo of an end result. In the case of history the butterfly does not always come from the caterpillar, although, on occasion, it may.

I invariably tell those of my students who have recently come from high school that they are about to taste the undiluted pleasure of investigating a body of knowledge which as a body of knowledge—not information—is absolutely useless. History, I explain, is an aggregation of truths, half-truths, semi-truths, fables, myths, rumors, prejudices, personal narratives, gossip, and official prevarications. It is a canvas upon which thousands of artists throughout the ages have splashed their conceptions and interpretations of a day and an era. Some motifs are grotesque and some are magnificent.

I confess to these young students that historians differ among themselves not only as to the nature of history but also as to the reliability of history. And at this point I enjoy quoting from the translator's preface of Abbé Clavigero's wondrous *History of Mexico*, which appeared in an English edition in 1807. "Partiality, prejudice, ignorance, credulity," wrote the translator, "have occasioned them [Spanish historians] all to blend so many absurdities and improbabilities with their accounts, that it has not been merely difficult, but altogether impossible, to ascertain the truth."

Up to this point many graduates from high school never had thought of history as a fragile reed, nor had they ever been introduced to it as a means by which to search for truth. For some students history always had been a vague something or other by which problems were solved. And the problems always seem rather insignificant. They may concern, for example, anything from the problem of building a frontier cabin to the problem of segregation or sectarian prejudice or nativism or any one of a dozen or more other "problems" that had been created by boards of education which produce "guides to the social studies," most of which are actually misguided attempts to set the educational pattern in a form more rigid than any ever conceived by the scholastics. It is difficult to demonstrate that the problems so neatly conceived in the guides ever are solved in classrooms. Indeed, many have never been solved by anyone.

History, like the fine arts and like literature, should be an adventure of the mind. Let it remain an act of faith. History is really the core of a liberal arts education. History as a problem-solver degenerates to an exercise, a soft bit of profitless time consumption as unreal and as artificial as curriculum-makers can manufacture.

In this connection, I invariably ask students to read John Franklin Jameson's letter of December 22, 1906, to Robert S. Woodward. Jameson was an historian and Woodward was a scientist with a great enthusiasm for astronomy. Woodward argued that the Carnegie Institution should grant larger sums of money to the physical sciences—because they were of greater utility—than to historical investigation and research. Jameson replied in this fashion:

> It is just as essential to clear the human mind of error and set it thinking correctly upon the relations of man to man and of nation to nation as upon the relations of man to the universe: . . . an establishment dispensing money for such purposes in the twentieth century neglects a large part of its duty if it makes no systematic provision for those philological and literary studies out of which in the last fifty years so much has come.

Let economics and political science and sociology, if they wish, become the practical problem-solvers. Permit them to be active, aggressive, militant. But separate them from history, for they do not belong together. If such a separation could be accomplished, it might relieve the history teacher from the profitless burden of concentrating so much upon beads of fact strung upon the ribbon of time. It might then be possible to see and think of history not only as an accumulation of events but also as a wide humanistic avenue leading to the gates of knowledge. Then might occur what Benedetto Croce describes in a chapter filled with dramatic suggestion:

> When the mind prepares itself for historical reflection and research, what the poet said happens. We climb the peak of the centuries whence our eye dominates countries and cities which were previously seen only sketchily and piecemeal, and aspects of life which were at first veiled by the smoke of action now seen limpid.[2]

This quotation does not mean that I advocate the substitution of speculation for the study of facts—whatever facts are. I am only suggesting that, perhaps too frequently, speculation suffers because of an overemphasis upon concrete, specific details. Knowledge of tangibles is significant if only to prove social conformity and adjustment. Thus, every child should know that George Washington was the first president of his country just as every child should learn how to knot the laces of his shoes, but which bit of knowledge is the more important is difficult to say. The point lies not in this oversimplified illustration, but in the fact that many teachers today seem unable to distinguish between the uselessness of useful knowledge and the usefulness of useless knowledge. In short, they lack an idea of history, or, perhaps, a philosophy of history.

The search for meaning in history is not easy, but neither is it beyond a student's capabilities. The student must collect a corpus of facts: he must master their historical anatomy; he must collect specimens of human events. But these facts, this anatomy, and these specimens do not in and of themselves constitute history, for as yet they have no meaning. They are quite useless—as meaningless as an exposed ulna in a dissecting room before the medical student knows that the ulna fits into the arm and that the arm is a part of a complete skeleton. . . .

Many of the philosophic schools have attempted to demonstrate the usefulness and the practicality of history. And each in large measure has failed, if only for the reason that not one among them has been able to agree with the others upon what constitutes the practical or the utilitarian. No one will deny that knowing a fact may be useful if one has a need for that particular and specific bit of information. Nor can it be denied that a series of facts are valuable if one has need for a knowledge of a string of apparently connected events. Yet neither a single fact nor a sequence of facts constitutes history— this is what too many teachers and students fail to appreciate.

Indeed, history is not necessarily an awareness of what happened in a certain place at a given moment of time. One may know, for example, that a Proclamation of 1763 stipulated that Englishmen should not migrate to certain lands lately acquired as the result of a war with France and still not possess any historical knowledge. It is possible to be in possession of complete details concerning the Trojan Horse and still lack historical knowledge. A student may have at his command all the biographical details of Jackson's career and still be completely lacking in an understanding of what Jackson represents as a man, as a symbol, and as a myth.

When history is smothered by the social sciences, the student receives the impression that history, because it is presented to him primarily as a practical tool for the solving of problems, is finite and fixable and a certainty. It is a completed and finished thing and all that is needed is to obey. Such a view brings almost automatically to mind a passage from Exodus: "Thus was all the work of the tabernacle of the tent of the congregation finished: and the children of Israel did according to all that the Lord commanded Moses, so did they."

But history, unlike the tabernacle, is never finished. Each generation sees it through new eyes. New men see it anew and record it with fresh insight. Agatha Christie in *The Moving Finger* allowed a young school girl to run on and on about history until she finally burst out: "Such a lot of things seem to me such rot. History, for instance. Why, it's quite different out of different books!" An older person replies, "That is its real interest."

I am concerned that we may be losing in this nation the leaven of the spirit of the liberal arts: that learning for learning's sake is, in some quarters, no longer considered desirable; that everything we do and think must be directed toward the solution of a practical formula. More and more we seem to try to reach how to make a living, how to adjust to society, and not how to live a good life.

Recently I took part in a panel discussion on the meaning of the liberal arts. I told an audience of college students that I was appearing as both serf and free man, for history demanded that I bind myself to laws of evidence and criticism and at the same time afforded me limitless opportunities to roam freely through all of man's past, to investigate what I chose, to ponder and to speculate without any shackles and without being bound by any loyalty oath.

History, I pointed out, belongs to the liberal arts because it is not a practical subject. It seeks not so much to impart information as it does to promote knowledge which may, in turn, result in a measure of wisdom. Pure history, like pure science, has no interest whatsoever in accomplishing anything; rather it permits the student to gain a perspective, to be an acute observer of man and his institutions, and to examine our mighty intellectual heritage which those who have gone before have shaped in their hours of persecution, of triumph, of supernaturalism and materialism, of scholasticism and humanism in the eras of monarchy and democracy.

History, whether in the grades or the high school or the college, should open—for the mere sake of curiosity—the story of art and literature, the annals of scientific change, the treasures of religion and philosophy. History exists to widen men's minds, to spread the intellect to the universe of subjective values as well as to the world of objective things. The liberalizing and gently beneficent influence of history brings wide understanding, and with comprehension comes patience and a tolerance that is beyond understanding.

The study of history should enable the student to observe calmly and dispassionately, to weigh judiciously, to maintain poise—to be, in short, a liberally-educated individual. Students should study history primarily because it is impractical, because it does not promise to add a single devaluated dollar to their income, because they burn with desire to know for knowing's sake. The history student is not learning to make a cigarette with a better filter, not removing the caffeine from coffee because the world's a nervous place, not designing a complex calculating machine, not touching-off a rocket whose destination lies in the misty realm of inter-stellar space.

All the liberal arts—each and every one—seek to transform savages into humanists. And history helps. The purpose of history is liberal and pliable. The purpose of the social studies seems narrow and brittle. In this distinction lies the difference between the educated man and the trained man. Eliseo Vivas, professor of moral and intellectual philosophy at Northwestern University, made the point this way:

> Education is something that happens to a mind when it awakens to the need to assimilate the spiritual and the intellectual heritage of our civilization, when it seeks to come into possession of its literature and arts, its philosophy, its theology, its science of nature and of man, and when it seeks to order its acquisitions in the proper historical perspective. An educated man in this sense is a man who is something the merely trained man is not. The trained man possesses his subject matter, uses it externally, instrumentally; his mind is well stocked with facts, ideas, theories. But neither fact, nor idea, nor theory can be part of a man; neither can they be incorporated into the person, to be constitutive of himself, nor can they be espoused as values can. For this reason the educated man is not necessarily the erudite, the walking encyclopedia. . . . The educated man does not possess theories or facts. He possesses art or literature, theology or philosophy, or science. These and not facts or theories can be an organic component of a personality—the very stuff of one's being.

The true task of the historian, like the fundamental obligation of the liberal arts, is to give to students on every level depth and breadth of insight. This means more than mere training. We need teachers in this country who know how to guide students to ask the hardest questions, "who make us teach, who fight us all the way, who go to the library because they want to and not because we send them, who are at least intellectual trouble-makers, who are exploring even the craziest ideas, who can teach us that we do not know the answers."

. . . Is education . . . today overemphasizing the acquisition of skills and the solving of problems? Study guides and teachers' manuals list initiatory activities, developmental activities, and culminating activities. With so many skills and activities, when is there time for thought, the very foundation of the educating process?

Some may charge that an emphasis upon thought is only a worthless ambition of eggheads. Others may criticize the hardboiled egghead as being insensitive and unsympathetic to what schools are attempting to do and what classroom teachers are accomplishing. But, before verdict is passed and sentence imposed, the plea needs to be finished and the argument concluded. To do this, it is necessary to turn Clio's wheel full circle, to return to the world of the Greek historians, to review both the writings and the points of view of Herodotus and Thucydides. To Herodotus, the major aim of the historian was to entertain an audience; hence he could blend truth with fancy and fiction with fabrication. Thucydides, on the other hand, was concerned with keeping a human record which was both truthful and accurate. It was he who gave man the first definition which showed the usefulness of history: "The accurate knowledge of what has happened will be useful, because, according to human probability, similar things will happen again."

So it was that history became practical instruction in statesmanship. It was a useful tool to be used in the art of war. It gave men a body of examples, principles, and precepts. When we talk about history building character or presenting man with a code by which to live, we have merely a hang-over from classical times.

History exists neither to be practical nor to be studied for its own sake. There is no contradiction in terms or thought here. In the first place, history, like any other discipline, cannot be divorced from the sum of man's experience and the total knowledge he has gained from those experiences. In the second place, history is disinterested even if we view it as a science, which it is not. And the teacher must be equally disinterested. Perhaps the task of the historian is simply to keep the record and attempt to find out how human events occurred.

Such a view does not deny, obviously, that someone somewhere may use history for his own practical ends and useful purposes. A breakfast food concern may want a history of itself or a railroad may desire a chronicle of its past. Perhaps these institutions desire narratives of their inception and growth as a part of a public relations campaign; perhaps they wish to celebrate a centennial with a book; perhaps they wish to justify or rationalize past policies and actions; perhaps they wish a history only to glorify a founder or a founding family. Who knows why some histories are written? But, whatever the reasons, the objectives are as practical as a ledger sheet.

Yet history never can be approached in the same spirit as the cereal manufacturer may approach it. In the final analysis, history must be studied and written as if, as Bury writes, "it has no bearing on anything beyond itself." This is the most difficult of all lessons to drive home to students.

History has value for man in precisely the identical manner that art and poetry possess eternal truths for man. And if, as in all wisdom, man's reach exceeds his grasp, is this not the true purpose of education? The historian, like Robert Browning, must embody successfully the complex variations of the human spirit, must give values substance, must make thought a personal experience. There is pathos and pain and frustration and exultation in learning and in finite hearts that yearn. Truth more frequently is mirrored in symbol than in fact. And students desperately need these dancing symbols to feed upon, for, without them, there is not much left.

Our knowledge is, indeed, a torch of smoky pine that lights the pathway but one step ahead.

References

1. Bertrand Russell, *Understanding History and Other Essays* (New York: Philosophical Library, 1957), 48.

2. See Benedetto Croce, *History as the Story of Liberty,* trans. Sylvia Sprigge (New York: Meridian Books, 1955), chap. 10, for a fuller discussion.

On Knowing the Past

Michael Kammen

Michael Kammen (b. 1936) is professor of American history and culture and director of the Society for the Humanities at Cornell University. Among the books he has written and edited are *A Rope of Sand: The Colonial Agents, British Politics, and the American Revolution* (1968); *People of Paradox: An Inquiry Concerning the Origins of American Civilization*, which won the Pulitzer Prize for History in 1973; *"What Is the Good of History?": Selected Letters of Carl L. Becker, 1900–1945* (1973); and *The Past Before Us: Contemporary Historical Writing in the United States* (1980). "On Knowing the Past" originally appeared in the *New York Times* (February 6, 1979).

Have we recently reached a critical juncture in our relationship to History? Abundant signs say yes. To judge by rising museum attendance, increasing book sales, successful television programs and historical-preservation activities, nostalgia is surely in the saddle.

Nostalgia would seem to be a mindless, if not headless horseman, however, because newspaper surveys reveal a woeful ignorance of the national past by Americans with above-average educational backgrounds. . . .

This problem exemplifies a more general American ambivalence about the past—an ambivalence that has been visible for three centuries. Americans who are policy-makers and opinion-makers, for example, have had a strangely ambiguous relationship to history.

Let us look at three of the most interesting Americans in our pantheon: Thomas Jefferson, Ralph Waldo Emerson and Henry Ford. Associated with each is a provocative statement about our need to be released from the burdens of an oppressive or meaningless past. Each statement is actually more complex than a one-line excerpt can reveal, but at least the one-liners serve to jog our memories:

"The earth belongs in usufruct to the living . . . the dead have neither powers nor rights over it." (Jefferson to James Madison, Sept. 6, 1789.)

"Our age is retrospective. . . . It writes biographies, histories, and criticism. The foregoing generations beheld God and nature face to face, we, through their eyes. . . . Why should not we have a poetry and philosophy of insight and not of tradition, and a religion by revelation to us, and not the history of theirs?" (Emerson, "Nature," 1836.)

"History is more or less bunk." (Ford in a newspaper interview, 1916.)

The problem with taking any of these pithy remarks too seriously is that they are not only misguided as declarations, in my opinion, but they are not even representative of the three men who offered them.

Consider the fact that Jefferson, in his 1781 "Notes on the State of Virginia," the only book he ever wrote and a classic of American thought, pleaded for the necessary centrality of History in the curriculum of secondary-school students. "History, by apprizing them of the past, will enable them to judge of the future; it will avail them of the experience of other times and other nations; it will qualify them as judges of the actions and designs of men."

Consider the fact that Emerson wrote an 1841 essay called "History" in which he declared that "Man is explicable by nothing less than all his history. . . . There is a relation between the hours of our life and the centuries of time."

And consider the fact that emblazoned on an iron sign in front of Greenfield Village and the Henry Ford Museum in Dearborn, Michigan, are these words from a Henry Ford grown wiser than the 1916 curmudgeon: "The farther you look back, the farther you can see ahead."

How are we supposed to make sense of such contradictory utterances?

First, of course, we must recognize that their views were as variable as ours. All lived long lives, witnessed and participated in the making of history, and changed their minds on certain key matters from time to time.

Second, we should appreciate that they distinguished between the desirability of knowing history and the imperative that we not be prisoners of the past.

Third, we must recognize that there is a tension contained within the cliché that we ought to learn from the lessons of the past. Do we learn from the so-called wisdom of the past, or do we profit from the follies of the past? Jefferson made that distinction, and preferred the second alternative.

One reason why Americans may frequently recite the negative statements of Jefferson, Emerson and Ford and prefer to neglect their affirmations of historical study is that we have been—most of us, most of the time—an optimistic and opportunistic people. We want to believe that "it" will all work out for the best.

The problem is that history shows us that "it" doesn't always. History, real history, isn't chock full of happy endings.

Listen to Walter Lippmann back in 1914: "Modern men are afraid of the past. It is a record of human achievement, but its other face is human defeat." How right he was—all the more reason why we must know and understand the past. We have at least as much to learn from our defeats as from our achievements.

Why, then, should we really want to know the past? Here are a few reasons that I find most compelling:

To make us more cognizant of human differences and similarities, over time and through space.

To help us appreciate far more fully than we do the nonrational and irrational elements in our behavior: what James Boswell called, in 1763, "the unaccountable nature of the human mind."

To enhance our awareness of the complexity of historical causation—the unanticipated intertwining of opinion and events—and their consequences for our understanding of that whirlwind we call social change.

To acknowledge more fully and critically than we do the consequences of what is at stake when powerful people interpret history for partisan purposes on the basis of insufficient or inaccurate information about the past.

To avoid the tendency to ascribe equal value to all relationships and events. Worse than no memory at all is the undiscriminating memory that cannot differentiate between important and inconsequential experiences.

It is the historian's vocation to provide society with a discriminating memory.

The Past and the New

Gordon Leff

Gordon Leff (b. 1926) has written on various topics in intellectual history and philosophy and is professor of history at the University of York. His books include *Medieval Thought* (1958), *Heresy in the Later Middle Ages* (1967), *Paris and Oxford Universities in the Thirteenth and Fourteenth Centuries* (1968), *History and Social Theory* (1969), *William of Ockham: The Metamorphosis of Scholastic Discourse* (1975), and *The Dissolution of the Medieval Outlook* (1976). "The Past and the New" originally appeared in *The Listener* (April 1969).

It used to be believed that we could learn from the past; and this belief provided history with its justification. Sixty years ago, history, together with classics, was considered the most suitable subject for training statesmen. An influential school of thinkers, especially in Germany, regarded it as the foundation of all human understanding and of the humanities. Today history has become another discipline and the social studies have become increasingly ahistorical. It is true that more history is written and read than ever before, but few of those doing either would claim any special status for history. Even when we invoke history's verdict it is meant more as a figure of speech than as a conviction that history will really judge.

The reasons for this change are obvious enough. On the one hand, we have largely lost any firm sense of the future, so that we no longer turn to the past for guidance or comfort. The age of belief in historical destiny, whether as the working of God's providence or as the realisation of a secular ideal such as progress or nationhood, itself belongs to history. Its passing has left a void that history as traditionally conceived cannot fill, just because we do not have a sense of direction. This development has been accompanied, on the other hand, by the turning away of the social sciences from history to the methods of the natural sciences. They seem to offer the certainty that history cannot give, with its relativism and seeming lack of coherence. Whereas history deals in endless concrete situations, from which universal laws cannot be drawn, the quantitative methods and general categories of the natural sciences provide just these universal laws which have become increasingly the preoccupation of the social studies.

Does this mean, then, that history has nothing to offer except as an academic discipline or bedside reading? I do not think so. On the contrary, I want to argue that it is precisely the dynamic, relative character of history, its preoccupation with the specific and the concrete, its lack of regularity, that makes it indispensable to all social and human understanding; and that the rejection of the old notion of historical destiny for that of the future as open gives history a greater importance now, when so much more depends upon our conscious choices, than in the past. In my view the present unsatisfactory state of the social studies, including much history, is directly attributable to the failure to recognise this. What we need is to reinstate the historical dimension into our thinking, not to escape from it into a world of non-temporal abstractions.

I have two grounds for saying this. The first is the opposite of the traditional defence of history: namely, that as the study of the past it offers us precedents for the present. I don't deny that it may, or that there is an obvious connection between the past and present. It is rather that this is largely irrelevant to understanding either the past or the present. No doubt, in certain situations, parallels with the past can provide a moral boost, as with the parallels drawn in 1940 between Britain's situation then and in 1800. But most of history does not revolve around such comparisons, and when it does the result is usually history at its most jejune. Why? Because history, although it is directed to the past, is essentially about the new. It is read and written as the unfolding of events which by definition have not occurred before. That is the only reason for their having a history. If Hitler's invasion threat in 1940 had been identical with Napoleon's in 1800, no separate study of Hitler's would be needed: we should merely say: "For Hitler in 1940 see Napoleon 1800." We don't do this, precisely because they were different, even if the circumstances were in each case similar.

Now the very need for precedents is evidence that we are confronted with something outside our previous experience, and the fact that we rarely find them beyond the most superficial and formal resemblances in history is no less evidence that history is the record of difference rather than of similarity. Let me develop that. Of course in one sense there is an overall similarity in history since it is about men; but this doesn't give it continuity. Indeed what distinguishes history and the human studies is that they are built around change, whether of a culture, a language, a system of law or institutions. Only when they are treated as abstractions can they be regarded as constant. But to see social phenomena exclusively in abstract and static terms does not make for superior knowledge: indeed often quite the reverse.

That is where history, indeed all social knowledge, is different from the natural and formal sciences. Where these last presuppose determinism, the repetition of the same processes given the same conditions, history presupposes contingency: that no two individuals or their circumstances will be exactly the same. Men's human history, as opposed to their natural history, is not the repetition of endless life cycles of individuals, but of repeated changes, which break the cycle and give it a new direction. History is written around these. Not every occurrence has to be a turning-point to be significant; but history can only be conceived in terms of difference, even if it is only the formal differences of one king succeeding another. And when it is only formal, so is the history written about it. Even the old-fashioned history books passed rapidly over the reigns of the unimportant kings to get to the highlights. We may not now agree with their criteria, but we make the same assumption that something is historically important in the degree to which it makes a difference. Whether this was for change or conservation is secondary to whether it represents something new. The so-called Carolingian Renaissance of the ninth century, for example, aimed merely at reviving education, not creating new knowledge; but this in itself was a striking development, even though it did not survive.

The presence of something that was not there before gives history its meaning. Charlemagne without his empire and his reforms would have been just another Frankish king. Through them he marks a new phase in the history of the earlier Middle Ages. We read and write the history of his reign in this light.

The same applies to any history. Its point is still to tell a story, or at least unfold a sequence. Like any sequence it is orientated to the future, which by definition is not revealed in the present, because there is no set way in which men are bound to act, even if they tend to act in certain ways at certain times. It is precisely in considering the possible alternatives within any situation that its history lies. Even if the predictable result is the one that emerges—say, that a strong army beats a small one—the result has still to be considered within the context of the other countervailing possibilities, which, until they were overcome, were part of the situation. No amount of knowing about Edward I's achievements can tell us how they turned to nothing in Edward II's reign, any more than we can know about Napoleon from knowing about the outbreak of the French Revolution in 1789. We cannot do so because at the time the future remained open. That is what makes us turn to history to understand how it came to be. Were we able to deduce Edward II's reign or Napoleon independently of the events which led to them, we should no more write their history than we write the history of the kettle which boils, to account for its boiling. It is the difference between determinism and contingency. The one gives the universal conditional laws of nature and the natural sciences; the other, in having a future which is different from the present, demands history to make it intelligible: to enable us to discover how and perhaps why men took one course rather than another when more than one course remained open to them.

But history doesn't just provide a context to what would otherwise be merely a shapeless succession of events: it enables us to measure what is common down the ages and what is peculiar to men at different epochs; to distinguish between what men are and have to suffer in virtue of being men, and what they can do and what they can become as individuals and members of diverse societies. This antinomy between the universal and the epochal is central to historical understanding. It doesn't take place in a void. It is we who put the questions about a particular segment of history, just as the scientist tests his hypothesis about a particular segment of nature. Neither is just an observer; both are actively involved in manipulating their data to bring order to it.

But with this difference: that the historian is concerned not just with facts but also with values. That is what makes his, and all social, knowledge different from that of nature and the natural sciences. To know about a rock crystal entails grasping the universal scientific laws under which it can be subsumed, and which therefore hold for all similar cases; knowledge of any kind of social phenomenon, on the other hand, from religion to banking, demands grasping the system of values to which it belongs; it is not enough to describe its operations, we have to penetrate to its meaning for those who operated it. I deliberately use the word *penetrate*, which has come to have pejorative associations with some kind of mystical or nonintellectual intuition, because this is what human actions involve. Just as we cannot understand an argument unless we know the meaning of the words used, so we cannot understand the way in which men act unless we know the ideals and interests which actuate them.

It is the tension between them, between how men conceive what they are doing and what happens, which forms the dialectic of history. By that I do not mean that it is a law of development, but that it is common to all human action and as such should be a datum of history as of any other social study. The way in which men evaluate reality is historically part of that reality. It is itself a fact. So there is not any question of a dichotomy between subjective interpretation and objective fact: for, as in any scientific law, the interpretation is part of the fact. So long as it holds they are inseparable; if not, it must be revised. But whereas the need to bring hypothesis and data into alignment is the condition of scientific knowledge, historical and social understanding rests upon accepting a built-in opposition between them. That is the difference between the two kinds of knowledge. For the human studies there is an element of myth inherent in human thinking and conduct. It represents man's response to his world, and runs in a spectrum from the image that we have of ourselves to that which we have of the cosmos. Much of it is not overtly conscious, but neither is it false consciousness. It is rather an amalgam of habit, tradition and experience which derives from a society's attitudes and practices; it owes as much to the past as to the present, to preconception as to perception, to the ideal as to the actual. The forms that it can take belong to the contingency of history, but its presence is one of the constants of history.

We inherit a body of beliefs and judgments which make up a kind of collective historical unconscious. It is one of the most formative elements in our lives. For not only does it colour our attitudes to the world but it produces a time-lag in our thinking which can persist over centuries. It is to be seen in conventions, practices, techniques, habits, institutions, which prevail within a society at any given time, and are often so far removed from their origins that they have become either mere ritual or a fetter upon new developments, especially in times of rapid change, as in our society today. But at the very least we are always one generation behind events, because each generation grows up under the influence of the ideas and experiences of the previous generation. It is a historical truism that the subalterns in the Flanders trenches from 1914 to 1918 were the generals who were confounded by Blitzkrieg in 1940, and that our rulers, brought up to believe in an empire on which the sun never set, can even now hardly bring themselves to preside over its final dissolution. The process is ineluctable. It gives rise at one level to the clash between generations: the laments about youth and our loss of values today can be matched almost word for word from any past epoch. But it also leads to the divergences within generations and society itself.

Here we meet with one of the paradoxes which history, not social theory, can reveal: namely, that the very conservatism which time-lag produces is also one of the sources of social change. Nothing, it seems to me, is more misleading than to treat society on an analogy with an organism just because of the discontinuities which can transform a society. These, far from being self-regulating, as in the change from a caterpillar to a butterfly, usually take place through opposition to change. For it is also a truism that we tend to react against anything which seems to violate the habits and expectations in which we have been brought up and which become our norms. Accordingly the more radical the change the more strongly we tend to oppose it.

It is this which helps to make myth so central to history. For if, on the one hand, history revolves round the emergence of the new, on the other this comes about from the diverse ways in which men interpret their situations: so that what emerges is almost invariably in spite of anyone's intentions. Indeed it is not too much to say that the almost endemic resistance to change produced by time-lag has more than anything else engendered change. The more radical developments have been repeatedly through the desire to keep things as they were or to restore them to some past ideal norm. It is in these conceptions that myth is so active. At one extreme it leads to the tension between precept and practice, ought and is, that has inspired all revolutionaries and reformers. Almost without exception they have appealed to a return to what they believed to have been the true state of affairs—whether the apostolic ideal of the Middle Ages, which demanded the restoration of the Church to its original pristine state of possessionlessness and humility, or the belief—of Rousseau and, in a different way, of Marx—that men are born free but are everywhere in chains. These and other ideal conceptions of restoring the true nature of things have dominated entire epochs, as we ourselves know. They lead men to believe and act upon them even when they are hopelessly at variance with the true state of affairs.

It is these beliefs which distinguish men and their history from the natural world. They are no less present at the other extreme, when they uphold the existing order, nor are they any less liable to lead to change, as the repeated holocausts fought in the name of one's country and the status quo show. In every case the ideal takes on a life of its own. It is when myth assumes these proportions that its advocates turn to history, which they mythologise in its support. That is an added reason for the study of history, to keep it from being misappropriated.

But whatever the level, myth is always at work; it is present as much among men who accept their miseries as part of God's dispensation as among those who revolt in fear of a non-existent famine; as much among those who accept the value of their currency as those who panic at the rumour of a devaluation. It is not that one is right and the other wrong, although they can also be that. It is rather that men are what they are, and history is what it is, in virtue of the beliefs which they hold and on which they act. Because these are contingent, as diverse as the possible outcomes and individuals who can realise them, history is indispensable to understanding what is indispensable to men.

History

Harold J. Hanham

Harold J. Hanham (b. 1928) received a Ph.D. from Cambridge University and has taught at the University of Manchester, the University of Edinburgh, Harvard, and the Massachusetts Institute of Technology. He has written about the history of New Zealand, Scotland, and England, and his works include *Elections and Party Management* (1959), *Scottish Nationalism* (1969), and *Bibliography of British History, 1851–1914* (1976). "History" was first published in the *Harvard University Handbook for Undergraduates* (Spring 1972).

*T*he historian is essentially an inquirer, an investigator. His (or her) subject matter is the past experience of mankind. The object of his investigation is the unraveling of the complexities of human behavior, both in individuals and in societies. The historian recognises that the past is as real as the present, that we often know more about it than we do about the present, and that only when we study the past do we see things in the round.

Historians differ in temperament and training. Some are natural storytellers who seek and find a popular market. Some are philosophers bent on elucidating the underlying factors that shape historical developments. Some are biographers preoccupied with individual characteristics. Some are scientists probing the past with relentless precision. Some are poets who see in the past beautiful forms and visions of grandeur. Some are hermits who wish to shut themselves away from imperfections of the present world. Some are politicians, ever conscious that history is constantly breaking into our lives demanding to be heard, some clamoring that past wrongs should be righted, others warning that we are losing touch with our roots.

The student who studies history does so because he, too, wants to become an investigator. He wants to know about the past—sometimes about men, sometimes about events, sometimes about historical processes. He wants to learn the skills that will enable him to write history that will satisfy him because it is a work of art. And history courses are designed for precisely that purpose. This does not mean that they are designed to produce professional historians: far from it. They must provide for the amateur as well as the professional, for the student whose primary interest is in the present, as well as for the student who really cares about the past; for the dilettante with a romantic interest in the history of the sailing ship or in Henry VIII's wives, as well as for the potential professional historian.

History, indeed, came into the undergraduate curriculum as an essentially nonprofessional subject. Its object was no less than the inculcation of wisdom. It took over from the classics as the most popular undergraduate study because it seemed to be a subject better fitted to enable men and women to come to terms with life than a subject confined to a narrow period of human experience, that of ancient Greece and Rome. And it carried with it a special cachet because it was so closely tied to the study of the living traditions of the nation. For the historians of the early twentieth century the history of the nation state was quite as much an epic as the *Iliad* or the *Odyssey* or the *Aeneid.*

All history departments are faced with one great problem: the subject matter of the discipline is so extensive that they must be selective. To give adequate coverage to East Asia they may have to neglect South Asia; if they are to cover the Middle East it may be at the price of neglecting Africa south of the Sahara. There are always student demands for more courses, more specialists, wider coverage, and these demands are always justified. The problem is made all the more acute by the fact that the interests of historians and students are constantly shifting. One generation cares nothing for witchcraft; the next is fascinated by it. One generation is skeptical about psychological history; the next is carried off its feet by Erik Erikson. One generation espouses scientific history and mathematical models; the next in reaction may go for impressionism.

Moreover, individual teachers differ greatly in their interests. I became a historian because I was conscious as a child of living in two worlds: the world of those of my elders who had left England in 1875 and for whom England was still the England of 1875, and the world of everyday life in New Zealand. I became preoccupied, and have remained preoccupied, with the phenomenon of the encapsulation of different value systems within a particular society. I began with the study of the importation of political ideas and institutions into New Zealand, and I moved on to the differences between urban and rural politics in late nineteenth-century England. In the last few years I have been working on a book on the different sets of values in Highland and Lowland Scotland in the nineteenth century, which led to a military occupation of the Western Isles in the 1880s, and last year I gave a course largely concerned with the continuing differences between French and English Canada. Other teachers have a similar history of individual preoccupations over and above those which are more directly involved in their courses.

What holds history together is a set of norms of investigation. The aim is to produce independent investigators, not stereotyped disciples of a particular historical school. The successful student of history is one who has learned to handle masses of data, to analyze them, to draw conclusions, and to write them up with a certain amount of literary skill. He is one, moreover, who can apply the techniques he has learned to other subjects and to other fields of activity. In all walks of life there is need for the man who can investigate skillfully and draw together the results of his investigations in such a form that others may use them.

The Uses of History

Harold Perkin

Harold Perkin (b. 1926) is a social historian who has taught at the University of Manchester and the University of Lancaster. A past president of the Association of University Teachers, he has written *The Origins of Modern English Society, 1780–1880* (1969); *The Age of the Railway* (1970); and *The Age of the Automobile* (1976). The following selection is from *History: An Outline for the Intending Student* (1970).

*W*hat is the use of history? That is a question you often hear from people, even people in universities, who think there is no answer to it. "That's past history," the same people tend to say when they mean something that is dead and gone and no longer relevant. History in the immortal words of *1066 and All That* is "What you can remember," and what most people can remember from their schooldays is a jumble of facts about kings, parliaments and battles which, even when they are correct, have little relevance outside a television quiz. Fortunately, school history is changing and now often deals in a more illuminating way with more interesting themes, but then what is the use of it beyond the pleasure it gives to amateur historians and the money it earns for professional ones? And why go on with it at the university when there are so many more modern and "relevant" subjects to study?

Well, pleasure has its uses, too, and most of the contributors to this volume will tell you of the pleasure and delight their own particular brand of historical study has given to them. "History" comes from a Latin word for a story, which comes from a Greek word for an enquiry, and there is a special kind of pleasure from seeing "what happened next," especially if the story is true rather than fictional, and a special kind of delight in enquiring and finding out for your-

self, especially something which no one living today has found out
before. "History for its own sake," as a pleasurable hobby or pastime,
like literature, art, science, sport or almost anything else, needs no
defence. If you like it, and increasing numbers of people with no
professional interest in it do, then you do it, and no one has any right
to question, as long as you do it in your own time. But there is the
rub: why should anyone be paid to do it by someone else, by their
parents or the taxpayer? What is the use of history to society or the
State? What is the use of it to you yourself in your post-university
life and career?

The answer is that history has many uses, from the very widest,
that it is all around us and we cannot escape it, to the narrowest,
that unless we know how a particular event came to happen we cannot begin to know what is likely to happen next. On the broadest
front, we are all of us faced with the question of Milton's Adam,
"How came I thus, how here?" Seen through the lens of a snapshot
camera the world of the instant present is a puzzling place. "The
moving finger writes and, having writ, moves on" but, contrary to
Omar Khayyam, immediately cancels most of the line, leaving only
the merest traces of evidence of what has happened in the permanent records of what immediately becomes the past. Anyone "born
yesterday," without experience of more than today's world, is at a
complete loss to understand it, to "know the ropes" and how they
came to tie themselves in such complicated knots. To ask in this
situation "What is the use of history?" is like asking "What is the
use of experience?" History is the summarized experience of society,
as experience is the condensed history of the individual. Without
experience the individual is as lost as a baby without a mother, a
learner driver without a qualified passenger, a potholer without a
torch. Without history a society scarcely exists, since it inheres only
in the continuing relationships between its members, which in turn
are merely the expectations that certain patterns of conduct and mutual service will continue in the future as they did in the past; and if
these patterns of conduct change, as they do in response to altered
circumstances such as war, economic crises, population growth, the
impact of new ideas, and the like, they do so not in a random or
arbitrary manner but within certain limits of possibility which an
experienced observer or a well-informed historian will recognize.
The experienced observer will know this intuitively, if his experi-

ence goes back far enough: the well-informed historian will know it consciously and systematically, because it is his job to find out and present it coherently. . . .

The importance of social and economic history for an understanding of the modern world, with its population explosion, its growing gap between the rich industrial nations and the poor agrarian ones, its split between East and West over how society and the economy should be organized, and its growing problem of race relations, is self-evident, and the teacher of history must obviously be equipped to deal with it. What is perhaps less evident is the need for historical understanding of our world at a much humbler level, in the local environment of our own immediate community. In spite of cars and aeroplanes, radio and television, we all spend a large part of our lives in the strictly local environment of our own village, suburb, town or city. This indeed is where history impinges upon us most, for the very fields and footpaths, streets and houses, pubs and churches, shops and public buildings have been placed where they are in relation to each other by men in the past, and for better or worse we still have to live with their decisions. When we wish to change the pattern even slightly we are constrained by living history and have to take account of it. Even more powerfully we are influenced by the community itself, the intimate web of personal relationships we thread our way through every day, and this too is a product of history and understandable only in its terms. . . .

. . . History at the university is not an attempt to learn everything about everything. It is not *what* is studied but *how* it is studied that matters. Contrary to popular opinion, it is not a factual subject, an exhaustive narrative of events, the record of "one damned thing after another." It is an analytical subject, an attempt to discover the *significant* things that have happened, and *why* they happened, what *caused* them and what *they* caused in their turn. Historical research is like crime detection: it addresses itself to solving problems, to finding out not merely the critical ordering of the relevant facts but their meaning and interconnection, the aims and motives of the protagonists, the constraints and pressures of the surrounding circumstances, the place of accident and coincidence, the part played by human charity or malice, skill or clumsiness, success or failure. Like detection, it does this by taking one problem at a time and studying it in depth: the microscope is more informative than the telescope, a prowl round the garden more relevant than a world cruise. Like detection, too, it is a kind of multi-factorial analysis: it cannot afford to ignore any factor, any kind of clue, whatever level of experience it comes from, whether it is labelled political, social, economic, religious, moral, intellectual, technological, scientific, medical, psychological, or just plain human, frivolous or whimsical. Dealing as it does with the whole life of man in past society, nothing human is alien to it, and nothing human escapes its net. Like no other subject it gives an insight into human behaviour in all its manifold aspects. For where else than in the collective experience of men in past society will a knowledge of the infinite possibilities of human conduct be found?

And this is what makes it of use not merely to the layman and the citizen and to the professionals who teach them, but to everyone who has to deal with human beings in complex situations. Business and government of all kinds require, in addition to specialist knowledge, a general capacity to deal with complex human situations, to solve problems, to ferret out the relevant facts and perceive their significance and interconnection, to balance many incompatible factors, financial, legal, technological, psychological and just plain human, against each other, and arrive at some sort of conclusion about them. Now this is what historians do all the time. Even the traditional weekly essay at the university is nothing more than an attempt to assemble the significant facts about a particular problem and arrive at some sort of conclusion, under the critical eye of a tutor. And how much of management and administration consists of just this, the rapid appraisal of the relevant facts and factors of a problem, and the writing of a memorandum or report for the critical eye of the chairman or the minister! It is not so surprising, then, as an *Observer* survey found a few years ago, that the highest-paid graduates in industry by their middle thirties are historians. Who else can get, outside industry itself, the necessary breadth of vision and general training?

The final and most important use of history, though, is neither professional nor utilitarian. It is the sheer enjoyment of the subject, and the wealth of meaning it gives to life in whatever career one pursues. For what historians sell is understanding, understanding of the world around us and the people in it, in all their variety and colour. I for one am profoundly grateful that I am paid for doing what is, after all, one of the noblest, most permanent and fascinating activities of man.

History, Values,
Self-Knowledge, and Identity

History can be helpful in forming the values by which we live, although disagreement exists over how the past relates to the development of values. The philosopher Morris R. Cohen argued that history "cannot prove any moral rules" but that "its study still has a vital ethical interest." For example, he contended, "a sense of history can save us from the habit of attributing our own motives to ancients who lived under conditions different from ours." History may not be able to "solve our ethical problems," Cohen believed, but it is "a necessary condition" for the "better understanding" of such problems. Hans Kohn reflected a more optimistic view about our ability to discover values in the past when he maintained that in the short time humans have recorded their history an ethical tradition has emerged. The study of the past, he said, "can teach us not to look on nations and classes as isolated phenomena but to see and to judge them in a universal context in the light of this ethical tradition." Henri-Irénée Marrou, in a carefully reasoned selection which appears later in this volume, also commented on the importance of history to values. He quoted the Roman Stoic, Seneca, who said that in history "no century is forbidden to us. . . . the force of our mind may go beyond the boundaries of the weakness of the solitary man. . . . We can dispute with Socrates, doubt with Carneades, enjoy the tranquility of Epicurus, with the Stoics conquer human nature, and bypass it with the Cynics. Since the structure of being. . . permits us to enter into communion with all the past, why not tear ourselves away from the narrow limits of our primary temporality and share with the finest minds . . . magnificent and eternal truths." We may not agree with Seneca, or Kohn, or Cohen, but it is difficult to escape the conclusion that some connection exists between our attitude toward history and the meaning we ascribe to the world around us. "If history is meaningless, the world as a whole is meaningless," writes a student of political thought, Glenn Tinder. "If history is absurd, man is a stranger in the universe."[1]

One writer in this section who speaks to the question of history and values is W. B. Gallie. In some ways, Gallie picks up on a theme implicit in the previous section when he says that "historical understanding can assist us, somewhat in the manner of practice for games of skill, . . . to achieve a 'masterful manipulation of the unforeseen.'" But Gallie also contends that "historical understanding can teach us, especially with regard to the institutional sides of life, what we are or where we stand in light of where we have come from" and that it can help us to know "what we ought to do or must never do in many important kinds of moral situations."

History provides us with self-knowledge, which can be important to the formation of values. The historian Arthur Bestor wrote that "there is no substitute for the study of history in the education of men who seek freedom through the understanding of themselves and the world they live in."[2] Self-knowledge and an understanding of our limitations is especially important in this scientific and technological age, according to George F. Kennan, because "the spectacular mechanical and scientific creations of modern man tend to conceal from him the nature of his own humanity and to encourage him in all sorts of Promethean ambitions and illusions." It is not required "that one should know or understand the whole unconscionable and spreading panorama of history," Kennan says. "A little bit, looked at hard and honestly, will do."

Knowledge of oneself is important to developing a sense of identity. Lester D. Stephens maintains that history "provides us with a sense of being," and without it "we would not know who we are, either individually or collectively." Stephens is cautious, though, about drawing moral lessons from the past and contends that "perhaps the single greatest abuse of history is committed by those who try to make it a repository of moral examples and caveats." He says, too, that if we are looking only for practical uses from history we invariably will be disappointed. But the study of the past is useful, he maintains. He agrees with many other writers in this volume that history does expose us to a wider variety of experiences and thus serves an important educational function. Gerda Lerner also thinks that history is necessary for modern societies and is important to gaining a sense of being. "By locating each individual life as a link between generations and by allowing us to transform the dead into heroes and role models for emulation, history connects past and future and becomes a source of personal identity." Although Lerner is speaking to a wide audience, she focuses attention on one field that has been too little studied—women's history.[3]

References

1. See Morris R. Cohen, *The Meaning of Human History* (LaSalle, Ill.: Open Court, 1947), 276–96 (quotations, 289, 291); Hans Kohn, "A Historian's Creed for Our Time," *South Atlantic Quarterly* 52 (July 1953): 347; and Glenn Tinder, "The Necessity of Historicism," *American Political Science Review* 55 (September 1961): 560–65 (quotations, 563). See also Gordon Wright, "History as a Moral Science," *American Historical Review* 81 (February 1976): 1–11.

2. See Arthur Bestor, "The Humaneness of History," *Western Humanities Review* 16 (Winter 1962): 3–9, reprinted in *The Craft of American History: Selected Essays*, ed. A. S. Eisenstadt (New York: Harper and Row, 1966), 9. See also R. G. Collingwood, *The Idea of History* (1946; reprint, New York: Oxford University Press, Galaxy Books), 10.

3. Many other writers have spoken about the past and identification. For example, Sidney Mead, the historian of religion, discusses the significance of history in establishing a "stable identity." Carol Kammen and Michael Kammen show how local history can enhance a "sense of rootedness." See Sidney Mead, *Identity and History* (Missoula, Mont.: Scholars Press, 1979), esp. 9–20, and Carol Kammen and Michael Kammen, "The Uses and Abuses of the Past: A Bifocal Perspective," *Minnesota History* 48 (Spring 1982): 11, 12. See also Page Smith's provocative chapter on "History and the Search for Identity," in *The Historian and History* (New York: Alfred A. Knopf, 1964), 232–49.

The Uses and
Abuses of History

W. B. Gallie

W. B. Gallie (b. 1912) studied at Oxford and Cambridge and taught philosophy at the University of Wales, the University of Keele, and Queen's University of Belfast in Northern Ireland. He was also professor of political science at Cambridge University. In addition to *Philosophy and the Historical Understanding* (1964), from which the following selection is taken, Gallie wrote *Peirce and Pragmatism* (1952) and *Philosophers of Peace and War: Kant, Clausewitz, Marx, Engels, and Tolstoy* (1978).

O ur account of explanations in history serves to reinforce the more general and familiar thesis that historical understanding is of a basically different kind from that achieved in the natural sciences by the discovery of new laws or by learning how to apply established laws to what seemed to be exceptional cases. At the same time, our account includes—and indeed stresses the indispensable service—of such general laws in supporting any new interpretation of the logic of some particularly puzzling historical situation. And equally, our account of historical understanding—of what it means to follow an evidenced narrative—certainly permits the use of any such narrative as a source of supply from which particular cases can be abstracted to suggest or to support this or that general law of the social (or in some cases the physical) sciences. In both these ways, therefore, historical understanding has important links with the kind of understanding that is gained in the sciences. But to grant this is in no way to subtract from our basic claim that historical understanding is something *sui generis*, inasmuch as it is the understanding of how some particular outcome came to be.

But if historical understanding is essentially of this kind, are we not forced to confess that the long-cherished idea of history as a guide to the future has been a sheer illusion? Must we not concede that history is, in itself, useless, or that its value is confined entirely within itself—to the intellectual satisfaction and self-discipline of those who study it, steeping themselves in a past whose intelligibility offers us no positive guidance for the ever-emerging future? Certainly, it seems to me, we should have to consent to this conclusion if the only way in which knowledge can be used or can prove itself useful were that exemplified by the application of scientific laws and formulae to help us meet the problems of practical life. Engineering, medicine, and the rapidly developing social sciences are in action every day before our eyes, to remind us of the importance—and indeed of the magnificence and the, humanly speaking, providential character—of this sort of "useful knowledge." But perhaps because of the very massiveness, as well as the comparative novelty, of what we owe to and expect from the applied sciences, we are all of us today liable to neglect other forms of useful knowledge: and to neglect them to our peril. Historical understanding, I shall now argue, can be of use to us, and needs must be used by us, in a variety of ways that are of the first importance to any form of civilised life.

In the first place, historical understanding can teach us, especially with regard to the institutional sides of life, what we are or where we stand in the light of where we have come from; more particularly understanding of what we are in the light of whence we have come can explain why there are certain things which we *cannot* do, let the future develop as it may. Secondly, historical understanding can assist us, somewhat in the manner of practice for games of skill, not indeed to foresee and forestall the difficulties that will face us, but to meet and cope with them, whatever forms they may take, with a kind of confidence, a kind of necessary carefreeness, such as no degree of scientific preparation can provide. Thirdly (and this will no doubt cause some eyebrows to rise) historical understanding can help us to see and can give us justifiable assurance regarding, not simply what we can or cannot do, but about what we ought to do or must never do in many important kinds of moral situation. . . .

First, then, the historical approach often helps us to see the importance of features of an institution which at first sight seems unjustifiable or arbitrary, since (apparently) they in no way help to fulfil the institution's most obvious functions or purposes. Nevertheless such factors may be among the necessary conditions of the institution's survival or efficiency. They may even—paradoxical though this at first sounds—express the very quick of its existence; that which not only keeps it in being but contains the seeds of its main future developments; that which will be remembered and cherished long after its currently accepted functions and purposes have become outmoded or forgotten.

Thus, for example, every political movement or party embodies, in addition to its official platform and its plans for legislative reforms, a number of vague, emotionally charged reminders of the past from which it has sprung. These may take the form of styles of address, the repetition of slogans and sacred names, ceremonies of remembrance, badges, banners, marching songs—all of which serve as cues for articulate or silent mass affirmations of loyalty and cohesion. The origin of such emotional cues may be remote or forgotten or fantastically misunderstood; or they may enshrine and echo personalities and incidents whose relevance to the practical issues of the day seems almost nil. Hence to practical forward-looking men the retention of these emotional cues may seem to be not simply useless but positively embarrassing and frustrating—it may seem describable only in pathological terms, as the expression of childishly wishful fantasies, or of unacknowledged aggressivenesses and phobias, or at best of ossified survivals from a more ignorant age. But the aptness of such descriptions does not mean that the emotional cues so described can be easily dispensed with. They may be essential to the party's continued existence as a reliable, recognisable unity. For, broadly speaking, every human association is formed to meet some particular need or danger or opportunity; and if it is really successful in uniting men for this first purpose, it will tend to be kept in being and made use of for other related purposes. Again, very broadly speaking, the greater the number of different purposes that a particular association can be used to serve the greater its chances of persistence, despite inward strains and anomalies and contradictions. It would therefore be the height of folly to regard all seemingly arbitrary features of a political movement or institution as negligible. They are there: and they cannot be ignored or disowned or flouted or sneered out of existence. Of course, it may always be possible—indeed, it is often a crucial task of statesmanship—to develop them, to canalise or direct them, to utilise them (or their names) for very strange purposes. But before any of these things can be done, such seemingly arbitrary features need to be understood: in particular the ways in which they have become interwoven with other aspects of the movement need to be understood. And it is difficult to see how such understanding is to be had, except by an historical appreciation of how the movement has developed, and by assessing, in the light of that development, the different relations of its many different strands. Such an appreciation will commonly show that the apparently arbitrary survival of some emblem or dogma from long ago in fact points back to some choice or alignment which was quite essential to the accepted orientation of today's rational and practical policies.

A closely similar point can be made from the other side, i.e. in terms not of popular acceptance and support of a particular institution or movement, but of its first, and subsequently, legendary founders or leaders. Admittedly, every political movement starts from some widely recognised danger or opportunity: but precisely which individual, of all the many individuals who might well give the new movement leadership and direction, will in fact be there and available, on the spot and with exactly the right status and record to meet the call of the hour—this is indeed almost entirely a matter of chance. But, on the other hand, once a first leader is recognised: once the movement has begun to develop under his hand and under his name, to be symbolised by his face or voice or known character and way of life, then commonly it will begin to take on features and qualities which had no necessary connection with the danger or opportunity which first brought it into being. Such personally attributable features, it might be thought, must be superficial and quickly lost and forgotten. But to assume this is to give way to a culpably shallow rationalism. The capacity of mankind, in its political actions, to make legends out of its leaders is a factor of immense historic importance. To admit this is not to subscribe to the foolish doctrine that great men make or determine the histories of the movements they initiate or the nations they lead. Every important chapter in human history is, of course, made by successive generations of men in their thousands or millions. But very commonly in making such a chapter together, and in order that they shall succeed in making it together, men must imprint upon it the image, complete with some arbitrary as well as with politically requisite features, of its first spokesman or protagonist or guide.

Besides helping us to see what we can and what we cannot do with our institutions in view of the ways they have come to be what they are, I believe that a study of their history can assist us in a more direct and positive fashion towards a wise use of them. Not, to be sure, by enabling us to foresee the dangers or difficulties with which our institutions may in future be faced, but rather—paradoxical although this again may sound—by preparing us to maintain and adapt them in the face of changes that are entirely unpredictable. History reveals on its every page the importance of contingencies— accidents, coincidences or other unforeseeable developments—in every human enterprise, relationship and institution: it would therefore be utterly illogical to expect it to aid us in anticipating and forestalling specifically predicted developments. Nevertheless, in spite of the seeming paradox, it can and does assist us to achieve a "masterful manipulation of the unforeseen."

As a rough analogy, to indicate how this can be, I would cite the use of practice in games of skill. To some extent, of course, practice is preparation for broadly predictable situations: it includes the building up of habitual moves and responses which are appropriate to recurrent features or moments of the game. But practice is something much more than this, especially for a player of some skill. Its chief purpose is to get the player into a state of general preparedness—of "form" as we say—which means an all-round readiness, quickness and flexibility of responses which enable him to introduce or combine moves or strokes or feints or what not as occasions demand, and such as he has never tried out before: to prepare him, in a word, so far as this is possible, for *whatever* shall happen. Now the oddness of such practice—and of its effectiveness—deserves far more serious consideration than it has hitherto received from either philosophers or psychologists. Here it will be sufficient to make good its reality by pointing to two of its principles or quasi-principles, which to date have remained nameless, but with which we are all perfectly familiar.

The first of these I shall call the principle of the reserve: the second, which looks, at first glance, the direct opposite of the first, I call the all-or-nothing principle. History affords us innumerable examples of both: indeed, to follow and to appreciate an instance of either principle is to enjoy one of the keenest and most characteristic pleasures that historical study can afford.

First, then, the principle of the reserve. When faced with any task, problem or impasse, we must be prepared for the possibility that the best, the most rationally and scientifically laid plans that we can contrive may go awry. We should therefore, if possible, retain the means and materials—or at the very least keep in mind the possibility—of other methods of pursuing our aim: methods that may be less convenient or less desirable, rougher or costlier, and whose working out we may have only vaguely envisaged. But, whatever their drawbacks, we must have them to hand, to avoid being guilty of that worst of practical shortcomings, being found entirely unequal to the event, being found entirely resourceless before the situation—no matter how freakishly fortuitous—that actually faces us. It is as a safeguard against such a contingency, which always threatens those who put their faith in some theoretically water-tight project, some prediction of how things are bound to turn out, that the principle of reserve is of such great practical value.

It is worth noting that, although this principle is most obviously pertinent to the conduct of public affairs, it has some perfectly good analogues among maxims or considerations which apply to the most personal and private sides of our lives: for example, that we must work, but without allowing ourselves to be entirely used up by our work; that while we should give all that we have to give in many of our personal relationships, we should never, so to speak, identify our lives with a relationship of any one particular kind; and that we should always keep something of our own—despite the principle of frankness and self-giving to others—that we "scarcely tell to ony." Quasi-principles of this kind are most easily stated in negative form: they are essentially vague, and it is inconceivable that we should ever be offered statements of the sufficient conditions of their just or appropriate employment. They have to be discerned and recognised through successive examples. Our endeavour to master and apply them is the very antithesis of any habitual or automatic application of a rule. Yet by means of the examples which histories afford, we certainly can create and constantly improve our capacity for dealing with tomorrow's contingencies when they arrive.

The all-or-nothing principle seems, at first, to make altogether contrary demands upon us. It rests upon recognising that, in certain extreme situations, it is necessary to put all one's fortune on a single cast, to dare to put it to the touch to win or lose it all. But how can such heroic recognition be squared with the cautious, the realistically adaptive, the sometimes (inevitably) opportunist spirit of the man who works on the principle of the reserve? This seeming contradiction can be removed, however, if we recall the special character of the two principles—they are expressly intended to deal with the contingent aspect of experience—and if we contrast them, in this respect, with other empirically grounded rules of prudence. The latter, which we find embodied in countless proverbs, maxims, practical tips, etc., are propounded as rules known to be true on the whole, or in the great number of usual or normal or standard cases, if not of this particular case; they are known to be true in the long run even if acceptance of them should prove disappointing in the short run in which we are actually engaged. But practical decision, although it will normally base itself on such generally true maxims, has also its own natural anxiety over the particular case with which it is currently engaged. To the man of action there come moments when the long run and the majority of cases begin to mean nothing, when his whole concern is with this particular case which is proving itself an obvious deviant, a twister, a freak, and upon whose outcome, good or ill, his whole future, his life, the cause he lives for, may depend.

This kind of situation might be illustrated by that of a skilled and usually reliable and indeed conventional card-player who for some personal reason must win a particular game, irrespective of distressing his partner, violating the usual conventions, etc., and equally irrespective of the extent of his loss if he loses. We may assume that he will begin play in quite orthodox fashion, e.g. in conformity with his bids if the game is bridge. But after a very few rounds it may be clear that orthodox play, although it may here as always minimise losses, is not going to guarantee victory. What, then, is to be done? If our player has the lead, we can imagine him proceeding to open up the game in a new and quite surprising way, in view of his earlier leads. And should this tactic disappoint, he may change yet again, despite raised eyebrows from partner or opponents. The unorthodoxy of his procedure, his offence against the conventions, may, however, be entirely justified in view of his own peculiar aim. Alternatively, we might imagine him staking all upon one enormous bluff at the outset; a bluff which might well cost him almost every trick in the game, but from which there is a real chance of attaining the narrow victory that he requires. On the former supposition he exemplifies the principle of the reserve; on the latter he exemplifies the all-or-nothing principle. Use of the former principle depends upon the ability to judge, in terms of one particular situation, the relative values of a number of approaches all of which are no doubt theoretically commendable: the latter depends upon the ability to see where the one small chance lies in a complex situation, and upon the ability, which Cardinal de Retz took to be the hallmark of practical genius, to distinguish the chance that is extraordinary from the chance that is truly impossible.

Now it requires no further arguing, I think, to derive from this description the conclusion which history is continually illustrating, although a too narrow logic may dislike it: namely that every successful man of action brings with him a mastery of both the above principles, and an almost instinctive skill in applying them, to any complex and serious situation.

Finally I want to suggest that historical understanding can often help us to decide which courses of action we are morally obliged to follow and which we are obliged to shun. This assistance is particularly important for those moral choices and resolves that arise because of our involvement in institutions, or our adherence to some important movement or cause: in a word, to the institutional side of morality, which contemporary moralists tend either to neglect or else to treat in the most perfunctory and hackneyed manner.

My claim in this connection can be introduced by recalling that we can hardly hope to man or serve an institution worthily unless we believe in it. Now, what does believing in an institution amount to? Not necessarily to believing that it has a future or that the future is with it; but rather that it deserves to have a future, that it has potential life in it and therefore might well have a great future if only we and others give it the support, and apply to it the energy and the intelligence, that it requires and deserves. But how, it may be asked, can historical understanding contribute to such positive, practical beliefs?

Certainly historical understanding will not suffice to ensure loyal support, intelligent service, faithful defence or careful development of any institution or cause. Nor, perhaps, in strictness, is it a logically necessary condition of such service, which conceivably might be given by some simple soul who had virtually no historical understanding of the institution that he was serving. For ultimately, it might be argued, loyal adherence to any institution or cause must be based upon some intuition or revelation of its worth, some direct and original appeal which it exercises upon the practical and imaginative sides of our natures. I am not myself altogether happy with this view, but for the argument's sake let us accept it. But now it must be admitted that the kinds of intuition or revelation that are here alleged, are notoriously—and indeed sometimes cruelly and even hideously—fallible. How, then, are they to be tested and secured? Not simply by a consideration or calculation of the foreseeable consequences of the actions and attachments which they commend; for some of these consequences will themselves have to be judged by the way they will play back upon and affect the future of the institution or cause whose value—or the rightness of our adherence to which—is the very thing that we are trying to confirm. Moreover, there are notorious practical difficulties in the way of such calculations of foreseeable consequences, unless made on the broadest and crudest scales. But by what other means can our moral intuitions and revelations be tested or confirmed? It is here, I believe, that historical understanding can make its contribution.

This can best be explained by an example. Suppose one had had the extraordinarily good fortune to be one of the original disciples of Socrates, considered as the first exemplar of the spirit of free criticism deployed to vindicate the autonomy of morals, or of Galileo, conceived as the first clear exemplar of the true method of hypothesis and experiment in physical inquiry. If one had had a modicum of intelligence, one could not but have recognised in either case something of immense importance, something most certainly with life in it and deserving a future. One would certainly have believed *in* what one heard and saw; and one might well have been fired to devote one's life and energies to furthering the aims and methods which either of these intellectual masters had begun, however laboriously and imperfectly, to disclose. Yet, in attempting this task, one would almost inevitably have run into innumerable and enormous difficulties: difficulties of a kind that would not simply have brought progress quickly to a halt, but would have made one feel entirely at a loss, in doubt, and intellectually and morally forlorn. What light, what guidance, one might well then ask, could the first fragmentary findings of either master afford to us when faced with *this* incomparably more complicated problem? How would *he* have envisaged the difficulties of applying here the method which seemed to him so lucidly inevitable in the first chosen simple cases?

But now, contrast this imaginary situation with that which we, in fact, enjoy: we who can look back across centuries of the continuing struggle for freedom of thought, containing so many noble reaffirmations of the autonomy of morals, or at the astonishing developments and successes of the method first descried by the genius of Galileo. Is it not far easier for us to see what Socrates and Galileo were respectively about than it was for the first of their disciples? Looking back along the line of development that stems from either name, surely it is now far easier for us to know what we mean by the spirit of free criticism or by the method of ideal and real experiment. And is it not now, correspondingly, far easier for us to know what it is that we believe *in* when we say that we believe in the spirit of free criticism or in the spirit of experimental inquiry? I do not say that our beliefs in these excellent things are necessarily stronger or more effective in producing appropriate attitudes and actions, or that they are more trustworthy, more deserving of faith and hope, than were the original beliefs first fired by the examples of Socrates and Galileo. What I claim is that any such belief, when it has been to some extent articulated through the history of its vicissitudes and revivals, its unexpected implications, its revolutionary extensions and triumphant reaffirmations, has one immense advantage over any direct, original acceptance of it—no matter how powerful, how penetrating, how full of prophetic promise the original apprehension and acceptance of that belief may have been. When our beliefs have been to some extent historically articulated we are in a very much better position to *describe* them, to indicate the differences—perhaps the many ranges of differences—that an acceptance of them makes to the rest of our conduct or view of the world. We are thus not only better equipped to defend the institutions and causes we believe in against polemical attacks, we are also in a better position to defend and discuss and reaffirm them *to ourselves*, to our critical perplexed selves, in moments—or decades or centuries—of difficulty, doubt and discouragement. In a word, it is often easier for us to act rightly because we have historical understanding to help us;

or, conversely, historically understanding can sometimes help us to decide what we ought to do and to do it.

I do not think it is necessary to pursue this argument beyond the example I have given. Certainly it is a form of argument that might admit of grave abuse, since it presupposes that we can distinguish those traditions which embody and develop an idea of unquestionable value, from those which may simply express some deep-seated and perhaps evil tendency in human nature. But despite this possible danger there can be no question in my mind, of the moral illumination which historical understanding can sometimes provide.

The Experience
of Writing History

George F. Kennan

George Kennan (b. 1904) is a specialist in international relations and now professor emeritus in the Institute for Advanced Study at Princeton University. Much of Kennan's early career was spent with the United States Foreign Service and the Department of State. He served as American ambassador to the Soviet Union and also to Yugoslavia. The primary architect of America's containment policy, Kennan writes mostly about diplomatic history and international relations. Among his publications are *American Diplomacy, 1900–1950* (1951) and the two-volume study *Soviet-American Relations, 1917–1920* (1956, 1958). "The Experience of Writing History" first appeared in the *Virginia Quarterly Review* (Spring 1960).

I just want to make a few very informal observations about the nature of history as a subject and about the condition of the historian. My excuse for doing so is simply that I came to this work unusually late in life, after a quarter of a century, in fact, in a wholly different sort of occupation. The impressions I have gained of these matters have something of the quality of the naïve. And since the naïve is occasionally amusing, whether or not it is instructive, I thought you might just possibly like to hear what these impressions are.

One of the first things that dismayed me, as I tried to put pen to paper with a view to relating historical events, was to discover the hopeless open-endedness of the subject of history itself: its multidimensional quality, its lack of tidy beginnings and endings, its stubborn refusal to be packaged in any neat and satisfying manner. I was soon brought to realize that every beginning and ending of every historical work is always in some degree artificial and contrived. No matter what you told, there was always something that had gone before, or came afterward, which you didn't have time to tell about, or which you didn't know about, and which was nevertheless essential to the completeness of the tale.

This open-endedness of the historical subject applied, I was brought to realize, not just to the longitudinal dimension of chronology, but also to the latitudinal dimension of related subjects and related happenings. No matter what field of human activity you selected for treatment, there were always a dozen other fields that had something to do with it, which you couldn't treat. And wherever you tried to draw the boundary between what you could write about and what you couldn't, it was always an artificial boundary, doing violence in some degree to the integrity of the presentation itself.

The perfect historical work, in other words, could not be written. If you were a great enough historian, if you were sufficiently learned in the environment of your subject as well as in its central core, then you might be able to do a good job of concealing from all but the most perceptive of your readers the untidiness of the outer limits of your presentation. But the untidiness would be there, nevertheless. There would always be a border, however well concealed, beyond which the firmness of your knowledge trailed off into the obscurity of your ignorance, or where the obvious limits on the patience of publishers and readers made it impossible for you to tell all you knew.

In addition to this diffuse quality of the subject, I was startled to discover how rigorous, when you stopped to think of it, were the limitations of perspective. History, it seemed, besides being open-ended, partook also of the nature of a sphere. You couldn't see it from all directions at once. You could see it only from some tiny, fixed point in its ample stratosphere. This point was always arbitrary in relation to the subject. An infinite number of other points could conceivably have been selected. Each would have revealed something which you, from the perspective of your particular point, were unable to reveal. Every point was, therefore, severely limited in its possibilities. Not only that, but there was a real question as to what latitude you really had in selecting the point you were going to use—whether, in fact, it was not already substantially selected for you.

This brought up, as you will readily see, the whole perplexing question of subjectivity. I had naïvely supposed, before I tackled this work, that there was a body of unrevealed or unappraised historical fact lying scattered around, like so many archaeological fragments, in the archival and bibliographical sediment of the ages, and that the historian's task was only to unearth these fragments, to order them, to catalogue them, and to arrange them in a manner that would permit them to tell their own tale. I was soon to learn that it was not this simple. These fragments were there, all right; but they had, it seemed, no single, definitive tale to tell. They could be arranged in an infinite number of ways, and each had its specific implications. Much was left to the powers of insight of the arranger. He had to do this arranging on the strength of his own good conscience, and to take personal responsibility for the product. This was the task of analysis and interpretation. And this meant that the fixed point from which one viewed history was actually none other than one's own self—one's self in the most intimate personal sense.

The describing of historical events, in other words, was partly an act of the creative imagination of the writer. You might know the bare skeleton of circumstance: that such and such occurred on such and such a day. The fact remains: you weren't there; you didn't see it. To arrive at its true significance—to understand its atmosphere, its meaning for those who experienced it, its relation to other events—you had to put yourself in the place of the people who were there; you had to apply to the historical record something which, however you tried to make it informed and dispassionate, was still an act of the imagination.

But then the question arose: was your imagination not the product of what you yourself had known in life? Of the things you had seen and experienced, as the inhabitant of a specific historical age? And if so, could you really visualize the happenings of another age? Could you conceive of things outside the range of your own experience? If not, then were you not really imposing a distorting lens upon the stuff of history by the very act of attempting to describe it? Was it not history which was serving as a framework for the product of your own imagination, rather than your imagination which was serving to illumine the facts of history?

I recall once seeing a performance of Gogol's *Revisor* (*The Inspector*) in one of the leading theatres in Stockholm. It was Gogol's old classic, all right. The words were correctly translated. The script was faithfully followed. Yet what was represented was not Russia but Sweden. Gogol's profound and despairing caricature of bureaucratic life in a Russian provincial administrative center of the early nineteenth century, with all its sad and despairing humor, had been somehow transformed into a jolly, colorful, little Swedish fairy tale, with characters who were like painted dolls—a very creditable performance, a very enjoyable and creative one, in its way; but it was Sweden, not Russia.

One was obliged to wonder whether this was not substantially what one did to any historical subject one touched, no matter how objective one tried to be. I wrote two volumes about certain phases of international life in 1917 and 1918. I did my best to describe things as I thought they looked to the actors in that drama. Sometimes I thought I had succeeded in tolerable degree. But I also had panicky moments of wonder as to whether I had done anything closer to reality than a sort of historical novel. In any case, I was forced to realize, when I looked at the volumes in retrospect, that however revealing they were as a record of the time to which they pertained, they were probably more revealing as a record of our own time—of the outlook and manner of thought of a citizen of the 1950s. I realized then why someone was once caused to remark that all history was contemporary history.

On the other hand, I did see that it was possible to do better or worse in this respect. It was possible to enhance one's capacity for visualizing history by means of the very effort of studying it. One thing supported another. The more you steeped yourself in the environment of your subject—the more, let us say, you supported a study of political events with a parallel study of the art, the religious beliefs, the folklore, the economics, and the manners of the times— the more your imagination could rise to the task. You could, in other words, lift yourself, to a degree, by your own intellectual bootstraps. But this meant that if you really wanted to get near to your subject, it was yourself you had to change. The mere amassing of more data would not do it. To understand a past episode, you had to make yourself to some extent a citizen of the epoch in question. You had to make its spirit, its outlook, its discipline of thought, a part of your own nature.

But this was something which you did only at a certain personal price; and the nature of this price was again one of the things that struck me very strongly about the writing of history. It was something which I can only describe—and I hope the term will not sound too bizarre to you—as its loneliness.

I do not mean to use this term in any self-pitying way. I have enjoyed no less than anyone else the company of my colleagues in the academic life—their company, that is, in the sense of the association one has with them in the odd moments of relaxation: over luncheon tables, and that sort of thing. I even discovered that scholars, so long as they have not constituted themselves a committee to deal with academic-administrative affairs (in which case something very strange indeed happens to them), are the most amusing and companionable of men. I should also like to stress that what I am about to say applies only to the studying and writing of history, not to the teaching of it. But it does appear to me that the studying and writing of history is a relatively lonely occupation.

The historian is lonely, first of all, vis-à-vis the historical personages who are the objects of his study. He lives for long periods among these people. They absorb his attention, his thoughts, sometimes even his sympathies and antipathies. Yet generally speaking, they are not really his companions. They surround him, silently and inscrutably, like figures in a wax museum. He can see them to one extent or another, in the literal sense, depending upon the stage of pictorial or photographic representation in the period when they lived. But they are inanimate. He sees them only frozen in poses—in a series of *tableaux morts*. Sometimes, to be sure, words are to be seen issuing from their mouths, hovering above their heads, so to speak, like the bubbles of utterance that emerge from characters in a comic strip. But one does not actually hear the voices; and one is often not sure whether the words were really theirs or those of the author of the comic strip. In any case, the human context of the utterance: the elusive nuances of circumstances, of feeling, of environment, of intuition and telepathy—the things that made that particular moment unlike any other moment that ever was or will be—all this is seldom to be recaptured. Only, perhaps, in cases of the most profound and selfless and erudite identification of the historian with the period of his study does there occur that intimacy of acquaintance which permits historical personages really to become alive again in their own right—not as products of the arbitrary imagination of the writer, but in reasonable resemblance to what they really were.

But even where such people become real for the historian, he, let us remember, does not become real for them. Their mutual relationship is a one-way street. *He* takes an interest in *them*. He supports them. He becomes their posthumous conscience. He tries to see that justice is done them. He follows their trials and experiences, in many instances, with greater sympathy and detachment than any of their egocentric and jealous contemporaries ever did.

But do *they* support *him*? Not in the least. They couldn't care less. Most of them would snort with contempt if they were to be made aware of the identity of those who would later undertake the effort to interpret their lives and strivings to future generations. Statesmen often conceive themselves to be working for posterity in the abstract, but they have little real respect for individual members of it, in a world where youth is never what age was and where the good old times will never be recaptured. Historical characters would have little solicitude for the brash member of a future generation who takes upon himself so presumptuously the burden of interpreting *their* doings and *their* difficulties.

The historian assists then, like a disembodied spirit, at the activities of his characters. To them, he has a duty, a responsibility, of understanding and of sympathy. But he himself remains unseen, unknown, unaided. This, for my money, is loneliness.

And it is not only vis-à-vis the inhabitants of the past that the historian is lonely. The study of history is something that cuts one off from the age in which one lives. It represents—let us face it—a certain turning of one's back on the interests and preoccupations of one's own age, in favor of those of another. This association with the past cannot occur, if only for reasons of time, otherwise than at the expense of the association with the present.

This is something which one's contemporaries, polite as they may be, rarely really understand or forgive. Every age is egocentric—and fiercely so. Every age thinks itself to be the most important age that ever occurred. Is not the present generation, after all, the occupant of that incomparably most important place in human history—the area between the past and the future? The very idea that one of the members of this generation should turn away from its absorbing and unprecedented concerns to give his attention, professionally and at length, to the affairs of people who suffer from the obvious inferiority of not being alive at all: this, to any normal and full-blooded contemporary, is little short of insulting. It implies that there were people long ago whose lives were so much more important and interesting than our own that the mere contemplation of them from a distance is held preferable to a direct participation in the affairs of our own age, despite all its obvious glories and mysteries. What body of the living, intoxicated by the illusion of progress and the belief in the uniqueness of its own experience, would ever forgive *that*?

The historian too often finds himself, I fear, in the position of the man who has left the noisy and convivial party, to wander alone on cold and lonely paths. The other guests, whom he has left behind, murmur discontentedly among themselves: "Why should he have left? Who does he think he is? Obviously, he doesn't like our company. He thinks us, plainly, a band of frivolous fools. But we are many; he is one of very few. We therefore are clearly right, and he is wrong. The devil take him. Let him sulk." So they say. And so he does.

So much for the historian's loneliness. Let me just mention one more thing that has grown upon me in the course of this work. It is the realization of how deeply one has to dig to find the justification for what one is doing. There are, after all, so many discouragements.

A librarian friend of mine told me the other day that it was most doubtful, in view of the inferior quality of present-day American paper, that anything I, or any of my colleagues, had recently written would still be legible fifty years hence. Since one of the few real consolations of writing history is the faint hope that perhaps one has accomplished something for the ages, this was a shattering thought.

Then, too, there is the atom, with all its grisly implications. I find it hard to forget that we live in an age when all sorts of people who haven't got the faintest concern for history—who don't even know, in fact, what it is—have it already in their power to put an end not only to great portions of the historical record (this, various military characters have done very successfully at frequent intervals in the past), but to both the writers and the readers. It is an uncomfortable reflection that this entire work of the study of the past—its subject, its rationale, its practitioners, its customers, its meaning—that all this is vulnerable, or soon will be, to the whims of brother Khrushchev or brother Mao or even certain of our American brethren that I could name, not to mention others who may, with time, come into the power of disposition over these apocalyptic weapons.

Even if men manage to avoid, by some unaccountable good fortune, the plunge over this particular abyss, one sees that humanity is now living, anyway, in the midst of some sort of a biological and technological explosion, by which the terms of life are being altered at an ever-increasing pace. A part of this explosive process is the multiplication of the historical record, particularly the recent one. Even the major events of the present century—events which appeared to people at the moment to be of major, headline significance—have accumulated in such volume as to place them quite beyond the apprehension of the layman. It is the rarest of persons who today has any comprehension of the series of events which, just in his own time and that of his father, has brought him where he is today. Even the historian feels increasingly inadequate to this task. He can only wander around, like a man with a tiny flashlight amid vast dark caverns, shining his little beam here and there for a moment on a tiny portion of the whole, but with the darkness always closing up behind him as it recedes ahead. More history is probably written today than at any time in the past; and with respect to distant ages, once largely lost to historical knowledge, we are no doubt making progress. But with respect to the doings of our fathers and grandfathers, or even our elder brothers, we are, I fear, fighting a losing battle. The dizzy pace of change is carrying us into the future faster than we can pay out the delicate thread of historical scholarship that is our only link to the past.

What, then, is the use? Has this pursuit of history become no more than a superfluous habit—something that people assume their children ought to study in school simply because this has always been done within their memory? Are the conditions of our lives being altered with such rapidity that the record of the past would have little to tell us even if we could keep up with the explosive expansion of its volume?

Each of us, I suppose, has to answer these questions for himself. I am personally convinced that they must be answered in the negative. It may be true that it is becoming increasingly difficult to reconstruct an adequate record of the past. It may be true that there never was a time when history was less susceptible of apprehension, in its entirety, by the layman. It may be true that we are condemned to explore only tiny and seemingly unrelated bits of a pattern already too vast for any of us to encompass, and rapidly becoming more so. All these things, to my mind, merely make the effort of historical scholarship not less urgent but more so.

It is clear that the spectacular mechanical and scientific creations of modern man tend to conceal from him the nature of his own humanity and to encourage him in all sorts of Promethean ambitions and illusions. It is precisely this person who, as he gets carried along on the dizzy pace of technological change, needs most to be reminded of the nature of the species he belongs to, of the limitations that rest on him, of the essential elements, both tragic and helpful, of his own condition. It is these reminders that history, and history alone, can give; for only history can expose the nature of man as revealed in simpler and more natural conditions, where that which was elemental was less concealed by artificialities. And to the supplying of these reminders, which is the historian's task, it is not necessary that one should know or understand the whole unconscionable and spreading panorama of history. A little bit, looked at hard and honestly, will do. In this little bit will be found, in the measure of the devotion applied to it, the compensation for all the essential imperfection of the historical art, for all the struggle with subjectivity, for all the loneliness, for all the questioning as to whether anyone will ever read what you wrote or whether it would do them any good if they did.

The Uses of History

Lester D. Stephens

Lester D. Stephens (b. 1933) is head of the Department of History at the University of Georgia. He has written articles that deal with such topics as history and education, slavery, agriculture, and evolution. His books include *Developing Competency in Teaching Secondary Social Studies* (1974), *Historiography: A Bibliography* (1975), and *Joseph Le-Conte: Gentle Prophet of Evolution* (1982). The following selection is taken from his book *Probing the Past: A Guide to the Study and Teaching of History* (1974).

O pinions on the usefulness of history range across a continuum to both extremes. Perhaps we have all seen the school pupil or the college student who states flatly that the study of history is a waste of time because it is totally irrelevant to present needs. From that extreme we can move to the opposite end of the continuum to find the metahistorian who swears with the strength of his soul that history is the fount of all wisdom and guidance. As with all dogmatic assertions, neither of these immoderate positions is really satisfactory, for somewhere in between lies the truth. History does serve some useful purposes, but it is not an infallible teacher. . . .

. . . As human beings we are forced to make decisions every day of our lives, and we act on the basis of those decisions. More often than not, these decisions are routine and of no great import, though occasionally we are compelled to make momentous decisions and to act in ways which may affect us deeply. The basis for such personal decisions is to be found in our beliefs, experience, and knowledge—or in a combination of all three. If we were suddenly deprived of all our beliefs, experience, and knowledge, that is, if our memory failed us completely, we would be forced to begin at the most elemental stage of man's existence to work out basic solutions to our immediate needs. And it would be a long time before we could through trial and error build up a system of beliefs, useful experience, and new knowledge which would save us from mistakes and gradually make life more bearable. Happily for us no such traumatic experience is likely to occur. What we may often fail to appreciate, however, is the value of the past to our lives.

A person can function on the basis of a very limited system of beliefs, a narrow background of experience, and a constricted amount of knowledge—at least where his decisions affect him primarily only in a personal way. As literacy spreads and as civilization becomes more complex, however, man is less and less left to himself. Consequently, he encounters life on a larger scale, and his actions have a greater bearing upon the society of which he is a part. Thus, the more he understands the world in which he lives, the greater the likelihood he will not be the victim of his own ignorance. And to understand the world and the present, one must have some knowledge of the past. Understanding the past, however, is more than possessing an unexamined mental image (or a myth, if you will) of what has gone before. When the past becomes history . . . then man is in a position to make more carefully reasoned decisions and to act in a rational way. That he will not necessarily do so is granted, but that he will be able to do so is justification enough for studying his past.

To argue for a knowledge of the past is not to defend the mere acquisition of historical facts. As Frederic Harrison noted some seventy years ago: "Facts are infinite, and it is not the millionth part of them that is worth knowing. What some people call the pure love of truth often means only a pure love of intellectual fussiness. A statement may be true, and yet wholly worthless."[1] History, as we have previously argued, is more than a compilation of facts. Its life depends on facts, of course, but its end is not the mere memorization of those facts. By a knowledge of the past we mean that one understands something about the processes of social change, possesses some insight into the multitude of factors which have shaped our present and how these have shaped the present of other societies in different ways, and, above all, sees the wisdom of having a critical attitude toward what men say about the past. It is a broad knowledge which can help us to see beyond the narrow confines of our own immediate and personal world, to grasp the concept of the great community of man from the time *homo sapiens* appeared until the present, which is ever becoming the past. To help us see ourselves in perspective is a task of history. And having properly seen ourselves in "time and space," [Henry Steele] Commager reminds us, we can moderate "our instinctive and pervasive parochialism" and subdue our intolerance "with different faiths, different loyalties, different cultures, different ideas and ideals."

History can help us shake off the shackles of excessive ethno-centrism and the debilitating bias of cultural and racial purity; it aids us to become "coterminous with humanity."[2] History helps to illuminate the human condition. Far from making us "unpatriotic," history helps us to know why we hold particular loyalties; it pro-motes in us the greatest kind of loyalty—a commitment to freedom of critical inquiry.

As creatures of our own immediate surroundings, we are naturally prone to believe that the light of culture shines brightest in our own circle. Our ideas, our beliefs, and our customs seem to us to be sanc-tified; those of others seem to suffer the defects of inferiority, or at the least they are viewed as unenlightened. As the philosopher Mor-ris R. Cohen has so meaningfully stated it: "History is necessary to control the exaggerated idea of our own originality and of the uniqueness of our own age and problems. To live from day to day without a wider vista is to fail to see all that is involved in the issues of the day." Surely, we cannot claim that the study of history alone can accomplish this goal: The study of literature, philosophical and religious systems, cultural anthropology, and a whole host of other activities of man in differing societies and at various times in his past—all are important to enlarging our perspective. History is one vital dimension of our reality, however, and it can aid us to appreci-ate our humanity.

Most of us recognize the value of experience, and we usually laud experience as a great asset in any man because it renders him more capable of making proper value judgments. It is not only the length of experience which we prize, however, but also its variety. As indi-viduals we can *personally* experience only so much—and naturally some individuals profit more than others from their experience. Thus history can expose us not only to more experience and a great-er variety of experience but also to the experience of men in past ages. "History," Ernest Scott informs us, "clarifies, criticizes, compares, co-ordinates experience, and makes it available for all."[3] If we are but willing, we can further expand our intellectual and humanistic horizons by partaking of the fruit of our historical experience.

NOT THE LEAST of the values of history is its existential function: It provides us with a sense of being. Without history we would not know who we are, either individually or collectively. True enough, we often identify ourselves by fantasies and myths, but the value of good critical history is that it helps us to acquire a more realistic identity. History viewed thus "is no mere complex of settled events, no museum of dead objects. History is a living thing, it is with us and in us every moment of our lives."[4] Through history we become conscious that we are links which connect the past, present, and future. We are particular men and women, existing in a particular historical time—continuants in one sense but shapers of the future in another sense. Thus we do not serve history by obeisance to the past, but history serves us by telling us who we are and by enlarging our prospects. For this reason, "history has to be periodically rewritten," as [Jacques] Barzun notes, so that we become capable of dealing "not with a crisis once every ten years, but for dealing with life itself, every day. . . ."[5]

Over the long span of his existence in civilized communities, man has endeavored to memorialize himself. This attempt to transcend his temporal life has taken a variety of forms, but one of the most persistent has been the recounting of his activities, sometimes on clay tablets or papyrus and at other times simply by oral story telling. Man did not begin to develop a sense of genuine historical consciousness, however, until he broke the bonds of cyclical recurrence and substituted a linear conception of purposeful, goal-oriented history. From the time of the Hebrews man began gradually to envisage a past which is a continuum with the present and the future. This notion has made it possible for man to transcend his own moment in time. "There is pleasure," says Paul Weiss, "in knowing that we are not alone, that we are part of a single totality, that we have in a sense lived a long time."[6] History can nourish this desire for memorialization, and it can do so within the confines of man's finite being. Religion permits us to transcend the mundane if we wish, but history can help to satisfy our craving for continuation as human beings. That in itself is no mean contribution.

History affords a source of pleasurable reading for some people, and thus we can extend its dimension as a source of identification to include its humanizing function. Certainly all history does not qualify as good literature, and surely all people do not enjoy reading even that history which is skillfully written. But some histories are masterpieces of literature, and many people derive personal pleasure from immersing themselves in such works. It may be true that the Gibbons and the Macaulays of historical writing are no more to be found among our modern-day historians, but the picture is not as bleak as some historians claim. The works of such historians as Samuel Eliot Morison, Garrett Mattingly, and C. V. Wedgwood, for example, are masterfully written, and they have proved themselves to be sources of great delight for a large number of people. It may well be, in fact, that it is not so much the lack of good historical writing which has stifled public interest in the reading of history as it is our failure to impart to students the excitement and joy which history has to offer. The excessive emphasis upon memorization of facts, the dullness of so many history lectures, and the stress upon history textbooks in our schools and colleges hardly serve to whet interest in reading history as a pleasurable activity. But the fault lies more in our approach than it does in historical writing itself.

IT IS EASY to claim too much for history, and the tendency to overstate its values has in no small measure reduced its credibility. Perhaps the single greatest abuse of history is committed by those who try to make it a repository of moral examples and caveats. The ascription of this function to history is typified in the statement of Lord Bolingbroke that "history is philosophy teaching by examples." The concept of history as instruction for good citizenship was further elaborated by Bolingbroke in the following statement: "An application to any study, that tends neither directly nor indirectly to make us better men and better citizens, is at best but a specious and ingenious sort of idleness . . . the study of history seems to me, of all other, the most proper to train us up to private and public virtue."[7] And so it is that the function of history in the school curriculum is frequently viewed solely as civic education. This is an unfortunate misuse of history, for while history may make us wiser citizens, it should not be used to entrench partisan and parochial impressions.

In the same vein history is abused by those who would select from it those elements which support their particular cause. Needless to say, the practice of "using" the past to sanctify change toward some revolutionary end, no matter how worthy, is to adapt it to authoritarian purposes. And, likewise, the "use" of the past to justify traditional institutions is a corruption of history. From our study of history we may see possibilities, potentialities, and alternatives, it is true. But we cannot use it as a source of ironclad authority.

A search for the *practical* use of history invariably ends in disappointment. That should not be taken to suggest that history is useless, however. Wisdom does not emanate solely from a study of utilitarian knowledge. History, properly understood and appreciated, is educative, and for that reason it is useful.

References

1. Frederic Harrison, *The Meaning of History* (New York: Macmillan, 1902), 10–11.

2. A. L. Rowse, *The Use of History*, rev. ed. (New York: Macmillan, 1963), 26.

3. Ernest Scott, *History and Historical Problems* (London: Oxford University Press, 1925), 6.

4. Erich Kahler, *The Meaning of History* (New York: George Braziller, 1964), 24.

5. Jacques Barzun, "History, Popular and Unpopular," in *The Interpretation of History*, ed. Joseph R. Strayer (Princeton, N.J.: Princeton University Press, 1943), 52.

6. Paul Weiss, *History: Written and Lived* (Carbondale: Southern Illinois University Press, 1962), 42.

7. Henry Saint-John, Viscount Bolingbroke, *Letters on the Study and Use of History* (Paris: Theophilus Barrois, Jr., 1808), 11–12. The statement was not original with Lord Bolingbroke; it was made by Dionysius of Halicarnassus, who seems to have borrowed the idea from Thucydides.

The Necessity
of History and
the Professional Historian

Gerda Lerner

Gerda Lerner (b. 1920) was born in Vienna, Austria, and became an American citizen in 1943. A pioneer in the establishment of programs in women's history, she is now professor of history at the University of Wisconsin, Madison. Lerner is a past president of the Organization of American Historians. Her books include *The Grimke Sisters from South Carolina: Rebels Against Slavery* (1967), *Black Women in White America: A Documentary History* (1972), and *The Majority Finds Its Past* (1980). The following are selections from her OAH presidential address, delivered in Philadelphia in 1982.

There is no adequate preparation for writing a presidential address. Trying to choose among the many urgent themes that demand attention, one is painfully aware of the wisdom of one's predecessors and one's own limitations. The audience to be addressed is the most critical and important one will ever face: a national audience of colleagues. For a woman, following a long line of male presidents, there is an added responsibility: one wishes to be representative of the profession as a whole and yet not neglectful of those long silenced.

Behind me stands a line of women historians, who practiced their profession and helped to build this organization without enjoying equality in status, economic rewards, and representation. Even the most exceptional among them, whose achievements were recognized and honored by the profession, had careers vastly different from their male colleagues. . . .

They and dozens of others did the best they could under the circumstances, opening the way for later generations. To remember them today is to honor their inspiration and to acknowledge their often distorted and diminished careers.

I would not be standing before you today, if it were not for the vision and perseverance of the nineteenth-century feminists, who treasured and collected the records and documents of female activity during their time. They laid the foundation for the study of women's history. This field would not have developed as rapidly as it did, if it were not for those determined intellectuals, not connected with any academic institution—Elizabeth Schlesinger, Miriam Holden, Mary Beard, Eugenie Leonard—who understood the need to preserve the record of the past of women in archives and who worked tirelessly for the inclusion of the history of women in academic curricula. The significant contributions to women's history scholarship of nonacademic historians, such as Elisabeth Dexter and Eleanor Flexner, also deserve to be remembered.

I would like to encompass as well the sensibilities and views of the present generation of women historians, who assume equality as their right and who expect to pursue their careers without experiencing economic disadvantaging, patronizing attitudes, and other forms of sex discrimination. They are the first generation of women professionals truly freed from the necessity of choosing between career and marriage. Having equal access to training and education at all levels, they enjoy the intellectual support offered by collegiality within their departments and by a network of women sharing common concerns. How am I, who have come from such different experiences, to speak for them?

As a Jewish refugee and an immigrant, I have never been able to take freedom and economic security for granted. As a woman entering academic life late, as a second career, I regard access to education as a privilege as well as an obligation. Having been an engaged participant in women's work in society all my life, I could not accept the truncated version of past reality, which described the activities and values of men and called them history, while keeping women invisible or at best marginal. My craft and my profession are inseparable from the road I have come and the life I have led.

. . . And so, speaking from the vantage point of a person long defined as marginal, I would like to address the issues I consider *central:* the necessity of history and the role of the professional historian.

To speak of the necessity of history is to say that history matters *essentially.* Human beings, like animals, propagate, preserve themselves and their young, seek shelter, and store food. We invent tools, alter the environment, communicate with one another by means of symbols, and speculate about our mortality. Once that level of social consciousness has been reached, we become concerned with immortality. The desire of men and women to survive their own death has been the single most important force compelling them to preserve and record the past. History is the means whereby we assert the continuity of human life—its creation is one of the earliest humanizing activities of *homo sapiens.*

But history is more than collective memory; it is memory formed and shaped so as to have meaning. This process, by which people preserve and interpret the past, and then reinterpret it in light of new questions, is "history-making." It is not a dispensable intellectual luxury; history-making is a social necessity.

History functions to satisfy a variety of human needs:

1. *History as memory and as a source of personal identity.* As memory, it keeps alive the experiences, deeds, and ideas of people of the past. By locating each individual life as a link between generations and by allowing us to transform the dead into heroes and role models for emulation, history connects past and future and becomes a source of personal identity.

2. *History as collective immortality.* By rooting human beings on a continuum of the human enterprise, history provides each man and woman with a sense of immortality through the creation of a structure in the mind, which extends human life beyond its span.

3. *History as cultural tradition.* A shared body of ideas, values, and experiences, which has a coherent shape, becomes a cultural tradition, be it national, ethnic, religious, or racial. Such a "symbolic universe" unites diverse groups. It also legitimates those holding power, by rooting its source in a distant past.

4. *History as explanation.* Through an ordering of the past into some larger connectedness and pattern, historical events become

"illustrations" of philosophies and of broader interpretative frameworks. Depending on the system of thought represented, the past becomes evidence, model, contrast to the present, symbol, or challenge.

Making history means form-giving and meaning-giving. There is no way to extricate the form-giving aspect of history from what we are pleased to call the facts. As Carl Becker said: "Left to themselves, the facts do not speak . . . for all practical purposes there is no fact until someone affirms it. . . . Since history is . . . an imaginative reconstruction of vanished events, its form and substance are inseparable."

Insofar as the historian chooses, evaluates, analyzes evidence, and creates models in the mind that enable us to step out of our own time, place, and culture into another world, his or her mental activity is akin to that of scientists and mathematicians, who "pop in and out" of different conceptual systems. But the construction of a coherent model of the past partakes of the imagination as well. The model created by the historian must not only conform to the evidence, it must also have the power to capture the imagination of contemporaries, so as to seem real to them. It shares this quality with the work of fiction. For both writer and historian, form is the shape of content.

History-making, then, is a creative enterprise, by means of which we fashion out of fragments of human memory and selected evidence of the past a mental construct of a coherent past world that makes sense to the present.

"Necessity," wrote Leopold von Ranke, "inheres in all that has already been formed and that cannot be undone, which is the basis of all new, emerging activity. What developed in the past constitutes the connection with what is emerging in the present."[1] We learn from our construction of the past what possibilities and choices once existed. Assuming, as Henri Pirenne says, that the actions of the living and those of the dead are comparable, we then draw conclusions about the consequences of our present-day choices.[2] This in turn, enables us to project a vision of the future. It is through history-making that the present is freed from necessity and the past becomes usable.[3]

History as memory and as a source of personal identity is accessible to most people and does not depend on the services of the professional historian. It is the story of one's life and generation; it is autobiography, diary, and memoir; it is the story of one's family, one's group of affiliation. As Wilhelm Dilthey wrote: "The person who seeks the connecting threads in the history of his life has already . . . created a coherence in that life . . . [which represents] the root of all historical comprehension. . . . The power and breadth of our own lives and the energy with which we reflect on them are the foundation of historical vision."[4]

By tracing one's personal roots and grounding one's identity in some collectivity with a shared past—be that collectivity defined by race, sex, class, ethnicity, religion, or nationality—one acquires stability and the basis for community. Recognizing this, conquerors have often destroyed historical monuments and the preserved record of the past of the conquered; sometimes, they have also destroyed the intellectuals who remember too much. Without history, no nation can enjoy legitimacy or command patriotic allegiance.

The necessity of history is deeply rooted in personal psychic need and in the human striving for community. None can testify better to this necessity than members of groups who have been denied a usable past. Slaves, serfs, and members of subordinate racial or national groups have all, for longer or shorter periods of time, been denied their history. No group has longer existed in this condition than have women. Groups so deprived have suffered a distortion of self-perception and a sense of inferiority based on the denigration of the communal experience of the group to which they belong. Quite naturally, each of these groups, as it moved closer to a position of sharing power with those ruling society, has asserted its claim to the past. Mythical and real heroes were uncovered; evidence of the group's struggle for rights was collected; neglected sources were made to yield information. In the process, inevitably, the established version of history has been revised. In the American setting, this has been the case in regard to Afro-American history and Native-American history, both fields that have moved from marginality to the mainstream and have, in the process, transformed and enriched our knowledge of the nation's past.

While at first sight the case for women appears to be similar, it is in fact profoundly different. All the other groups mentioned, except for colonials, although of varying sizes, have been minorities in a larger whole. In the case of colonials, subjects of imperial powers, who often are majorities dominated by powerful minorities, there has always been a legitimate past prior to the conquest from which the oppressed group could draw its identity and historical perspective. Jews, ethnics, African slaves could look back on a heroic, though distant, past, on the basis of which they could make claims to the future. During the time of being "out of history" oppressed groups have also been "out of power" and therefore have felt solidarity among themselves as victims of oppression.

Women have had a historical experience significantly different from that of men. Women are not a minority, although they have been treated as if they were members of minority groups. Women appear in each class and rank of society, and they share, through the connection they have with males of their family groups, the fate, values, and aspirations of their class or race or ethnic group. Therefore, women frequently are divided from other women by interests of class, race, and religion. No other subordinate group with a common experience has ever been so thoroughly divided within itself.

Women have participated in civilization building equally with men in a world dominated and defined by men. Thus, women have functioned in a *separate* culture *within* the culture they share with men. Mary Beard wrote in 1932 that women "have never been solely on the side lines observing passively or waiting for men to put them to needed work. In every crisis women have helped to determine the outcome. . . . No story of cultural history is adequate which neglects or minimizes women's power in the world."

Yet women's culture has remained largely unrecorded and unrecognized. It must be stressed that women have been left out of history not because of the evil intent of male historians, but because we have considered history only in male-centered terms. We have missed women and their activities, because we have asked questions of history that are inappropriate to women. To rectify this we must, for a time, focus on a woman-centered inquiry, considering the possibility of the existence of a female culture within the general culture shared by men and women. As we ask new questions and consult formerly neglected sources, we uncover the record of women's unrecognized activities. For example, when we ask the traditional question, "What have women contributed to reform activities, such as the abolition movement?" we assume that male activities are the norm and that women are, at best, marginal to the male-defined movement. In answer to such a question we learn that abolitionist women demanded the right to lecture in public and to hold office in antislavery societies and thereby, in 1840, provoked a crisis that split and weakened the antislavery movement. What is ignored in this interpretation is the fact that the increased participation of women and their greater activism actually strengthened antislavery ranks. Had we asked the question, "What was women's role in, perception of, and experience in the antislavery movement?" the answers would lend themselves to a somewhat different interpretation. If one looks at the impact of the antislavery movement solely in terms of voting behavior and politics (male activities), the contribution of women may seem unimportant. But reform movements in antebellum America can also be seen as efforts to adjust personal values and public morality to the demands of a rapidly industrializing society. Moral reform, sexual purity, temperance, and abolition became the symbolic issues through which women expressed themselves in the public sphere. Antislavery women's activities—organization building, the spreading of literature, petitioning, participation in slave rescues—helped to create changes in the climate of opinion in the North and West that were essential to the growth of the political antislavery movement. Men and women, even when active in the same social movements, worked in different ways and defined issues differently. As historians are uncovering the record of women's activities and correcting the bias in the interpretation of the past, which has assumed that man is the measure of all that is significant, we are laying the foundation for a new synthesis. Women's history is a tool for allowing us to see the past whole and entire.

Such an enterprise, however, exciting as it is, lies some time ahead. Meanwhile, women must live with the effect of having been deprived of a usable past. As we have noted, history as memory and history as a source of personal identity have presented women with a world in which people like ourselves were, with a few exceptions, invisible in all those activities valued highly as "contributions" to civilization. The actuality—that women, as Mary Beard so confidently asserted, have always been a force in history and have been agents, not subjects, in the process of civilization building—has been obscured. Thus, women have been deprived of heroines and role models and have internalized the idea of their own victimization, passivity, and inferiority to men. Men, similarly miseducated through a distorted image of the past, have been reinforced in their culturally created sense of superiority and in the conviction that a sex-based division of labor justifies male dominance.

Speaking of the psychological tensions under which Afro-Americans have existed in a white world, W. E. B. Du Bois described this "peculiar sensation, this double-consciousness, this sense of always looking at one's self through the eyes of others. . . . One ever feels his two-ness—An American, a Negro; two souls, two thoughts, two unreconciled strivings; two warring ideals in one dark body." Although in many decisive respects the condition of women cannot be compared with that of Afro-Americans, all women have partaken of a kind of "double-consciousness," a sense of being central and yet defined as marginal, essential and yet defined as "the Other," at the core of historical events and yet left out of history.

The complexities of the experience of black women, who are subject to discrimination both as women and as members of a racial minority group, cannot be discussed here. All women have in common that their history comes to them refracted through the lens of men's observations and refracted again through a male-centered value system. The historic condition unique to women is that, for over five thousand years, they have been excluded from constructing history as a cultural tradition and from giving it meaning. In the period when written history was being created, shortly after the formation of the archaic states, women were already in a subordinate condition, their roles, their public behavior, and their sexuality defined by men or male-dominated institutions. From that time on, women were educationally deprived and did not significantly participate in the creation of the symbol system by which the world was explained and ordered. Women did not name themselves; they did not, after the Neolithic era, name gods or shape them in their image. Women have not held power over symbols and thus have been truly marginal to one of the essential processes of civilization. Only in the last two hundred years have the societal conditions been created that would afford women equal access to educational opportunity and, later, full participation in the definition of intellectual fields and disciplines. Only in the past two hundred years have groups of women been able, through organized activities and social sharing, to become conscious of their group identity and with it the actuality of their historical experience, which would lead some of us to begin to reclaim our past. For women, all history up to the twentieth century has truly been prehistory.

If the bringing of women—half the human race—into the center of historical inquiry poses a formidable challenge to historical scholarship, it also offers sustaining energy and a source of strength. With the case of women we can best illustrate that history matters. By contemplating, in the case of women, the consequences of existing without history, we can renew our faith in and commitment to the work of the professional historian.

TODAY, what does it mean to be a professional historian? . . .

As we examine our relationship to the society at large, we see that insofar as we function as fact finders about the past and as re-creators of past worlds (or model builders), the need of society for our skills is as great as ever. It is our function as interpreters of the past, as meaning givers, that has become most problematical. History as cultural tradition and legitimizing ideology and history as explanation have increasingly come under questioning. Again, the causes are societal and historic. The scientific revolution of the twentieth century has undermined the claim of history to being, together with philosophy, the universal field of knowledge for ordering the human experience. The facile slogan of the 1960s, which declared history "irrelevant," reflected a perceived discontinuity between industrial and postindustrial society. The explosion of scientific knowledge and of technical control over the environment has made it possible to envision a future dominated by scientific knowledge and technical expertise. For such a future, it appears, the past cannot serve as a model. In its most pragmatic manifestation, this kind of thinking has led to the substitution of "Social Studies" for history in many American school systems.[5] At a more advanced and theoretical level, this kind of thinking is evident in a debate among sociologists, philosophers, and historians, some of whom argue that history has been superseded by science as a means of ordering human experience and orienting the individual within society. Most historians would answer that, despite great strides in science and technology, human nature has not essentially changed. Historically formed institutions continue to provide the structures within which the new knowledge and technologies are organized. Historically determined political institutions continue to allocate labor and resources to science and technology, so that those holding and organizing "the new knowledge" operate within the constraints of tradition.

Those arguing the irrelevance of history define history too narrowly, by focusing on history as the transmitter of tradition, as the means for legitimizing the status quo, as the ideology of a ruling elite. But history, as we have discussed earlier, has many other than merely legitimizing functions. It is possible that what we now perceive as "the crisis of history" is merely the coming to an end of the function of history as elite ideology.

Another important strand of twentieth-century thought can help us in reorienting history in the modern world. The major upheavals of our time—wars, the holocaust, the nuclear and cybernetic revolutions, and the threats to the ecological balance—have made us aware of the limited use of rational thought in politics and social planning. Irrationality in political and social behavior may make it more urgent than ever to understand the process of Becoming and the limits placed upon the present by past decisions and choices. Psychoanalysis has directed our attention to the power of the irrational and unconscious in motivating human behavior. Sigmund Freud showed us how the past of the individual, suppressed and made unconscious through faulty interpretation, can exert a coercive force over present behavior. "Healing" of such compulsive behavior occurs through the mental process of bringing past events to awareness and reinterpreting them in light of a new—and better—understanding derived from present circumstances. This process is akin to the work of the historian in reinterpreting past events in light of present questions. The denied past of the group, as well as of the individual, continues to affect the present and to limit the future. We, as historians, might take up the challenge offered by analytic theory and seek to work toward a "healing" of contemporary social pathology, using the tools of our craft imaginatively and with a new sense of direction. We are, after all, not a small group of clerks and mandarins guarding secret knowledge in the service of a ruling ideology, but people with special skills, who translate to others the meaning of the lives and struggles of their ancestors, so that they may see meaning in their own lives.

We do this best in our function as teachers. Most of us, for much of our professional lives, are teachers; yet this activity is the one we seem least to appreciate in ourselves and in others. Our habitual performance at the lectern has, in some aspects, been superseded by the intervention of printing, and many of us, sensing the basic incongruity of the manner in which we conduct our work, have fallen back on being performers, seeking to catch the reluctant attention of an audience more accustomed to the frenetic entertainment style of the mass media.

In fact, the teacher as performer acts within an ancient and valid tradition. Above all, we seek to tell a story and tell it well—to hold the audience's attention and to seduce it, by one means or another, into suspending disbelief and inattention. We seek to focus concentrated attention upon ourselves and to hold it long enough to allow the students' minds to be directed into unexpected pathways and to perceive new patterns. There is nothing shabby about this performance aspect of the teacher's skill, this trick of the magician and the artist. When we succeed in our performance role as teachers, we extend the learner's thoughts and feelings, so that he or she can move into past worlds and share the thoughts and values of another time and place. We offer the student the excitement of puzzle solving in our search for evidence and the sense of discovery in seeing general design out of the mass of particulars.

Lastly, we also teach, as master craftsmen and craftswomen, imparting particular skills to the uninitiated. The ability to think and write with clarity, the habit of critical analysis, the methodology of history, the painstaking patience of the researcher—all these skills are transmitted by the ancient method of transference from master to apprentice. As we allow students to see the historian at work, we become role models, and if we are so inclined, we lighten the students' task by demystifying our knowledge, sharing its "tricks" and openly acknowledging its shortcomings. The craftsmanship aspect of teaching connects us with the craftsmanship of other workers, those who labor with their hands and those who work with their minds. As teaching and researching historians, we work as did the master stonemasons and wood-carvers on the great medieval cathedrals and the ancient Mayan or Buddhist temples or the women who embroidered the great Bayeux tapestry: we do our own particular work, contributing to a vast, ongoing enterprise. In our own performance and in the standards we set for students we can represent dedication to understanding the past for its own sake and in its own light. In an age of alienation we can impart a sense of continuity to the men and women we teach. And we can help them to see the discontinuities in a larger perspective.

The problem of discontinuities has never loomed larger than in this generation, which is the first generation in history forced to consider the possibility of the extinction of humankind in a nuclear war. The possibility of discontinuity on such a vast scale staggers the imagination and reinforces the need of each individual to know his or her place in history. Now, as never before, we need to have a sense of meaning in our lives and assurance of a collective continuity. It is history, the known and ordered past, that enables us to delineate goals and visions for a communal future. Shared values, be they based on consensus or on the recognition and acceptance of many ways of form-giving, link the individual to the collective immortality of the human enterprise.

The historian professes and practices such knowledge and imparts it to others with passion and an abiding confidence in the necessity of history. In these times, more than ever, it is good to be a historian.

References

1. Leopold von Ranke, "A Fragment from the 1860's," in *The Varieties of History: From Voltaire to the Present*, ed. Fritz Stern (New York: Meridian Books, 1956), 61.

2. Henri Pirenne, "What Are Historians Trying to Do?" in *Methods in Social Sciences: A Case Book*, ed. Stuart A. Rice (Chicago: University of Chicago Press, 1931), 435–45.

3. "Intelligent understanding of past history is to some extent a lever for moving the present into a certain kind of future." John Dewey, *Logic: The Theory of Inquiry* (New York: Holt, 1938), 239.

4. Wilhelm Dilthey, *Pattern and Meaning in History: Thoughts on History and Society*, ed. H. P. Rickman (New York: Harper, 1962), 86–87.

5. Daniel J. Boorstin ascribes this to the influence of the media: "When in our schools the study of 'current events' (that is, what is reported in the newspapers) displaces the facts of history, it is inevitable that the standard of knowledge propagated by newspapers and magazines and television networks themselves . . . overshadows all others. When to be informed is to be knowledgeable about pseudo-events, the line between knowledge and ignorance is blurred as never before." Daniel J. Boorstin, *The Image; or, What Happened to the American Dream?* (New York: Atheneum, 1962), 231–32.

History:
Stimulus to the Imagination,
Instrument of Freedom

Historical knowledge can stimulate the creative imagination, as both Henry Steele Commager and Henri-Irénée Marrou show. The imagination, Commager tells us, "like a taste for music, or for painting, can be cultivated."[1] History enriches our lives in other ways, too, as these writers tell us, by improving our perspective, by making us aware of others and thus pulling us away from self-centeredness, and by allowing us to recapture cultural values from earlier times. Commager, Marrou, and Boyd C. Shafer, like Carl Becker, observe that the study of the past expands personal experience. This extension of experience can release us from the bonds of the present and reveal increased possibilities for action. Marrou and Shafer especially emphasize the liberating qualities of history.[2] "A historical awareness," Marrou writes, "brings about a veritable *catharsis*." But history does not guarantee liberation. It can either encumber us by reinforcing passivity, Howard Zinn writes, or it can enhance our freedom by untying "our minds, our bodies, our disposition to move." Through "a judicious culling of past experience" we can become more active, sensitive, and effective participants in society, Zinn maintains.

References

1. Richard W. Van Alstyne argued that "the essence of history is speculative thought. . . . Ascertaining 'the facts' and interpreting them are part of the . . . process of imaginative re-creation." See Richard W. Van Alstyne, "History and the Imagination," *Pacific Historical Review* 33 (February 1964): 2, 6.

2. History, says Myron A. Marty, liberates man "from the shackles that hold him in the present moment." See Marty, "Teaching History as a Liberating Art," in *New Directions in Community Colleges: Merging the Humanities*, ed. Leslie Koltai (San Francisco: Jossey-Bass, 1975), 32.

The Nature of History

Henry Steele Commager

Henry Steele Commager (b. 1902) is widely recognized as one of America's most distinguished teachers and historians. He has taught at many of the leading universities in the United States and abroad and is now professor emeritus at Amherst College. Among his many works are the widely used *Growth of the American Republic* (1930), written with Samuel Eliot Morison, and *The American Mind* (1951). The following selection is from *The Nature and Study of History* (1965).

*T*he first thing to be said about History is that the word itself is ambiguous. It means two quite distinct things. It means the past and all that happened in the past. It means, too, the record of the past—all that men have said and written of the past, or, in the succinct words of Jacob Burckhardt, "what one age finds worthy of note in another." Sometimes it is said that these two things are in fact much the same: that the past exists only in our record of it, or our awareness of it, and that without such a record, there would be no meaningful past at all. Thus the great Italian philosopher-historian, Benedetto Croce, asserted that all history was contemporary history. There is, as we shall see, a germ of truth here. But this view is not so much wrong as confused and, in a sense, perverse. The past is not dependent on us for its existence, but exists in its own right. It happened even though historians failed to record it, just as the tree fell in the forest even though no one was there to hear the sound of its fall. History does not suddenly spring to life when some historian gets around to discovering it or recording it. The historian who clears up some puzzle about the past, or who discovers new material and fills in some gap in our knowledge of the past, does not in fact create the past, though he may recreate it. What happened, happened independently of him, and the consequences of whatever happened ensued independently of him. James Madison's *Notes on the Federal Convention*, for example, was not published until 1836; only then were historians able to penetrate into the very chamber of the Convention, to know, and to explain, what had occurred. Yet what had happened at the Convention—what delegates had said, for example—had in fact happened, and had made history. The consequences of the debates in the Convention did not wait upon the publication of Madison's *Notes*.

But if the debates in the Federal Convention were history, so was Madison's *Notes*. Just as what happened at the Convention had consequences, so the publication of the *Notes* fifty years later had consequences. It clothed with flesh and blood the skeleton of formal resolutions and conclusions with which historians had previously solaced themselves, and inaugurated both a more realistic and a more nationalistic interpretation of the Constitution.

What this suggests is that the historian, by discovering some lost ingredients in the past, or by illuminating dark areas of the past, can in a real way re-make the past. History is *there*—there in the fact that it did occur; there, too, in the conscious or the unconscious memories of men. The memory can be jogged, the consciousness can be stimulated, the image of the past can be changed. When the historian does these things he makes history.

History, then, is the past. History is also the memory of the past. Needless to say it is with the second of these meanings that we are concerned.

Let us consider history as memory.

For a people to be without history, or to be ignorant of its history, is as for a man to be without memory—condemned forever to make the same discoveries that have been made in the past, invent the same techniques, wrestle with the same problems, commit the same errors; and condemned, too, to forfeit the rich pleasures of recollection. Indeed, just as it is difficult to imagine history without civilization, so it is difficult to imagine civilization without history. As Frederic Harrison has written:

Suppose that all knowledge of the gradual steps of civilization, of the slow process of perfecting the arts of life and the natural sciences, were blotted out; suppose all memory of the efforts and struggles of earlier generations, and of the deeds of great men, were gone; all the landmarks of history; all that has distinguished each country, race, or city in past times from others; all notion of what man had done or could do; of his many failures, of his successes, of his hopes; suppose for a moment all the books, all the traditions, all the buildings of past ages to vanish off the face of the earth, and with them the institutions of society, all political forms, all principles of politics, all systems of thought, all daily customs, all familiar arts; suppose the most deep-rooted and sacred of all our institutions gone; suppose that the family and home, property, and justice were strange ideas without meaning; that all the customs which surround each of us from birth to death were blotted out; suppose a race of men whose minds, by a paralytic stroke of fate, had suddenly been deadened to every recollection, to whom the whole world was new. Can we imagine a condition of such utter helplessness, confusion, and misery?* . . .

WE ARE ALL acquainted with the young man who earnestly assures us, with a mixture of vanity and zeal, that he has always "hated history." It is all dates, he tells us, or it is all a lot of rather tiresome problems—the problem of the "fall" of Rome, the problem of the French Revolution, the problem of Secession and Civil War. And it never gets you anywhere; you are no better off when you have finished than when you began.

Some of this attitude may be confidently set down to poor and uninspiring teaching—teaching which never challenged the interest nor excited the imagination of students. Some of it—perhaps a good deal—may be put down to the same kind of uninspired teaching embodied in textbooks in which the authors try to please everybody, avoid the "controversial," ignore the dramatic, concentrate on problems which are never solved or whose solution is of no interest, and, like so many of the novels and dramas of our time, eschew narrative and leave out heroes and villains. Some of it can be ascribed to the individual himself; his inability to respond imaginatively to the drama of the past. In all likelihood he is one of those of whom Wordsworth wrote:

> A primrose by the river's brim,
> A yellow primrose was to him,
> And it was nothing more.

*Frederic Harrison, *The Meaning of History and Other Historical Pieces* (New York: Macmillan, 1914).

But after we have done all this explaining, there remains a stubborn residuum of intelligent and open-minded students who still find nothing to nourish them in history. They may agree with Gibbon that history is "the register of the follies and misfortunes of mankind," or with Napoleon that it is a "lie agreed upon," or with Carlyle that it is "a great dust-heap," and they do not stop to read those marvellous volumes in which Gibbon recorded the "follies and misfortunes" of man, or discover how Carlyle proved that history was charged with life and passion, nor are they excited by the challenge to separate truth from lies about Napoleon himself.

What are we to say to all this? Why should the young study history? Why should their elders read history, or write it?

That is a question which recurs again and again: What use is history? Let us admit at once that in a practical way history has no use, let us concede that it is not good for anything that can be weighed, measured, or counted. It will not solve problems; it will not guarantee us against the errors of the past; it will not show nations how to avoid wars, or how to win them; it will not provide scientific explanations of depressions or keys to prosperity; it will not contribute in any overt way to progress.

But the same can be said, of course, of many other things which society values and which men cherish. What use, after all, is a Mozart sonata or a painting by Renoir, or a statue by Milles? What use is the cathedral of Siena or the rose windows of Chartres or a novel by Flaubert or a sonnet by Wordsworth? What use, for that matter, are a great many mundane things which society takes for granted and on which it lavishes thought and effort: a baseball game, for example, or a rose garden, or a brocade dress, or a bottle of port?

Happily, a civilized society does not devote all of its thought and effort to things whose usefulness can be statistically demonstrated. There are other criteria than that of usefulness, and other meanings to the term "useful" than those acknowledged by the Thomas Gradgrinds of this world.

History, we can confidently assert, is useful in the sense that art and music, poetry and flowers, religion and philosophy are useful. Without it—as without these—life would be poorer and meaner; without it we should be denied some of those intellectual and moral experiences which give meaning and richness to life. Surely it is no accident that the study of history has been the solace of many of the noblest minds of every generation.

The first and doubtless the richest pleasure of history is that it adds new dimensions to life itself, enormously extending our perspective and enlarging our experience. It permits us to enter vicariously into the past, to project our vision back over thousands of years and enlarge it to embrace all the races of mankind. Through the pages of history we can hear Pericles deliver his Funeral Oration, look with wonder as Scipio and Hannibal lock forces in that desperate field of Zama, trek with the Crusaders to the Holy Land, sail with Columbus past the gates of Hercules and to a new world, sit with Diderot as he edits the Encyclopédie, share the life of Goethe and Schiller at the little court of Weimar, stand and listen to those stirring debates in those dusty prairie towns which sent Douglas to the Senate and Lincoln to the White House, share the agony of General Lee as he surrenders the Army of Northern Virginia at McLean's Court House, stand beside Winston Churchill as he rallies the people of Britain to their finest hour. History supplies to us all those elements which Henry James thought essential to the life of the mind: density, variety, intricacy, richness, in the pattern of thought and of action, and with it "the sense of the past."

This immense enlargement of experience means, of course, that history provides us with great companions on our journey through life. This is so familiar a consideration that it needs no elaboration. Wherever the historian or biographer has been, he has given new depth and range to our associations. We have but to take down the books and we are admitted to the confidence of Voltaire and Rousseau, Johnson and Boswell, Thomas Jefferson and John Adams, Justice Holmes and William James. We can know them with more of an intimacy than their contemporaries knew them, for we can read their letters, journals and diaries. This is not just one of the pleasures of history, it is one of the indispensable pleasures of life.

A third, and familiar, pleasure of history is the experience of identifying the present with the past, and thus adding a new dimension to places and events. It was Macaulay who observed that "the pleasure of History is analogous in many respects to that produced by foreign travel. The student is transported into a new state of society. He sees new fashions. He hears new modes of expression. His mind is enlarged by contemplating the wide diversities of laws, of morals, and of manners." . . .

Everyone who has visited historic towns, in the Old World or the

New, knows that when he looks at them through the eyes of history they cease to be museum pieces and pulse with life and with vigor. Nestling between its ancient hills, bisected by the gleaming Arno, its domes and towers piercing the skies, Florence is beautiful to the eyes of even the purblind. But how it springs into life when we people its piazzas and narrow streets with the men and women of the past: when we conjure up the spectacle of Savonarola burned at the stake in the great Piazza de la Signoria where the mighty David now stands; Bruneleschi erecting the giant Duomo; Ghiberti carving the great bronze doors of the Baptistry, a lifetime work, this; Giotto and Fra Filippo Lippi and Raphael and Leonardo and Michelangelo painting those pictures which now hang in such lavish profusion from the glittering walls of the Uffizi and the Pitti palaces; Machiavelli pondering the history of the condottieri while he writes the *Prince*, and Galileo seeing a new universe through his telescope and opening up a new universe of the mind as well. Did ever a city boast a comparable galaxy of genius; did ever a city publish itself more generously in its monuments, or impress itself more richly on the eye and on the mind?

Nor is it only the great centers of art and letters, like Florence or Venice or Salzburg, that take on new dimensions when seen through the eyes of history; the same miracle transforms even the most modest of towns. Henry James observed, somewhat condescendingly, that Emerson had "dwelt for fifty years within the undecorated walls of his youth"; but to Emerson those rooms were redolent of the past, as was the little village of Concord. And as for Hawthorne, how, wrote James, could he have found materials for his stories, living where he did, where "the coldness, the thinness, the blankness . . . present themselves so vividly that our foremost feeling is that of compassion for a romancer looking for subjects in such a field." But Hawthorne himself looked out of his attic window on a Salen rich in history and tradition and found in it the ingredients for *The Scarlet Letter* and *The House of Seven Gables*, and a dozen other stories that are a precious part of our literature.

Consider the little town of Salem in Massachusetts, now no more than a suburb of Boston. It is a lovely town in its own right, there by the sea and the rocks, its handsome old houses still standing sedately along Chestnut and Federal Streets. As we look at it through the eyes of history we conjure up a straggling village busy with fish-ing and with theological disputes and remember that Roger Williams preached here those heresies which brought him banishment from the Bay Colony, and so too Mistress Anne Hutchinson. We look at Gallows Hill and recall the dark and terrifying story of Salem witchcraft which haunted Nathaniel Hawthorne, who grew up here, and whose spirit still broods over the town. We recreate it in its heyday, when its captains sailed all the waters of the globe and its flag was thought to be the flag of an independent nation, and the spoils and rewards of the China trade glittered in every drawing room. For at the turn of the century Salem was like one of the famous city states of Italy—Florence or Venice or Pisa. It had its own architects, like Samuel McIntyre who built the stately mansions of the sea captains and the merchant princes, mansions which still stand; its own preachers, like the famous William Bentley of the East Church, reputed to be the most learned man in America; its own jurists, like Samuel Putnam and Samuel Sewall who became Chief Justices of the Commonwealth, and Joseph Story who joined the Supreme Court of the United States at thirty-two. Samuel Bowditch was a boy here, watching the sailing ships come in to India Wharf and learning celestial mathematics and navigation from a library which had been captured from a British ship during the War for Independence; he sailed on a Salem merchantman, and grew up to write the *Practical Navigator*. So was George Crowninshield who built the magnificent Cleopatra's Barge and sailed it through the Mediterranean, and the dour Timothy Pickering who lived in the oldest house in town—which still stands—and grew up to be the most reactionary politician in the country; so too the astonishing Benjamin Thompson who grew up to be Count Rumford of the Holy Roman Empire and to live in state in Munich and found the Royal Institution in London, and so too William Prescott who played as a boy along India Wharf and Derby Wharf, and swam in the cold waters of the harbor and picnicked on Hog Island, and who became the historian of Mexico and of Peru.—Then another generation, and Salem entered its long decline, its harbors silted up and its wharfs falling into decay and grass growing up between the cobblestones of its ancient streets, while the paint peeled off the proud McIntyre houses. It is all there—in Nathaniel Hawthorne's stories, in the reminiscences of Joseph Story and Rufus Choate, in the historical romances by Joseph Hergesheimer and Esther Forbes, so faithful to the spirit and the reality of the old town—all there for us to recapture through the pages of history.

Needless to say, all this makes great demands upon the imagination, the imagination of the historian and of the student alike. "At bottom," George Macaulay Trevelyan has said, "the appeal of history is imaginative," and he gives us, as an example of this, one of Carlyle's recreations of the past—it is in his essay on Boswell's Johnson:

> Rough Samuel and sleek wheedling James *were*, and *are not*. Their Life and whole personal Environment has melted into air. The Mitre Tavern still stands in Fleet Street; but where now is its scot-and-lot paying, beef-and-ale loving, cocked-hatted, pot-bellied Landlord; its rosy-faced assiduous Landlady, with all her shining brass-pans, waxed tables, well-filled larder-shelves; her cooks and bootjacks, and errand boys and watery-mouthed hangers-on? Gone! Gone! The becking Waiter, who, with wreathed smiles, was wont to spread for Samuel and Bozzy their supper of the gods, has long since pocketed his last sixpence; and vanished sixpences and all, like a ghost at cock-crowing. The Bottles they drank out of are all broken, the Chairs they sat on all rotted and burnt; the very Knives and Forks they ate with have rusted to the heart, and become brown oxide of iron, and mingled with the indiscriminate clay. All, all has vanished; in very deed and truth, like that baseless fabric of Prospero's air-vision. Of the Mitre Tavern nothing but the bare walls remain there; of London, of England, of the World, nothing but the bare walls remain; and these also decaying (were they of adamant), only slower. The mysterious River of Existence rushes on; a new Billow thereof has arrived, and lashes wildly as ever round the old embankments; but the former Billow with its loud, mad eddyings, where is it?—Where?—
>
> Now this *Book* of Boswell's, this is precisely a revocation of the edict of Destiny; so that Time shall not utterly, not so soon by several centuries, have dominion over us.

A dangerous thing, this, for once we introduce the element of imagination we imperil the integrity of the historical record. Yet how can we possibly exclude it? What is history, after all, without imagination? Imagination comes to our aid at every moment; it is what permits us to clothe the bare bones of history with life. It throws a glow over the most impersonal, the dullest, of the data of history. It infuses even a statistical table with color and life: who can read the statistics of the population growth of the western territories and states of the United States in the nineteenth century without seeing, in his mind's eye, the Conestoga wagon, and the canal boats on the Erie Canal, the railroad puffing its way across the Appalachians, weather-beaten men with their wives and children and cattle, beating out a trail to Oregon or to the Mormon utopia at the Great Salt Lake?

Imagination brings home to us that the names in the history books represent real people, that the decisions which were made involved the same fears and hopes and uncertainties and courage as those which we ourselves make, that Latimer at the stake and Lord Nelson at Trafalgar suffered the same agonies and exaltations which we ourselves experience, that to a man like Robert E. Lee the decision to stay with his state was no abstract "problem" of secession, but just such a spiritual and moral crisis as would plunge us into despair if we confronted it today. Alas, many historians are like the preacher of whom Emerson writes:

> A snow-storm was falling around us. The snow-storm was real, the preacher merely spectral, and the eye felt the sad contrast in looking at him, and then, out of the window behind him into the beautiful meteor of the snow. He had lived in vain. He had no one word intimating that he had laughed or wept, was married or in love, had been commended, or cheated, or chagrined. If he had ever lived and acted, we were none the wiser for it. The capital secret of his profession, namely to convert life into truth, he had not learned. . . . This man had ploughed and planted and talked and bought and sold; he had read books; he had eaten and drunken; his head aches, his heart throbs; he smiles and suffers; yet was there not a surmise, a hint, in all the discourse, that he had ever lived at all.

It might be thought that imagination like—let us say—an ear for music, is something you either have or have not. If you have it, well and good; if not, there is nothing to be done about it. But the imagination, like a taste for music, or for painting, can be cultivated. How can the historical imagination be cultivated? It can be cultivated through drama and poetry. Shakespeare suffused the stuff of history with his glorious imagination; no wonder Winston Churchill said that he had learned all of his English history out of Shakespeare! How history comes alive in the novels of Walter Scott—such varied historians as Prescott and Carlyle and Trevelyan have acknowledged his inspiration. With what insight does Wordsworth read its moral lessons, in the sonnet "On the Extinction of the Venetian Republic," for example, or in "To Toussaint L'Ouverture," or in *The Prelude*. Imagination can be cultivated, too, by the study of art and architecture. Who can wander through the National Portrait Gallery in London and not feel stirred by the spectacle of these men and women who have made England; how exhilarating to visit such great Palladian palaces as the Villa Rotonda and the Villa Malcontenta outside Vicenza, and to see Jefferson's Monticello emerge out of these models.

This does not exhaust the pleasures of history; they are, indeed, inexhaustible. We may, without too gross an impropriety, paraphrase Dr. Johnson's observation on London, that anyone who is tired of history is tired of life.

The Usefulness of History

Henri-Irénée Marrou

The philosopher-historian Henri-Irénée Marrou (b. 1904) was born and educated in France and spent much of his life teaching and writing about ancient Rome as well as early church history and theology. His books include *A History of Education in Antiquity* (1948) and *St. Augustine and His Influence Through the Ages* (1958). The following selection is from *The Meaning of History* (1959).

*A*s the limited, incomplete nature of historical truth (and therefore of history itself) becomes more apparent, the question so often discussed by our predecessors—without a satisfactory resolution—imposes itself with ever greater urgency. In what sense is history useful? What role should it assume in our culture?

Our reply will be qualified, as well as complex, for history in fact serves ends, and at several levels of being. . . .

True, we have agreed with Heidegger and all existentialism that "there is no history except in and through the historicity of the historian." That is, the past can only be known if it is brought in some way into a relationship with our existence. But we must immediately add this further (and to us, fundamental) qualification: if the past matters to us, this contact may sometimes be made from a great distance and in a very indirect fashion—at the cost, as Plato was fond of saying, of a "long detour," μαχρὰ ἡ περίοδος.

Is it not true that the historian may be obsessed by his involvement in change, and seek to understand his present situation only to direct his very next action? I am distressed by the excesses to which an egocentric notion such as Dilthey's may lead, organizing, as he does, the entire concept of history from the starting point and focus of the knowledge of the ego. On the contrary, we have found that historical knowledge is based on a dialectic between the Self and the Other, necessarily implying an essential element of otherness.

In the very narrowest perspective, history may aim at nothing but the comprehension of my historical situation by reconstructing the line, in a genealogical sense, of my antecedents. Obviously, in this case, I come to know these previous stages, these ancestors—even these immediate predecessors through an autobiography of my self of yesterday. Yet I also know them as different (since past), and as irreducibly other than that present self of mine which is straining toward the future.

Thus historical knowledge always implies a detour, a circuitous route. It supposes an initial centrifugal movement, an *epokhè*, a suspension of my most urgent existential preoccupations, a movement outside myself, an exile, a discovery and an encounter with the other.

It is here that it is important to distinguish levels and scope. In its most superficial form, history will appear to the moralist as the result of simple curiosity. It is, first of all, the discovery of sheer otherness. In those days, in that country, men lived who were this or that. They spoke such a language, had a certain type of social organization, practiced such and such techniques of production; such was their clothing, their cooking.

First there is what might be called the elementary level, that of the child learning for the first time in primary school: "In the past, our country was called Gaul." Then, on a secondary level, there is the person discovering the Pharaonic civilization. And the same thing also exists on a higher plane: the other day I was listening to Mr. Charles Virolleaud lecture at the Academie des Inscriptions on the results of Russian excavations at Kamir-Blour in Armenia. We discover the existence of the kingdom of Urartu with the same curiosity that our children discover the Gauls.

This is the equivalent of the botanist's effort to observe and classify the different species which comprise the flora of a newly explored region: he must first know that they exist and what they are before being able to see the really interesting problems they create.

As long as it remains on this first level, history will always be open to the moralist's severe charge of idle curiosity, whether he be St. Augustine, Descartes or (the heir to them both) Bossuet:

". . . This insatiable greed to know history! If it aims to derive some useful example for human life, well and good. One can bear with it and even praise it, provided that some sobriety is brought to this research. But if, as is the case with most curious people, the end is merely to feast the imagination on vain objects, what is more useless than to linger over what no longer exists, than to seek out all the follies that have passed through a mortal's head, than to recall with so much care the images that God destroyed in his holy city—the shadows that he dispersed, vanity's entire apparatus, that plunges back into the nothingness from which it came?"

When it is a question of practical morality, we must always distinguish each specific case. As is evident from the idle questions that readers address to popular magazines specializing in this sort of question, there certainly exists a peripheral zone where historical knowledge sinks into mere vanity. But Augustinianism too, in the name of the seriousness of existence and our stake in it, can sink into a narrow and crass utilitarianism. Human success lies in a balance between opposing demands that is difficult to achieve and always unstable. In culture, health and wealth, commitment and breadth of views are not always compatible. . . .

If we consult the psychologist, he will declare that curiosity (no matter how gratuitous it may appear) implies an existential value at its core. This, of course (the moral problem remains untouched), may perfectly well be morbid—escapism, daydreaming, the need to have fantasies that we are someone else, or the need to defy another person.

Consequently, even if history were only the "aesthetic contemplation of singularities" as it has sometimes been defined, it would not be useless or without a cultural function. I should like to stress this specifically aesthetic character. We need think about it for only a moment to see the analogy that exists between the matter of history and the subjects—themes, characters, situations—at work in epic, tragic, dramatic, romantic, or comic literature. Viewed from this angle, history is a grab bag of good stories to tell, a magnificent collection of inexhaustible richness.

Is there a Racinean tragedy that compares, in the intensity and nobility of its passion, to the true story of Heloise's loves? For romantic adventure, what could be better than that of King Giannino, the Sienese merchant who was persuaded by Cola di Rienzi that he was King John I of France, the posthumous son of Louis X the Headstrong, deprived of his heritage by his uncle, Philip V? What detective story is equal in suspense to a real espionage story such as the "Cicero Affair" in Ankara during the last war?

There is more than an analogy here. It is always surprising to realize the role historical knowledge has played in world literature as ferment to the creative imagination, from Homer to our own time.

Roger Martin du Gard would never have conceived of the dénouement of *Summer, 1914* if he had not heard of the historical suicide of Lauro de Bosis, the young Italian who flew over Rome in 1932 or 1933 distributing anti-Fascist tracts, and died in the venture.

And what about Balzac? Without Vidocq we would not have Vautrin, nor *A Shadowy Affair* without the kidnaping of Senator Clément de Ris (which occurred in October, 1800), and Esther Gobseck's liaison with Lucien de Rubempré borrows one of its most human episodes from Juliette Drouet's affair with Hugo. This characteristic is not peculiar to realistic novelists; Stendhal's imagination would never have conceived *The Charterhouse of Parma* if it had not been sparked by an old Roman chronicle.

These comparisons will help us become aware of another, and more profound, function of historical knowledge. It is one that theoreticians have too often neglected or dismissed summarily. We have by no means said everything once the term "aesthetic value" has been pronounced. True, we often study history as we read Balzac. But what mind is superficial enough to dare claim that the reading of Balzac is not weighted with existential seriousness? In both cases, we derive a lesson in humanity from our experience. In reply to the moralist whose narrow intransigence is founded on ignorance, the lover of literature will join the historian in defending the legitimacy and, above all, the fruitfulness of this human experience. Whether it is real or fictitious, and even if vicarious, it represents a true broadening of my personal experience, my experience with man. Much more surely than through literature (whose humanity is always somewhat uncertain), knowledge of history extends—in practically unlimited measure—my knowledge of man in all his many-sided reality, in his infinite capacities, well beyond the necessarily narrow confines of my own personal experience.

And let it be clearly understood that when we say "man" we mean everything that reflects human nature in its personal aspects as well as in its collective manifestations. History studies and knows Roman civilization and the culture of antiquity as well as Cicero's personality.

We study history as we read literature seriously, and as we seek above all to meet and know men in life— "in order to learn what we did not know and what would be practically impossible to find out by ourselves without being precisely the man who is teaching it to us. When we have known and understood him, we have become that man, and we know what he knows. Even if he has lived long ago and far away, we henceforth possess his experience with man and with life."

Similarly, I will assign to history, as one of its essential functions, the enrichment of my internal universe by recapturing cultural values salvaged from the past.

By the deliberately vague term "cultural value" we will signify, in the most general possible fashion, all that we may know and understand of the true, the beautiful, and the real in the domain of human life. We will let it extend from the most elementary products of civilization (any artifact whatever, a tool or instrument, a work of art, a concept, a feeling) to the vastest syntheses, those "ideological superstructures" bequeathed to us by great civilizations organizing themselves about a collective ideal.

We discover these values first under the category of the Other, meeting them as already existing among men of the past, in the bosom of lost societies or civilizations. But to the extent that we are capable of grasping and understanding them, they again come to life in us. In a sense, they acquire a new reality and a second historical existence, in the womb of the historian's thought and in the contemporary culture to which he reintroduces them. The historian seems to me comparable to a man who, without fear of wasting time (this is *epokhè*), leisurely pokes the ashes of the past. This is literally true in looking for papyrus, when we poke around the heaps of *sebakh* (household refuse) heaped up at the gates of the large towns of Greek and Roman Egypt and find there drachmas left by oversight or golden staters struck in the king's likeness, as fresh and shining as if they were newly minted.

It is not necessary to waste time in demonstrating how real this recovery is—so obvious, for example, in the domain of the history of philosophy or the history of art. Each may judge for himself, in considering his own artistic experience, the contribution of history to the enrichment of our aesthetic consciousness and to the deepening of our taste. . . .

I would like to give a personal example, as usual. Moved by a purely historical curiosity, I once studied the Augustinian treatise *de Musica*, which is a disconcerting work the first time it is read and is often neglected. Its study has its place in a survey of the ancient origins of the medieval cycle of the Seven Liberal Arts. While reading it, I was most struck by the fact that Saint Augustine used the word *musica* to denominate not the art which we call "music," but the science of its mathematical acoustical and rhythmic bases. The commentary I gave insisted that this was a misconception which should be avoided, and did not admit that the treatise in question might contain anything of use to the present-day musician.

A few years later I happened to draw up for myself a theory of musical art. I realized after a while, without grasping it entirely in the beginning, that the doctrine which I formulated as the truth (and for which I assumed responsibility as an aesthetician) was nothing more than the doctrine of Saint Augustine himself. It had demonstrated its own validity in this field, needing only some slight transpositions and a few adaptations (which I had made unconsciously).

I am convinced (and the unfortunate experience of certain of my predecessors proves it) that I would never have had this unlooked-for advantage if I had read Saint Augustine with a less open mind, or if I had been too eager to question it about present-day musical problems.

Thus in order to have a genuine history of philosophy we must convert the philosopher to the idea of the historical adventure. We must persuade him that he has both a right and a duty to take a few days off, "a legitimate holiday." During this time he should allow himself the curiosity necessary to discover other philosophies. It has sometimes been tried by adopting a moral point of view: in the name of the virtue of *docilitas*—which is none other than the fundamental virtue of humility applied to things of the mind. The philosopher in search of truth should begin by asking himself whether others have not by chance discovered something of it ahead of him. But here again we shut ourselves into a prejudiced perspective. I prefer to emphasize another argument: truth is not the only predicate which can define a doctrine. There are thoughts which though true are narrow, poor, strict, barbarous. Historical culture is not an instrument of truth, properly speaking, but a factor of culture.

I can be understood more easily if I make a comparison. Paleography, epigraphy, numismatics and other studies of this type are not sufficient unto themselves (the paleographer who is only that and no more has a very small mind), but offer themselves humbly as sciences auxiliary to history. And it is in the same way, I will say, that history appears as an auxiliary science of thought for the philosopher. In itself it is not all-sufficient, but it is careless not to make use of its services. History teaches the philosopher that he must enlarge his horizons, become more aware of the complexity of problems and of their implications; it proposes to him solutions—or objections—that he might not have imagined or foreseen. It rescues him from the inevitable narrowness that isolation implies, and integrates him into the vast society of minds by means of a constantly enriching dialogue.

That is what Seneca expressed in a fine page, dear to the humanist: "No century is forbidden to us: [through history] the force of our mind may go beyond the boundaries of the weakness of the solitary man: *egredi humanae imbecillitatis angustias*. We can dispute with Socrates, doubt with Carneades, enjoy the tranquility of Epicurus, with the Stoics conquer human nature, and bypass it with the Cynics. Since the structure of being (*rerum natura*) permits us to enter into communion with all the past, why not tear ourselves away from the narrow limits of our primary temporality and share with the finest minds these magnificent and eternal truths" *quae immensa, quae aeterna sunt?*

Against this last idea certain of my readers will protest. Is this not an anti-historical way of using history? Will we not find here again that false *philosophia perennis* in which, in a sham décor of the Champs-Elysées, Socrates in tunic and barefooted, Descartes in Louis XIII lace, Kant in powdered wig, and Comte in formal black have a discussion in which they each advance against the others disincarnated arguments? But I reply: No. If I am truly a historian, I seize each of these doctrines (and their truth—eternal in itself) in its concrete historicity, within the web of that human reality which is situated in space and in time. I take them in their chronological order and (what is more) in the civilization, in the culture, in the political, economic, and social context which was that of the men Socrates, Descartes, Kant or Auguste Comte. "We have treasure in earthen vessels." Philosophical truth—and all truth (the revealed truth of religious faith is transmitted to me through a Church, a tradition, a Book: *fides ex auditu*)—does not come to us in the form of bits of raw metal in the pure state, but as an alloy or in combination with a human reality.

Our comprehension of a doctrine will be all the more authentic and the more profound to the extent that we grasp it better within the structure of its orginal reality. We may always have the right to abstract it from this complex, but indeed the surgical operation is so delicate that many of the fine points and the most delicate nuances—those in which the truth resides—risks being damaged or destroyed in the course of the operation.

What progress there is from the *Système d'Aristote* by Hamelin to Werner Jaeger's *Aristotle.* In this work we follow the thought as it is being born; we see it developing and revealing itself through literary forms and on various occasions. For here again the historian puts his preliminary question to the too systematic mind of a Hamelin: about this System, what do you know and how do you know it?

At this point, I imagine, it will be the philosophers who will be upset, should they be listening: "Given (such) a history of philosophies—is there still a question of philosophy?" If we insert the thought too intimately into the life of the men who have conceived it, shall we not dissolve the truth (and hence the reality of the thought) in the temporal flux, and fall into the relativism of *Historismus?* Here we reach that profound reticence (which we have so often observed) of true philosophers in regard to history.

But what shall we say about the theologians! In their eyes you will easily be viewed as a "relativist" if by any chance you are too keenly interested in the past stages of theology—in Origen for instance, or St. Maximus the Confessor, or even St. Thomas, if you go so far as to insist on the fact that he lived in the thirteenth century.

In this sometimes ridiculous, sometimes dramatic misunderstanding, certainly all the faults are not on the side of the historians. If the philosopher dislikes Clio's interference, it is often because she tears him away from his comfortable dogmatism, all ignorance and naïveté. He reproaches her with endlessly complicating problems instead of trying to solve them. But, as we have seen, the mission and the fruitfulness of history consists precisely in constantly re-calling: "There are more things in heaven and earth—in the thought of your predecessors—than can at first be imagined by your simple philosophy." She makes us understand that nothing is simple. Con-fronted by two doctrinal positions which appear to clash head on, the first reaction of the philosopher will be expressed in brutal terms: "If one is true and the other contradicts it, then the second must be false." The historian, an unexpected heir to this situation, will endeavor to seize the original intention of these two thoughts from within, and will often be led to suggest that there is no contra-diction, properly speaking, "because it is clear that if these two doc-trines are worked out according to two quite different original preoc-cupations, they will never envisage the same problems from the same viewpoint, and consequently the one will never reply to the precise question posed by the other"; hence, "they can neither ex-clude nor coincide with each other."

All this is certainly not designed for calming our adversary, the dogmatist. If the effect of disinterested sympathy (in which we have recognized the specific quality of the true historian) causes the mere possibility of a contradiction to disappear, what will become of the notion of absolute Truth? If my effort of comprehension succeeds in recomposing each doctrine according to the perspective in which it appeared as true to its author, it will also appear to me in the same light of truth again—at least as long as I will allow myself to look at it in that perspective. If I succeed in seeing the problem of salvation as Saint Augustine saw it, the mystery of predestination will cease to scandalize me, and I will tend to admit even its most extreme consequences. But on the contrary, if I adopt the theory of Pelagius or that of Julien d'Eclane, here I am once more about to become a Pelagian. The peril is not an imaginary one. Let us remember the formulas, so generous but so imprudent, which Péguy used in his *Bar-Cochebas:*

"But the whole assembly of the great metaphysicians of history, who live on in the memory of humanity, must appear again . . . and a gathering of all the great peoples and races of the earth—in a word, an ensemble of all the great cultures; we must call up a people of languages, a concert of voices that often (?) harmonize and some-times (!) are in dissonance, but which are heard again and again, forever." And earlier, criticizing the philosophy of history which locates successive doctrines according to a linear and continuous progression and shows that they are abolished one after the other, "surpassed" by a progressive movement: "It does not seem that any man—nor any humanity . . . can ever intelligently boast of having surpassed Plato." Or again: "A mind which begins to *surpass* a philosophy is quite simply a soul which is beginning to fall out of harmony with the tone and the rhythm, the language and the resonance of that philosophy. . . ." Then follows the magnificent eulogy of Hypatia, that soul "so perfectly attuned to the Platonic soul . . . and to the Hellenic soul generally . . . , that . . . when everyone, an entire world, was in discord . . . she alone remained attuned even unto death."

It is now the historian who seems to speak the impious word, *Larvatus prodeo*, and who comes forward in a mask. In what we might term the arsenal of thought, he can borrow at his every whim this or that new mask, or some cast-off costume ("défroque"), and each time play the role perfectly as a good actor—until he is taken in by his own acting. The temptation is great. Once an interest in historical research has been aroused, the philosopher runs the risk of being carried away (by curiosity, laziness, or a truly humble devotion to some great master of former days)—and so may forget his mission, his personal vocation, *his* problem. He holds back, restricting his ambition little by little, in order to reconstruct another philosopher's teaching, and no longer dares think for himself in his own name. In the end, the perfect historian of philosophy identifies himself with that Other whom he knows so well. He no longer thinks, he rethinks. He plays (the game may be played seriously without ceasing to be a game) at contemplating the world and life "through the other's glass," and with his eyes. He becomes Plato, Plotinus, or Saint Thomas . . . and no longer is himself.

There is a simple remedy once the disease has been diagnosed. He must keep alive in himself an awareness of the existential engagement of the thought, and he must constantly strengthen and renew this awareness. He must not passively allow himself to be invaded by that foreign personality, nor accept this other man's principles or viewpoint as one accepts the rules for bridge or chess. In that dialectic, he must not allow his own self to be suffocated by the other, he must not cease to exist, he must always be someone.

This is where the true danger that history presents lies in wait for the philosopher: in dilettantism—not in relativism. It is not historical experience that is responsible for the ravages of *Historismus*, wherever they may be found, but it is rather an internal disease of philosophic thought that has lost the sense of Truth. Historicist relativism (everything is true only for a time—its time) is the inevitable response to a problem whose wrongly stated terms have been dictated by an already existing, fundamental scepticism. If the philosopher abandons his elaboration of a table of truth-values (for it is also a criterion of past truth), if he adventures lightly into the thickets of the past, how can history lead him to discover—how can it reveal to him—what he was not able to see in his own existential situation?

If he is resolved not to be unfaithful to his vocation, the real philosopher must first of all confront the difficult problem of Truth on the genuinely philosophical level. When he has resolved it (and if he does not resolve it, no one can do it for him), he can then confront the diversity of the past without danger. The differences between the philosophers, his predecessors, will not intimidate him any more than the criticisms of his contemporaries, for the true philosopher is one who knows that he has seized the truth—sure of his position, he is resigned (if necessary) to be right even in the face of or against all others.

Here I will invoke the fable of the troubadour Peire Cardenal, *Una ciutatz fo, no sai cals . . .* : Once there was a city in which all the citizens went mad after an accident, except one of them: "Great is his surprise to see them thus, but even greater is theirs to see him still sane; it is he whom they take for a madman. . . . This fable is the image of the world, which is this city full of madmen." If he too is ever alone, the philosopher should know how to resist the *consensus* of the deranged!

If a man does not abandon his personality, he is not unarmed when he confronts history. He reacts to his predecessors as he does to his contemporaries. He weighs their reasons and judges, accepts them or rejects them. But his thought emerges from the dialogue enriched by that confrontation (or reinforced, if it has not been altered), and strengthened through the trial he has accepted and victoriously overcome. . . .

Through a fear of depersonalizing his hero when studying a philosopher, a thinker, the historian will insist enthusiastically on the

irreducible difference that distinguishes him from every other philosopher. As he is anxious to grasp his object in its concrete reality,
he will tend to overemphasize too easily whatever goes to form his
individuality. And it is very true that the "continuity of the Platonic
tradition" can never be reduced to any kind of permanent abstract
Platonism, defined as a pure essence that passed from hand to hand,
unaltered. It is incarnated in the series of particular personalities
(who are in the final analysis incomparable): Plato, Plotinus, Por-
phyry and on down through Giordano Bruno and Marsilio Ficino.

For example, in order to grasp the originality that is responsible for
the fact that the "lack of faith" of Rabelais is not that of a Lucian, a
Voltaire or an Anatole France, the historian will try to "explain"
them—that is to say, to understand their mentality, their way of
thinking and of feeling—as a function of the cultural and social milieu which formed them.

I have just quoted Lucien Febvre: somewhere he says that Calvin
and "the character of a totally gratuitous and unconditional gift
which the granting of grace to the chosen assumes (in his writings)"
can be compared with the royal conception of justice and of royal
"grace" that was in effect in France in the sixteenth century: "Let us
recall any account of that time; the guilty man is kneeling, blind-
folded, his head on the block . . . the man in red has already
brandished his fearsome naked blade. . . . And at that precise moment a horseman dashes into the square waving a parch-
ment . . . *grace . . . grace!* The very word. For the king grants his
grace. He does not take any merit into account. Such is the God of
Calvin."

Now here is something alive, something "true." The historian
smiles with pleasure—but what exactly is the value of such approx-
imations? Let us pass over all the fundamental ambiguity in such a
comparison. (Is it Calvin who has been subjected to the influence of
the justice of this day or rather is it not this very justice that has
produced a theological and moral climate to which Calvin is not the
only witness?) We must insist at least once more upon the "facile"
and the arbitrary element in such a type of explanation.

In imitation of L. Febvre, I might undertake to explain for you the
harshness of the theory of predestination as seen by St. Augustine,
and his indifference to the inequality of the lot between the Chosen
and the Damned by the social climate of ancient slavery. But I could

just as well see there a consequence of his physiological constitution—of the distress of the asthmatic that apparently he once was. On the other hand I might embark in the psychoanalyst's vessel, and talk to you of his "Oedipus." Of course that is not all: there is still the racial hypothesis, which would explain the thing to you by the traditions of the Berbers. And how many other possibilities!

But most important, though such hypotheses take into account the *how*, and possibly (let's be optimistic) the *why*, they can never explain the *Quid* of the thought. That cannot be reduced to the empirical conditions which accompanied and, if you like, conditioned its appearance. Whatever may be the reasons that led Calvin to formulate his doctrine, whatever were the ways and means which brought him to that day, Calvinism exists and has an internal coherence, a meaning, a value—a degree of truth which the thinker (here the theologian rather than the philosopher, it matters little) must work out. And what goes to prove all of this is the fact that there have been, there still are and there will continue to exist for a long time Calvinists living in an entirely different milieu from that of sixteenth-century France to whom, despite this difference of environment, his "truth" will be similarly evident. Hence it is insufficient to say that "to restore by an intellectual effort, for each of the epochs which he studies, the mental arsenal of the men of that epoch . . . there is the supreme ideal, the historian's final goal." To explain Cuvier by Montbeliard or the French Revolution—that is to stabilize historical research at a superficial and exoteric level.

Such is not the fine point of our effort. As a matter of fact, if the historian studies a thought of another day by devoting himself with restless and punctilious curiosity to the man who conceived it, to his person and what surrounds him—it is not for the pleasure of collecting anecdotes. It is not that he is moved by the illusory ambition to "reduce" that thought to the conditions of its first appearance—but there is a need to comprehend. And for the same reason he studies the occasions (often futile, always extraordinarily contingent in regard to the doctrinal content) which led the philosopher to formulate it; he studies the works in which it is expressed, their literary type, the vicissitudes of their text—not omitting, as we saw concerning Plato, the least particle of any possible connection.

What is it that we seek, what should we seek to grasp? is, if I may put it so boldly (to talk like the chemists), it is the truth at the very moment of birth, in that "original intuition" of which Bergson has spoken so effectively—that central flash, or *Ursprung*. It is from this core (no matter, once again, what the contingencies may be) that the idea took shape in the thinker's consciousness and demanded his attention. Here I appeal to the experience of all those who, with a docile and sincere heart, ever leaned over a page—whether written yesterday or two thousand years ago—that at last understood, revealed to them its authentic, its eternal truth. They will testify unanimously: no, historical study, carried to its limits, is not a school of relativism. No, it does not end by dissolving a thought in its cultural or social (or any other) environment. It is the occasion and the means of a rediscovery, of a revival, of an enriching experience.

It was before I studied St. Augustine historically that this thought seemed to me relative, curiously odd and quite peculiar. I clashed with him as I might with a foreigner. He was to me that learned man of the decadence, a representative of a civilization now long gone and of a superseded stage in the social, intellectual, and religious evolution of humanity. It is only now, on the contrary, that I have learned to know him, to understand him, to think somewhat like him. It is only now that I can grasp from within how and why it was that he had been led to assume such a doctrinal position and to express it in one fashion or another (here hardening it to the paradoxical in the heat of battle, there expressing it with a popular and even smiling simplicity, as in the *Sermon* addressed to his own people of Hippo). It is only now that the value of his thought is really accessible to me—its value sometimes as Truth, and sometimes as an intimidating objection that it is necessary to confront and conquer.

It is with this original historicity (which was his reality) that my own historicity establishes the rapport which constitutes history. It is a complex rapport, and the reader should not forget that all I can know of the historicity of intermediate ages intervenes. I do not grasp the Augustinian doctrine of predestination only in the instant in which it finishes by taking form under the fire of Julien d'Eclane's objections, but I think it by assuming at the same time all that rightly or wrongly it may have become in the thought of Gottschalk, Luther or Jansenius.

In this rapport there is established a fraternal dialogue. His spirit

and mine communicate what is most profound in each of our existences because we are, the two of us, souls enamoured of—and capable of—Truth.

I have dwelt on this matter of the history of philosophy at some
length because it seems to me typical: *ab illo disce omnes*. We can
see that historical knowledge has an analogous function in whatever
sphere it may be exercised. We must not demand of a thing more
than it can furnish—nor anything different. History will not relieve
the philosopher of his responsibility in formulating a judgment concerning the truth. And neither can it pretend to dictate to the man of
action for example a decision of a political nature (in virtue of the
precedents or analogies which it has revealed to him). History cannot undertake the role of a central vivifying force in human culture
or in life. Its true role (infinitely more humble but on its own level
very real and very precious) is to furnish the alert mind of feeling and
thinking and acting man with an abundance of those materials on
which he may exercise his judgment and his will. Its fruitfulness
resides in the practically unlimited extent to which it can obtain
these from our experience and understanding of man. Therein lies
its greatness, its "usefulness."

Let us not hesitate to return once more—in a new and vitalized
sense—to the ancient conception of *historia, magistra uitae*. We
know what a narrow and ridiculous application the old rhetoricians
made of this. In their hands history was reduced to a repertoire of
topical anecdotes, of examples designed for the use of the moralist,
of precedents for the jurist or statesman, of well-tested stratagems
for the tactician or the diplomat.

But this expression is susceptible of a quite profound meaning. It
is by investigating men—by meeting men other than myself—that I
learn to understand better what man is (and the man that I am, with
all his potentialities—now splendid, now frightful). This is clearly
evident in the experience of everyday life. Who would dare say it is in
vain that we have encountered these men, in vain that we have
sought to know them, to understand them—to love them? Since it
is itself a Meeting with Others, history reveals to us infinitely more
things—on all the aspects of being and of human life—than we
could discover in only one lifetime. It is in this way, too, that it
renders our creative imagination more fertile, and opens a thousand
new paths for our efforts in thinking as it does for our action. (Here I

use the word "action" in its widest sense, annexing to it for instance the sentimental life: by listening to the troubadors I can discover, or deepen, the art of love.)

History liberates us from the impediments, the limitations that are imposed on our experience of man when we situate him in a certain place in a certain society at a certain moment of his evolution—and thus it becomes in a certain sense an instrument and a means to our liberty.

But there is more. I have continued to insist on the fact that history is not only the reconstruction of my genealogical tree and of my biological antecedents, but I have not denied that it is. Yet it is very evident that it is also—and in a sense it is first of all—*my* history. It is the reconstruction and through this the realization of the human development that has made me what I am, that has led to this cultural, economic, social, and political situation in which I am enmeshed by all the fibers of my being.

It is here that a difference appears. And it is capital from the point of view of *historiodicy* (the "justification of history"). It is a difference at the very heart of culture and of life—between biological evolution and what we proposed to call, by analogy, the evolution of humanity. If a horse, for example, could become aware of the avatars of his distant tertiary ancestors (the Hyracotherium, the Orohippus, etc.) that would change nothing in his bone structure, nor in his racing technique (and the same is true of man when he reconstitutes his phylogenesis).

But the evolution of humanity as well has transmitted to us a heritage that at first is imposed on us with the same "natural" and tyrannical necessity. Yet from the moment that this evolution becomes history—from the moment when I become conscious of that heredity, when I know what I am, and why and how I have become it—that knowledge liberates me with respect to that heritage, and I can now consider it simply under the aspect of an inventory. I can accept it or reject it (to the extent that it is a question of things within my power). As for whatever is beyond me, I can at least judge it bravely, opposing it with indignant condemnation, for example—and this act in the sphere of thought can in turn inspire and animate a whole line of action with a view to transforming things.

If Stalin had been able to discover where his police technique came from (through a historical study of the notion of personal liberty of the type that Lord Acton had dreamed of bringing about), he might have drawn back in horror when confronted with all that survived in him of Ivan the Terrible and of the Byzantine Basileus. It might have led him to modify the regime of the M.D.V., that heir of the N.K.V.D., of the O.G.P.U., of the Tcheka, of the Okhrana, and so on right down to the *agentes in rebus* of the Later Empire and to the *frumentarii* of Hadrian.

A historical awareness brings about a veritable *catharsis,* a liberation of our sociological subconscious somewhat analogous to that which psychoanalysis seeks to establish on the psychological level. I have been somewhat ironic with regard to their aggressive pretensions when they invade our domain, but it is with the greatest seriousness that I here invoke this parallel. In the one case as in the other, we observe this mechanism (at first view surprising) by which "the knowledge of the past cause modifies the present effect." In each case man frees himself from a past which up until that moment had weighed upon him obscurely. He does this not by forgetfulness but by the effort of finding it again, by assimilating it in a fully conscious way so as to integrate it. It is in this sense, as has so often been repeated from Goethe to Dilthey and to Croce, that historical knowledge frees man from the weight of the past. Here again history appears as a pedagogy, the exercise ground and the instrument of our liberty.

I cannot insist too strongly that history, of its nature, is not capable of claiming that directive and dominating role which the men of the nineteenth century dreamed for it. Nevertheless, its presence within the framework of human culture can confer upon this culture a characteristic and very precious value, which is sufficient to determine the whole atmosphere of thought and life. I will gladly define man the historian: he is the man who delights in history and knows how to nourish himself with that knowledge, who has an authentic grasp of its object (even though it is always a partial one). In contrast to him there is the man of the Philosophy of History— that barbarian—the man who knows (or imagines that he knows) the last word on the mystery of time. A victim of his own illusions, he forgets the arbitrary selections and the deforming mutilations by means of which he has been able to draw up his schematic image of the past and future of humanity. Drunk with a desire for power, he rushes into action with a blind fanaticism. Ah! It is not a good thing to be found crossing his path, nor even (as a reluctant ally) to associate with his drive, if only partially. Suspicious and soon convinced of your opposition to the movement of "History," he will shortly sweep you aside, liquidating you without mercy. At the same time—it is a painfully ironic compensation—this same man is obliged to adhere instant by instant to the very sinuous line which the realization of the Idea traces in the course of time. When he loses the sense of Truth with its absolutes, he loses all his internal framework, autonomy and dignity—he howls with the wolves, adores the powerful, spits upon the conquered.

The real historian, on the contrary, knows that he cannot know everything. He does not try to be more than a man, and he accepts with simplicity the fact that he is not God. He knows things incompletely, in his little mirror—not only in limited fashion but often obscurely. Yet he also knows that he does not know; he estimates and locates the immensity of what escapes him. And in this way he acquires a keen sense of the complexity of being and of the situations of man, in all their tragic ambivalence.

What is our twentieth century in the process of accomplishing? Will it see the emancipation of the laboring class (and of the colored peoples)? Or will we only witness a simple shift of imperialism, sanctioning the decline of Western Europe to the advantage of North America or of the Slavic peoples (while awaiting Asia's moment)? Are the sufferings of the present the foreshadowing of the birth of a humanity that is at last truly fraternal, living on a unified planet in universal peace? Or are we definitely entering upon an era of total war, with all its uncontrollable unleashing of the forces of destruction? Are we to see the dreams cherished by our fathers during the liberal period fulfilled and finally carried out—will there be the triumph of the human person, the recognition of man by man in its fullness and completeness? Or have we instead arrived at the threshold of a new world of terror through the emergence of the totalitarian or police state, and the dictatorship of the technocrats? Will we see a labor civilization develop under that very name, where the servitude of the slave to his task is so sinister and deceptive that he comes to bless and adore the very signs of his servitude? Will we see a base materialism or a spiritual advance? And if a new impetus, will it be a renaissance of the noblest forms of religious life, or rather the triumph of the mongrel and vulgar forms of the collective Sacred? Who knows?

As he struggles with this irreducible ambiguity, the historian acquires the sharpest sense of his responsibility and realizes the meaning of his involvement, the value of his free decision. At the same time, he gains a more profound and much wider knowledge of the immense inherent potentialities that exist for him to choose from. He is man become aware—who walks with open eyes, and who cannot be deceived. He does not go forward like a laboring ox, his neck straining toward the furrow but, head held high, he contemplates the immense horizon open to the four winds of the spirit. He knows that nothing is simple, that the die is not cast, that many possibilities exist which may or may not be fulfilled. He chooses and he judges. He is a man who does not become intoxicated with victory, for he measures its precarious nature, its uncertainty, and its limitations. He is also a man who is not broken by defeat. And when there is nothing more that he can do, he knows how to say: *No.* Unyielding, he knows how to suffer with nobility and how to preserve hope.

History, Not Art, Not Science, but History: Meanings and Uses of History

Boyd C. Shafer

Boyd C. Shafer (b. 1907) is a past executive secretary of the American
Historical Association and editor of the *American Historical Review*
(1953–63). He is one of the leading authorities on the history of nationalism, and his books include *Nationalism: Myth and Reality*
(1955) and *The Faces of Nationalism: New Realities and Old Myths*
(1972). The following essay was first published as an article in the
Pacific Historical Review (May 1960).

A good many years ago when I was a graduate student in
history we used to argue whether history was a science or an
art. I still hear this argument, an argument that incidentally
began with Burckhardt and Croce before I was born. Thirty years ago
I thought the argument futile though enlightening. I still do. Because it will serve as a vehicle for ideas I am going to ride it once
more in this paper.

Historians, like scientists, seek truth and use objective techniques
of fact finding and arriving at generalizations. The writing of history
has some of the appearances of art. It refines experience and gives it
artificial shape and form, a kind of meaningful unity. But . . . the
study of history is neither fully scientific nor neatly artful. History
has its own methods and purposes, its own meanings and uses.

History is all that has happened to men: all of man's experiences, all of man's actions, political strivings, economic organizations, social groupings; all of man's ideas, good and bad, logical and illogical. In short, it is everything in man's past. A historian is first of all a technician and a storyteller who tries to recount what happened during some particular time in the past, who puts together the pieces of a period of historical time, or perhaps describes but a segment of this time. A historian is a good historian if like Ssú-ma Ch'ien or Ranke he tries to reconstruct the past as it actually happened, *wie es eigentlich gewesen;* if like Charles Beard he imaginatively assembles his facts and data while making clear his prejudices and points of view, his frame of reference (one cannot ask that he be just a *tabula rosa*): and if like Parkman he can so beautifully narrate the events of the past that men will enjoy reading about them. And a historian is a great historian, if like Thucydides, Tacitus, Gibbon, Tocqueville, Burckhardt, and perhaps our own Carl Becker, he can think about the past in so informed a fashion that it not only becomes in a sense recaptured but illumines and makes meaningful the present of his contemporaries and the many "presents" of those who follow.

The great historian is not only a historian but a man of culture and of conscience. To paraphrase Matthew Arnold, the historian, like any humanist, wants to know the best that has been thought (and I might add the worst), and through this knowledge to turn a "stream of fresh and free thought upon a stock of notions and habits." He can do this, he can perceive, comprehend, and communicate only in the degree that he himself is a man of deep learning and vast experience (direct and vicarious). . . . To be a historian, one must attempt to know everything, to be a universal man. As H. I. Marrou, the French philosopher-historian, has written, the "more [the historian] is intelligent, cultivated, rich in lived experience, open to all the values of man, the more he will be able to recover the things of the past, the more his knowledge will take on richness and truth." The richness of historical knowledge is indeed "directly proportional to the personal culture of the historian," to the degree that he knows the world's humanistic and scientific literature, to the extent, depth, and quality of his own experience.

The best historian is not only a cultured man; he is also a special being with consciousness of his responsibilities to other men. Precisely because, as the English historian George Unwin had it, the "ultimate aspect of history" is "that widening and deepening of community which is the correlative of the moral and spiritual growth of man as individuals," the great historian recognizes and fulfills his obligations to other men by seeking truth about their (and his own) past and then teaching and publishing his findings, no matter how popular or unpopular these may be. But that the historian is a man of culture and conscience does not make him a scientist or an artist.

The historian uses the scientific method. He systematically observes, he develops hypotheses, he organizes and orders his data, he tests his evidence, he arrives at tentative generalizations, he tests again, he organizes and orders. But he can never arrive at exact or definite laws. He cannot because he cannot fully control himself and he cannot fully control his data. He is, even though a Ranke or a Beard, a victim of prejudice or his climate of opinion; those of his class, his nationality, his community, his religion. However desirable complete objectivity would be, no historian can write history without some bias. Ranke of Germany, for all his seeming objectivity, was ultimately a German, a Protestant, and a patriot. And Beard, in his zeal for an America free of "Europe's basalts" finally seemed to succumb to the devil theory of history he once scorchingly blasted. The historian who attempts to write without having a point of view has at least that point of view and he still interprets within the philosophic scheme or frame of reference of the economic and political ideologies of his time, whether of democracy and capitalism or egalitarianism and communism. Further, the historian is compelled always to work with variable subjects in a variable environment, neither of which he can actually recreate. Historiographers, like Bernheim of Germany in his *Lehrbuch der Historischen Methode,* have evolved complex techniques for externally ascertaining and determining the validity of evidence, but we historians can never test or isolate our evidence as can a scientist in a laboratory. As Justice Holmes wrote to Pollard, "The trouble with all explanations of historic causes is the absence of quantification. You never can say how much of the given cause was necessary to provide how much effect, or how much cause there was."

As historians, we go back for our basic evidence to what we call the primary sources, the manuscripts, published letters and memoirs of eyewitnesses, the public documents, the newspapers, the pamphlets, the books, and the material remains of the time about which we are writing. Like prosecuting attorneys, we cross-examine the eyewitnesses, attempt to determine their trustworthiness, and check them against each other. Ideally we never accept the actuality of an event or fact unless two or more sources agree. Then we check upon the eyewitnesses by circumstantial evidence, by imaginative induction and logical deduction. But unfortunately some of the facts always escape us. We can never exactly create again the historical circumstances, have our actors live again and repeat a performance. And even with the facts available to us, we are unable to use instruments of delicate precision to measure what made the actors act. No matter, then, how carefully we discover and study the facts, we can never recover them all, we have no micrometers to determine motivation or causation, and no way of testing our generalizations so that other historians may take them for granted. Through complete mastery of the facts and by being able to see and read Henry VIII's mind at the time of action, we would like to know what made him act. Since we cannot do so, we can never be certain whether he was motivated by the eyes of Ann Boleyn, by avarice for church property, or by ideals of national patriotism when he divorced Catherine, or if by all three, in what degree by each. In consequence we must be satisfied with only tentative hypotheses concerning the nature of human action.

Even if a historian arrives at objective interpretation of evidence, he cannot with certainty use this interpretation for the purpose of prediction. Historians may arrive at historical laws like Cheyney's law of continuity that "all events, conditions, institutions . . . come from immediately preceding events, conditions, institutions." These laws usually have been either so general and obvious that they are of little use, or so formed by the views of the time that they can be described as little more than intelligent insights valid only at a certain time and in a certain place and in a certain context of thought. This is not to assert that historians may not someday be able to develop laws of historical development with which they may be able to predict, within reasonable limits, future developments within human societies. It is only to say that out of the mass of historical data, out of the varying and complex flow of human life, historians have not yet been able to arrive at universally applicable or acceptable generalizations which may be used for the purposes of prediction.

History is as deep, as rich, as complex as life itself—in fact, it is life as lived in the past, ceaseless, moving, changing life. It includes "every trace and vestige of everything man has done or thought since he first appeared on earth." Recorded history is simply what the men who are historians have been able to find or have chosen to remember of the past of men. From history, as from memory, almost anything can be "proven," but at the same time it would be equally true to say that nothing can be "proven" from history. Though history contains all mankind's experience, hence contains the future as well as the past, it cannot in consequence be used to predict with any certainty that this or that action or institution will always succeed or always fail, for while it is true that men are human and therefore much alike through all history, it is never true that the circumstances of one time exactly repeat those of a previous time. . . .

If history is not a science, perhaps, then, it is an art. Historians indeed employ many of the devices of the literary arts, intuition, imagination, evaluation, narration, analogy. Historians employ these devices to give meaning to the succession of events and ideas. Since they can never hope to portray exactly what happened, they must give an artificial or artful shape and form to these events or ideas. This form, which we may call artistic if it is good, is like and yet unlike what has happened; it is a form which not only reflects like a mirror but reveals the shape of the historian's own mind. Hence it is not actuality that is reproduced but an imaginative, plausible, and at best artful likeness. But the analogy of history and art may easily be stretched too far. The task of the historian differs from that of the artist. The artful historian, the Parkman or the Morison, does not, like the novelist, create his subject matter, he tries to re-create it. He must take his subject, the past, as he finds it. But there is no end, no beginning of history, no certain sequences of events leading to a denouement, no rounded development, though chance or the historian's own mind may supply them.

The writing of a novel is an art which requires the imaginative construction of a plot according to rules laid down (this is history) long ago. There must be a dichotomy or plot, conflict, the unravelling of a story through depiction of character. Fact is not as important as insight. The novel can, if the writer is great, be true to life, afford insights perhaps deeper and more significant than the historical monograph. The historian, however, is first of all obligated to see his subject, the past, *wie es eigentlich gewesen.* His plot, if any, was constructed by God or the fates. He must accept it—he cannot imaginatively create it. The historian must, it is true, exercise imagination, but the imagination necessary to reconstruct what happened rather than dichotomy, plot, conflict, character. As Aristotle said of poetry, the novel may be higher than history in that it requires the great insight, perhaps even the greater intellect, though this I do not believe. But whether or not a volume of history is inferior to a novel or poem is beside the point. The artist and the historian have different functions: fundamentally the one artificially constructs anew, the other recreates and interprets an already existing past.

History is neither art nor science. But if it is neither, has it meaning, any use? Is it not just another of the academic studies selected by universities for intellectual gymnastics: a study to befuddle and fool, an academic exercise of Erewhonian professors, full of illusions and delusions, of propaganda and lies, sounds and fury signifying nothing but professional vanity? . . . Perhaps, indeed, the very best that can be said for history is that we learn from history that we do not learn from history. But this old retort of a historian tired of trying to convince his fellows makes no more sense than the jibes of the wit, the mechanic, and the scholar.

History, as has often been said, is to the community what memory is to the man. Like memory, history may be obscure, dimly perceived, and our knowledge of it but a chaos of faulty impressions. In the ultimate sense, indeed, history may be meaningless. But as men cannot think or act without memory, so a society is lost without its social roots, without its traditions, its history. As a man may hate a memory, men may hate history, but they cannot get along without it. It is the facts of the past, true, imagined, or false, that fill our minds. Nothing, in fact, is a fact unless it is of history. Whether we will or not it is only with historical facts, then, be these real or imagined, that we can think. Without the facts of history we resemble Vanbrugh's Lord Foppington, who, satisfied with the sprouts of his own brain, had mighty small potatoes. Like memory, historical knowledge may be inaccurate or wrong, but at any one moment, it is our only ground for thought and action. We may go further. Like the individual and his memory, the richer and fuller a society's knowledge of history, the richer and fuller the society. As Sir Winston Churchill put it, "The further and deeper you look back, the more you can see forward."

All analogies are inexact, but an old one of Becker's which I paraphrase here is worth repetition. Suppose this morning when you awakened you were the victim of amnesia. You see no familiar sights, you have no familiar feelings, not even the most familiar one of all, the pang of hunger. You do not know what you should do, or even if you should do. You are scarcely "aware" because you have nothing in your mind with which to be aware. Perhaps you instinctively begin to stuff something in your mouth, though you do not know what will satisfy the unfamiliar pang in your middle. What will it be, the wool comforter, the leather in the shoe beneath the bed? You learn very likely then and there that wool does not taste good and that leather cannot easily be chewed. You are acquiring experience, a memory, a history. In the future you may again try wool or leather but you now have a basis for judgment. In a real sense you are liberated. You now have, though your experience still binds you, a certain freedom of choice, which, without this experience, you would not have. To Sir Winston's observation, I would add, the further and deeper you can look back, the broader the range of possibilities of intelligent and useful thought and action you may conceive.

If intelligently interpreted, the greater the remembered experience the better the ground for action. Knowledge of experience will not necessarily tell us what we should do, or how we will act. It does increase the possibilities of action, hence freedom of action, and of right action. As individuals in society have knowledge of history the possibilities of that society to survive and develop may be enhanced. For as experiences of men are remembered so that the number of choices confronting men may be increased, so the depth of understanding may be enlarged, so the chances of growth may be multiplied. History's greatest and most useful role, if I may again quote Marrou's *De la connaissance historique,* is "to furnish the man who feels, who thinks, who acts, an abundance of material upon which to exercise his judgment and his will; its fecundity resides in this practically indefinite extension of our experience and of our knowledge of man."

Each one of us is, in Dilthey's words, a historical being. The study of history tells us how we have "become." It tells us what we are, peculiar as that may be. Knowing history, a man can better explain and understand himself. If he is an English Protestant, a French Catholic, or a Chinese Buddhist, he has inherited certain ways of looking at the universe, certain political traditions, certain ways of housing and clothing himself, certain habits of eating and drinking, certain attitudes toward women, and certain standards of fairness in play. However much this English Protestant, French Catholic, or Chinese Buddhist might like to forget his past, he cannot understand his present nor imagine his future unless he understands the long history of the community from which he springs. Even if he is a revolutionist and wishes to break with the past, he cannot, unless he knows history, know how he would like his society or himself to differ. History is the only foundation upon which he can build any kind of a structure, whatever his dreams. Whether an individual is conscious of it or not, history is the pavement upon which he must set his feet and take such steps as he is able. Only by knowing the past can a man discern the directions he may walk, the highways that may be open and the likely consequences of travel upon any one of them. Recorded history enlarges a man's perceptions so that he may find his world and himself more spacious and more understandable "than the narrow confines of the fleeting present." Knowledge of history, then, liberates us from our own narrow experience, our own time, our own society, and thus becomes an instrument of freedom.

History may have more utilitarian ends. When a man leaves his bed and walks in a dark room in the middle of the night, he misses furniture and avoids stubbed toes only because he is a historian and has learned . . . where the obstacles are placed. In the same way each modern problem, institution, and each individual has a history from which something can be learned. . . .

From history we cannot prove that man is either warlike or peaceful. From history we cannot draw the conclusion that "peace is only a pause in war," or that lasting peace, except that of death, will inevitably come to man. We can learn, if we will, however, that some ways of trying to avoid war may, under certain circumstances, possibly work better than others. We can find, for example, in the works of Machiavelli that there are three ways of treating a conquered nation if we do not wish to fight them again. We can obliterate that conquered nation as Rome did Carthage. We can send wise governors who by becoming citizens of and part of that country govern it as natives and yet are friendly. Or we can punish the conquered country quickly and lightly, get out, and maintain friendly relations. But if we follow none of these policies, as with Germany in 1919, we, following Machiavelli, may expect war again. . . .

We may hope that the study of history will widen any man's experience, will enable him further to understand his practical, everyday problems, may help him avoid errors of conduct and thought, and at times therefore will have utilitarian value. History, as we all know, may also have the value literature has for entertainment. Since prehistoric times the old men of the tribes and nations have told tales of valor and courage, of cowardice and hypocrisy. There may not be much ethical or pecuniary value in these tales but, if they are well told, they give men an escape from the present which at times is too much with them. If history had not ethical value, if it brought no monetary rewards, men would still be historians, bards, storytellers. For the tale of man's past is a good tale, full of shocks, surprises, and suspense.

Finally, perhaps the study of history has ethical value. In making a man aware of his past it makes him aware, be he scientist or philosopher or bricklayer, of his relations to and reliance upon other men. In itself it may not make him feel a sense of responsibility to other men. That, probably, is the function of philosophy and religion. But once a man is aware of what he has inherited from the past, of his debt to other men, of his meaninglessness and insignificance without history and without other men, he cannot but realize that he is part of all men. This in itself may be justification enough for history.

History is not a science, not an art. It is the essential preliminary, the accompanying study of both. It is not science. It is not art. It is remembered experience, and remembered experience is the beginning of all understanding, of any action whether intelligent or not.

What Is Radical History?

Howard Zinn

Howard Zinn (b. 1922) teaches at Boston University. His teaching and research interests are in the field of American history and political theory. A strong antiwar activist in the 1960s and a proponent of racial and economic justice, Zinn has tried to write history from the perspective of the disadvantaged. His works include *La Guardia in Congress* (1959), *The Southern Mystique* (1964), *SNCC: The New Abolitionists* (1964), *Vietnam: The Logic of Withdrawal* (1967), *Postwar America, 1945–1971* (1973), and *A People's History of the United States* (1980). The following selection is from *The Politics of History* (1970).

*H*istorical writing always has some effect on us. It may reinforce our passivity; it may activate us. In any case, the historian cannot choose to be neutral; he writes on a moving train.

Sometimes, what he tells may change a person's life. In May 1968 I heard a Catholic priest, on trial in Milwaukee for burning the records of a draft board, tell (I am paraphrasing) how he came to that act.

> I was trained in Rome. I was quite conservative, never broke a rule in seminary. Then I read a book by Gordon Zahn, called *German Catholics and Hitler's Wars*. It told how the Catholic Church carried on its normal activities while Hitler carried on his. It told how SS men went to mass, then went out to round up Jews. That book changed my life. I decided the church must never behave again as it did in the past; and that I must not.

This is unusually clear. In most cases, where people turn in new directions, the causes are so complex, so subtle, that they are impossible to trace. Nevertheless, we all are aware of how, in one degree or another, things we read or heard changed our view of the world, or how we must behave. We know there have been many people who themselves did not experience evil, but who became persuaded that it existed, and that they must oppose it. What makes us human is our capacity to reach with our mind beyond our immediate sensory capacities, to feel in some degree what others feel totally, and then perhaps to act on such feelings.

I start, therefore, from the idea of writing history in such a way as to extend human sensibilities, not out of this book into other books, but into the going conflict over how people shall live, and whether they shall live.

I am urging value-laden historiography. . . . [Many] still rebel at this—despite my argument that this does not determine answers, only questions; despite my plea that aesthetic work, done for pleasure, should always have its place; despite my insistence that our work is value-laden whether we choose or not. . . .

What kind of awareness moves people in humanistic directions, and how can historical writing create such awareness, such movement? I can think of five ways in which history can be useful. That is only a rough beginning. I don't want to lay down formulas. There will be useful histories written that do not fit into preconceived categories. I want only to sharpen the focus for myself and others who would rather have their writing guided by human aspiration than by professional habit.

1. *We can intensify, expand, sharpen our perception of how bad things are, for the victims of the world.* This becomes less and less a philanthropic act as all of us, regardless of race, geography, or class, become potential victims of a burned, irradiated planet. But even our own victimization is separated from us by time and the fragility of our imagination, as that of others is separated from us because most of us are white, prosperous, and within the walls of a country so over-armed it is much more likely to be an aggressor than a victim.

History can try to overcome both kinds of separation. The fascinating progression of a past historical event can have greater effect on us than some cool, logical discourse on the dangerous possibilities of present trends—if only for one reason, because we learn the end of that story. True, there is a chill in the contemplation of nuclear war, but it is still a contemplation whose most horrible possibilities we cannot bring ourselves to accept. It is a portent that for full effect needs buttressing by another story whose conclusion is known. Surely, in this nuclear age our concern over the proliferation of H-bombs is powerfully magnified as we read Barbara Tuchman's account of the coming of the First World War:

> War pressed against every frontier. Suddenly dismayed, governments struggled and twisted to fend it off. It was no use. Agents at frontiers were reporting every cavalry patrol as a deployment to beat the mobilization gun. General staffs, goaded by their relentless timetables, were pounding the table for the signal to move lest their opponents gain an hour's head start. Appalled upon the brink, the chiefs of state who would be ultimately responsible for their country's fate attempted to back away but the pull of military schedules dragged them forward.

There it is, *us*. In another time, of course. But unmistakably us.

Other kinds of separation, from the deprived and harried people of the world—the black, the poor, the prisoners—are sometimes easier to overcome across time than across space: hence the value of historical recollection. Both the *Autobiography of Malcolm X* and the *Autobiography of Frederick Douglass* are history, one more recent than the other. Both assault our complacency. So do the photos on television of blacks burning buildings in the ghetto today, but the autobiographies do something special: they let us look closely, carefully, personally behind the impersonality of those blacks on the screen. They invade our homes, as the blacks in the ghetto have not yet done; and our minds, which we tend to harden against the demands of *now*. They tell us, in some small degree, what it is like to be black, in a way that all the liberal clichés about the downtrodden Negro could never match. And thus they insist that we act; they explain why blacks are acting. They prepare us, if not to initiate, to respond.

Slavery is over, but its degradation now takes other forms, at the bottom of which is the unspoken belief that the black person is not quite a human being. The recollection of what slavery is like, what slaves are like, helps to attack that belief. Take the letter Frederick Douglass wrote his former master in 1848, on the tenth anniversary of his flight to freedom:

> I have selected this day to address you because it is the anniversary of my emancipation. . . . Just ten years ago this beautiful September morning yon bright sun beheld me a slave—a poor, degraded chattel—trembling at the sound of your voice, lamenting that I was a man. . . .

When yet but a child about six years old I imbibed the determination to run away. The very first mental effort that I now remember on my part, was an attempt to solve the mystery, Why am I a slave. . . . When I saw a slave driver whip a slave woman . . . and heard her piteous cries, I went away into the corner of the fence, wept and pondered over the mystery. . . . I resolved that I would someday run away.

The morality of the act, I dispose as follows: I am myself; you are yourself; we are two distinct persons. What you are, I am. I am not by nature bound to you nor you to me. . . . In leaving you I took nothing but what belonged to me . . .

Why do we need to reach into the past, into the days of slavery? Isn't the experience of Malcolm X, in our own time, enough? I see two values in going back. One is that dealing with the past, our guard is down, because we start off thinking it is over and we have nothing to fear by taking it all in. We turn out to be wrong, because its immediacy strikes us, affects us before we know it; when we have recognized this, it is too late—we have been moved. Another reason is that time adds depth and intensity to a problem which otherwise might seem a passing one, susceptible to being brushed away. To know that long continuity, across the centuries, of the degradation that stalked both Frederick Douglass and Malcolm X (between whose lives stretched that of W. E. B. Du Bois, recorded in *The Souls of Black Folk* and *Dusk of Dawn*) is to reveal how infuriatingly long has been this black ordeal in white America. If nothing else, it would make us understand in that black mood of today what we might otherwise see as impatience, and what history tells us is over-long endurance.

Can history also sharpen our perception of that poverty hidden from sight by the foliage of the suburbs? The poor, like the black, become invisible in a society blinded by the glitter of its own luxury. True, we can be forcefully reminded that they exist, as we were in the United States in the 1960's when our sensibilities had been sharpened by the civil rights revolt, and our tolerance of government frayed by the Vietnamese war. At such a time, books like Michael Harrington's *The Other America* jabbed at us, without going back into the past, just supplying a periscope so that we could see around the corner, and demanding that we look.

Where history can help is by showing us how other people similarly situated, in other times, were blind to how their neighbors were living, in the same city. Suppose that, amidst the "prosperity" of the

1950's, we had read about the 1920's, another era of affluence. Looking hard, we might find the report of Senator Burton Wheeler of Montana, investigating conditions in Pennsylvania during the coal strike of 1928:

> All day long I have listened to heartrending stories of women evicted from their homes by the coal companies. I heard pitiful pleas of little children crying for bread. I stood aghast as I heard most amazing stories from men brutally beaten by private policemen. It has been a shocking and nerve-racking experience.

Would this not suggest to us that perhaps in our time too a veil is drawn over the lives of many Americans, that the sounds of prosperity drown out all else, and the voices of the well-off dominate history?

In our time, as in the past, we construct "history" on the basis of accounts left by the most articulate, the most privileged members of society. The result is a distorted picture of how people live, an underestimation of poverty, a failure to portray vividly the situations of those in distress. If, in the past, we can manage to find the voice of the underdog, this may lead us to look for the lost pleas of our own era. True, we could accomplish this directly for the present without going back. But sometimes the disclosure of what is hidden in the past prompts us, particularly when there is no immediate prod, to look more penetratingly into contemporary society. (In my own experience, reading in the papers of Fiorello LaGuardia the letters from the East Harlem poor in the twenties, made me take a second look at the presumed good times of the fifties.) . . .

2. *We can expose the pretensions of governments to either neutrality or beneficence.* If the first requisite for activating people is to sharpen their awareness of what is wrong, the second is to disabuse them of the confidence that they can depend on governments to rectify what is wrong.

Again, I start from the premise that there are terrible wrongs all about us, too many for us to rest content even if not everyone is being wronged. Governments of the world have not been disposed to change things very much. Indeed, they have often been the perpetrators of these wrongs. To drive this point at us strongly pushes us to act ourselves.

Does this mean I am not being "objective" about the role of governments? Let us take a look at the historical role of the United States on the race question. For instance, what did the various American governments do for the black person in America right after the Civil War? Let's be "objective," in the sense of telling *all* the facts that answer this question. Therefore we should take proper note of the Thirteenth, Fourteenth, Fifteenth Amendments, the Freedman's Bureau, the stationing of armed forces in the South, the passage of civil rights laws in 1866, 1870, 1871, and 1875. But we should also record the court decisions emasculating the Fourteenth Amendment, the betrayal of the Negro in the 1877 Hayes-Tilden agreement, the nonenforcement of the civil rights acts. Ultimately, even if we told all, our emphasis in the end would be subjective—it would depend on who we are and what we want. A present concern, that citizens need to act themselves, suggests we emphasize the unreliability of government in securing equal rights for black people.

Another question: to what extent can we rely on our government to equitably distribute the wealth of the country? We could take proper account of the laws passed in this century which seemed directed at economic justice: the railroad regulation acts of the Progressive era, the creation of the graduated income tax in the Wilson administration, the suits against trusts initiated in the Theodore Roosevelt and Taft administrations. But a *present* recognition of the fact that the allocation of wealth to the upper and lower fifths of the population has not fundamentally changed in this century would suggest that all that legislation has only managed to maintain the status quo. To change this, we would need to emphasize what has not so far been emphasized, the persistent failure of government to alter the continuing inequities of the American economic system.

Historians' assessments of the New Deal illustrate this problem. We can all be "objective" by including in any description of the New Deal both its wealth of reform legislation and its inadequacies in eradicating poverty and unemployment in America. But there is always an emphasis, subtle or gross, which we bring to bear on this picture. One kind of emphasis adds to a feeling of satisfaction in how America has been able to deal with economic crisis. Another stimulates us to do more ourselves, in the light of the past failure at dealing with the fundamental irrationality by which our nation's resources are distributed. The needs of the present suggest that the second kind of historical presentation is preferable. . . .

A radical history, then, would expose the limitations of governmental reform, the connections of government to wealth and privilege, the tendencies of governments toward war and xenophobia, the play of money and power behind the presumed neutrality of law. It would illustrate the role of government in maintaining things as they are, whether by force, or deception, or by a skillful combination of both—whether by deliberate plan or by the concatenation of thousands of individuals playing roles according to the expectations around them.

Such motivating facts are available in the wealth of data about present governments. What historical material can do is to add the depth that time imparts to an idea. What one sees in the present may be attributable to a passing phenomenon; if the same situation appears at various points in history, it becomes not a transitory event, but a long-range condition, not an aberration, but a structural deformity requiring serious attention. . . .

3. *We can expose the ideology that pervades our culture—using "ideology" in Mannheim's sense: rationale for the going order.* There is the open sanctification of racism, of war, of economic inequality. There is also the more subtle supportive tissue of half-truths ("We are not like the imperialist powers of the nineteenth century"); noble myths ("We were born free"); pretenses ("Education is the disinterested pursuit of knowledge"); the mystification of rhetoric ("freedom and justice for all"); the confusion of ideals and reality (The Declaration of Independence and its call for revolution, in our verbal tradition; the Smith Act and its prohibition of calls for revolution, on our lawbooks); the use of symbols to obscure reality ("Remember the *Maine*," vis-à-vis rotten beef for the troops); the innocence of the double standard (deploring the violence of John Brown; hailing the violence of Ulysses Grant); the concealment of ironies (using the Fourteenth Amendment to help corporations instead of Negroes).

The more widespread is education in a society, the more mystification is required to conceal what is wrong; church, school, and the written word work together for that concealment. This is not the work of a conspiracy; the privileged of society are as much victims of the going mythology as the teachers, priests, and journalists who spread it. All simply do what comes naturally, and what comes naturally is to say what has always been said, to believe what has always been believed.

History has a special ability to reveal the ludicrousness of those beliefs which glue us all to the social frame of our fathers. It also can reinforce that frame with great power, and has done so most of the time. Our problem is to turn the power of history—which can work both ways—to the job of demystification. I recall the words of the iconoclast sociologist E. Franklin Frazier to Negro college students one evening in Atlanta, Georgia: "All your life, white folks have bamboozled you, preachers have bamboozled you, teachers have bamboozled you; I am here to debamboozle you."

Recalling the rhetoric of the past, and measuring it against the actual past, may enable us to see through our current bamboozlement, where the reality is still unfolding, and the discrepancies still not apparent. To read Albert Beveridge's noble plea in the Senate January 9, 1900, urging acquisition of the Philippines with "thanksgiving to Almighty God that He has marked us as His chosen people, henceforth to lead in the regeneration of the world," and then to read of our butchery of the Filipino rebels who wanted independence, is to prepare us better for speeches about our "world responsibility" today. That recollection might make us properly suspicious of Arthur Schlesinger's attempt to set a "historical framework" for Vietnam comprised of "two traditional and entirely honorable strands in American thinking," one of which "is the concept that the United States has a saving mission in the world." In the light of the history of idea and fact in American expansionism, that strand is not quite honorable. The Vietnam disaster was not, as Schlesinger says, "a final and tragic misapplication" of those strands, a wandering from a rather benign historical tradition, but another twining of the deadly strands around a protesting foreign people. . . .

4. *We can recapture those few moments in the past which show the possibility of a better way of life than that which has dominated the earth thus far.* To move men to act it is not enough to enhance their sense of what is wrong, to show that the men in power are untrustworthy, to reveal that our very way of thinking is limited, distorted, corrupted. One must also show that something else is possible, that changes can take place. Otherwise, people retreat into privacy, cynicism, despair, or even collaboration with the mighty.

History cannot provide confirmation that something better is inevitable; but it can uncover evidence that it is conceivable. It can point to moments when human beings cooperated with one another (the organization of the underground railroad by black and white,

the French Resistance to Hitler, the anarchist achievements in Cata-
lonia during the Spanish Civil War). It can find times when governments were capable of a bit of genuine concern (the creation of the
Tennessee Valley Authority, the free medical care in socialist countries, the equal-wages principle of the Paris Commune). It can disclose men and women acting as heroes rather than culprits or fools
(the story of Thoreau or Wendell Phillips or Eugene Debs, or Martin
Luther King or Rosa Luxemburg). It can remind us that apparently
powerless groups have won against overwhelming odds (the abolitionists and the Thirteenth Amendment, the CIO and the sit-down
strikes, the Vietminh and the Algerians against the French).

Historical evidence has special functions. It lends weight and
depth to evidence which, if culled only from contemporary life,
might seem frail. And, by protraying the movements of men over
time, it shows the possibility of change. Even if the actual change
has been so small as to leave us still desperate today, we need, to
spur us on, the faith that change is possible. Thus, while taking
proper note of how much remains to be done, it is important to compare the consciousness of white Americans about black people in
the 1930's and in the 1960's to see how a period of creative conflict
can change people's minds and behavior. Also, while noting how
much remains to be done in China, it is important to see with what
incredible speed the Chinese Communists have been able to mobi-
lize seven hundred million people against famine and disease. We
need to know, in the face of terrifying power behind the accusing
shouts against us who rebel, that we are not mad; that men in the
past, whom we know, in the perspective of time, to have been great,
felt as we do. At moments when we are tempted to go along with the
general condemnation of revolution, we need to refresh ourselves
with Thomas Jefferson and Tom Paine. At times when we are about
to surrender to the glorification of law, Thoreau and Tolstoi can revive our conviction that justice supersedes law. . . .

In sum, while there is a value to specific analysis of particular
historical situations, there is another kind of value to the unearthing
of ideals which cross historical periods and give strength to beliefs
needing reinforcement today. The trouble is, even Marxist historians
have not paid sufficient attention to the Marxian admonition in his
Theses on Feuerbach: "The dispute over the reality or nonreality of
thinking which is isolated from practice is a purely scholastic ques-

tion." Any dispute over a "true" history cannot be resolved in theory; the real question is, which of the several possible "true" histories (on that elementary level of factual truth) is *true*, not to some dogmatic notion about what a radical interpretation should contain, but to the practical needs for social change in our day? If the "political ends" . . . are not the narrow interests of a nation or party or ideology, but those humanistic values we have not yet attained, it is desirable that history should serve political ends.

5. *We can show how good social movements can go wrong, how leaders can betray their followers, how rebels can become bureaucrats, how ideals can become frozen and reified.* This is needed as a corrective to the blind faith that revolutionaries often develop in their movements, leaders, theories, so that future actors for social change can avoid the traps of the past. To use Karl Mannheim's distinction, while *ideology* is the tendency of those in power to falsify, *utopianism* is the tendency of those out of power to distort. History can show us the manifestations of the latter as well as the former.

History should put us on guard against the tendency of revolutionaries to devour their followers along with their professed principles. We need to remind ourselves of the failure of the American revolutionaries to eliminate slavery, despite the pretensions of the Declaration of Independence, and the failure of the new republic to deal justly with the Whiskey Rebels in Pennsylvania despite the fact a revolution had been fought against unjust taxes. Similarly, we need to recall the cry of protest against the French Revolution, in its moment of triumph, by Jacques Roux and the poor of Gravillers, protesting against profiteering, or by Jean Varlet, declaring: "Despotism has passed from the palace of the kings to the circle of a committee." Revolutionaries, without dimming their enthusiasm for change, should read Khrushchev's speech to the Twentieth Party Congress in 1956, with its account of the paranoid cruelties of Stalin.

The point is not to turn us away from social movements but into *critical* participants in them, by showing us how easy it is for rebels to depart from their own claims. . . .

The history of radical movements can make us watchful for narcissitic arrogance, the blind idolization of leaders, the substitution of dogma for a careful look at the environment, the lure of compromise when leaders of a movement hobnob too frequently with those in power. . . . Searching histories of radical movements can deter the tendency to make absolutes of those instruments—party, leaders, platforms—which should be constantly subject to examination.

That revolutionaries themselves are burdened by tradition, and cannot completely break from thinking in old ways, was seen by Marx in the remarkable passage opening *The Eighteenth Brumaire of Louis Bonaparte:*

> Men make their own history, but they do not make it just as they please; they do not make it under circumstances chosen by themselves, but under circumstances directly found, given and transmitted from the past. The tradition of all the dead generations weighs like a nightmare on the brain of the living. And just when they seem engaged in revolutionizing themselves and things, in creating something entirely new, precisely in such epochs of revolutionary crisis they anxiously conjure up the spirits of the past to their service and borrow from them names, battle slogans and costumes in order to present the new scene of world history in this time-honored disguise and this borrowed language. . . .

How to use the past to change the world, and yet not be encumbered by it—both skills can be sharpened by a judicious culling of past experience. But the delicate balance between them cannot come from historical data alone—only from a clearly focused vision of the human ends which history should serve.

HISTORY is not inevitably useful. It can bind us or free us. It can destroy compassion by showing us the world through the eyes of the comfortable ("the slaves are happy, just listen to them"—leading to "the poor are content, just look at them"). It can oppress any resolve to act by mountains of trivia, by diverting us into intellectual games, by pretentious "interpretations" which spur contemplation rather than action, by limiting our vision to an endless story of disaster and thus promoting cynical withdrawal, by befogging us with the encyclopedic eclecticism of the standard textbook.

But history can untie our minds, our bodies, our disposition to move—to engage life rather than contemplating it as an outsider. It can do this by widening our view to include the silent voices of the past, so that we look behind the silence of the present. It can illustrate the foolishness of depending on others to solve the problems of the world—whether the state, the church, or other self-proclaimed benefactors. It can reveal how ideas are stuffed into us by the powers of our time, and so lead us to stretch our minds beyond what is given. It can inspire us by recalling those few moments in the past when men did behave like human beings, to prove it is *possible*. And it can sharpen our critical faculties so that even while we act, we think about the dangers created by our own desperation.

These criteria I have discussed are not conclusive. They are a rough guide. I assume that history is not a well-ordered city (despite the neat stacks of the library) but a jungle. I would be foolish to claim my guidance is infallible. The only thing I am really sure of is that we who plunge into the jungle need to think about what we are doing, because there *is* somewhere we want to go.

HISTORY
AND SOCIETY

History, Civic Virtue, and the Schools

hether history should be used to teach citizenship is currently at issue; certainly the questions raised in this controversy deserve serious reflection. Thoughtful observers believe that teaching enlightened citizenship, educating people to become more perceptive and effective participants in the world about them, remains a legitimate function of studying the past. History should play some part, they say, in self-government and in helping us preserve our intellectual freedom amidst the complexities of modern life. They maintain that this is not a call for inculcating unthinking allegiance. Nor is it an effort to fuse blind patriotism and citizenship, which has so inflamed national passions and characterized much history teaching in elementary and secondary schools during this century. The argument for using history to teach enlightened citizenship has merit, although many people who came of age during the 1960s and 1970s remain skeptical. Too often they feel, as Lester Stephens observed in a previous selection, that the past has been misused "to entrench partisan and parochial impressions." Surely the decline of history in public schools in recent years is, in part, a result of this skepticism. A considerable number of teachers today apparently doubt that good citizenship is sufficient justification for including history in the curriculum at the elementary and secondary levels.

The following essays deal with several themes, but each touches on the relation between history and citizenship. Frederick Jackson Turner and George Macaulay Trevelyan, writing before the First World War, saw many benefits from studying the past, and the development of civic virtue was important among them. Trevelyan believed that reading history is important to the creation of political wisdom and that it can produce "a new state of mind," one that is better prepared to discern what is important from what is not. The

Canadian writer David Pratt, however, questioned whether history necessarily promotes good citizenship and believed that many of the traditional reasons given for teaching history are no longer convincing "while powerful arguments for history in the schools are being overlooked." The British historian Herbert Butterfield maintained that history "can be used to broaden our consciousness of citizenship, whether in a nation or in the world." But Butterfield was not talking about the kind of history that can be tested in memory examinations, and he was critical of the abridged histories that some people read in the hope of finding a shortcut to historical knowledge. Studying the past often involves "a process of unlearning," Butterfield said, and history in no way should be trivial pursuit. Both Trevelyan and Butterfield thought that if the wrong kind of history is disseminated the world can easily be "plunged into bloodshed."

The Significance of History

Frederick Jackson Turner

Frederick Jackson Turner (1861–1932) was one of the most influential American historians of the late nineteenth and early twentieth centuries. He first taught at the University of Wisconsin and then later at Harvard. Although he wrote primarily about the American past, he was also widely informed about European and ancient history. His publications include *The Rise of the New West* (1906), and he is perhaps best remembered for his seminal essay "The Significance of the Frontier in American History," which appeared in 1893. "The Significance of History" first appeared in 1891 in the *Wisconsin Journal of Education*.

The conceptions of history have been almost as numerous as the men who have written history. To Augustine Birrell history is a pageant; it is for the purpose of satisfying our curiosity. Under the touch of a literary artist the past is to become living again. Like another Prospero the historian waves his wand, and the deserted streets of Palmyra sound to the tread of artisan and officer, warrior gives battle to warrior, ruined towers rise by magic, and the whole busy life of generations that have long ago gone down to dust comes to life again in the pages of a book. The artistic prose narration of past events—this is the ideal of those who view history as literature. To this class belong romantic literary artists who strive to give to history the coloring and dramatic action of fiction, who do not hesitate to paint a character blacker or whiter than he really was, in order that the interest of the page may be increased, who force dull facts into vivacity, who create impressive situations, who, in short, strive to realize as an ideal the success of Walter Scott. It is of the historian Froude that Freeman says: "The most winning style, the choicest metaphors, the neatest phrases from foreign tongues would all be thrown away if they were devoted to proving that any two sides of a triangle are not always greater than the third side. When they are devoted to proving that a man cut off his wife's head one day and married her maid the next morning out of sheer love for his country, they win believers for the paradox." It is of the reader of this kind of history that Seeley writes: "To him, by some magic, parliamentary debates shall be always lively, officials always men of strongly marked, interesting character. There shall be nothing to remind him of the bluebook or the law book, nothing common or prosaic; but he shall sit as in a theater and gaze at splendid scenery and costume. He shall never be called upon to study or to judge, but only to imagine and enjoy. His reflections, as he reads, shall be precisely those of the novel reader; he shall ask: Is this character well drawn? is it really amusing? is the interest of the story well sustained, and does it rise properly toward the close?"

But after all these criticisms we may gladly admit that in itself an interesting style, even a picturesque manner of presentation, is not to be condemned, provided that truthfulness of substance rather than vivacity of style be the end sought. But granting that a man may be the possessor of a good style which he does not allow to run away with him, either in the interest of the artistic impulse or in the cause of party, still there remain differences as to the aim and method of history. To a whole school of writers, among whom we find some of the great historians of our time, history is the study of politics, that is, politics in the high signification given the word by Aristotle, as meaning all that concerns the activity of the state itself. "History is past politics and politics present history," says the great author of the *Norman Conquest.* Maurenbrecher of Leipzig speaks in no less certain tones: "The bloom of historical studies is the history of politics;" and Lorenz of Jena asserts: "The proper field of historical investigation, in the closer sense of the word, is politics." Says Seeley: "The modern historian works at the same task as Aristotle in his Politics." "To study history is to study not merely a narrative but at the same time certain theoretical studies." "To study history is to study problems." And thus a great circle of profound investigators, with true scientific method, have expounded the evolution of political institutions, studying their growth as the biologist might study seed, bud, blossom, and fruit. The results of these labors may be seen in such monumental works as those of Waitz on German institutions, Stubbs on English constitutional history, and Maine on early institutions.

There is another and an increasing class of historians to whom history is the study of the economic growth of the people, who aim to show that property, the distribution of wealth, the social conditions of the people, are the underlying and determining factors to be studied. This school, whose advance guard was led by Roscher, having already transformed orthodox political economy by its historical method, is now going on to rewrite history from the economic point of view. Perhaps the best English expression of the ideas of the school is to be found in Thorold Rogers' *Economic Interpretation of History*. He asserts truly that "very often the cause of great political events and great social movements is economical and has hitherto been undetected." . . .

Viewed from this position, the past is filled with new meaning. The focal point of modern interest is the fourth estate, the great mass of the people. History has been a romance and a tragedy. In it we read the brilliant annals of the few. The intrigues of courts, knightly valor, palaces and pyramids, the loves of ladies, the songs of minstrels, and the chants from cathedrals pass like a pageant, or linger like a strain of music as we turn the pages. But history has its tragedy as well, which tells of the degraded tillers of the soil, toiling that others might dream, the slavery that rendered possible the "glory that was Greece," the serfdom into which decayed the "grandeur that was Rome"—these as well demand their annals. Far oftener than has yet been shown have these underlying economic facts affecting the breadwinners of the nation been the secret of the nation's rise or fall, by the side of which much that has passed as history is the merest frippery. . . .

Today the questions that are uppermost, and that will become increasingly important, are not so much political as economic questions. The age of machinery, of the factory system, is also the age of socialistic inquiry.

It is not strange that the predominant historical study is coming to be the study of past social conditions, inquiry as to landholding, distribution of wealth, and the economic basis of society in general. Our conclusion, therefore, is that there is much truth in all these conceptions of history: history is past literature, it is past politics, it is past religion, it is past economics.

Each age tries to form its own conception of the past. *Each age writes the history of the past anew with reference to the conditions uppermost in its own time.* Historians have accepted the doctrine of

Herder. Society grows. They have accepted the doctrine of Comte. Society is an organism. History is the biography of society in all its departments. There is objective history and subjective history. Objective history applies to the events themselves; subjective history is man's conception of these events. "The whole mode and manner of looking at things alters with every age," but this does not mean that the real events of a given age change; it means that our comprehension of these facts changes.

History, both objective and subjective, is ever *becoming*, never completed. The centuries unfold to us more and more the meaning of past times. Today we understand Roman history better than did Livy or Tacitus, not only because we know how to use the sources better but also because the significance of events develops with time, because today is so much a product of yesterday that yesterday can only be understood as it is explained by today. The aim of history, then, is to know the elements of the present by understanding what came into the present from the past. For the present is simply the developing past, the past the undeveloped present. As well try to understand the egg without a knowledge of its developed form, the chick, as to try to understand the past without bringing to it the explanation of the present; and equally well try to understand an animal without study of its embryology as to try to understand one time without study of the events that went before. The antiquarian strives to bring back the past for the sake of the past; the historian strives to show the present to itself by revealing its origin from the past. The goal of the antiquarian is the dead past; the goal of the historian is the living present. Droysen has put this true conception into the statement, "History is the 'Know Thyself' of humanity— the self-consciousness of mankind."

If, now, you accept with me the statement of this great master of historical science, the rest of our way is clear. If history be, in truth, the self-consciousness of humanity, the "self-consciousness of the living age, acquired by understanding its development from the past," all the rest follows.

First we recognize why all the spheres of man's activity must be considered. Not only is this the only way in which we can get a complete view of the society, but no one department of social life can be understood in isolation from the others. The economic life and the political life touch, modify, and condition one another. Even the religious life needs to be studied in conjunction with the political and economic life, and vice versa. Therefore all kinds of history are essential—history as politics, history as art, history as economics, history as religion—all are truly parts of society's endeavor to understand itself by understanding its past.

Next we see that history is not shut up in a book—not in many books. The first lesson the student of history has to learn is to discard his conception that there are standard ultimate histories. In the nature of the case this is impossible. *History is all the remains that have come down to us from the past, studied with all the critical and interpretative power that the present can bring to the task.* From time to time great masters bring their investigations to fruit in books. To us these serve as the latest words, the best results of the most recent efforts of society to understand itself—but they are not the final words. To the historian the materials for his work are found in all that remains from the ages gone by—in papers, roads, mounds, customs, languages; in monuments, coins, medals, names, titles, inscriptions, charters; in contemporary annals and chronicles; and, finally, in the secondary sources, or histories in the common acceptance of the term. Wherever there remains a chipped flint, a spearhead, a piece of pottery, a pyramid, a picture, a poem, a coliseum, or a coin, there is history.

Says Taine: "What is your first remark on turning over the great stiff leaves of a folio, the yellow sheets of a manuscript, a poem, a code of laws, a declaration of faith? This, you say, was not created alone. It is but a mold, like a fossil shell, an imprint like one of those shapes embossed in stone by an animal which lived and perished. Under the shell there was an animal, and behind the document there was a man. Why do you study the shell except to represent to yourself the animal? So do you study the document only in order to know the man. The shell and the document are lifeless wrecks, valuable only as a clue to the entire and living existence. We must reach back to this existence, endeavor to recreate it."

But observe that when a man writes a narration of the past he writes with all his limitations as regards ability to test the real value of his sources, and ability rightly to interpret them. Does he make use of a chronicle? First he must determine whether it is genuine; then whether it was contemporary, or at what period it was written; then what opportunities its author had to know the truth; then what were his personal traits; was he likely to see clearly, to relate impartially? If not, what was his bias, what his limitations? Next comes the harder task—to interpret the significance of events; causes must be understood, results seen. Local affairs must be described in relation to affairs of the world—all must be told with just selection, emphasis, perspective; with that historical imagination and sympathy that does not judge the past by the canons of the present, nor read into it the ideas of the present. Above all the historian must have a passion for truth above that for any party or idea. Such are some of the difficulties that lie in the way of our science. When, moreover, we consider that each man is conditioned by the age in which he lives and must perforce write with limitations and prepossessions, I think we shall all agree that no historian can say the ultimate word.

Another thought that follows as a corollary from our definition is that in history there is a unity and a continuity. Strictly speaking, there is no gap between ancient, medieval, and modern history. Strictly speaking, there are no such divisions. Baron Bunsen dates modern history from the migration of Abraham. Bluntschli makes it begin with Frederick the Great. The truth is, as Freeman has shown, that the age of Pericles or the age of Augustus has more in common with modern times than has the age of Alfred or of Charlemagne. There is another test than that of chronology; namely, stages of growth. In the past of the European world peoples have grown from families into states, from peasantry into the complexity of great city life, from animism into monotheism, from mythology into philosophy; and have yielded place again to primitive peoples who in turn have passed through stages like these and yielded to new nations. Each nation has bequeathed something to its successor; no age has suffered the highest content of the past to be lost entirely. By unconscious inheritance, and by conscious striving after the past as part of the present, history has acquired continuity. Freeman's statement that into Rome flowed all the ancient world and out of Rome came the modern world is as true as it is impressive. In a strict sense imperial Rome never died. You may find the eternal city still living in the Kaiser and the Czar, in the language of the Romance peoples, in the codes of European states, in the eagles of their coats of arms, in every college where the classics are read, in a thousand political institutions.

Even here in young America old Rome still lives. When the inaugural procession passes toward the Senate chamber, and the president's address outlines the policy he proposes to pursue, there is Rome! You may find her in the code of Louisiana, in the French and Spanish portions of our history, in the idea of checks and balances in our constitution. Clearest of all, Rome may be seen in the titles, government, and ceremonials of the Roman Catholic church; for when the Caesar passed away, his scepter fell to that new Pontifex Maximus, the Pope, and to that new Augustus, the Holy Roman Emperor of the Middle Ages, an empire which in name at least continued till those heroic times when a new Imperator recalled the days of the great Julius, and sent the eagles of France to proclaim that Napoleon was king over kings.

So it is true in fact, as we should presume a priori, that in history there are only artificial divisions. Society is an organism, ever growing. History is the self-consciousness of this organism. "The roots of the present lie deep in the past." There is no break. But not only is it true that no country can be understood without taking account of all the past; it is also true that we cannot select a stretch of land and say we will limit our study to this land; for local history can only be understood in the light of the history of the world. There is unity as well as continuity. To know the history of contemporary Italy we must know the history of contemporary France, of contemporary Germany. Each acts on each. Ideas, commodities even, refuse the bounds of a nation. All are inextricably connected, so that each is needed to explain the others. This is true especially of our modern world with its complex commerce and means of intellectual connection. In history, then, there is unity and continuity. Each age must be studied in the light of all the past; local history must be viewed in the light of world history.

Now, I think, we are in a position to consider the utility of historical studies. I will not dwell on the dignity of history considered as the self-consciousness of humanity; nor on the mental growth that comes from such a discipline; nor on the vastness of the field; all these occur to you, and their importance will impress you increasingly as you consider history from this point of view. To enable us to behold our own time and place as a part of the stupendous progress of the ages; to see primitive man; to recognize in our midst the undying ideas of Greece; to find Rome's majesty and power alive in present law and institution, still living in our superstitions and our folklore; to enable us to realize the richness of our inheritance, the possibility of our lives, the grandeur of the present—these are some of the priceless services of history.

But I must conclude my remarks with a few words upon the utility of history as affording a training for good citizenship. Doubtless good citizenship is the end for which the public schools exist. Were it otherwise there might be difficulty in justifying the support of them at public expense. The direct and important utility of the study of history in the achievement of this end hardly needs argument.

In the union of public service and historical study Germany has been preeminent. For certain governmental positions in that country a university training in historical studies is essential. Ex-President [of the American Historical Association] Andrew D. White affirms that a main cause of the efficiency of German administration is the training that officials get from the university study of history and politics. In Paris there is the famous School of Political Sciences which fits men for the public service of France. . . .

Nor does England fail to recognize the value of the union of history and politics, as is exemplified by such men as Macaulay, Dilke, Morley, and Bryce, all of whom have been eminent members of Parliament as well as distinguished historical writers. From France and Italy such illustrations could easily be multiplied.

When we turn to America and ask what marriages have occurred between history and statesmanship, we are filled with astonishment at the contrast. It is true that our country has tried to reward literary men: Motley, Irving, Bancroft, Lowell held official positions, but these positions were in the diplomatic service. The "literary fellow" was good enough for Europe. The state gave these men aid rather than called their services to its aid. To this statement I know of but one important exception—George Bancroft. In America statesmanship has been considered something of spontaneous generation, a miraculous birth from our republican institutions. To demand of the statesmen who debate such topics as the tariff, European and South American relations, immigration, labor and railroad problems, a scientific acquaintance with historical politics or economics would be to expose one's self to ridicule in the eyes of the public. I have said that the tribal stage of society demands tribal history and tribal politics. When a society is isolated it looks with contempt upon the history and institutions of the rest of the world. We shall not be altogether wrong if we say that such tribal ideas concerning our institutions and society have prevailed for many years in this country. Lately historians have turned to the comparative and historical study of our political institutions. The actual working of our constitution as contrasted with the literary theory of it has engaged the attention of able young men. Foreigners like Von Holst and Bryce have shown us a mirror of our political life in the light of the political life of other peoples. Little of this influence has yet attracted the attention of our public men. Count the roll in Senate and House, cabinet and diplomatic service—to say nothing of the state governments—and where are the names famous in history and politics? It is shallow to express satisfaction with this condition and to sneer at "literary fellows." To me it seems that we are approaching a pivotal point in our country's history. . . .

Again, consider the problems of socialism brought to our shores by European immigrants. We shall never deal rightly with such problems until we understand the historical conditions under which they grew. Thus we meet Europe not only outside our borders but in our very midst. The problem of immigration furnishes many examples of the need of historical study. Consider how our vast Western domain has been settled. Louis XIV devastates the Palatinate, and soon hundreds of its inhabitants are hewing down the forests of Pennsylvania. The bishop of Salzburg persecutes his Protestant subjects, and the woods of Georgia sound to the crack of Teutonic rifles. Presbyterians are oppressed in Ireland, and soon in Tennessee and Kentucky the fires of pioneers gleam. These were but advance guards of the mighty army that has poured into our midst ever since. Every economic change, every political change, every military conscription, every socialistic agitation in Europe, has sent us groups of colonists who have passed out onto our prairies to form new self-governing communities, or who have entered the life of our great cities. These men have come to us historical products, they have brought to us not merely so much bone and sinew, not merely so much money, not merely so much manual skill, they have brought with them deeply inrooted customs and ideas. They are important factors in the political and economic life of the nation. Our destiny is interwoven with theirs; how shall we understand American history without understanding European history? The story of the peopling of America has not yet been written. We do not understand ourselves.

. . . Gladstone's remark that "the American constitution is the most wonderful work ever struck off at a given time by the brain and purpose of man" has been shown to be misleading, for the constitution was, with all the constructive powers of the fathers, still a growth; and our history is only to be understood as a growth from European history under the new conditions of the New World. . . .

If any added argument were needed to show that good citizenship demands the careful study of history, it is in the examples and lessons that the history of other peoples has for us. It is profoundly true that each people makes its own history in accordance with its past. It is true that a purely artificial piece of legislation, unrelated to present and past conditions, is the most short-lived of things. Yet it is to be remembered that it was history that taught us this truth, and that there is, within the limits of the constructive action possible to a state, large scope for the use of this experience of foreign peoples.

I have aimed to offer, then, these considerations: History, I have said, is to be taken in no narrow sense. It is more than past literature, more than past politics, more than past economics. It is the self-consciousness of humanity—humanity's effort to understand itself through the study of its past. Therefore it is not confined to books; the *subject* is to be studied, not books simply. History has a unity and a continuity; the present needs the past to explain it; and local history must be read as a part of world history. The study has a utility as a mental discipline, and as expanding our ideas regarding the dignity of the present. But perhaps its most practical utility to us, as public school teachers, is its service in fostering good citizenship.

The ideals presented may at first be discouraging. Even to him who devotes his life to the study of history the ideal conception is impossible of attainment. He must select some field and till that thoroughly, be absolute master of it; for the rest he must seek the aid of others whose lives have been given in the true scientific spirit to the study of special fields. The public school teacher must do the best with the libraries at his disposal. We teachers must use all the resources we can obtain and not pin our faith to a single book; we must make history living instead of allowing it to seem mere literature, a mere narration of events that might have occurred in the moon. We must teach the history of a few countries thoroughly, rather than that of many countries superficially. The popularizing of scientific knowledge is one of the best achievements of this age of book-making. It is typical of that social impulse which has led university men to bring the fruits of their study home to the people. In England the social impulse has led to what is known as the university extension movement. University men have left their traditional cloister and gone to live among the working classes, in order to bring to them a new intellectual life. Chautauqua, in our own country, has begun to pass beyond the period of superficial work to a real union of the scientific and the popular. In their summer school they offer courses in American history. Our own state university carries on extensive work in various lines. I believe that this movement in the direction of popularizing historical and scientific knowledge will work a real revolution in our towns and villages as well as in our great cities.

The schoolteacher is called to do a work above and beyond the instruction in his school. He is called upon to be the apostle of the higher culture to the community in which he is placed. Given a good school or town library—such a one is now within the reach of every hamlet that is properly stimulated to the acquisition of one—and given an energetic, devoted teacher to direct and foster the study of history and politics and economics, we would have an intellectual regeneration of the state. Historical study has for its end to let the community see itself in the light of the past, to give it new thoughts and feelings, new aspirations and energies. Thoughts and feelings flow into deeds. Here is the motive power that lies behind institutions. This is therefore one of the ways to create good politics; here we can touch the very "age and body of the time, its form and pressure." Have you a thought of better things, a reform to accomplish? "Put it in the air," says the great teacher. Ideas have ruled, will rule. . . . Of one thing beware. Avoid as the very unpardonable sin any one-sidedness, any partisan, any partial treatment of history. Do not misinterpret the past for the sake of the present. The man who enters the temple of history must respond devoutly to that invocation of the church, *Sursum corda,* lift up your hearts. No looking at history as an idle tale, a compend of anecdotes; no servile devotion to a textbook; no carelessness of truth about the dead that can no longer speak must be permitted in its sanctuary. "History," says Droysen, "is not the truth and the light; but a striving for it, a sermon on it, a consecration to it."

Clio, a Muse

George Macaulay Trevelyan

George Macaulay Trevelyan (1876–1962) was a major British historian and master stylist. He taught modern history at Cambridge University between 1927 and 1940 and later at Trinity College (1940–51) and was chancellor of Durham University from 1951 to 1958. His many works included *England Under the Stuarts* (1904), *History of England* (1926), and the multivolume *England Under Queen Anne* (1930–34). In addition to writing about the history of the British people, Trevelyan also wrote about Italy. The following selection is taken from *Clio, a Muse, and Other Essays Literary and Pedestrian*, which first appeared in 1914.

It is necessary to ask, "What is history and what is its use?" We must "gang o'er the fundamentals," as the old Scotch lady with ear trumpet said so alarmingly to the new minister when he entered her room on his introductory visit. So I now ask, what is the object of the life of man *qua* historian? Is it to know the past and enjoy it forever? Or is it to do one's duty to one's neighbour and cause him also to know the past? The answer to these theoretic questions must have practical effects on the teaching and learning, the writing and reading of history.

The root questions can be put in these terms:—"Ought history to be merely the Accumulation of facts about the past? Or ought it also to be the Interpretation of facts about the past? Or, one step further, ought it to be not merely the Accumulation and Interpretation of facts, but also the Exposition of these facts and opinions *in their full emotional and intellectual value* to a wide public by the difficult art of literature?"

The words in italics raise another question which can be put thus:—

"Ought emotion to be excluded from history on the ground that history deals only with the science of cause and effect in human affairs?" . . .

The functions of physical science are mainly two: direct utility in practical fields, and in more intellectual fields the deduction of laws of "cause and effect." Now history can perform neither of these functions.

In the first place it has no practical utility like physical science. No one can by a knowledge of history, however profound, invent the steam-engine, or light a town, or cure cancer, or make wheat grow near the arctic circle. For this reason there is not in the case of history, as there is in the case of physical science, any utilitarian value at all in the accumulation of knowledge by a small number of students, repositories of secrets unknown to the vulgar.

In the second place history cannot, like physical science, deduce causal laws of general application. All attempts have failed to discover laws of "cause and effect" which are certain to repeat themselves in the institutions and affairs of men. The law of gravitation may be scientifically proved because it is universal and simple. But the historical law that starvation brings on revolt is not proved; indeed the opposite statement, that starvation leads to abject submission, is equally true in the light of past events. You cannot so completely isolate any historical event from its circumstances as to be able to deduce from it a law of general application. Only politicians adorning their speeches with historical arguments have this power; and even they never agree. An historical event cannot be isolated from its circumstances, any more than the onion from its skins, because an event is itself nothing but a set of circumstances, none of which will ever recur. . . .

. . . There is no utilitarian value in knowledge of the past, and there is no way of scientifically deducing causal laws about the action of human beings in the mass. In short, the value of history is not scientific. Its true value is educational. It can educate the minds of men by causing them to reflect on the past.

Even if cause and effect could be discovered with accuracy, they still would not be the most interesting part of human affairs. It is not man's evolution but his attainment that is the great lesson of the past and the highest theme of history. The deeds themselves are more interesting than their causes and effects, and are fortunately ascertainable with much greater precision. . . .

It is the tale of the thing done, even more than its causes and effects, which trains the political judgment by widening the range of sympathy and deepening the approval and disapproval of conscience; that stimulates by example youth to aspire and age to endure; that enables us by the light of what men once have been, to see the thing we are, and dimly to descry the form of what we should be. "Is not Man's history and Men's history a perpetual evangel?" . . .

One day, as I was walking along the side of Great Gable, thinking of history and forgetting the mountains which I trod, I chanced to look up and see the top of a long green ridge outlined on the blue horizon. For half a minute I stood in thoughtless enjoyment of this new range, noting upon it forms of beauty and qualities of romance, until suddenly I remembered that I was looking at the top of Helvellyn! Instantly, as by magic, its shape seemed to change under my eyes, and the qualities with which I had endowed the unknown mountain to fall away, because I now knew what like were its hidden base and its averted side, what names and memories clung round it. The change taking place in its aspect seemed physical, but I suppose it was only a trick of my own mind. Even so, if we could forget for a while all that had happened since the Battle of Waterloo, we should see it, not as we see it now, with all its time-honoured associations and its conventionalised place in history, but as our ancestors saw it first, when they did not know whether the "Hundred Days," as we now call them, would not stretch out for a Hundred Years. Every true history must, by its human and vital presentation of events, force us to remember that the past was once real as the present and uncertain as the future.

Even in our personal experience, we have probably noticed the uncanny difference between events when they first appear red hot, and the same events calmly reviewed, cold and dead, in the perspective of subsequent happenings. I sometimes remember, each time with a shock of surprise, how the Boer War and the Election of 1906 appeared to me while they were still portents, unsettling our former modes of thought and expectation. Normally I cannot recollect what I then felt. It comes back to me only at chance moments when my mind has let slip all forms and pressures stamped on it in later days.

days. It is not that my worthless "opinions" have altered since then. I am speaking of something much more subtle and potent than "opinions"; I mean the pangs felt by the soul as she hastily adapts herself to new circumstances, when some strange joy or terror, with face half hid, ineluctably advances. I have forgotten most of it, but I remember some of it sometimes, as in a dream.

Now, if so great a change of emotional attitude towards an event can take place in the same person within a few years, how very different must our view of the Battle of Waterloo and of the Reform Bill of 1832 be from the aspect which first they bore to our grandfathers and great-grandfathers, men so very different from ourselves, brought up in habits of thought and conduct long passed away. Deeply are they buried from our sight

> Under the downtrodden pall
> Of the leaves of many years,

and sometimes deeper still under the formulae of conventional history. To recover some of our ancestors' real thoughts and feelings is the hardest, subtlest and most educative function that the historian can perform. It is much more difficult than to spin guesswork generalisations, the reflex of passing phases of thought or opinion in our own day. To give a true picture of any country, or man or group of men in the past requires industry and knowledge, for only the documents can tell us the truth, but it requires also insight, sympathy and imagination of the finest, and last but not least the art of making our ancestors live again in modern narrative. Carlyle, at his rare best, could do it. If you would know what the night before a *journée* in the French Revolution was like, read his account of the eve of August 10, in the chapter called "The Steeples at Midnight." Whether or not it is entirely accurate in detail, it is true in effect: the spirit of that long dead hour rises on us from the night of time past. . . .

But since history has no properly scientific value, its only purpose is educative. And if historians neglect to educate the public, if they fail to interest it intelligently in the past, then all their historical learning is valueless except in so far as it educates themselves.

WHAT, then, are the various ways in which history can educate the mind?

The first, or at least the most generally acknowledged educational effect of history, is to train the mind of the citizen into a state in which he is capable of taking a just view of political problems. But, even in this capacity, history cannot prophesy the future; it cannot supply a set of invariably applicable laws for the guidance of politicians; it cannot show, by the deductions of historical analogy, which side is in the right in any quarrel of our own day. It can do a thing less, and yet greater than all these. It can mould the mind itself into the capability of understanding great affairs and sympathising with other men. The information given by history is valueless in itself, unless it produce a new state of mind. The value of Lecky's Irish history did not consist in the fact that he recorded in a book the details of numerous massacres and murders, but that he produced sympathy and shame, and caused a better understanding among us all of how the sins of the fathers are often visited upon the children, unto the third and fourth generations of them that hate each other. He does not prove that Home Rule is right or wrong, but he trains the mind of Unionists and Home Rulers to think sensibly about that and other problems. . . .

. . . When a man of the world reads history, he is called on to form a judgment on a social or political problem, without previous bias, and with some knowledge of the final protracted result of what was done. The exercise of his mind under such unwonted conditions sends him back to the still unsettled problems of modern politics and society, with larger views, clearer head and better temper. The study of past controversies, of which the final outcome is known, destroys the spirit of prejudice. It brings home to the mind the evils that are likely to spring from violent policy, based on want of understanding of opponents. When a man has studied the history of the Democrats and Aristocrats of Corcyra, of the English and Irish, of the Jacobins and anti-Jacobins, his political views may remain the same, but his political temper and his way of thinking about politics may have improved, if he is capable of receiving an impression.

And so, too, in a larger sphere than politics, a review of the process of historical evolution teaches a man to see his own age, with its peculiar ideals and interests, in proper perspective as one among other ages. If he can learn to understand that other ages had not only a different social and economic structure but correspondingly different ideals and interests from those of his own age, his mind will have veritably enlarged. I have hopes that ere long the Workers' Educational Association will have taught its historical students not to ask, "What was Shakespeare's attitude to Democracy?" and to perceive that the question no more admits of an answer than the inquiry, "What was Dante's attitude to Protestantism?" or, "What was Archimedes' attitude to the steam-engine?"

The study of cause and effect is by no means the only, and perhaps not the principal means, of broadening the mind. History does most to cure a man of political prejudice, when it enables him, by reading about men or movements in the past, to understand points of view which he never saw before, and to respect ideals which he had formerly despised. Gardiner's *History of the Civil War* has done much to explain Englishmen to each other, by revealing the rich variety of our national life, far nobler than the unity of similitude. Forms of idealism, considerations of policy and wisdom, are acceptable or at least comprehensible, when presented by the historian to minds which would reject them if they came from the political opponent or the professed sage.

But history should not only remove prejudice, it should breed enthusiasm. To many it is an important source of the ideas that inspire their lives. With the exception of a few creative minds, men are too weak to fly by their own unaided imagination beyond the circle of ideas that govern the world in which they are placed. And since the ideals of no one epoch can in themselves be sufficient as an interpretation of life, it is fortunate that the student of the past can draw upon the purest springs of ancient thought and feeling. Men will join in associations to propagate the old-new idea, and to recast society again in the ancient mould, as when the study of Plutarch and the ancient historians rekindled the breath of liberty and of civic virtue in modern Europe; as when in our own day men attempt to revive mediæval ideals of religious or of corporate life, or to rise to the Greek standard of the individual. We may like or dislike such revivals, but at least they bear witness to the potency of history as something quite other than a science. And outside the circle of these larger influences, history supplies us each with private ideals, only too varied and too numerous for complete realisation. One may aspire to the best characteristics of a man of Athens or a citizen of Rome; a Churchman of the twelfth century, or a Reformer of the sixteenth; a Cavalier of the old school, or a Puritan of the Independent party; a Radical of the time of Castlereagh, or a public servant of the time of Peel. Still more are individual great men the model and inspiration of the smaller. It is difficult to appropriate the essential qualities of these old people under new conditions; but whatever we study with strong loving conception, and admire as a thing good in itself and not merely good for its purpose or its age, we do in some measure absorb.

This presentation of ideals and heroes from other ages is perhaps the most important among the educative functions of history. For this purpose, even more than for the purpose of teaching political wisdom, it is requisite that the events should be both written and read with intellectual passion. Truth itself will be the gainer, for those by whom history was enacted were in their day passionate.

Another educative function of history is to enable the reader to comprehend the historical aspect of literature proper. Literature can no doubt be enjoyed in its highest aspects even if the reader is ignorant of history. But on those terms it cannot be enjoyed completely, and much of it cannot be enjoyed at all. For much of literature is allusion, either definite or implied. And the allusions, even of the Victorian age, are by this time historical. For example, the last half dozen stanzas of Browning's *Old Pictures in Florence,* the fifth stanza of his *Lovers' Quarrel,* and half his wife's best poems are already meaningless unless we know something of the continental history of that day. Political authors like Burke, Sydney Smith, and Courier, the prose of Milton, one-half of Swift, the best of Dryden, and the best of Byron (his satires and letters) are enjoyed *ceteris paribus,* in exact proportion to the amount we know of the history of their times. And since allusions to classical history and mythology, and even to the Bible, are no longer, as they used to be, familiar ground for all educated readers, there is all the more reason, in the interest of literature, why allusions to modern history should be generally understood. History and literature cannot be fully comprehended, still less fully enjoyed, except in connection with one another. I confess I have little love either for "Histories of Literature," or for chapters on "the literature of the period," hanging at the end of history books like the tail from a cow. I mean, rather, that those who write or read the history of a period should be soaked in its literature, and that those who read or expound literature should be soaked in history. . . .

The value and pleasure of travel, whether at home or abroad, is doubled by a knowledge of history. For places, like books, have an interest or a beauty of association, as well as an absolute or aesthetic beauty. The garden front of St. John's, Oxford, is beautiful to everyone; but, for the lover of history, its outward charm is blent with the intimate feelings of his own mind, with images of that same College as it was during the Great Civil War. Given over to the use of a Court whose days of royalty were numbered, its walks and quadrangles were filled, as the end came near, with men and women learning to accept sorrow as their lot through life, the ambitious abandoning hope of power, the wealthy hardening themselves to embrace poverty, those who loved England preparing to sail for foreign shores, and lovers to be parted forever. There they strolled through the garden, as the hopeless evenings fell, listening, at the end of all, while the siege-guns broke the silence with ominous iteration. Behind the cannon on those low hills to northward were ranked the inexorable men who came to lay their hands on all this beauty, hoping to change it to strength and sterner virtue. And this was the curse of the victors, not to die, but to live, and almost to lose their awful faith in God, when they saw the Restoration, not of the old gaiety that was too gay for them and the old loyalty that was too loyal for them, but of corruption and selfishness that had neither country nor king. The sound of the Roundhead cannon has long ago died away, but still the silence of the garden is heavy with unalterable fate, brooding over besiegers and besieged, in such haste to destroy each other and permit only the vile to survive. St. John's College is not mere stone and mortar, tastefully compiled, but an appropriate and mournful witness between those who see it now and those by whom it once was seen. And so it is, for the reader of history, with every ruined castle and ancient church throughout the wide, mysterious lands of Europe. . . .

IN THIS VEXED QUESTION whether history is an art or a science, let us call it both or call it neither. For it has an element of both. It is not in guessing at historical "cause and effect" that science comes in; but in collecting and weighing evidence as to facts, something of the scientific spirit is required for an historian, just as it is for a detective or a politician.

To my mind, there are three distinct functions of history, that we may call the *scientific,* the *imaginative* or *speculative,* and the *literary.* First comes what we may call the *scientific,* if we confine the word to this narrow but vital function, the day-labour that every historian must well and truly perform if he is to be a serious member of his profession—the accumulation of facts and the sifting of evidence. "Every great historian has been his own Dry-as-dust," said Stubbs, and quoted Carlyle as the example. Then comes the *imaginative* or *speculative*, when he plays with the facts that he has gathered, selects and classifies them, and makes his guesses and generalisations. And last but not least comes the *literary* function, the exposition of the results of science and imagination in a form that will attract and educate our fellow-countrymen. For this last process I use the word literature, because I wish to lay greater stress than modern historians are willing to do, both on the difficulty and also on the importance of planning and writing a powerful narrative of historical events. Arrangement, composition and style are not as easily acquired as the art of typewriting. Literature never helps any man at his task until, to obtain her services, he is willing to be her faithful apprentice. Writing is not, therefore, a secondary but one of the primary tasks of the historian. . . .

. . . Now history can prove the truth or falsehood of facts but not of opinions. When a man begins with the pompous formula—"The verdict of history is—" suspect him at once, for he is merely dressing up his own opinions in big words. Fifty years ago the "verdict of history" was mainly Whig and Protestant; twenty years ago mainly Tory and Anglo-Catholic; today it is, fortunately, much more variegated. Each juror now brings in his own verdict—generally with a recommendation of everyone to mercy. There is even some danger that history may encourage the idea that all sides in the quarrels of the past were equally right and equally wrong.

There is no "verdict of history," other than the private opinion of the individual. And no one historian can possibly see more than a fraction of the truth; if he sees all sides, he will probably not see very deeply into any one of them. The only way in which a reader can arrive at a valuable judgment on some historical period is to read several good histories, whether contemporary or modern, written from several different points of view, and to think about them for himself.* But too often the reading of good books and the exercise of

---

*Biography is very useful for this purpose. The lives of rival statesmen, warriors and thinkers, provided they are good books, are often the quickest route to the several points of view that composed the life of an epoch. *Ceteris paribus*, a single biography is more likely to mislead than a history of the period, but several biographies are often more deeply instructive than a single history.

individual judgment are shirked, while some vacuous text-book is favoured on the ground that it is "impartial" and "up-to-date." But no book, least of all a text-book, affords a short cut to the historical truth. The truth is not grey, it is black and white in patches. And there is nothing black or white but thinking makes it so. . . .

In the Victorian age the influence of historians and of historical thinkers did much to form the ideas of the new era, though less of course than the poets and novelists. Today almost all that is characteristic in the mind of the young generation is derived from novelists and playwrights. It is natural and right that novelists and playwrights (provided we can count among them poets!) should do most to form the type of mind of any generation, but a little steadying from other influences like history might be a good leaven in modern gospels and movements.

The public has ceased to watch with any interest the appearance of historical works, good or bad. . . .

If, as we have so often been told with such glee, the days of "literary history" have gone never to return, the world is left the poorer. Self-congratulation on this head is but the mood of the shorn fox in the fable. History as literature has a function of its own, and we suffer today from its atrophy. Fine English prose, when devoted to the serious exposition of fact and argument, has a glory of its own, and the civilisation that boasts only of creative fiction on one side and science on the other may be great but is not complete. Prose is seldom equal to poetry either in the fine manipulation of words or in emotional content, yet it can have great value in both those kinds, and when to these it adds the intellectual exactness of argument or narrative that poetry does not seek to rival, then is it sovereign in its own realm. To read sustained and magnificent historical narrative educates the mind and the character; some even, whose natures, craving the definite, seldom respond to poetry, find in such writing the highest pleasure that they know. . . .

The Functions
of Teaching History

David Pratt

David Pratt (b. 1939) received a Ph.D. in educational theory from the
University of Toronto in 1969 and at the time this essay appeared was
an associate professor of education at Queen's University in Kingston,
Ontario. He also taught history in high school for five years. He is co-
author of *Teaching Prejudice* (1971), a study of Canadian social studies
textbooks. "The Functions of Teaching History" was originally published in *The History Teacher* (May 1974).

For the teacher of history it is the best of times, it is the worst of
times. It is a time when fortunes are made in the production
of historical epics; it is also a time when the quintessence of
ahistoricism has been distilled into a popular slogan: "Today is the
first day of the rest of your life."

In the struggle to survive in an increasingly overcrowded curriculum, history teachers oscillate wildly between tradition and fashion
in justifying their subject. On the one hand, lies the Scylla of the
discipline reduced to a ritual; on the other, the Charybdis of the
discipline riding the coattails of the younger sciences. This paper
contends that current justifications for the teaching of history, besides often being at variance with the nature of the subject, are generally either invalid or insufficient, while powerful arguments for
history in the schools are being overlooked.

This inquiry is concerned with history at the pre-university level,
that is, for history as part of general education. The objectives of
specialist and professional training in history are narrower and, if it
is taken for granted that society needs a continuing supply of histo-

rians and university teachers of history, easier to justify. It is at the elementary and secondary school level that the place of history in the curriculum is most open to question. It is also at the secondary level (elementary school children still being a captive audience) that the subject is undergoing the greatest attrition.

Despite the urgent need to find valid and persuasive reasons for engaging students in the study of history, a common feature that strikes the observer of history teaching in the schools is the absence of an explicit rationale for teaching the subject. While few history teachers are at a loss for words when their subject is directly challenged, history as actually taught in the classroom tends to resemble a ritual above justification. This deficiency is more serious than the catalogue of pedagogical delinquency uncovered by Hodgetts and his team in their observation of 900 social studies classes, for it is apparent in the behavior of teachers who are competent as instructors as well as those who are incompetent, and in teachers with substantial academic training as well as in historical amateurs. An examination of university history programs provides at least one clue to this enigma, revealing the low priority accorded even in honors programs to the philosophy of history. This makes less surprising the rarity with which one encounters a history teacher who has been obliged during his academic training to confront squarely the question: What is the value of the study of history?

It is a question with which historians themselves have difficulty. "Most disturbing of all," wrote Charles Sellers of his experience on a California curriculum committee, "was the difficulty we historians had in coming up with a rationale for history in the schools that was clear and convincing even to ourselves."[1] The British historian, Arthur Bryant, went even further during a B.B.C. radio discussion in 1972. "Speaking as a historian," he remarked, "I'm very doubtful whether history teaches anyone anything."

But the question can hardly be avoided much longer. For while the flood of refugees from ritualistic history courses shows no sign of abatement, the pressure on history in the school curriculum is probably only beginning. Teachers of traditional school subjects are accustomed to respond to skeptical students or colleagues by citing what they consider to be valuable outcomes of instruction in their subject. But the important question (as Herbert Spencer pointed out in 1860) is not whether there is any absolute justification for a cur-

riculum subject, but whether the subject is relatively more important than subjects presently not included in the curriculum. At a
time when the number of skills and knowledges necessary for citizens to maintain a degree of control over their lives is rapidly expanding, the status of all school subjects must be continually
reappraised.

Many students at the present day still arrive at—and graduate
from—a university knowing perhaps how Athens defended herself
against Persia but ignorant as to how to defend themselves against
violence in the street, fraud in the market-place, or injustice in the
courts. Most of the neophyte teachers I instruct are unable to use a
typewriter, let alone a computer. Few secondary schools deliberately
prepare their students for what will, for many of them, be their most
important social role, raising children of their own. We deplore the
pace of life, yet give no place to relaxation training in the school
curriculum. We claim to be developing rational skills and coherent
values, but we firmly resist the introduction of school programs in
logic, epistemology, or ethics. We assert that schools cannot become
more efficient until there are more jobs for graduates, but we still
maintain a curriculum aimed to produce consumers of jobs rather
than generators of jobs or of alternatives to jobs. With so many critical areas excluded from the curriculum, what is included should be
subjected to even closer scrutiny than is presently the case. Such
scrutiny, one suspects, is on the way. Will history be able to with-
stand it?

Given that this is the context in which those who seek to rationalize the school curriculum operate, and also to some extent the
context in which school students themselves grope for authentic
educational experiences, many of the proponents of history weaken
their case by the extent of their claims. History is in many jurisdic-
tions obligatory or strongly recommended in secondary schools despite the fact that many pupils have already studied the subject for
four years or more at the elementary level. Yet secondary school
history teachers, like their university counterparts, comport themselves as if no significant learning in the subject had taken place at
the lower level. In such a case, there must be redundance, either at
the higher or the lower level. And, in fact, if most of the universally
significant objectives of the study of history cannot be achieved in
two or three years, one is inclined to doubt that any further incre-

ment of compulsory study will make a radical difference. But for purposes of the argument herein, the question at issue is not how much history should be taught, but whether any history should be taught in the schools.

There are hundreds of specific objectives that history teachers collectively claim to be pursuing. Only six of the more basic arguments for the study of history will be examined here: the argument that history should be studied "for its own sake"; that studying history promotes "good citizenship"; that it promotes "tolerance and international understanding"; that it contributes to the development of certain intellectual skills; that it allows students to develop useful generalizations; and that specific facts from the past are instrumental to "understanding the present."

That history should be studied "for its own sake" is an argument heard from school teachers less frequently today than twenty years ago when it was a cornerstone of Professor Neatby's onslaught on "the socialized approach" to history teaching in Canadian schools.[2] It is, however, still alive and well in higher education, where recent writers deplore the decline of "the principles and practices according to which the university as an institution has operated since its emergence in the Middle Ages. The basic credo is that knowledge is important and must be pursued—knowledge per se, not *practical* or *relevant* knowledge." The position further merits consideration because it is the implicit rationale of every lesson that seeks to do no more than transmit historical information.

Most human activity may be classified as having either instrumental or intrinsic value. An activity having instrumental value is pursued "to obtain some thing or condition other than itself which is considered to be of value." An activity having intrinsic worth is valuable in and for itself. While both objects and activities may have instrumental value, only experiences can have intrinsic value. It is illogical to speak of the value of "knowledge per se"; knowledge cannot be intrinsically valuable in the absence of a knower. In the above quotation, "knowledge per se" is presumably an ellipsis for "the study of knowledge per se," or learning.

Necessary and sufficient conditions of an experience being intrinsically valuable are that the experience be perceived by the subject as pleasurable, enjoyable, satisfying, etc. While there are circumstances in which such a description may apply, it must be admitted that this is rarely the case with the typical adolescent studying history, least of all perhaps under the tutelage of those teachers most prone to use this argument. Incantation of the catch-phrase "intrinsic value" does not make an activity intrinsically valuable; to make this the case, both the activity and the argument must be deliberately developed.

When, on the other hand, a teacher admits that a student may not enjoy his present study of history but argues that such study will at some later date facilitate enjoyable experiences, or even "lead to positions of considerable emolument," he is arguing for the instrumental value of history. The five other common justifications to be discussed all fall within this latter category.

We need not be concerned with the public-relations merit of claiming to promote good citizenship, for where the stated rationale for an objective is purely political it is usually recognized as spurious even by its proponents. Nor need the use of "good citizenship" as the expression of a general good be discussed here. Insofar as good citizenship is defined in terms of development of tolerance, intellectual skills, or understanding of the world, it is discussed later in the paper. The interpretation of the term that does need to be examined, however, is that related to a rather crude concept of socialization— the idea that studying history will promote acceptance or support of the social and political status quo, that knowledge of the past, rather than ignorance as in Santayana's dictum, will lead men to repeat it.

While it is clear that history *may* be used in this way, as it is in the Soviet Union, and as it has been in most countries, there appears to be no necessary reason why this outcome should result from the study of history. In fact, the nature of the discipline appears rather to dictate the reverse. History involves the study of men and human institutions over time, in a word, the study of change. Only if we assume that time, and change, have stopped (or if we assume a totally determinist position) can we represent existing social and political arrangements as ideal or essential. The student trained in history may not necessarily want to give history a nudge, but he will expect change as a matter of course. For similar reasons, there are no grounds for expecting that history will necessarily promote patriotism or national loyalty, with which "good citizenship" is often associated.

Historians and history teachers, advancing the argument that the study of history promotes tolerance, rarely attempt to define tolerance, but they implicitly assume that tolerance is equivalent to a favorable attitude towards out-groups,[3] and in official curricula the term is often juxtaposed to such expressions as neighborliness, cooperation, and international goodwill. It is doubtful that history can in principle promote these attributes, and it is evident that in practice it usually does not. There is a good deal of evidence to show that school textbooks in history, on which much instruction is based, far from rejecting contemporary prejudices, simply reinforce the prejudices and stereotypes current twenty years previously. Political history in particular, in [David F.] Kellum's words, often produces little more in students than "a lethal innoculation of us-themism." But more importantly, can history, conscientiously taught, ever have as its necessary objective or outcome an increase in tolerance as defined above? Does a close and reasoned study of Nazism make one like Nazis better? Does an analysis of British rule in India, or Turkish rule in Armenia, or United States influence in Central America increase one's regard for these powers? Does a review of Canada's role in the demise of the League of Nations compel greater respect for Canadians? Those who would argue that "to understand is to forgive" are usually assuming a deterministic premise without accepting the logical conclusion—if one takes a deterministic position, forgiveness and tolerance are equally irrelevant.

Tolerance is not the most visible product of the knowledge of history acquired by Ulstermen, Cypriots, or Quebecois. For Nietzsche "the bridge to the highest hope" was "that men may be delivered from revenge"; in a commentator's words, "the recovery from that sickness is not simply from the disasters of his own instincts, but the recovery from the long history of revenge in the race." I believe it was V. S. Pritchett who first suggested that the rage and frustration seething in American life was the outcome of the nation's knowledge of its own history of lost opportunities, breeding nostalgia not for a lost past but for a lost future. And the experience of Victor Frankl in Auschwitz gave rise to a new school of psychotherapy aiming at a reorientation of the patient away from preoccupation with his past. Stephen Daedalus spoke for more than Irishmen in declaring "History is a nightmare from which I am trying to awake."

Historical knowledge, like all self-knowledge, promises peace neither within nor among individuals. At best, it may bring about the realization that the "crimes, follies, and misfortunes of mankind" are not limited to any single race or nation.

The use of history as a vehicle for developing intellectual skill is fashionable. A leading protagonist is Edwin Fenton, who maintains that history should be taught primarily to develop "inquiry skills," and that the chief of these is the ability to develop and test hypotheses. In the sense that the historian must begin any endeavor by asking a specific question, Fenton is directly in the tradition of [R. G.] Collingwood, and Fenton's criticisms of conventional history teaching likewise parallel Collingwood's strictures on "scissors-and-paste history." Fenton, however, is not using the word "hypothesis" merely as an approximate synonym for "question," but attempts to employ the term in its scientific sense. One is therefore forced to inquire: in what ways is history more suited to developing skill in hypothesis formulation and testing than the disciplines in which this approach to evidence has been most exactly developed, namely the physical and social sciences? Reflection suggests that history cannot, in fact, develop or practice these skills as effectively as, say sociology, because the historian is as a rule unable to perform the basic procedure for testing hypotheses—empirical experiment. The problem is not resolved by classifying history as a social science or as part of the "social studies." If history is no more than one of the social sciences, then its place in the curriculum must depend on its being able to perform some social science functions better than any of the other social sciences. This is a position that would be difficult to sustain.

Similar problems afflict the argument that the primary purpose of history teaching is to develop "critical thinking" or "value clarification." These attributes, poorly defined though they usually are, appear in themselves to be laudable objectives. But the most appropriate subjects for teaching "critical thinking" are logic and epistemology, not history, and for teaching "value clarification," ethics. If such valid objectives are to be achieved in the schools, then the appropriate subjects should be introduced into the school syllabus. This is unlikely to come about so long as history teachers are claiming, albeit on dubious grounds, that these objectives lie within their territory.

The tendency to appropriate to history intellectual skill objectives legitimately within the province of other disciplines appears to have a twofold motivation. First is the belief that the chief function of an area of study is to produce verifiable propositions. [B. G.] Massialas and [C. B.] Cox make this belief explicit: "One must reject the conception of history as chronology, and minimize the (so-called) aesthetic and poetic values of history . . . social studies is primarily concerned with the systematic inquiry into publicly testable propositions." I hope to show in due course that this is a narrow and mistaken conception of history. The second reason that history teachers purloin intellectual objectives properly belonging in other areas of study is because they tacitly recognize that history itself uses, and hence can train people in, few specialized techniques. As one of the oldest of the disciplines, it has enriched and been nourished by conventional wisdom, and its methods are the methods of common sense. It may be used to teach students certain research and reporting skills, but other disciplines may perform this function as well, and some better. Lukacs is under no illusions as to his role as a university teacher of history: "I can impart the 'method' of historical research," he asserts, "to a group of intelligent students in about twenty minutes."[4] All in all, it seems unlikely that history can be sustained primarily on the grounds that it promotes the growth of specific intellectual skills.

The argument that the study of history enables the student to derive generalizations about human behavior is frequently proposed. Like some of the previous arguments, it rests in part on a failure to distinguish between history and the social sciences, for one of the principal distinctions is in the approach of these disciplines to generalizations.

A century ago this issue did not arise. Historians produced generalizations as a legitimate part of their professional role; the social sciences were as yet infants in the historian's nursery. But in the past hundred years, the social sciences have developed and claimed for themselves most of the areas of investigation productive of generalizations. Thus, if a modern historian makes a statement, such as "economic instability is the prelude to political instability," he is not functioning *qua* historian, but *qua* economist or political scientist. Nevertheless, a historian may still legitimately make a statement, such as "the development of towns in Europe was inimical to feudal relationships." The difference in kind between the two generalizations points to the difference between history and the social sciences.

The social scientist analyzes events in order to generate wider and wider generalizations, building ultimately into a theory predictive of human action. The historian's interest is as much in the unique as in the general, in discontinuity as much as continuity. His generalizations are descriptive and historical and seek to explain only particular events; any predictions emerging from his work are by extrapolation, not by theory.

The development of sociology, psychology, political science, economics, anthropology, and the other social sciences has resulted in progressive delimitation and hence clearer definition of the historian's role. Even in his own shrunken terrain he is not unchallenged. Statisticians have decisively solved problems of the authorship of significant historical documents which had divided historians for decades. Similarly, the major works on medical history have been written by medical men with an amateur interest in history, not vice versa; there are obvious reasons why this should be so. But this delimitation is not necessarily to be deplored by the historian. For while on the one hand the historian who knows nothing but history is now an anachronism, the role of the historian who can draw on and coordinate the insights of the other social sciences is now more important than ever. The role of the historian has developed in a century from that of one-man band to that of conductor of a symphony orchestra. Only a distorted vision would view this as a decline in status. Such distortion, applied to school history by having the teacher or student of history ape the social scientist, would logically result not in securing the place of history in the curriculum, but in its total replacement by the social sciences.

"Relevance" is so pervasive a contemporary slogan that it is not surprising that history teachers feel obliged to pay homage to it. One way they do so is by proposing that the study of history enables students to derive generalizations about mankind that are useful for understanding the present. The complement to this argument holds that the present is better understood through knowledge of particular events in the past. This reasonable point of view, which rightly deplores the kind of history teaching which consists of "guided tours through the historical dustbin," is unfortunately often used as a basis from which to argue that only those events are worthy of study which illuminate man's present. This position, and the educational practices it engenders, are the product of ahistorical thought.

The history of school history is in this regard itself instructive. In the English-speaking world, history gained its place in the curriculum during a period of social stability, and under the influence of historians who saw human development as a steady process of evolution towards the liberal institutions of late nineteenth century England. Times changed; even Collingwood's modest claim of thirty years ago that "the only clue to what man can do is what man has done," now rings false in an age in which (as Jules Verne once said) the key to man's future is not what he has done but what he can imagine. School history, however, remained unchanged. This is in part because the belief that the past is the key to the present is more than half true.

Human history manifests both continuity and discontinuity. Neither is ever found uncontaminated by the other. Ignorance of continuity is a product of ignorance of history, as illustrated by public discussion which treats of conflicts in the Middle East, Ireland, or Southeast Asia as if they originated in the past decade. It is the lack of a diachronic dimension of thought which leads observers to interpret genocidal acts by American forces abroad as products of the Cold War; the historian recognizes them as the expression of a continuity stretching back at least to the Spanish-American War, perhaps to the first ingression to America of the Puritans, who, in the words of W. M. Evarts, "first fell upon their knees, and then upon the aborigines."

The relationship between the continuities and the discontinuities of history have rarely been better expressed than in Mark Twain's epigram, "The past does not repeat itself, but it rhymes." Yet the accelerating rate of change in the late twentieth century has made the rhymes less than perfect. Nuclear weapons, space exploration, and genetic engineering are only three of numerous developments which represent historical discontinuities so radical that the past offers little guidance even to an understanding of their implications, let alone to their management.

The role of the historian is to elucidate the interaction of continuities and discontinuities in man's development. His interest in continuity obliges him to pay attention to similarities and generalities. His interest in discontinuity leads him to seek the unique, the novel, and the particular. The teacher of history who elucidates only historical continuity is performing not so much half the historian's role as a parody of that role.

The belief that the study of the past should and will result in understanding the present leads teachers to select for study only those periods of history that can be made to show continuity with the present. Hence, fifth century Athens is usually studied in North American schools as "the cradle of democracy" on the shaky assumptions that i) fifth century Athens was a democracy; ii) the word "democracy" meant the same thing to fifth century Athenians as it does to modern Westerners; iii) Canada and the U.S.A. are democracies; and iv) modern North American political institutions are descended from those of fifth century Athens. By concentrating on and, where necessary, inventing continuities, while ignoring discontinuities in human history, the activity itself becomes ahistorical.

Study of the past is often a necessary condition for fully understanding the present. This is one valid justification for the study of history. The argument becomes pernicious when study of the past is considered a sufficient condition for understanding the present. To expand its role to this point is to distract the learner from a search for pragmatic solutions to contemporary problems. History enhances our understanding of the present only so long as its limitations are recognized. In the words of C. Wright Mills: "In our attempt to understand any society we come upon images which have been drawn from its past and which often confuse our attempt to confront its present reality. This is one reason why history is the shank of any social science: we must study it if only to rid ourselves of it."

The combined merit of the arguments summarized above would scarcely entitle history to more than a peripheral role in the school curriculum. It is now time to turn to a different approach.

One approach to the question, what unique contribution can a discipline make to the education of an individual, is to ask the related question, in what way is the discipline itself unique? Clearly there are few components of the structure of the discipline of history which are unique. The techniques it uses in collection, selection, synthesis, and reporting of evidence are common to many disciplines. Even its terminology is unspecialized. Its subject matter, the actions of man, is the subject matter of a score of disciplines. But what is unique to history is the nature of its concern with time. While time is an important element in such disciplines as physics, astronomy, geology, biology, and anthropology, only history is specifically and exclusively concerned with the actions of man on the dimension of time. As this is what makes history a discipline in its own right, it is here that one may find its unique importance as a school subject. Thus, it may be argued, a major function of history teaching is to give students a sense of their identity on the dimension of time.

Modern man, deracinated and transient, lives in the present and for the future, partly is and wholly hopes to be. He possesses neither the temporal nor the geographical anchor eloquently described by Steinbeck's sharecroppers facing eviction from their land:

> Grandpa took up the land, and he had to kill the Indians and drive them away. And Pa was born here, and he killed weeds and snakes. . . . An' we was born here. . . . It's our land. We measured it and broke it up. We were born on it, and we got killed on it, died on it. Even if it's no good, it's still ours. That's what makes it ours—being born on it, working it, dying on it.

The individual identity of contemporary man is the product of the memories within his skull. In unhistorical man, these memories are personal and stretch back to infancy. In historical man, memories extend personally to infancy, and vicariously back through the past of mankind. "I am not one person, I am many people," says a character in one of Virginia Woolf's novels. Historical man knows that he is not of one age but of many ages, an entity and a link in a process stretching backwards in time.

All identity is historical; students of history into whose consciousness the past has become incorporated have in this way achieved a more complex identity. Yet the limitations on this identity are commonly extreme. The typical graduate of a university honors history program has been schooled to think of history as beginning with the discovery of America or the British conquest of Canada. Even within that tiny slice of time, the subject of study is one small sample of the activities (political and economic) of a small elite segment of the population. Few university departments of history offer courses dealing with periods prior to 400 A.D., and the professional historian's obsession with written records almost invariably restricts him to the last 5000 years of man's past. It is ironic that the modern historian should date the origin of history at approximately the same point as Bishop Ussher did three centuries ago in his famous Chronology. The modern historian's pre-Darwinian posture is further manifested, as [George] Grant points out, by his assumption that only man has a history. For not only is Neanderthal man as much our ancestor as Elizabethan man, the history of man and of the world leads back through the lower forms of life to the inorganic compounds of the earth and ultimately to the burning gases of the sun. Every pupil in every classroom bears in his biological structure and functioning tangible evidence of having developed from an aquatic creature. A serious and exacting examination of the origins and development of human life is a legitimate and perhaps a critical part of a school history program, which could add new dimensions to students' historical identity.

Conventional history teaching, particularly with the survey approach, is unlikely to have a deep or permanent effect. "If one can really penetrate the life of another age," wrote T. S. Eliot, "one is penetrating the life of one's own." And, one might add, one's own life. When one finds and rereads a letter or diary written years previously, this penetration takes the form of immediate insight into the discrepancies between what one thinks one is now, what one thinks one was then, and what one thought one was then. The study of man's past should enable us to compare what man thinks he is now with what he thought he was then. But how is the classroom teacher to achieve this?

Let us suppose that a teacher were to discard his textbook on "The world from Egypt to the Reformation," and replace it by a single work of art, perhaps Sophocles' *Oedipus Rex*, and that for an entire semester or year the attention of the class were to be focused on this work. Students design and make Greek costumes, build a Greek stage, fabricate Greek instruments to make Greek music, study and learn the parts, and ultimately produce the play. By the end of the program they eat, drink, think, and dream the life of Athens at the time of Sophocles. Such an activity differs from those found in conventional history programs in that it is not an intellectual exercise intended to enable students to understand or control the present, but an experience intended to develop their insight into the diversity of human consciousness, which is a part of their own identity. In this sense it accords with Acton's statement that "the study of history is not to make us cleverer for next time, but to make us wiser, forever."

"Those who study history are concerned with the occurrences of passed times; those who conceive time as history are tuned to what will happen in the future. . . . To enucleate the conception of time as history must then be to think our orientation to the future together with the will to mastery." If the historian is an anachronism in a future-oriented society, it is because of his misconception of history as comprehending only the dimension of the past. Definition of history as the actions of man on the continuum of time necessitates inclusion of the future within the scope of the discipline. Man's natural egocentrism leads him to consider himself the culminating point in evolution, rather than a phase in a continuing process. Such egocentrism is paralytic: study of the past, which is irrevocable, need engage only the intellect; study of the future implies engagement of the will. Grant's concern with "the will to mastery" sets him apart from pre-Marxian historians who seek only to understand the world, and pre-Marxian history teachers who believe that understanding the world is a sufficient condition for changing it.

"I like men who have a future," said Oscar Wilde, "and women who have a past." Unlike ladies of the fin-de-siecle, history with a past is safe and respectable. Prospective history is suspect if not actually disreputable. Clearly study of the future opens the way for spurious extrapolation of "lessons of history" and for facile prognostication (so, for that matter, does study of the past). But more is at stake than the desirability of amateur speculation. Responsible behavior, according to G. E. Moore's definition, entails the intelligent prediction of the practical consequences of actions; and in this, indeed, inheres the very possibility of man's being a rational agent. In a society still dominated by the ideology of the Reformation and the introspective psychology it engendered, history provides an ideal vehicle for conveying Mill's argument that the worth of an action should be judged from its effects, not from the motives of the agent. The student of history who is taught to condemn the nineteenth-century entrepreneurs who set in motion the chain of events culminating in the present condition of world-wide pollution, but to praise the nineteenth-century medical missionaries, who share responsibility for twentieth-century overpopulation, is not developing a moral outlook that is socially functional.

Retrospective history can teach students to consider the long-term effects of human actions, but such learning will remain information unless they are taught to project the long-term effects of actions at the present, including their own actions. . . .

For most students of history, there is an inevitability about the past which obscures the role of human choice. This may be offset by the study of the future, which enables a student to perceive historical events as the products not of fate or accident but of human choice. The insight and practice which such study can give into the definition and selection of alternatives in the light of estimated effects is educative in the highest sense, in that it has the potential to enlarge the scope of the individual's self-determination.

Earlier in this paper, the argument that the study of history was "valuable for its own sake" was rejected on the grounds that the activity of studying history is rarely perceived as pleasurable, satisfying, or enjoyable by students. As intimated earlier, however, there are conditions under which this may be the case.

An activity is inherently valuable if the agent experiences it as interesting. A contemporary increase in popular interest in history suggests that some people do in fact find history interesting. Such individuals find such subjects as the changes in the self-image of European man between 1600 and 1700, or between 1910 and 1920, as inexhaustible a source of fascination as others find trigonometry or detective stories.

For an even smaller number of people history provides an additional and more elusive value in the area of aesthetics. Discussion of the aesthetic value of history is usually limited to the role of history as ancillary to the arts: one can understand Chopin more fully by becoming familiar with the cultural context of Romanticism. But contemplation of the past or the relics of the past, for those so attuned, can be an aesthetic experience in its own right. A display case in a museum, containing a helmet each from Plataea, Marathon, and Thermopylae, will to most people be no more than a collection of ancient army surplus. To a few it will be a stimulus to contemplation and speculation about the men who wore such armor, the motives which caused them to fight in these battles, and the aspirations for themselves and for Greece which these motives reflected. Such an experience is not so much cerebral and cognitive as comparable to the effect produced by painting or music on an appreciative subject.

Both an interest in and an aesthetic appreciation for history are no doubt the responses of a minority. Unlike a taste for poetry, which appears to be present in all young children and to be extinguished in all but a minority by their schooling, the study of history can probably have the kind of intrinsic value outlined above only for the few. The more experiences a person finds interesting or satisfying, the happier his life will be. For this reason the school has an important role to play in nourishing minority tastes; but at the same time it must avoid the hopeless and wasteful attempt to impose minority tastes upon the majority.

It has been the intention of this paper to suggest that the study of history in general education needs a more convincing and coherent rationale than is usually presented. Without such a rationale, non-specialist history teaching tends to wither, and indeed deserves to wither, when it competes with curricula whose justification has been better substantiated. Effective leadership in this task by competent historians and metahistorians has been conspicuous by its absence. The future of the specialist study of history in the universities does not depend on the quality of history teaching in the schools, and any involvement in school history by philosophers of history is therefore likely to be altruistic. It is probable that, unless such altruistic leadership emerges, the issue will soon no longer be that of saving history, but of re-introducing it into the school curriculum.

References

1. Charles G. Sellers, "Is History on the Way Out of the Schools and Do Historians Care?" *Social Education* 33 (1969): 510.

2. Hilda Neatby, *So Little for the Mind* (Toronto: Clarke Irwin, 1953), 168.

3. This definition, though common, is unsatisfactory because it represents tolerance as a kind of positive prejudice; on the other hand, tolerance usually means something other than pure neutrality. A more useful definition might be: a predisposition to counteract egocentrism by a provisionally favorable response to dissonant subjects pending their objective evaluation. This is an attitude that history could very well promote—but so could many other disciplines. See Bertrand Russell, *History of Western Philosophy* (London: Allen and Unwin, 1961), 58.

4. John Lukacs, *Historical Consciousness* (New York: Harper and Row, 1968), 37.

The Dangers of History

Herbert Butterfield

Herbert Butterfield (1900–1979) spent much of his career teaching modern history at Cambridge University. He wrote many books including *The Historical Novel* (1924), *The Peace Tactics of Napoleon* (1929), *The Statecraft of Machiavelli* (1940), *The Origins of Modern Science* (1949), *Christianity in European History* (1951), and *George III and the Historians* (1957). Of particular interest to readers of this anthology is Butterfield's *The Whig Interpretation of History* (1931), which examined how historical understanding is obstructed when the past is studied with too close a reference to the present. The following selection is from Butterfield's *History and Human Relations* (1951).

In spite of the development of technical historical enquiry during the seventeenth century, and the recognised importance of historical study in the systems of eighteenth-century thought, it would seem to be true that the modern rage for history was born out of the morbidities and nostalgias of the Romantic Movement. It was assisted by the reaction against the French Revolution, which in England—particularly in the teaching of Edmund Burke—tended to confirm the nation in its attachment to its own past and its belief that the liberties of the country went back to times immemorial. Englishmen have particularly prized the continuity of their history, and have found something rich and fruitful in the very fact of continuity; all of which was to have its effect on our interpretation of our national story. In Germany, on the other hand, during the Romantic Movement, men were particularly conscious of the tragic political situation of the country in modern centuries and they tended to contrast it with the glories of the Holy Roman Empire of medieval times.

In general, we see in the nineteenth century one of the most important movements in the whole story of European thought: namely, the great development of history and of historical thinking. Not only did history become a principal branch of study, but it affected all other departments of mental activity. As an English writer once said, in the nineteenth century human thought in every field seemed to run to history; and this was true for example of philosophy in Hegel and of a great deal of Protestant theology. The movement was one in which Germany held the intellectual leadership. Furthermore, it is chiefly to Germany that we owe the great advance which was achieved in the development of a more scientific study of the past, the evolution of a higher and more austere form of scholarship; all of which made it a much more serious matter than it had ever been before to write about past events. Partly because Germany was so large a country, she was able to reach a higher degree of impartiality than most other people. If she had some historians who were inclined to support Prussia, for example, there would be other historians in different parts of the country who were opposed to Prussia; and somewhere or other in Germany both sides of the question would be stated, and the truth was more carefully tested as a result. In the development of high and austere standards of scholarship English students in particular set out to be the disciples of the great German writers of history, so producing what for a long time was a remarkable intellectual alliance. Lord Acton once suggested that this German historical movement in the nineteenth century was a more fateful step in the story of European thought than even the famous Italian Renaissance of the fifteenth century. It seems to me that we must agree with this view, for the Renaissance did not add a new ingredient to our Western civilisation in the way that the historical movement of the nineteenth century was able to do.

The twentieth century has not been so happy for the historical sciences, and these sciences are gravely injured by two things which have turned out to be the great plagues of our time—namely, wars and revolutions. In all countries the very interest that governments have come to have in history—government patronage of historical study—has proved to carry with it hidden dangers. The very popularity of history amongst new classes of people (who are sometimes lazy readers, sometimes unaware of the necessity for the older critical canons, and sometimes unconscious of the way in which wishful thinking operates in the study of history) has produced many new embarrassments, especially in a world where men have learned how powerful history can be for purposes of propaganda. The establishment of many new nation-states since 1918 has also proved to be not always a good fortune for historical study in Europe. New nations are particularly sensitive about their historical past, particularly jingoistic in their national pride. And it seems that small nations, especially if they are new nations too, are liable to be more intense and local in their prejudices—they are sometimes more narrowly self-concentrated than the greater ones. It is going to need a harder struggle everywhere to keep up the standards of academic scholarship in future than it did before 1914.

We are now in a position to survey the influence which something like a hundred and fifty years of historical study has exercised on the development of modern Europe. It is not clear that as yet we have learned all that there is to learn from this particular aspect of the history of historical science, or fathomed all the effects that the study of the past has itself had on nations and their policies. Concerning historians as interpreters and guides in the affairs of their own generation, I have read some severe things that Englishmen have written about German scholars, and there are similar things that the Germans have said about us. But the world still waits for the wag who will scientifically examine the nineteenth and twentieth-century writers of history and show us how far their studies and researches really did raise them above the fevers and prejudices of their time—how far in reality it is plausible to argue that historians are wiser than the rest of their contemporaries on political matters. And a more scientific age than ours may even find materials for an analytical treatment of associated questions; for, to take one example, it would be interesting to see it demonstrated whether it is always prudent to rely for political advice on the kind of "expertness" which the "regional historian" possesses—at any rate the one who, through the knowledge of one of the obscurer languages, has happened to acquire something approaching a monopoly in his field, without having to face any great clash of scholarship in his own country. And if we say that a given expert on Ruritania must be right provided he is accepted by the Ruritanians themselves, the history of historiography will be able no doubt to raise a debate even on this issue.

At any rate it is possible even now to make certain comments on the part which historical reflection has played in the development of the errors that have been so tragic for the twentieth century. And in this connection there is one law which makes itself apparent if we examine the events of the last one hundred and fifty years; and that is the paradox that a great deal of what people regard as the teaching or the lessons of history is really an argument in a circle. In reality the historian is in the habit of inserting some of his present-day prejudices into his reconstructions of the past; or unconsciously he sets out the whole issue in terms of some contemporary experience—he has what we might call the modern "set-up" in his mind. In this way English writers once tended to see the ancient Greeks as modern Whigs; the Germans would read something of modern Prussia even into ancient Rome. Magna Carta would be interpreted in the nineteenth century in the light of modern English constitutional problems. Those who dealt with the medieval Holy Roman Empire too often envisaged it with the nineteenth-century conflict of Austria and Prussia in their minds. Sometimes there has been a tendency to project the prejudices of the present day into the structure of the past as it was envisaged in long periods and in general terms—the tendency for the British to say, when France was the enemy, that France had been the "eternal enemy of mankind." In England the view once prevailed that German history was particularly the history of freedom, for it was a story that comprised federation, parliament, autonomous cities, Protestantism, and a law of liberty carried by German colonists to the Slavonic east. In those days it was the Latin States which were considered to be congenial to authoritarianism, clinging to the Papacy in Italy, the Inquisition in Spain and the Bonapartist dictatorships in militaristic France. The reversal of this view in the twentieth century, and its replacement by a common opinion that Germany had been the aggressor and the enemy of freedom throughout all the ages, will no doubt be the subject of historical research itself some day, especially as it seems to have coincided so closely with a change in British foreign policy. The historian, then, can even deepen and magnify present-day prejudices by the mere fact that he so easily tends to throw them back and project them on to the canvas of all the centuries. And the more the historian seeks to please his generation or serve his government or support any cause save that of truth, the more he tends to confirm his contemporaries in whatever they happen to want to believe, the more he hardens the age in its favourite and fashionable errors.

Before 1919 I was taught a kind of history which saw in the sovereignty of national states the culmination of the progress of centuries—the very end towards which history was moving. I remember how the Reformation itself would be applauded for having released the nation-states from "the fetters of internationalism"; and it was the custom to show that history, especially in the nineteenth century (the "Holy Alliance," for example), had demonstrated the folly and futility of attempts to form anything like a League of Nations. From 1919, however, one saw the teaching of history reorganised and text-books rewritten—the events of the past now marshalled to serve a different purpose, and in particular the course of nineteenth-century European history reshaped—this time for the purpose of proving that all the centuries had been pointing to a different kind of consummation altogether, namely the League of Nations. I am not concerned with the question which of these views was the true one. But I should have been more impressed if on both those occasions the historian had not been so inclined to ordain and dispose his subject-matter, and lay out the whole course of centuries, for the purpose of ratifying the prejudice that already prevailed for other reasons at the time. It can easily be seen, therefore, that the historian who most desires to please his age—the historian whom we most applaud because he chimes in with our views—may be betraying us, and may rob us of one of the possible benefits of historical study, namely the advantage of an escape from merely contemporary views and short-range perspectives. On the other hand, Burckhardt and Acton gave the nineteenth century certain warnings which the lapse of time has proved to be of great significance. It appears, however, that a generation does not take much notice of a message that it happens to dislike.

The things which happened in England have taken place in the historiography of all other countries; and of course the Englishman sees the error when German historians make it, and the German sees the error in the foreigner too, but none of us seem able to jump out of our own skins and to see our own position with a certain relativity. And for the most part there is much too little disposition even to attempt the task. Sometimes historical students take tremendous trouble with the details of their researches, but when they come to the important point where they build up the larger framework of their story or draw their final conclusions, or pretend to extract from the narrative its teaching value, they are liable to become very casual and to be totally unaware of the processes that are taking place in their minds. They do not realise that very often they are smuggling into history the things they eventually imagine themselves to be extracting from it—the penny that they draw out of the slot-machine is the very penny that they first put in. Even after the historian has collected data and sifted his materials with industry and discrimination, a very minute addition of wishful thinking may deflect the whole organisation of the results. A desire for self-justification may set the historian at a slightly wrong angle; and the extension of the lines of the picture may mean that this apparently small deflection will ultimately have the effect of carrying him far away from the central course. Indeed, history can be very dangerous unless it is accompanied by severe measures of self-discipline and self-purification—unless we realise that there is something that we must do with our personalities. Let us note, then, that historians have developed a remarkable scientific apparatus for the discovery, handling and sifting of historical evidence. They have not always remembered that this leaves vast areas of historical reconstruction and historical thinking which have not yet been brought under the same scientific control, though the history of historiography may enable us to make further advances even here.

The situation is more serious than anything that has so far been stated, however; for I think it is true to say that in the European politics of the last two centuries certain errors are discoverable which were born out of historical reflection as such—errors which would not have been made if people had not been so interested in the past and so concerned with it. The influence of historical study in the nineteenth century led to the creation of what we can only regard as new kinds of myths—things which came with the mysterious halo of religion about them and were almost made to serve as substitutes for religion. Amongst these I should put the myth of romantic nationalism, the modern religion of exaggerated nationalism, which is a perversion of such principle of nationality as had existed hitherto. That myth had historians as its high priests while its prophets were a particular type of student of the past who enquired into the history of languages and interested themselves in early folk-literature. Moreover, ideas which are introduced into historical scholarship at a high level soon become degraded into myths. Instead of being developed in a flexible manner with the passage of time, they are repeated with rigidity, dragged into different contexts, tossed to and fro in the market-place and generally hardened and coarsened in the rough-and-tumble of the world's affairs. Historical memories, especially in Eastern Europe—and also in Ireland—have engendered much of the national animosity of modern times. In a far wider sense than this the over-stressing of the historical argument in modern European politics has been unfortunate both for historical study and for diplomacy. One must wonder sometimes whether it would not have been better if men could have forgotten the centuries long ago, and thrown off the terrible burden of the past, so that they might face the future without encumbrances. And above all, when history has been accompanied by a tendency to regard the past as an independent source of rights, or when it has been accompanied by a tendency to worship the primitive stages of one's national culture and the uniqueness of a national mentality, it has made its contribution even to that serious drift of the modern world in the direction of irrationalism—the flight from the old ideal of a universal human reasonableness.

It would seem that history possesses certain initial attractions which will prevent it from being overlooked in any consideration of a scheme of general education. It is one of the subjects which purport to produce a "well-informed mind," and it answers many of the requirements of ordinary curiosity. It is capable of easy discussion across a table without necessary resort to any long-term intellectual system. It gives an extension to the material which the mind can gather for the purpose of manufacturing into experience. And it imparts the kind of knowledge which throws light on the problems of the present day, and which can be used to broaden our consciousness of citizenship, whether in a nation or in the world.

On the other hand, against mathematics (for example), it has the disadvantage that mere progress from one chapter to another—the mere perusal of a larger area of the subject-matter—does not in itself constitute or impose an intellectual discipline. The mere reading of history, the mere process of accumulating more information in this field, does not necessarily give training to a mind that was initially diffuse. For this reason it is not wise to learn history by a hasty accumulation of information, so that the mass of data clutters up the memory and the growth of knowledge too greatly outstrips the general development of the mind. Furthermore, in the case of mathematics we start with our feet on the hard earth, learning the simplest things first, firmly establishing them at each point before we go any further, and making our argument good and watertight at each step of the way. In other words, we begin with strong foundations of concrete, and we gradually build our skyscrapers on the top of this. In the case of history, on the other hand, we start up in the clouds, at the very top of the highest skyscraper. We start with an abridged story, seen in the large and constructed out of what in reality are broad generalisations. It is only much later, when we reach the actual work of research, that we really come down to earth and arrive at the primary facts and primary materials. Only at the end of many years of training do we come to know what it means genuinely to establish the assertions that we make. For this reason, history is dangerous as an educational subject; and the best kind of history-teacher is not the one who tells us most clearly what to believe—not the one who seeks merely to transfer a body of knowledge from his head into the heads of his pupils. The best kind of history-teacher is the one who realises the danger of the subject itself and construes it as his function to redeem and rescue it as far as possible.

If our Western civilisation were to collapse even more completely than it has done, and I were asked to say upon which of the sins of the world the judgment of God had come in so signal a manner, I should specify, as the most general of existing evils and the most terrifying in its results, human presumption and particularly intellectual arrogance. There is good reason for believing that none of the fields of specialised knowledge is exempt from this fault; and I know of no miracle in the structure of the universe that should make me think even archbishops free of it. But it is the besetting disease of historians, and the effect of an historical education seems very often actually to encourage the evil. The mind sweeps like the mind of God over centuries and continents, churches and cities, Shakespeares and Aristotles, curtly putting everything in its place. Any schoolboy thinks that he can show that Napoleon was foolish as a statesman, and I have seen Bismarck condemned as a mere simpleton in diplomacy by undergraduates who would not have had sufficient diplomacy to wheedle sixpence out of a college porter. I do not know if there is any other field of knowledge which suffers so badly as history from the sheer blind repetitions that occur year after year, and from book to book—theses and statements repeated sometimes out of their proper context, and even sometimes when they have not been correctly understood; and very supple and delicate ones turned by sheer repetition and rigidity of mind into hard dogmatic formulas. I have seen historians condemn the Middle Ages for their blindness in quoting and requoting earlier authorities and so perpetuating an original error; when it was in fact these self-same historians who were doing just that very thing—repeating judgments at second-hand—in the very act of stating that particular case. I do not personally feel that in modern times technical history, in spite of all the skill that has gone to the making of it, has ever been taken up by a mind that I should call Shakespearean in its depth and scope, save possibly in the remarkable case of Ranke. I think that, compared with the novelists, the historians have even been coarse-fingered and too lacking in subtlety in their handling of human nature; so that, if he had only the novelists and the historians to judge from, a visitor from another planet would think that they were talking about two different kinds of substance.

In any case, though we had an Aristotle or a Shakespeare as an historian, the best that any of us can do at a given moment only represents the present state of knowledge in respect of the subject with which we are dealing. There is a profound sense in which all histories—like all scientific interpretations of the universe—are only interim reports; and in history the discovery of a small fact that may be pivotal is calculated to produce a drastic reshaping of the whole field of study. It is not so much the concrete facts—like the date of the battle of Waterloo—that are liable to such drastic revision, but rather the whole organisation of the story. In other words, the effect of the revision falls most of all on that region where our moral lessons, our teaching-conclusions and our verdicts have their roots. In a manner that we cannot imagine or quite foretell our historical conclusions are liable to be transformed and wrenched into a different shape when for fifty years English, German, French and American scholars have co-operated in the gigantic task of historical revision. Professor Trevelyan said in his Inaugural Lecture in Cambridge that the world would be liable to be plunged into bloodshed if teachers and students disseminated wrong history. There can be no doubt of this; but any generation that looks back to any previous generation can hardly close its eyes to the fact that wrong history is being taught in all countries, all the time, unavoidably.

Research is being constantly conducted by thousands of people over the globe for the purpose of correcting it. And the corrections—especially in the case of comparatively recent history—are often very surprising and disconcerting.

History, in fact, is so dangerous a subject—and so often it is the sinister people like a Machiavelli or a Napoleon or a Lenin who learn "tricks of the trade" from it, before the majority of people have thought of doing so—that we might wonder whether it would not be better for the world to forget all of the past, better to have no memories at all, and just to face the future without ever looking back. We must teach history, however, precisely because so much bad history exists in the world already. Bad history is in the air we breathe, and even those who do not pretend to know any history behind the days of their grandfathers are dangerous sometimes, for they too are the slaves of unconscious assumptions or concealed perversities on the subject of the past. From one point of view we must say that none of us learns history—none of us ever attains a final understanding or the kind of knowledge in which he can safely rest. From another point of view, however, we may say that there is great need for history all the same, provided we conceive it as a process of unlearning. Something can be achieved if we can sweep away only a single layer of the tremendous crust of error that already has the world under its grip. Perhaps we may say that we sweep away one layer of error from our minds when we are at school; another layer when we study history at the University; and a further layer still if we reach so far as actual research. Indeed, supposing we continue the study of history all our lives we may sweep away a further layer of this crust of error every ten years, if we can keep our freshness of mind. But we do not complete the process. We do not reach the stage when we can say that we comprehend a particular subject in a final manner. For this reason it is better that men, when they leave the University, should forget the history of Louis XIV as they learned it there, unless they are prepared to continue the process of "unlearning." It is better that they should not allow the knowledge to freeze in their minds, while the world changes, and historical science changes—better that they should not thirty years later be holding too rigidly in their memory the things learned so long before. For historical knowledge is valuable only while it is, so to speak, liquid—it is worse than lumber if it freezes and hardens in the mind. We may say, then, that it is better for men to forget what they have actually learned of Louis XIV and cling rather to the experience they gained in the study of history and in historical exercises. History is more useful when transmuted into a deeper wisdom that melts into the rest of experience and is incorporated in the fabric of the mind itself.

The dangers of history are liable to become much greater if we imagine that the study of this subject qualifies us to be politicians or provides us with patterns which we can immediately transpose into the context of contemporary politics. . . .

The argument that history qualifies men for the practice of politics is one which had a certain relevance and validity when it was used by the aristocrats who ruled England in the eighteenth century; but they were thinking of history as an additional acquirement for people who were supposed to have had their real education already. In any case, those English gentlemen of the eighteenth century were brought up from their very childhood to be rulers and politicians. They saw the practice of administration, heard political discussion, learned the arts of management in their local estates and observed the conduct of public affairs at first hand from their earliest days—they were being educated all the time in the actual practice of politics. For these people history came in its proper context—it was the one additional thing which would widen their horizon. Since they knew so much about the practical working of current affairs they were politicians already, and the study of history was calculated to make them better ones precisely because it broadened their horizon. I should seriously question the validity of a parallel argument for the modern democratic world and our modern educational system. We are wrong to think that the study of history itself is sufficient to turn us into competent politicians. And it is perhaps a tragedy that nowadays so many people—even if unconsciously—are in reality building up their political outlook from what they have read in books.

Some of the best diplomatic historians I ever met were almost the worst diplomats in the world when it came to transacting business in real life. It is often said in England that history is useful, and that it qualifies people to take part in politics, because it enables them to see how such things as politics and diplomacy work. I once had to induce the governing body of my college in Cambridge to try to come to an agreement on the colour of a carpet for a college library. A person who has had to undertake such a task and who has dis-

covered all the manœuvrings, all the delicate tactics, the persuasions, the whole science of give-and-take, that are necessary to get
twelve men to agree on the colour of a carpet—such a person may be
said to have had his first lesson in diplomacy. A person who merely
reads a life of Bismarck is liable to be deceived a hundred times over,
owing to the sheer fact of unavoidable abridgements, even if for no
other reason. In our condensed version of the story a host of little
shiftings and successive adjustments and minute manœuvrings
made by Bismarck over the course of a number of weeks get com-
pressed and telescoped together—so that they cake and solidify into
one big thing, a mighty instantaneous act of volition, a colossal
piece of Bismarckism. My teacher, Professor Temperley, once reminded us in Cambridge that when the research student goes to
manuscript sources, to the original diplomatic correspondence, for
example, he does not go merely in order to have a scoop and to uncover some surprising secret; he goes to the sources primarily in
order that by an actual day-to-day study of the whole correspondence
he shall learn the way in which diplomacy works and decisions are
arrived at. Only the research student really studies things at close
enough quarters to understand the complexity of these processes.

Indeed, abridged history—through the mere fact that it is necessarily so abridged—is having the effect of leaving the world with
many serious misconceptions. By foreshortening the picture and
making Bismarckian strokes of policy more trenchant than they really were, abridged history gives men a greater appearance of sovereignty over events than they actually possess; and it tends to magnify the controlling power of governments over the next stage in the
story. With the decline of religion, and in the absence of anything
else that seems authentic, men and nations rely on the abridged history they have learned to give them their impression of their place in
the sun, their purposeful intent, and their idea of what they can do
with their destiny. They acquire an academic dream-impression of
what statesmen can do in the world, what governments achieve,
what their national mission is, and what can be brought about by
sheer self-assertion and will.

In any case, the world rarely remembers to what a degree the pretended "lessons" which are extracted by politicians from history are
judgments based on the assumption that we know what would have
happened if some statesman in the past had only acted differently.

When historians so often assert that the Congress of Vienna made a mistake in neglecting the "principle of nationality," we may wonder whether they have really faced for a single moment the question: What would have happened in Europe if the Congress of Vienna had followed the twentieth-century view? There was much talk in 1919 of the necessity of "avoiding the mistakes of 1815"; and when a person has been fed with the apparently self-evident verdicts of abridged history, it is difficult to convince him that in any event this is a fallacious formula for policy. What you have to avoid in 1919 are not the mistakes of 1815 but the mistakes of 1919. What you have to avoid is too blind an immersion in the prejudices of your own time. Those who talked of "avoiding the mistakes of 1815" were using history to ratify the prejudices they had already. In any case, men are slow to count their blessings and quick to see the faults and short-comings of the world into which they are born, and in 1919 it was the general cry that Europe must not be saddled with the burden of a settlement as unsatisfactory as that of the Congress of Vienna. It took our knowledge of the difficulties, weaknesses and ephemerality of the Versailles settlement to make us realise that the state of the question is entirely different. What we want to learn now is why the Congress of Vienna was so much more successful than we have known how to be.

Not only do historical judgments rest so often on an assumption concerning what would have happened if a certain statesman had acted differently—if only Metternich had done *the other thing*, for example—but there is a rigidity that occurs in our treatment of the possible alternatives, for we so often imagine that there was only one alternative, when in reality there was a great range of them. We overlook, therefore, the complexity of the mathematics that will be required to work out the displacements which a different event would have produced, as in the case of the problem of what would have happened if Napoleon had won the battle of Waterloo. So from an armchair every Tom, Dick and Harry in England can conduct a facile course of reasoning which will satisfy him that he could easily have thwarted Hitler at an earlier point in the story, because he, for his part, would have done *the other thing*; as though in such a case a man like Hitler would not have done something different too at the next remove, and a host of other factors would have to be altered, the historical process quickly complicating all the calculations that require to be made. Indeed, history adds to the errors of a rigid mind and only serves us when we use it to increase our elasticity.

Over a quarter of a century ago Paul Valéry produced a serious criticism of historical study, and it is not clear that his main charge has been answered—his criticism is certainly applicable to that kind of historical education which is directed merely to the "learning" of history, the acquisition of the sort of knowledge which is examined in memory tests. He put his finger on a critical point, indeed on what perhaps is the very crux of the matter, when he suggested that the effect of historical study was to produce a certain lack of mental elasticity. This, as he showed, was liable to be particularly harmful in a world where changes were coming in such rapid cascades that the mind could hardly be expected to move quickly enough to catch up with them. I believe it is true to say that many people in England in 1919 looked back upon the previous hundred years of European history, and saw that during that period events had been moving in a certain curve—moving in the direction of "liberalism" and "nationality," for example. Too easily and unconsciously they assumed that in the coming years the course of history would continue that curve: so that their knowledge of the past, especially of the very recent past, robbed them of a certain flexibility. They would have been better equipped to meet the developments of the succeeding decades if they had studied in ancient history the deeper processes that political bodies have been observed to undergo over long periods. When Norway was invaded in 1940 the view was put forward in English official quarters that Hitler had broken one of the laws of history, in that he had conducted an invasion across water without possessing the command of the sea. Again the rigidities to which historical thinking are liable were the cause of deception. Even if a thing has never proved possible in the past we are not justified in inferring directly that history has proved such a thing to be impossible. When France collapsed in 1940 many Englishmen regarded it as self-evident that that country had made a tragic mistake in preparing only for defensive warfare and putting her trust in the Maginot Line. A French statesman said, however, that he, for his part, regretted not the construction of the Maginot Line but the failure to continue something of the sort to the sea. Other alternatives still were open, for the explanation of the downfall of France—including the possibility that her armies had made the reverse of the mistake generally imputed to them, by rushing with too great *élan* into Belgium when hostilities were opened in that region. On occasion it might require very subtle calculation and a microscopic sifting of evidence to decide the choice between the alternative interpretations that are possible in a situation of this kind. Few people take this trouble, and it is exactly in choices of this type that a very slight insertion of "wishful thinking" carries the majority of men to what is apparently a self-evident conclusion. One of the dangers of history lies in the ease with which these apparently self-evident judgments can be extracted from it, provided one closes one's eyes to certain facts. The person who is incapable of seeing more than one thing at once—incapable of holding two factors in his mind at the same time—will reach results all the more quickly and will feel the most assured in the judgments that he makes.

I imagine that if we wish to study the effect of historical study on the actual conduct of affairs, one of the appropriate fields in which we can pursue the enquiry is that of military strategy. In general, it is not possible to have a war just for the purpose of training the leaders of an army, and it has been the case that the teaching of strategy was for a long time carried on by means of historical study—for a hundred years by a continual study of the methods of Napoleon. Since the time when Machiavelli inaugurated the modern science of war there have been grave misgivings about this use of history. Machiavelli himself was open to the reproach that since he required the detailed imitation of the methods of the Romans, he refused to believe in artillery. Similarly, it would appear to be the case that if men shape their minds too rigidly by a study of the last war, they are to some degree unfitting themselves for the conduct of the next one. If a nation decides conversely that it will set out with the particular purpose of avoiding the mistakes of the last war, it is still liable to be the slave of history and to be defeated by another nation that thinks of new things. Historical study, therefore, has sometimes had a deadening effect on military strategists; and it has often been a criticism of them that they were too prone to conduct the present war on the method of the previous one, forgetting how times had changed.

It seems true, however, that many of the errors which spring from a little history are often corrected as people go on to study more and more history. If a man had a knowledge of many wars and of the whole history of the art of war, studying not merely the accounts of battles and campaigns, but relating the weapons of a given period to the conditions of the time, relating policies to circumstances, so that he came to have an insight into the deep causes of things, the hidden sources of the changes that take place—if he allowed this knowledge not to lie heavily on his mind, not to be used in a narrow and literal spirit, but to sink into the walls of his brain so that it was turned into wisdom and experience—then such a person would be able to acquire the right feeling for the texture of events, and would undoubtedly avoid becoming the mere slave of the past. I think he would be better able to face a new world, and to meet the surprises of unpredictable change with greater flexibility. A little history may make people mentally rigid. Only if we go on learning more and more of it—go on "unlearning" it—will it correct its own deficiencies gradually and help us to reach the required elasticity of mind.

History and the Present

*K*nowing about past events can help to orient us in the present, although the path to understanding the contemporary world through history is often uncertain. Herbert Butterfield warned that merely organizing history around the present can result in nothing more than "a gigantic optical illusion." His caveat is worth considering and has been restated in various ways by others. The Dutch historian Pieter Geyl believed the past reveals that current political problems emerge from historical issues still alive. But, he said, "the present is not elucidated merely by connecting it with trends in the immediate preceding period, from which it may be seen to issue." It is, rather, "the whole of history" that will help us comprehend the world we live in. Geyl continued: "A mind that has established contact with forms of life remote and unfamiliar, that has come to know great events and personalities of some particular period, pondering motives and evidence, watching the ever surprising shapes in which greatness and character appear, or studying the curious changes of social habits and the impact of economic factors—such a mind is likely to see more deeply into contemporary phenomena and movements, be it of culture or of politics."[1]

Among the writers in this book, Allan Nevins also believed that contemporary problems are influenced by the past and that history shapes the present and allows us to create the future. "The uses of history are almost endless," Nevins maintained, and "it may be read for a hundred reasons," among them inspiration and enlightenment. Along similar lines, Carl G. Gustavson contended that the past is woven into the very fabric of many fields of knowledge and that knowing about history makes the present more comprehensible by adding depth and meaning to our surrounding environment. Clearly, as David S. Landes and Charles Tilly argued, "the present is a child of the past" and "our options are limited by what has gone before."

Nothing, they wrote, "is understandable except as seen through time." The discussion by Landes and Tilly of the historian as social scientist and as humanist gives, incidentally, some idea of the variety of ways historians approach their work and the different expectations they have for their craft.[2]

If history can help us to understand the contemporary world, we nevertheless must always be wary about how the past is used to explain the present. If Clio enables us to confront the unpredictable present more rationally, she also can be easily prostituted, especially when historians allow themselves to be subservient to the state or bureaucracy. "The only durably satisfactory present that we can fashion," Donald M. Dozer declared, "must be constructed upon a frank appreciation of the realities of the past."

Perhaps because history is so frequently prostituted, many historians are understandably reluctant to enter into contemporary analysis. The lack of sufficient perspective and available evidence makes such work tricky if not downright impossible. Still, as the intellectual historian H. Stuart Hughes once noted, "*somebody* must interpret our era to our contemporaries" and why should those functions be abdicated to those less well trained?[3] Historians have a vital function to play, if not in the analysis of the present, then in evaluating the use of history by those who do attempt to explain the world of today. Much of our contemporary dialogue is saturated with historical arguments, as Allan Lichtman and Valerie French show in their discussion of history and contemporary analysis. Sometimes such arguments are explicit. More often, however, they are not, and if one is to make sense of them one must know something about the past.

References

1. See Herbert Butterfield, *The Whig Interpretation of History* (London: G. Bell, 1931), 29, and Pieter Geyl, *The Use and Abuse of History* (New Haven, Conn.: Yale University Press, 1955), 83–85 (quotation, 83–84). Also see the discussion on the relationship between past and present by the French historian Marc Bloch in *The Historian's Craft*, trans. Peter Putnam (New York: Alfred A. Knopf, 1953), 35–47. Bloch's account was originally written in 1941 in the midst of World War II. Bloch was later executed by the Nazis.

2. Another excellent discussion of what historians do and their use of other disciplines is Lawrence Stone, "History and the Social Sciences in the Twentieth Century," in *The Future of History: Essays in the Vanderbilt University Centennial Symposium*, ed. Charles F. Delzell (Nashville, Tenn.: Vanderbilt University Press, 1977), 3–42.

3. Some historians believe that one of the best ways to stimulate interest in history among very young students is to draw parallels, however tentatively, between the past and the present. See H. Stuart Hughes, "Is Contemporary History Real History?" *American Scholar* 32 (Autumn 1963), esp. 524–25 (above quotation, 525). See also William L. Langer, "The Historian and the Present: We Must Not Abdicate Our Function to Journalists and Commentators," *Vital Speeches* 19 (March 1, 1953): 312–14; and Geoffrey Barraclough, *History in a Changing World* (Norman: University of Oklahoma Press, n.d.), 222.

A Proud Word for History

Allan Nevins

Although Allan Nevins (1890–1971) never received a Ph.D. in history, he was widely regarded as one of America's premier historians. He was an editorial writer for various publications including the *New York Evening Post, The Nation,* and the *New York World.* In 1927 he began teaching history at Cornell, and the following year he moved to Columbia University, where he remained until his retirement. He was president of the American Historical Association in 1960. He won Pulitzer Prizes for his biographies of Grover Cleveland and Hamilton Fish and was awarded the Bancroft Prize for *Ordeal of the Union* (1947). In addition, he wrote and edited many other books, including *The Gateway to History* (1938, 1963), from which the following selection is taken.

A cartridge bag is unstrapped from the sweaty horse, and a brown hand pulls out a thick volume; it is Theodore Roosevelt in East Africa about to give half an hour at the end of a day's hunting to Carlyle's *Frederick the Great.* His object—relaxation, entertainment, instruction. A clean-cut naval officer in blue uniform sits in the English Club in Lima, Peru, a history of Rome on his knee, pondering, and then opens the book again at a chapter telling how Hannibal crossed the Alps. He is Alfred T. Mahan, he has reflected how much more easily the Carthaginian army might have reached Central Italy by water, and he looks for more facts on a theory that has just struck him—the idea of the decisive potency of sea power in wars. An earnest woman of sensitive face looks up from a page of manuscript which she is intently writing, and quickly consults a book labeled Parkman; it is Willa Cather halfway through *Shadows on the Rock,* and trying to recall a bit of color in *The Old Regime in Canada.* A schoolboy emits a merry laugh; he has just found J. J. Jusserand's account of medieval vagabonds, minstrels, out-laws, and peddlers in *English Wayfaring Life* richly comic.

The uses of history are almost endless. It may be read for a hundred reasons, and when read merely for amusement, or for its rich pageantry and drama alone, it insensibly serves other ends. But to understand its more important values we must approach it on an elevated level, and measure it not in relation to individuals, but to societies and nations.

Although when we use the word history we instinctively think of the past, this is an error, for history is actually a bridge connecting the past with the present, and pointing the road to the future. This fact Daniel Webster wrapped into the majestic exordium of his reply to Hayne. "Mr. President," he began, "when the mariner has tossed for many days in thick weather, and on an unknown sea, he naturally avails himself of the first pause in the storm, the earliest glance of the sun, to take his latitude and ascertain how far the elements have driven him from his true course." Webster here indicated one of the cardinal utilities of history. Since mankind is always more or less storm-driven, history is the sextant of states which, tossed by wind and current, would be lost in confusion if they could not fix their position.

History enables bewildered bodies of human beings to grasp their relationship with their past, and helps them chart on general lines their immediate forward course. And it does more than this. By giving peoples a sense of continuity in all their efforts, red-flagging error, and chronicling immortal worth, it confers on them a consciousness of unity, a realization of the value of individual achievement, and a comprehension of the importance of planned effort as contrasted with aimless drifting.

This conception of history as a lantern carried by the side of man, moving forward with every step taken, is of course far ampler than the concept of a mere interesting tale to be told, a vivid scene to be described, or a group of picturesque characters to be delineated. It is essentially western and modern. To the Oriental, and even to the ancient Greek, history was an incomprehensible chaos of happenings, or a repetitive wallpaper pattern. Present-day citizens of America, Britain, and France, however, especially when harried and perplexed by the sweep of events, peer earnestly into history for some illumination of their predicament and prospects. They may only read magazine articles or listen to TV discussions upon what Lincoln or Theodore Roosevelt did in some analogous crisis, or they may verse themselves as deeply in history as Woodrow Wilson and Winston Churchill did; but at any rate, they feel the meaning of history for the present.

It is when great events rouse men to their most responsible temper, and fierce ordeals awaken them to a new sense of their capacities, that they turn readily to the writing of history, for they wish to instruct, and to its reading, for they want to learn. Nineteen hundred years ago the Greek essayist Lucian was writing: "From the beginning of the present excitements—the barbarian war, the Armenian disaster, the succession of victories—you cannot find a man but who is writing history; nay, everyone you meet is a Thucydides, a Herodotus, a Xenophon." It was no accident that the First World War fostered such an interest in history that for a time the number of books devoted to it in English exceeded the titles in fiction; that much the same phenomenon appeared after the Second World War; and that the period between the two conflicts produced a number of the most ambitious efforts ever made to find a meaning in the whole course of world history, ranging from H. G. Wells's *Outline of History* to Arnold Toynbee's *The Study of History*, both in very different ways enormously popular.

Democratic peoples of wide popular education, where the feeling of progress toward some goal is strong, inevitably display a specially keen interest in history as an illuminant of present and future. Democracy gives every thoughtful citizen a sense of being a participator in history, education sharpens his curiosity, and belief in progress teaches him to look for continuing patterns. The United States was born at a time when a tradition of interest in history was easily established. Modern historical writing in spirit and method is largely a product of the nineteenth century Enlightenment, and it was just as the Enlightenment began to merge in the Industrial Revolution that the republic emerged. Various writers, such as Lord Morley in his *Voltaire* and *Burke*, have pointed out how great a part historical composition played in the mature phases of the Enlightenment.

The literate generation contemporaneous with the American and French Revolutions in Western Europe and the United States steeped itself in history. When the eighteenth century ended no gentleman's library was complete without Thucydides, Livy, and Tacitus, and few cultivated men on either side of the Atlantic could not discuss the historical works of Hume, Voltaire, Mabillon, and Gibbon. Henry Adams in his life of John Randolph of Roanoke speaks of the immutable "literary standards" of the day to which Randolph's education conformed: "He read his Gibbon, Hume, and Burke; knew English history. . . . " Even at an earlier period three works, Raleigh's eloquent *History of the World*, Bishop Burnet's *History of the Reformation*, and Clarendon's history of the Puritan rebellion, had been widely diffused throughout the American colonies. But as the Enlightenment widened its appeal to the intellectual aristocracy of the time, and the currents of political revolt stimulated a search for precedents, books written on a higher plane came into use. Young John Adams slaked a burning thirst in More's *Wolsey*, Clarendon, Hume, Walton's biographies, and Goldsmith's historical compilations. John Dickinson in Pennslyvania and George Mason in Virginia were not behind him.

In short, the men who took the leadership of our nation, believing in history as an exponent of current events, were well acquainted with the works then standard. Law and political thought were their primary study, but history maintained an almost equal place.

Thus it was that we find Washington after the Revolution ordering from England a small library of historical works: Robertson's *Charles V* and *History of America*; Voltaire's *Charles XII*; Sully's *Memoirs*; lives of Peter the Great, Louis XV, and Gustavus Adolphus, and histories of Rome and Portugal. Hence it is that we find John Adams, in describing the qualifications of a good Secretary of State, writing a little later: "He ought to be a Man of universal reading in Laws, Governments, History." Thus it is, again, that we find Chancellor Kent stating in his autobiography that in 1782, at Poughkeepsie, he brightened his study of law by reading Smollett's and Rapin's histories of England. "The same year I procured Hume's *History*, and his profound reflections and admirable eloquence struck most deeply on my youthful mind." Alexander Hamilton's library included not only Greek and Roman historians, but well-thumbed sets of Gibbon, Hume, and Robertson. Few well-educated Americans, indeed—ministers, editors, attorneys, physicians as well as political leaders—then failed to regard history as a necessary discipline. Most of them would have agreed with Jefferson, himself a lover of the best British historians, in what he wrote of the proper requirements of Virginia's educational law:

> But of the views of this law none is more important, none more legitimate, than that of rendering the people the safe, as they are the ultimate, guardians of their own liberty. For this purpose the reading in the first stage, where *they* will receive their whole education, is proposed, as has been said, to be chiefly historical. History, by apprising them of the past, will enable them to judge of the future; it will avail them of the experience of other times and other nations; it will qualify them as judges of the actions and designs of men; it will enable them to know ambition under every guise it may assume; and knowing it, to defeat its views.

The spell which history, not as entertainment but as an interpretive guide, exercised over the better instructed groups of Americans, remained undiminished for generations. Charles Sumner, for example, with a career as statesman in view, wrote a friend just after his Harvard graduation in 1830: "I have marked out for myself a course of study which will fully occupy my time— namely, a course of mathematics, Juvenal, Tacitus, a course of modern history, Hallam's *Middle Ages* and *Constitutional History,* Roscoe's *Leo* and *Lorenzo,* and Robertson's *Charles V."* Even pioneer America felt that a familiarity with history befitted the leader; after the log cabin campaign Webster spent a weary day deleting Greek heroes and Roman consuls from William Henry Harrison's inaugural address. We might extend the roster to the first Roosevelt and Woodrow Wilson, who wrote history as well as read it omnivorously, and acted steadily by its light; to Harry Truman, who referred part of his confidence in discharging his Presidential labors to a wide early reading of history, and who when he faced the intractable MacArthur thought of what Lincoln had done with the intractable McClellan; and to John F. Kennedy, whose *Profiles in Courage* covered a wide historical range, and whose general knowledge of the American and European past is not easily matched.

I

BUT HISTORY is more than a guide for men in their daily round; it is a creator of their future. The conception which men have of their record in generations past shapes their dreams and ambitions for the generations to come. The Israel that Herzl helped to found owed most of its force to the Zionist image of the older Israel, as the new Italy of which Mussolini dreamed was partly a reincarnation of Rome of the Caesars.

Consider how great a purpose history has served as a womb or matrix of nations. The strongest element in the creation of any human organization of complex character and enduring strength is the establishment of a common tradition by the narration of its history. The common literature may be important, especially a common poetry; a common religion will knit its members together by its gospel. But even literature and religion contain historical elements; and members of a nation of uneven literary tastes and of mixed religions can be tightly bound together by reverence for the tale of their past. The Greek who thrilled over Thermopylae, the Roman exulting over the devotion of Curtius or the conquests of Caesar, the Briton reading of Nelson at Trafalgar, the American following the epic story of pioneering from Captain John Smith to Kit Carson, have all responded to the same emotion. When Treitschke resolved to revive the national spirit of the Germans he began by writing their history; when Vienna wished to hinder the growth of patriotism among the Czechs it threw obstacles before the publication of Palacky's history of Bohemia.

To give a people a full sense of their future we need first the historians who give them a full sense of their past. The school texts that told of Plymouth Rock, Valley Forge, and the Alamo, the rhetorical pages of George Bancroft, the historical poems of Longfellow on Miles Standish and Paul Revere, and Cooper's historical romance *The Spy,* helped immeasurably in making America a nation. Turner's essay on the historical influence of the frontier, by deepening our understanding of the uniqueness of our past, strengthened our nationalist feeling. "Laws die, books never"—and the nation-builder may well say that he cares not who writes the laws of a country so long as he can write its history.

If history has been a maker of nations, her role as their continuing inspirer is almost equally important. The nature of the inspiration is highly varied, but its central importance is this, that it tends to make each individual a sharer in the great deeds, ideas, and movements of his ancestors or forerunners, and to awaken an emulative passion in his breast. It tends also, since history tells a very mixed tale, to awaken healthy doubts, repulsions, and condemnations, which may be nearly as valuable; but the positive side is more important than the negative. "My only regret is that I have but one life to give for my country"—the country schoolmaster who said that had done his country service in braving almost certain death to gain information for the patriot armies. But in flinging that golden sentence to the historians, to be repeated till every child knows it, he performed a service far greater. We could add many illustrations of the kind. The best inspiration of history, however, outruns mere national feeling and applies to all humanity, fortifying its higher resolves.

"All learners, all inquiring minds of every order," wrote Carlyle of history, "are gathered round her footstool, and reverently pondering her lessons as the true basis of wisdom." But more than wisdom resides in her teachings. The grandeur of the historical record confers a certain grandeur upon ourselves. All thoughtful men tend in some degree to identity themselves with the figures and forces of history. We realize that each individual mind is one more incarnation of a universal mind. The past was wrought by men and women basically like ourselves. What Shakespeare and Lincoln accomplished, what Caesar Borgia and Stalin perpetrated, what Hannibal and Gustavus Adolphus dared and endured, are illustrations of the powers, debasements, and fortitudes of our common human nature. In the larger accomplishments of the race we feel we have a share. "We sympathize in the great moments of history," writes Emerson, "in the great discoveries, the great resistances, the great prosperities of men; because there law was enacted, the sea was searched, the land was found, or the blow was struck, *for us*, as we ourselves would have done in that place or have applauded."

This conception of history as a creative and inspiring force has always been essentially a literary conception. Such history can effect little unless it is widely read, which means that it must possess color, suspense, warm human interest, and an infusion of romance or poetry. James Anthony Froude deliberately essayed to nurture patriotic feeling by his history of England from the accession of Queen Elizabeth, and by such essays as his stirring account of "England's Forgotten Worthies," a resuscitation of the exploits of Tudor captains like Drake, Hawkins, and Raleigh. Possessing vigorous literary talent, and able to simplify and dramatize complex transactions effectively, he won and still holds a wide following. Guizot in his history of France, written primarily for precocious youth, had a similar goal in view. George Bancroft envisaged his history of the English colonies in America, their developing freedom, and their final struggle for complete liberty as a sort of prose epic, he too telling an oversimplified and sometimes melodramatic story for its inspiring effect. His success in his own long generation was enormous, and hard as it may seem to believe now, it was primarily a literary success.

All the eminent literary historians of the nineteenth century, in fact, believed earnestly in history as a guide to the present and a shaper of the future. Such a writer as Macaulay wished to instill a feeling for Whig and liberal values in English civilization. Because he passionately desired to see these values prevail in the future, he believed he could illustrate their validity by an examination of the past. Anxious for all literate persons to read his work, he thought that the art of Walter Scott's historical romances could be combined with the severe truthfulness of the annalist, and plumed himself on the fact that his history displaced the latest novel on the dressing table of fashionable women. Such glowing literary artists as Motley and Parkman were less consciously and obviously, but just as firmly, animated by a like ambition. Each celebrated in his own way a triumph of the ideals of free, democratic, and Protestant New England, which they hoped would continue to prevail; Motley the victory of Dutch and English libertarians over Spain, Parkman the victory of the free individualistic Anglo-Saxons over the regimentation and intolerance of New France.

Indeed, literary history used for inspiration as well as instruction and entertainment once became a great popular possession in the United States, as in other lands. It is a salient and creditable fact of the American cultural record that from 1830 to 1880 history was one of the most continuously popular forms. Prescott's *Conquest of Mexico* sold 5000 copies in four months in the United States, and went through edition after edition; his *Conquest of Peru* sold 7500 copies in the same brief period; his Spanish histories, indicting obscurantism and tyranny, nearly as well. The works of Bancroft and Motley never ceased to sell. Irving's life of Washington, the ablest study of the Revolution made up to that time, was one of the notable successes of American publishing prior to the Civil War. When we recall that meanwhile the histories of Macaulay, Carlyle, and Grote were not merely brought out by authorized publishers but extensively pirated, while translated works like Charles Rollin's ancient history sold widely, we can comprehend why the American mind received a distinct historical bias during most of the century.

Whenever history is invoked to shape the present and future, however, it obviously runs very real perils. Any participant in current affairs must face some rough hauling and buffeting. The Behistun Rock on the road from Babylon to Ecbatana carries an inscription by Darius the Great asserting that he had destroyed "the Reign of the Lie"; the currency, that is, of a view of history propagated by a usurper who had claimed that he was the son of Cyrus and hence the rightful ruler of the Persian Empire. Every fresh political campaign in democratic lands finds candidates assailing "the reign of the lie"—that is, the misrepresentations of rivals with respect to the history of recent events. We live amid a constant clash of ideas, and they all grow out of historic experience. It is almost impossible to name a political, economic, or social preconception which is not molded and colored by history. It is equally impossible to name a piece of real history which is not molded and colored by political, economic, or social beliefs. The two interact.

II

. . . IT IS OBVIOUS that the fusion of past and present in historical study results in an unending controversy over many aspects of written history, and in a constant coloration or perversion of historical truth. History is never above the melee. It is not allowed to be neutral, but forced to enlist in every army. Lincoln sadly pointed out during the Civil War that both sides prayed to the same God for victory. Each side also appealed to the same national history for support of their belief that a just God would give the victory to its special tenets: the belief of Southerners that the American past justified a people in battling for self-determination and independence, the belief of Northerners that the past required a struggle to vindicate national integrity. The conviction of Darius that he had to combat a lie is paralleled by the conviction of Western nations in the twentieth century that they too must overthrow foul and potent lies. A great deal of national policy in Britain and America during the last generation is, from one point of view, an implementation of historical criticism.

The Nazi lie, propagated by Hitler with the aid of a tremendous apparatus, was an imperialist claim that history proved Germans to be a *Volk* of superior gifts and discipline, entitled to rule as a master race over inferior peoples. It was an assertion that after suffering a long series of terrible historical wrongs, this master race should assert its power, and reduce to vassalage the Gauls, the Slavs, the Jews, and the colored hordes. Teutonic domination, in an empire to last a thousand years, would crown civilization with new glories. The racial interpretations of history presented by Count Gobineau, Houston Stewart Chamberlain, and others were mingled with the anti-Christian, anti-humanitarian interpretations of Nietzsche, and the classic exaltations of German virtues by Hans Zwiedineck von Südenhorst and Wilhelm Oncken. Standards of accepted morality were cast aside as historically unjustified. Anything that promoted Nazi ambition was inherently good, while anything which obstructed it was wicked. Had Hitler conquered Europe, a vast amount of history would have been rewritten in an effort to make the Nazi lie stand as truth. . . .

IV

THE ONLY HISTORY that can truly nourish, inspire, and guide a people over a long period of time is written in a different spirit. It is produced with a high, not a low, intention; in an earnest effort to ascertain the truth objectively. The servant of truth cannot be slave of party or nation. If men allowed history to sink for long to the fascist or communist level, we would have not an integral European history, but a West German type of history written for West Germans, a French type of history written for Frenchmen, and a Scottish type of history written for Scots. To an unfortunate extent, such distorted history does exist, but not with the sanction of true scholars or tolerance of critical readers. No greater place exists for a Spanish type of European history, or an Italian or Dutch type, than for an Italian physics and a Dutch physics. Of course perfect objectivity is never achieved, but English historians of integrity, like Lecky and George Otto Trevelyan, have gone a long way toward it in granting the justice of the patriot cause in the Revolution, while American historians have gone equally far in granting the purity and strength of the Tory cause.

Not only is the intention of true history high, but the method is scientific. The historian, that is, collects his data fairly, observes it systematically, organizes it logically, and tests its parts thoroughly. Then by inductive logic and the use of hypothesis he reaches provisional generalizations, and only when he has carried out a final search for new data, and made fresh tests, does he commit final conclusions to paper. In all this he casts off, so far as possible, the prejudices of race, nationality, class, and faction. If his method falls short of the test-tube precision of the chemist, it is at any rate as scientific as he can make it. He will go to the primary sources for as many facts as possible, and restrict his reliance on secondary accounts. He will give each category of evidence its proper valuation: the official document, the letter, the memoir, the newspaper story, the pamphlet, the artifact. He will put every witness, every scrap of paper, under cross-examination. And when he finishes his reconstruction of the past, he will give it as veracious a glow of life as his art can encompass.

This standard history is the only type that a cultivated people will in the long run cherish. Fortunately it exists in Western nations in abundance. Our shelves are loaded with its treasures. Some of its values change with the climate of opinion, but the value of its basic integrity remains immutable. It stands ready to give the casual reader sound amusement, the student instruction, the philosopher ideas, and the statesman parallels and prophecies; ready, more importantly, to give any nation a sense of the union of past, present, and future.

Its vitality is constantly quickened by the interaction of past and present, and the changing hues which each gives the other. It is obviously clear that we can learn something about the frenzy of McCarthyism and its faked exposure of plots from a careful reading of Macaulay upon the frenzy that surrounded Titus Oates and his particular faked conspiracy. We can learn a good deal about the criminal folly of Hitler's maltreatment of the Jews from a study of the criminal folly of the Spanish expulsion of the Moors as related by Henry Charles Lea in his vivid book on the Moriscoes. The interaction, however, often gives us a converse profit. Thus one English historian has remarked that it is no longer easy to call the mild repressions and exactions of Charles I "tyranny," as older writers did, since Hitler and Stalin have shown how monstrous a tyranny can really be under a modern dictator. We have to take a more moderate view of

Stuart oppressions—or those of George III. It is certainly easier now to understand the history of ideological conflict in sixteenth-century Europe over religious beliefs, for we have the history of twentieth-century ideological conflict over politico-economic beliefs to cast light upon it. In each instance the struggle aroused profound and bitter emotion, making men ready to kill and be killed.

Nearly all historians of the first rank have reflected this complex relationship of yesterday, today, and tomorrow, making their work a bridge. Why did Gibbon choose his particular subject of the *Decline and Fall?* A man of independent means, philosophical outlook, and contemplative pleasure in learning for learning's sake, he might have regarded his theme as divorced from all current interests. Actually he did not. He chose it in part because he believed that a harmonious relationship and even general resemblance existed between Rome of the Antonines, and Britain of the Hanoverians, and he felt confident that great numbers of literate people in Western Europe would be interested in a delineation of Roman politics and society which brought out the resemblance. He was also fascinated by the question whether any of the causes which had brought about the fall of Rome could operate to bring about the fall of British civilization, and thought that an exploration of this question would also interest many readers. He was right. It was not alone his mastery of facts, his critical angle of vision, or his style which gave his history an immense vogue; it was its close relationship to the situation of Britain at the time. Men may read it even today thinking of a resemblance between the positions of the Roman and American nations.

History, over the long period since Hume and Voltaire, has become steadily more useful to peoples as it has broadened its scope, and gained an eclectic use of new tools. It has learned to take all possible profit from the other social studies—statistics, sociology, economics, psychology, geography—in presenting a complete and exact picture of the past. . . .

. . . The historical and biographical work of the last generation not only illuminates our past, but suffuses a radiance which more than any other body of books—more than the writings of sociologists, economists, or political experts—casts rays upon our immediate future. The American who ignores this work has neglected what might be the most vital part of his education.

Were history as nearly static as some branches of learning it would be a drab affair, but it is alive in every aspect. It is most of all alive in that it is constantly being reborn like the phoenix from its own ashes. As mankind lengthens its experience, perspectives change. The lenses through which we look at the past have to be refocused from generation to generation. What seemed wisdom to our fathers is often folly to us, and what is dramatic to our age may seem naive or banal to the next. While the best history has enduring elements, there is a sense in which every generation has to have history rewritten new for it, and in this fact lies much of the fascination which historical activity will always offer thoughtful men. As the history written in any age bodies forth the form and spirit of that age, a succession of histories is a record of the stages through which thought and feeling have passed. In its protean forms, history touches the realm of ideas at more points than any other study, and in the best of its forms it is compact as much of ideas as of fact. There was a profound and not merely superficial meaning in the last instructions Napoleon left for the King of Rome: "Let my son often read and reflect on history; this is the only true philosophy."

A Most Dangerous Product: History

Carl G. Gustavson

Carl G. Gustavson (b. 1915) has taught at several colleges and universities, including Lake Forest College, Miami University, and Ohio University. He is a past president of the Ohio Academy of History and
among his books are *The Preface to History* (1955) and *Europe in the
World Community Since 1939* (1971). The following selection is from
Gustavson's *The Mansion of History* (1976).

*T*he scene: the government palace in Futureville. The year: 20—.
The occasion: a cabinet meeting, presided over by Dictator
Won Ahl de Marbles. The minister of propaganda, Dr. Boeggels,
is speaking:

". . . and now that the Future has arrived and the Splootch Telepather has given us control of the world, we must take further measures to ensure our mastery. Among our more urgent priorities, we
must make the people forget the past, we must abolish history.

"We are now the masters of 178 former countries, each with its
own history. As long as they remember their past achievements as
separate peoples, the Americans, the Russians, the Chinese and all
the others are not going to be loyal subjects of our global empire. We
must obliterate these divisive memories permanently."

The minister of culture spoke up: "I quite agree. The memories of
the past also help to keep the various religions alive. If we abolish
history, Islam, Christianity, Judaism, Shintoism, and the other religions will be easier to destroy. Marxism, too, depends upon history
and will be snipped at the roots."

"If we can abolish their recollections of past struggles, the labor organizations will be much easier to quash," contributed the minister of labor.

The dictator turned to Dr. Splootch, inventor of the Splootch machine. "Well, then, have all the preparations been made?"

Splootch responded, "All is in readiness, Your Excellency, for a trial run. It will be limited, at first, to the capital city, where we have already carried on intensive indoctrination. The public has been repeatedly warned that thinking historically is a heresy and that those guilty of it will be splootched—vaporized—without further warning. The telepather has been programmed, for the time being, to the telepathic waves of the inhabitants of this city. It will work exactly as when we splootched everyone in Washington, the American capital, which—ah—persuaded all other governments to capitulate immediately."

"Good," said the dictator, "turn it on." Splootch walked over to the huge panel blinking with many lights on one side of the room and pushed a button. A faint whirring sound pervaded the room.

"And now to the next item on the agenda," began Won Ahl, after a brief admiring pause, but a door burst open, and an excited attendant gestured urgently to the dictator. "Your Excellency, those architects in the anteroom have vanished, just disappeared into thin air."

"What? Heretics so close at hand! Good to have found them out. Now back to the agenda. Mr. Precedence, as minister of justice, what do you . . ." He stopped. A trail of vapor curled where Mr. Precedence had sat. The ministers looked hastily about—four other seats were also empty.

"Traitors! In the cabinet itself! . . . What do *you* want?" This was directed to an attendant looking out the window who had started muttering incoherently to himself. He swung around, a terrified look on his face. "Your Excellency, the people in the Great Square, the people, the . . . they . . ."

The telephone started ringing. The chief of police answered it, then turned to the cabinet. "Someone is calling from the war department. It seems that the chiefs of staff were having lunch together and have suddenly all disappeared."

The phone was already ringing again. A moment of listening, then "There's an emergency at the hospital. Some of the doctors cannot be located." He hung up, whereupon the phone started clamoring again. "It's from the university. They claim something mysterious is going on down there, professors disappearing from in front of classes and most of the students also. Only some environmentalists and a couple behaviorists still seem to be teaching."

A cabinet minister rose, shouting at Dr. Splootch: "How is that contraption hooked up? Turn off . . ." Even as he spoke, he vanished. So did three other ministers. The attendant at the window was yammering, "The Square, the Square! All that's left is a boy and girl standing there smooching."

Dr. Splootch snarled defensively, "I am a technician, not an ideologue. I do what I am told—program the machine to vaporize anyone thinking about the past!" The telephone was ringing incessantly, an attendant rushed into the room, started to shout, and vanished. Only three cabinet ministers were now left. Dr. Boeggels roared: "You idiot, couldn't you tell the difference between . . ." and became a cloud of vapor.

"Turn it off!" ordered the dictator. Splootch started for the machine, saying, "I don't see what's wrong. When I hooked it up to vaporize Washington . . ." and vanished. So did everyone else in the room except the dictator, who was now screaming too loudly to hear anyone else: "Turn it off! Turn it off!"

The dictator stopped for breath, stared at the vapor clouds with unbelieving eyes, and went into hysterics: "I am Emperor of the World! I am the greatest conqueror in hist . . ."

THE ROOM WAS EMPTY.

Preposterous? In a sense, it actually did happen once. The Emperor Shih Huang Ti (246–210 B.C.), forcefully reorganizing China after the end of the Chou dynasty, tried to obliterate the traditions of the past by ordering all works of history and literature destroyed. Hundreds of manuscripts were burned and numerous scholars executed. He survived for a few more years, but after his death Chinese history was at least partially restored from hidden books and the memories of surviving scholars.

Dr. Splootch seems to have received faulty instructions. The intent must have been to eliminate the history of countries and groups as it is taught in formal classes or as it may be used to inculcate loyalty. Apparently these people did not understand that history is inextricably woven into the context of many areas of knowledge. Lawyers work with precedences; a long legacy out of the past guides the varied skills of architects, generals, and physicians, while geologists and professors of literature may be as much involved in the past as historians themselves.

Equally distressing, the cabinet evidently overlooked that everyone is his or her own historian, that our daily life is cluttered with our personal past, and that we rely upon our own experiences in facing today's happenings. Where is the dividing line between now and the past? Many times a day we all encounter the past, last week or ancient, in such forms as living memory, personal records, published allusions, habitual group conduct, and artifacts in our material environment.

"History" is most often defined as "the remembered past" or as "the memory of things said and done." One more precise version suggests that it is "the story of the deeds and achievements of men living in societies." It is the story of the past, the memory of human beings recollected, usually, in the form of narrative. We often refer to the past itself as "history," and the technician in Futureville, obviously confused over usage, hooked up his machine to this, rather than to any organized body of knowledge about it. That is, when we allude to history, we may be thinking of the happenings themselves or of the *recorded* memories of these events. There is also a third kind, the inchoate public memory of the past, full of myths and half-truths, which politicians often invoke while trying to win elections; in its more mystic, rather sacerdotal, form, the losers are apt to appeal to it, to posterity, for a more just judgment of themselves and their deeds.

These people in Futureville also made a very common error by regarding history as a burden, as an obstacle to their future. This is being much too selective, forgetting that the good things and the dynamic forces that power our age have also come out of the past.

Many have condemned history. Everyone knows that Napoleon Bonaparte once said history is a "lie agreed upon." The historians Thomas Carlyle and Edward Gibbon declared, respectively, that it was a "great dust-heap" and an account of the "crimes, follies, and misfortunes of mankind." Voltaire called it a pack of tricks played upon the dead. Henry Ford swept the whole business aside with the simple declaration that history was "bunk."

For sheer power of invective, however, one must particularly admire the denunciation by Paul Valéry, the French poet: "History is the most dangerous product evolved from the chemistry of the intellect. Its properties are well known. It causes dreams, it intoxicates whole peoples, gives them false memories, quickens their reflexes, keeps their old wounds open, torments them in their repose, leads them into delusions of grandeur or persecution, and makes nations bitter, arrogant, insufferable, and vain."

Whatever its merits or demerits, history must be of extraordinary importance in order to earn such sweeping broadsides. Furthermore, Napoleon's opinion did not prevent him from creating more of it, nor did Carlyle or Gibbon stop writing about the past. And apparently the bunk did not extend to the history of automobiles, for Ford's museum at Dearborn Village contains a magnificent collection of vehicles illustrating the evolution of modern transportation.

HISTORY COMES in many varieties and has many uses. It can be exciting or tedious, instructive or misleading, an intellectual discipline or blatant superstition. Properly practiced and reflective of the diversities of human experience, "the mansion of history," in the words of Cicely V. Wedgwood, "has enough rooms to accommodate all of us."

History's oldest and persistent service has been for entertainment, the enjoyment of stories of actual happenings as a pastime. Customarily regarded as a branch of literature until the middle of the nineteenth century, it still usually retains the form of a narrative and continues to provide material for cinema, television, and books of fiction. Vicarious experiences of the past invite us to partake of adventures in which we cannot ourselves adventure and to view broadening human panoramas otherwise unseen. For those too despondent over the trials of the present, the past may offer healing surcease. The future we cannot visit, but journeys to other peoples in other times are readily available.

Posterity, through history, memorializes those who have gone before, confers an earthly immortality as recognition of individual achievement. History is not for those who may accept the work of a hundred generations without acknowledging any debt to their predecessors; perhaps, they, too, will have descendants who will regard us as too benighted to be worth remembering and for whom the past will also be such a shadowy limbo that only *their* Now will seem imperishable.

Nations, institutions, and social groups use it to inspire loyalty to themselves and to create a sense of shared community by the telling of stories about past struggles, victories and defeats, and the sacrifices made for the benefit of posterity. Heroes are held up for emulation, and villains paraded as warnings. Lacking earlier traditions, American writers soon after their country's independence created their own versions of their country's past and have continued to do so. The growth of European nationalism in the nineteenth century inspired a long series of historians to write about the past in terms of their respective peoples' glories and destinies. Clearly subject to extreme abuse, this was the kind of history denounced so vehemently by Paul Valéry. Newly independent countries in Asia, Africa, and the West Indies quickly began to produce their own histories in order to give themselves a separate identity, a sense of mission, and to engender pride in their nationhood. Ghana and Mali, formerly the Gold Coast and the French Sudan, adopted proud historical names of earlier empires when they became independent. American blacks, seeking self-awareness and a fair place in society, demanded their own history and a more just description of their past role in the community.

Though the past is often, much too often, depicted as a struggle between the Good Guys (ourselves, naturally) and those Bad Guys in the Outer Darkness, history, in more objective forms, also describes the origins of things. The more background we know, the better we comprehend our contemporary world and our own place in it. As these lines are being written, a small child is running up the path of our little Canadian island; for her, the path that we hacked out and everything that was recently built are "given," they simply exist, the island has no past. Cicero commented, a couple thousand years ago, that a person who does not know what happened before he was born will remain forever a child. Each generation in turn, like explorers arriving in a strange land, must familiarize itself with the world of the living, and history, the collective memory of the community, serves as one guide for learning the contours of reality and how they came to be there.

Are the "lessons of history," beloved of political orators, useful? Back in 1934 and 1937, groups of German mountain climbers, full of the reckless zeal of Nazi Germany, staged onslaughts on Mount Nangi Parbat in the Himalayas for the greater glory of the Third

Reich. Both expeditions met grim fates, eleven dying in 1934 and sixteen being buried in an avalanche in 1937. Mountain climbers, like all groups, have their own history, the stories of their achievements and tragedies, a collective memory of experiences helpful in confronting problems inherent in such endeavors. Those two groups ignored the lessons of mountaineering history, and they "met the fate they deserved." Shortly thereafter, Adolf Hitler led the Nazis in a greater onslaught, the military and political conquest of Europe, and for a few years the Fuehrer seemed to be a magically successful wizard of history. After spectacular early successes, however, the venture suffered total disaster. Had Hitler, like the mountain climbers, failed to consult history properly?

Although the answer to that particular question may seem easy, the factors involved are usually so diverse and interrelated that using lessons of history is about like trying to figure the trajectory of a space rocket to Jupiter with only elementary arithmetic. A prefatory "History teaches that . . ." should generally be taken as a signal that the speaker or writer is about to peddle his or her pet nostrum. Perhaps Sir Lewis Namier summed up a sensible answer best by saying that history gives an "intuitive understanding of how things do *not* happen." John H. Plumb put it another way, suggesting that history reveals what may be prudent.

History's importance often looms the most starkly in episodes in which it has beem omitted from the calculations. This is exemplified, in two often-cited examples, by a Neville Chamberlain, bereft of much historical knowledge, thinking he could do business with Hitler, or a Colonel Edward House at the Paris peace conference in 1919 assuming that he could ignore the historical factors represented by the statesmen there and deal successfully with these men on a purely personal basis. History reveals the limitations of any one specific action by presenting the numerous factors that are involved in any current problem. It engenders a "feel" for the probabilities, on the basis of rather similar circumstances, and warns of simplistic solutions based on a too-limited selectivity of facts or excessive faith in one particular creed.

IS HISTORY ACTUALLY RELEVANT to our problems in an age of rapid change? Why study the past if, as some insist, it is obsolete? This argument could be reversed: if change is this rapid, then a student focusing only on the present will discover, a few years later, that *this* has also become obsolete, that he or she was concentrating on a transitory moment in history. When individual events follow in rapid sequence, the sensible procedure is to study the patterns, the direction of development over a period of time, in order to gain orientation. In horse and buggy days, we could watch the fence posts go by, but when we now drive on a highway, we must be aware of the contours of the road and the pattern of traffic.

Put another way, studying only the present is comparable to looking at a still picture from a stopped movie projector, seeing only the suspended animation of action that had begun much earlier, one moment only out of a continuing story on the reel of time. We live in a community whose social groups and institutions usually have much longer longevity than we do and whose habitual conduct can only be understood by watching their behavior over a lengthy period. Our Now is only one historical moment in the drama, an instant in an "infinity of present instants" (George Kubler). That child on the island path may live only in the Now, but she is also curious, fulfilling a natural need for explanations which usually must reach back to events that happened earlier.

Then, too, perhaps we are overly impressed by the rate of change because we happen to be participants. The synthetic rush of the news media contributes to this feeling, although the impression of fast-breaking events often reflects the imperatives of journalists' work rather than what really is out there. As a consequence, in our journey through life many of us keep watching the fence posts whiz by, not the broader panorama. Did immigrants traveling overseas from Europe perhaps face as much or more change? Or European peasants going to work in a factory town? Are recent technological developments actually more revolutionary in their impact than those of the nineteenth century?

Sometimes we delude ourselves about the nature of change itself. We may be deceived by old ideas masquerading under new labels or become excited about a new proposal to solve an old problem, not realizing that this proposal, in its essentials, has been tried before, perhaps many times. Our circumstances may seem novel if, lacking the collective memory of humanity, we do not often recognize basically similar circumstances that we share with our ancestors. Paradoxically, to be purely present-minded is to risk being entrapped in the past without even recognizing it as such.

History alleviates the fear of the unknown. The vicarious experience of history is good training for confronting the crises of our own age because, even though history does not repeat itself exactly, the happenings often have an evocative similarity. Community experiences do recur in various guises, and they can provide the perspective for seeing our own trials in the light of earlier crises and tribulations. In the midst of the brawling American scene at the beginning of the 1970s, the president of the American Historical Association told his fellow historians at their annual convention that they might "find some comfort" and perhaps also some enlightenment by looking at the crises of the fourth and fourteenth centuries. Others have pointed to the sixteenth century for similarities to the disorientation and mood of our own times. Knowing about the past makes not only the present but also the immediate future much less uncharted.

History, properly used, teaches respect for reality, an ability to discern and trace out the existing contours and the social forces at work in society. This is also a hard saying for those who either prefer to employ it as ammunition for special causes or who do not like recollections of the past because earlier experiences argue against their particular panacea. History is a good corrective for those who are constantly camped at the river Jordan, impatiently waiting to be led into the Promised Land. The historian's past does have a future, and we know what it is; we read about the American Revolution and are aware of what its future would bring. The historically minded know that the future is part of Time, part of our world, and that basically similar processes will still be at work. History soberly tells us the expectancy, the unlikelihood that we will suddenly encounter a secular Second Coming, either a sudden end of our world or an equally abrupt entry into a blessed Millennium. In the words of Jacques Barzun, history "molds minds strong enough to stand without flinching the terror and confusion of existence."

BEYOND THESE SPECIFIC USES, however, the most significant contribution of history to our contemporary world lies in its mode of thought, that is, in historical-mindedness. As one of the intellectual tools of the modern mind, it provides a dimension of human life, like the artistic or the spiritual, a way of enriching our perceptions of the environment. A virtually indispensable attribute of the civilized individual, a lack of historical-mindedness is comparable, in some ways, to being color-blind or tone-deaf. Not that all can be historically minded, any more than all of us can be musical or poetic, but the acquisition of its magical powers effectively transform our perceived surroundings in depth and meaning.

A mature sense of historical-mindedness stimulates self-identity, enabling the individual to surmount, intellectually, his or her immediate environment and emancipating the individual, to some extent, from the pressures to conform to this year's vogues. He or she ceases to be a pawn of the social forces and their representatives. The words of C. V. Langlois and Charles Seignobos, in a history manual written at the end of the last century, still carry conviction: the "practice of the historical method . . . is very hygienic for the mind, which it cures of credulity."

We cannot escape history, which is as omnipresent as the air about us, and we are often no more aware of its presence. The only question is whether individuals use it in a rudimentary sense or develop it into a tool useful for themselves as human beings and citizens. Even the most adamant hillbillies, in the time sense, who are determined not to leave their own cherished parochial valley because it is manifestly the best valley, cannot abolish history; they can merely reduce it to superstitions. Like any other skill, whether cultural, technical, or athletic, historical-mindedness as a discipline requires a certain amount of training in order to be a useful, satisfying possession.

What Is History?

David S. Landes and Charles Tilly

David S. Landes (b. 1924) and Charles Tilly (b. 1929) have attempted to employ methods from statistics and quantitative analysis in their efforts to recover the past. Landes has a broad background as a scholar; he has taught at Columbia, Berkeley, and Harvard. He is particularly interested in history and economics and has written on European and Middle Eastern history. He was formerly associate editor of the *Journal of Economic History*, and his works include *Bankers and Pashas: International Finance and Economic Imperialism in Egypt* (1958), *The Unbound Prometheus: Technological Change and Industrial Development in Western Europe from 1750 to the Present* (1969), and *Revolution in Time: Clocks and the Making of the Modern World* (1983). Tilly has taught at the University of Delaware, Princeton, Harvard, and the University of Toronto, and is now Theodore M. Newcomb Professor of Social Science in the Departments of Sociology and History at the University of Michigan. Tilly has written or edited *The Vendee* (1964), *Measuring Political Upheaval*, with James Rule (1965), *The Formation of National States in Western Europe* (1975), and *As Sociology Meets History* (1981). The following selection is from *History as a Social Science* (1971), edited by Landes and Tilly.

History is, first of all, the custodian of the collective memory and as such performs the important function of nourishing the collective ego. Second, it is in all societies a primary vehicle of the socialization of the young, teaching them the past so that they may know who they are and behave appropriately in the present. Third, it is the branch of inquiry that seeks to arrive at an accurate account and valid understanding of the past.

The third function is in large part a response to and corrective of the other two. Precisely because history has critical social, psycho-

logical, and educational functions; precisely because we are all prisoners of our past, in the sense that our options are limited by what
has gone before and our preferences are shaped by our image of who
we are and have been, it is of the utmost importance that we try to
free our history from myth and error. Otherwise we are liable to self-
deception or manipulation. It is no coincidence that authoritarian
regimes have typically found it desirable and even necessary to censor works of history and to rewrite the record of the past to their
convenience and advantage; that even democratic societies have
chosen history texts for their children that would inculcate sentiments of pride and patriotism; or that the "emerging nations" of
today, like those of yesterday, should all be engaged in a systematic
effort to recreate (or create) their past in order to enhance their present and future.

The attempt to eschew the path of indoctrination or self-delusion,
to develop history as an intellectual discipline seeking an objective
truth independent of the seeker, is a typically Western rationalistic
response to a problem that most other cultures have treated very
differently. We are a historicist civilization. Our sacred books—the
Old and New Testaments—are essentially histories, as are some of
the oldest and greatest of our literary classics. By common consent,
the greatest of the ancient historians was Thucydides, whose claim
to immortality rests in large part on his efforts to free himself from
romanticism and myth and to treat history not as a source of passion
and psychic gratification but rather as a doorway to experience and
wisdom.

Further, Western civilization is optimistic. We have almost unlimited faith in man's ability to know and, by knowing, to do. This
almost narcissistic confidence in ourselves has had its greatest confirmation in the realms of natural science and technology. By contrast, our relative ignorance of human behavior and our impotence
in dealing with it are lamentable; even so, we cherish the conviction
that as we know more, we shall do better; and in that case, we shall
never do better unless we know more.

Know more about what? Every one of the social sciences has its
own contribution to make to our knowledge of man. The contribution of history is *perspective*. This is no small matter. It is only too
easy and too tempting for each generation, especially the more sensitive members of each generation, to see the tests and troubles of
their own time as unique. For many, what is past is past, and what

matters is now and sometimes later. This is particularly true of social engineers, who, however much they may be motivated by the
recollection of past *wrongs*, do not want to be discouraged by the
record of past *mistakes*. In defense of this "ostrich approach," it
must be admitted that history has been misused as a stick to beat
reformers and to block change. Yet never is the perspective of history
so valuable as when men try to shape their destiny, that is, try to
change history. Then, if ever, man has to know how he came to this
pass; otherwise he is condemned to repeat his errors or, at best, to
blunder through one difficulty only to arrive at another. In this
sense, history, if read correctly, should help make men wise.

Not everyone would agree. There has always been a body of opinion within the historical profession that has denied the possibility of
an objective history—for the very cogent reason that it is simply
impossible for the historian to perceive the past except through eyes
distorted by personal values and sympathies. Each man, in this view,
is his own historian. As for the lessons of history, men choose these
to their purpose—like the devil citing scripture. De Gaulle called on
France's tradition of greatness and power to justify his break with
NATO; his adversaries pointed to the experience of two world wars
to show the necessity of European cooperation. Israelis cite Jewish
history to demonstrate the justice and passion of their attachment
to the Holy Land; Palestinians point to their own history—as recorded in the Bible—to argue that they were there first. Supporters
of the American military intervention in Vietnam have drawn an
analogy to Munich and the appeasement of the 1930s to justify
firmness in the face of totalitarian aggression; while their opponents
have gone back to ancient Athens for lessons in the folly of arrogance. History is not alone in this respect: one could cite any
number of other examples of self-serving analogy, even of conflicting
inferences from the same body of evidence, from any of the behavioral and social sciences. A lawyer might even remark that this is
the human condition: people will always see things differently;
that's what keeps the courts busy.

It would be a serious mistake, however, to infer from these difficulties that our ignorance is inevitable and irreducible. Just as courts
have developed over time adversary procedures and principles of evidence designed to promote the pursuit of truth and justice, so the
social sciences, including history, have invented techniques for the
collection, verification, and appraisal of evidence as a means of un-

derstanding man's motivations and behavior. The social scientist shares in the understanding that results cannot be complete or definitive: he typically deals in a realm of probability; but as his techniques have become more refined and powerful, the probabilities and usefulness of his answers have increased. The gains have been greatest in those areas where the social scientist has been able to simplify his problems by exclusion of all but a few paramount variables; the best example is economics. History, by comparison, has and will always have a hard time: the matter to be studied is inherently complex (some would say, infinitely complex) and resistant to simplification. That, however, only makes the task harder and the results of inquiry necessarily looser. It does not rule out a closer approach to the goal of truth.

History is no different from other intellectual disciplines in having to fulfill several roles at once; but it is more multifarious and hence more divided than the others. There is no such thing as an introductory core course that aims to convey the essence of the subject. Nor is there any pretence to an orthodoxy—whether in the problems to study, the methods to employ, or the standards to meet. Because of this highly valued freedom from norms, the range of performance is extremely wide. Thus, although history is first and foremost a story—and to this day this is what the average person thinks of as history—there are all kinds of stories: dull or exciting, scrupulously careful or wildly imaginative, painfully naive or subtly interpretive. At one extreme is the simple chronicle that strings events one after the other like separate stones on the strand of time; at the other is the account that tries to explain each event as the result of what went before, including in the explanation such enduring circumstances, environmental and internal, as influence the behavior of the actors in the story. Needless to say, most histories fall not at the extremes, but somewhere between.

The same range of variation is found in that kind of history that treats, not of a sequence of change through time, but of a state of affairs or the condition of persons at a moment in time. At one extreme is the antiquarian approach, which simply collects bits and pieces of data, more or less without regard to their importance or interrelationships. At the other is the highly schematized or focused analytical model, which is all articulation and interrelationships. Again, most descriptive histories fall somewhere in between. . . .

Be that as it may, it would be useful for the purpose of the present inquiry to define our terms, and the clearest way to do this is to present the social science and humanist modes as ideal types at opposite poles of the spectrum of methodology. This does violence to the real character of historians and the history they write: historians are typically men of caution and moderation who do their best to avoid extremes. Still, if we keep in mind that the antinomies that follow are a heuristic device, a figment, they will help clarify the divisions within the historical profession and the problems confronted by social science history as one of several complementary, yet often competing, approaches to the subject.

1.A. THE SOCIAL SCIENCE APPROACH is problem-oriented. It assumes that there are uniformities of human behavior that transcend time and place and can be studied as such; and the historian as social scientist chooses his problems with an eye to discovering, verifying, or illuminating such uniformities. The aim is to produce general statements of sufficiently specific content to permit analogy and prediction.

1.b. The humanist views any such extraction of human experience from its matrix of time and place as an insult to the integrity of the historical process. He feels that human beings and their life in society are far too complex to be simplified in this manner; and without simplification, there is no generalization. As Isaiah Berlin has said, it is the job of a science to concentrate on similarities; whereas the historian is interested in what differentiates. The effort to abstract generalizations, "if it were feasible [and Berlin clearly has his doubts], would be the task of sociology, which would then stand to history as a 'pure' science to its application."

Many historians, moreover, would argue that complexity, far from being a disadvantage, is a source of intellectual pleasure and stimulation. Again, to quote Isaiah Berlin:

> If we ask ourselves what historians have commanded the most lasting admiration, we shall, I think, find that they are neither the most ingenious, nor the most precise, nor even the discoverers of new facts or causal connections, but those who (like imaginative writers) present men or societies or situations in many dimensions, at many interesting levels simultaneously, writers in whose accounts human lives, and their relations both to each other and to the external world, are what (at our most lucid and imaginative) we know that they can be.

2.A. IN HIS EFFORT to derive generalizations that will fit into the larger corpus of social and behavioral science, the historian as social scientist aims self-consciously at methodological rigor. He defines his terms, states his hypothesis, clarifies his assumptions (in so far as he himself is aware of them), and stipulates the criteria of proof. If possible—and for the moment this is largely confined to a field like economic history—he states his hypothesis in the form of an explanatory model, preferably in mathematical language and so framed that the criteria of proof are measurable.

2.b. The historian as humanist has no need of this elaborate procedure (though he would pretend to no less methodological rigor). Since he starts with the subject rather than with a question, he often does not begin with a preliminary hypothesis. Rather he derives his conclusions in the course of research and then writes his story in accordance with the evidence, framing the exposition in such a way as to convey his interpretation and the reasons for it. Even if he does begin with a hypothesis, he prefers to avoid what he believes to be the literary infelicities inherent in the elaboration of an explicit model. His primary concern remains the story, and he prefers to weave his assumptions and interpretations into the account in such a way as not to detract from its fluency and interest. In general, he prizes subtlety more than precision.

3.A. THESE DIFFERENCES in approach show up perhaps most clearly in the use and treatment of numerical concepts. Both kinds of historian use such concepts, though the humanist is sometimes not aware of the quantitative implications of such words as "usually," "many," "most of," "often," and the like. The historian as social scientist is keen to measure, and although he would not go so far as to say that only what can be measured is science, he would argue (or at least some would argue) that some number, however approximate, is better than no number—so long as one has some notion of the range of error.

3.b. The historian as humanist is, first of all, skeptical: he knows that many aspects of human behavior are simply not reducible to numbers; and knowing the credence that readers are liable to give to anything that gives the appearance of precision, he prefers no number to what he feels is the spurious assurance of an approximate number. Secondly, his preoccupation with the personages of his story, his concern for their individuality, his effort to accomplish an empathic migration and put himself in their place—all these make him hostile to anything that reduces his subjects to digits. Numbers constitute an artificial normalization of selected characteristics of intrinsically unique persons or events; hence they dehumanize. . . .

4.A. THE DISAGREEMENT about numbers is related to a difference in esthetic priorities. The historian as social scientist knows that tables of statistics do not scan well. They break the rhythm of the text, and comments on numerical matters are often tedious in their factuality. Still, he is reconciled to these failings. His primary virtues are clarity, precision, and analytical rigor. Besides, some subjects simply do not lend themselves to dramatic or elegant presentation.

4.b. The historian as humanist cherishes the ideal of history as literature. He wants to be an artist as well as a scholar. Style, pace, and elegance are important, and even ambiguity may be cultivated for its power to stimulate thought. As for numbers, there are humanists who would confine them to pagination; they break the rhythm of the prose.

THESE ARE THE ANTITYPES AND, like all such ideal versions of a diversity of specimens, they verge on caricature. Most historians, we have noted, fall somewhere in between, combining in their work and intellectual stance elements of both schools. What is more, the social sciences–humanities dichotomy is only one of several divisions within the profession. There are those who are drawn to history primarily by a psychological affinity for distant times and places, and those who want to understand their own time or the nature of change through time. Similarly, there are those who seek, however vainly, the ideal of an objective truth (all the social-scientific historians would presumably be included in this camp); while others, as we have seen, deny the existence of this objective, autonomous truth and insist that history is a subjective perception of the historian, who inevitably alters his subject in the course of studying it.

. . . Historians of all stripes do have two things in common: the assumption, first, that the present is the child of the past and that nothing is understandable except as seen through time; and second, that the truth is always complex.

History as Force

Donald M. Dozer

Donald M. Dozer (1905–1980) taught Latin American history at several universities, including the University of Maryland and the University of California at Santa Barbara. In addition, he worked several years in various government positions including in the National Archives and the United States Department of State. Among his books are *Latin America: An Interpretive History* (1963) and *The Monroe Doctrine: Its Modern Significance* (1965). "History as Force" originally appeared in the *Pacific Historical Review* (November 1965).

T he role of the historian in American life has been steadily declining. John Spencer Bassett noted this decline in 1926 when he wrote:

Fifty years ago historians like Bancroft and Prescott stood side by side with the great poets at the top of the world of letters. . . . They lived like proconsuls over provinces of literary expression. Today the historian's influence has waned. He is no longer to be compared with the lordly proconsul, but rather to the hard-working centurion, whose labors held together the military units on which rested the Roman authority in the province.*

As a result, history guides our judgments less than it used to do. As our society takes on more and more the characteristics of the society of George Orwell's *1984*, it becomes a society without history or rather a society in which history is considered to be serviceable mainly as a tool of political action. . . .

We are passing through an era of historical nihilism. "The past does not exist," cries one of the characters in Jean Paul Sartre's *La*

*Jean Jules Jusserand, Wilbur C. Abbott, Charles W. Colby, and John S. Bassett, *The Writing of History* (New York: Scribner's, 1926), pp. vi–vii.

Nausée. "The world we are living in is totally new," pontificates Robert M. Hutchins. We are, as it were, in flight from history. We have ignored the fact, familiar to us in earlier, more sober times, that only history can explain how the present has come to be what it is. We no longer see the present as part of a living and rational whole, and we seem either unable or indisposed to relate the past creatively to the present. We have come to feel that today has sprung unexpectedly out of a void of yesterday and that we are consequently called upon to deal with problems that have never before confronted mankind. A society such as our own that has abandoned its sense of historical continuity is ripe for social innovation, even revolution.

A sense of history is an acquired characteristic of man. Perhaps it is an unnecessary encumbrance. Friedrich Nietzsche argued in his earliest philosophical work that the historic sense only inhibits the genius of man and paralyzes his will to action. A nation obsessed with a sense of the past may, for that reason, lack a sense of presentness and may fail to develop its potential greatness in the present. Communities and families that live on their history stagnate. Only when man throws off the shackles of the past, it is argued, only when, as in George Santayana's sonnet, he ceases to ponder "the ruin of the years and groan beneath the weight of boasted gain" can he fully liberate his energies and fashion a satisfactory present for himself.

History is the whole of human experience in time. It is the study of all that man has ever done, or thought, or felt. It is the biophysical record of his experience preserved and related in sequence. History is the minutes of previous meetings. It is the recorded "tut-tut." It is the nagging counterfoil to rashness. It is, if you please, the line that forms on the right. In history we travel backward in time to learn the interaction of men and events in the past that created our present world. Men and women long since dead who lived in a world that seemed modern to them acted or were acted upon in ways that vitally affect our lives today. If we know what they did we will be better able to understand our problems today and will not have to approach each problem as if it were unique. We shall also have a clearer vision of prospects and possibilities as we travel forward into an unknown future.

Nietzsche's dramatic challenge to history, like other similar criticisms of the value of history, assumes a fundamental conflict between action and thought. This assumption is easily refuted, for thought of some kind, as modern psychology has shown, always precedes action. The question then is whether it will be merely impulsive thought or informed thought and whether the action that it produces will be hasty, ill-considered action or intelligent action based upon experience. Mere actionists who have had no sense of history have strewn man's past with their follies.

But what is more dangerous, historical nihilism denies the idea of progress derived from experience which underlies the empiricism of our age, at least in the field of the physical sciences. As it rejects empiricism it also rejects intellectualism. An appeal to history in moments of crisis is an appeal to reason—the accumulated reason of the past. When the citizens of a state are ignorant of history they will become victims of ambition and intrigue, they will accept illusions as reality, they will mistake license for liberty, they will identify treachery with patriotism. They can easily be converted into a blind instrument of their own destruction. But on the other hand, if we absorb history and at the same time retain our critical faculties we shall know better how to introduce reason into man's career as it unfolds in the future. And we shall be able to do so without emotionalism, without prejudice, and without revolution. Historians cannot be revolutionists. They know that it is impossible for any people, in Alfonso Reyes' words, "to live skipping epochs" (*vivir saltando épocas*). The secular pressures of history will ultimately prevail, and changes that are too abruptly undertaken do not solve problems but only create new inequities.

History itself is a record of a long tug-of-war between man's logic and man's experience. All of his efforts at rational living are subsumed in his historical experience. Those who attempt to impose their own dialectical systems upon society, therefore, must reckon with the alarms of the past. Without these echoed warnings their logic can become too logical; it may become a systematic way of going wrong with confidence. Both reason and experience together are needed to produce the fullest logic, the highest pragmatism. History, in other words, supplies its own dialectics.

History is the legislation of the past. The cumulative experiences of mankind may not seem as real as the experiences of any single individual, but they are more conclusive even for that individual than anything in his own experience. This is not to say, however, that the lives of individuals are ruled by a rigid historical determinism, for history is a record of actions by individuals. But in history man only proposes and acts; he does not fix the ultimate pattern.

History is inseparable from chronology. Now, a sense of chronology, like the sense of history itself, is an acquired characteristic. Time as a concept is unfamiliar to very young children and to the senile aged. Not until a child has advanced several years from birth does he begin to differentiate between the present and the past. To him his parents were contemporary with all that happened before he was born, and all times are embraced in the concept of "olden times." The thing that makes a child an ineffective member of society is his inability to see the relatedness of things in time. Similarly the principal factor that makes the senile aged incompetent and unable to contribute to social progress is that they have lost their sense of chronology. The time sequences in their own lives have become meaningless. To them all time is one as they begin to merge with the eternal. The grandmother talks as if her own grandfather and grandmother, her uncles and aunts, are still living on the old farm.

Only mature individuals, therefore, are able to particularize about the past, to see the sequences and consequences in history and to relate them to present living. It is our consciousness of this relatedness between the past and the present that makes us adults. Lacking it we remain half men or children, and our actions both as individuals and as members of society are impulsive, short-range, and blundering.

History may be thought of as a union of memory and intelligence. When we acquaint ourselves with history, when we learn why our predecessors acted as they did, and when we study the outcome of their actions we alert ourselves to all the elements in new situations that may confront us and we face the unpredictable with a greater wealth of experience than we had before. An understanding of the past, explains Ernst Cassirer, "gives us a freer survey of the present and strengthens our responsibility with regard to the future." It frees us to be more vigorously contemporary. History, it is true, may not furnish specific guidance for each daily crisis, yet it will enable us better to meet these crises by enlarging our perspective, by making us wiser. It is a means, concludes George H. Sabine, "by which society is enabled to understand what it is doing, in the light of what it has done and of what it hopes to do."

How difficult it is for a man to view objectively the times in which he lives! Current history is an anomaly, for if it is current it is not history. And yet only by viewing our own times *sub specie aeternitatis* or in the perspective of past and future can we hope to relate ourselves wisely to our world. The historian, if he conceives his function thus, can become, in Friedrich Schlegel's phrase, "a retrospective prophet." If historians are not fulfilling this exalted role today, it is, in part, because they have yielded to the blandishments of political power. History has its political uses, and during the past generation these have been discovered and flagrantly exploited. No more than passing reference needs to be made here to the historians of Germany who prostituted their craft to the Nazi political power or to the historians of Soviet Russia who first exalted Joseph Stalin and then, at the command of his successor, Nikita Khrushchev, obligingly dropped from their histories all mention of the former Russian leader. . . .

"Historians" who thus prostitute their science place themselves in fundamental conflict with historicism, indeed with history itself. They are no longer men thinking. They are only man defending. They push a servile pen. The only coherence which their "history" possesses is imposed upon them by authority, which subordinates originality to conformity, ideas to details, substance to shadow, free inquiry to a new scholasticism. They place history at the service of what they regard as a cause, namely, the preservation of the reputation of men whom their contemporaries call great.

When history is declared to be only what the ruling clique, that is, the bureaucracy in any country, says it is, it ceases to be history in any terms that free men understand. This kind of history becomes only a fiction agreed upon among the principal participants. As the official truth is thus promulgated, history stops. The aim is, in Orwell's words, to "freeze history at a chosen moment." It is only one further step for the historian, who thus selectively construes his facts, to insist that we must only fall in step with history and become completely decisionless before its inexorable futurity.

This is the type of lore that meets the needs of certain societies that lack a written objective history. For example, Pochacuti, the great leader of the completely socialized Inca empire of Peru in the fifteenth century, seeing the need for an official organization of the history of his people and of his royal house, suppressed some of the existing lore, elaborated those parts of it which supported his house, and declared it treason to depart from this official corpus of belief. As the latest chronicler of Incan history, Burr Brundage, tells us, "this falsified Pachacutean view of history is a historical fact of major importance, for it served to steer the course of future events." Thus the history of the nation, continues Brundage, was "totally taken over as a royal prerogative." Upon his coronation an emperor named three or four "bards as his official historians who were to compose and record in lay form each great action of his reign as it occurred. . . . On his death, his successor ordered the totality sung to him and had those he approved added to the canon. Popular history, probably in prose form, there must have been, contradicting in many ways the glorified state presentation, but these were of course driven underground."

History that is thus preserved only by the "official" rememberers is at best a compound of fiction, legend, and myth. As such it can serve as the basis for the propagation of a cult and for the maintenance of tribal solidarity, for it is only the record that the old-timers of the tribe remember or wish to have remembered. They can use the "official" history to influence the current actions of the tribe, remembering only such parts of it as will serve their own immediate ends. By means of this selective history the tribal leaders can control the tribe swaying it in this or that direction, against this or that enemy, behind this or that leader. In the absence of the full historical record the only history that remains is official history—that is, the history that is remembered by those who participated in it and is passed on by them in the form of memoirs.

In more sophisticated societies the pressure to write this type of official history is felt especially by those who are employed as government historians. They enjoy a monopoly of historical sources and can therefore determine what and how much shall be made available to scholars, to the public, and to the formulators of public policy. If the historian employed by government arranges the data of history to suit the prejudices of his employers and does not show the past as it really was, he degenerates into a bureaucratic time-server. He may be competent, industrious, and intelligent, but he always remains thoroughly disciplined and never critical of his superiors. He thus becomes a member of the claque and acquires a vested interest in perpetuating a forced and biased interpretation of history.

He is the "rememberer" who stands behind the man of action to provide historical sanction for his decisions, whether wise or unwise. He shows or at least pretends to show a kind of "protective stupidity," in Orwell's phrase, which will guarantee him both personal security in his job and security for the bureaucratic party of which he is a member. He does not deviate in either opinion or action from official orders, and even when orders are not issued he divines them by a kind of extrasensory perception and obeys them. He agrees that all policy decisions that have been made in the past by his superiors have been perfect decisions and that his bureaucratic masters have a record of complete infallibility. All he must do is dig up the evidence that will sustain their infallibility and suppress that which does not sustain it. As he thus resolves every question in favor of withholding information he ceases to be a historian and reduces his role to that of a public censor.

As a censor he follows the maxim: *éraser l'infame*. When he finds something in history that offends him or his official heroes, he obliterates it. He presents the past in the light of his own purposes or the preoccupations of his own age. If he conspires to perpetuate only the facts that are officially acknowledged, he and his historical craft can be made to serve the same purposes as the official rememberers in primitive societies. He will use history as a means not of seeking and publishing the truth about the past but of establishing and maintaining authority. In any contest between moral integrity and power, he will support the latter and will allow his historical skills to be used as an instrument of power politics. . . .

History, particularly official history, may therefore be used to condition the people to the supposed requirements of a political situation, not to enlighten them. It aims at converting them to an official point of view. The historian's synthesis of the past envisages predicatorily what ought to be in terms of what he says has been. He uses his science to shape the future by selective editing of the past or by perversion and destruction of historical records. He thus reduces history to a single lifetime—his own—and foreshortens the whole vast term of man's experience on this earth. The best that can be said for him is that he has fallen into the rut of a "presentist subjectivism," the worst that he betrays his calling for hire and willfully fails to illustrate the present by showing up its problems in accurate and full perspective. His history then becomes only an apology for state policy. By reason of the suppression and perversion of historical information, the realities of our world vanish in part. As we lose the rationale of our present, we lose also a part of our past, to our own misfortune.

Our scientific age has been made possible by the discovery of the method of the working hypothesis as a substitute for dogma. By this method, scientists formulate conclusions on the basis of all available evidence, and as new evidence appears they scrap their old conclusions in favor of new ones. If the physical scientists had never questioned the Ptolemaic theory of the universe, their science would undoubtedly have disappeared and the atomic age would still perhaps be four hundred years in the future. This method of "dogma eat dogma" has opened up to modern man expanding and seemingly illimitable visions of new truth.

This is a method which history, as one of the sciences—a word which in the literal sense, *sciencia,* means simply knowledge—shares with all the other sciences. Historians cannot afford to be any more satisfied with truths discovered in the past than can the natural scientists. They should not be content simply to repeat traditional ideas but must push beyond the old frontiers into new areas of research and interpretation. For "the truths of history," as Goldwin Albert Smith has written, "are usually wild and leaping things. They do not lie asleep and still when we peer behind the curtain of the night. They are always joined to other truths, many of which we do not understand." A historian who makes an unconditional commitment to a certain set of historical formulas forgets that absolute truth is not found in any one historical work or in any one historical school, or indeed in all of them put together. The reality of life can never be captured or imprisoned in a system.

Historians reject this principle when they base their history not upon the facts but upon their preconceptions. Repudiating their science, they fall back upon the will to believe. They make history an act of faith. Their science then becomes only intuitive and emotional. It moves into the realm of the romantic and becomes doctrinaire, oracular, and intellectually irresponsible. It concerns itself no longer with the meanings of things or even with things themselves but is content to parrot the accepted jargon about things. The genuine historian is distinguished from the historical charlatan by the tentativeness of the conclusions which he holds, for history cannot be dogma. Embalmed truth, in history as in every other science, is falsehood.

History therefore must be a science in perpetual evolution. It must take account of all the hard resilient facts of human experience. It must adapt old experience to new situations and necessarily must be at the same time both destructive and constructive—destructive of outmoded historical concepts and constructive of new patterns of action for the future based upon experience.

The bridge over which history—and indeed all science—moves from the orthodoxy of yesterday to the orthodoxy of tomorrow is known as revisionism. We all acknowledge in our saner moments that no advancement in insight and wisdom is possible unless we continue to call in question and reconsider what we have previously taken for granted. Professor Samuel Eliot Morison, in paying tribute to Edward Channing, observed that "Channing's most striking characteristic as an historian was his ability to wipe his mind clear of preconceived interpretations and theories, even if he had been teaching them all his life; to study every question and period anew, from the sources, and to reach fresh conclusions."

The function of the historian is to be constantly correcting and completing the image of the past. He is concerned not only with what is true in the past but also with what is false. Indeed he does not think in terms of true and false, because he is concerned with everything that has happened in the past, with analyzing and explaining it, and with showing its relatedness to the present. He must be ready to penetrate beneath conventional expressions and disguises. For him no subject is taboo and hence closed to further discussion. To represent history as more dignified than human nature is to tamper with the truth. "The historian," J. R. Pole of University College, London, has written, "has a responsibility to the past, but it is not that of deciding within what limits he can recommend it to the approbation of his readers." . . .

. . . When a historian . . . closes his mind, he makes it his only object to erect a structure that can be admired even though it may not represent reality. It becomes all white, and his critics become all black. He presumes to have imprisoned reality for all time. But in fact he has become the captive of his own myths.

Myth has its uses, and as long as it is believed it may be a powerful instrumentality for governing men. It represents a crystalization of primitive truth and serves as the justification for ritual and cult. But, as soon as it ceases to be believed, the priestcraft who perpetuate it lose their authority, the hero-cult upon which it is based loses its sanctity, and the world of myth is seen to be only an artificial world, a mere make-believe. One of the functions of the true historian is to strip away the falsities of myth and to reveal it as mere myth. He should never conspire to manufacture a myth or to perpetuate it as the truth. . . .

. . . When historians become accomplices to bureaucrats, history becomes a means not of enlightening the people but of keeping them in ignorance.

"The historian who pretends to an independent authority to certify the documents or verify the claims of a government department must be as jealous and importunate as the cad of a detective who has to find the murderer amongst a party of his friends," writes Professor Herbert Butterfield of the University of Cambridge. And, he continues, "if an historian were to say: 'This particular group of documents ought not to be published because it would expose the officials concerned to serious misunderstandings,' then we must answer that he has already thrown in his lot with officialdom—already he is thinking of their own interests rather than ours." Furthermore, he adds, "supposing there are gaps anywhere in the documentation . . . then there should be no limit to the detective work put into the matter and no limit to the precision in the account that is given to historical students."

What is even more serious, Butterfield declares, is the effort of official historians "to lull us to sleep" by telling us that the materials which are withheld "do not matter for purposes of historical reconstruction. Here is a point," he concludes, "that goes to the very basis of historical science." It also goes to the very basis of the principle of the right of the people to know the full truth and to have the information necessary to exert an effective and intelligent control over the officials to whom they have temporarily entrusted the powers of government. After all, public officials are only custodians of the official records. They are not the owners. What will become of our system of government if the facts on which the people must base their decisions are suppressed or distorted and then only a partial record is promulgated by "historians" as the full truth?

It is here, in this spadework of the profession, that the historian working in the official bureaucracy has an immense responsibility. By his selection of the documents revealing the experience of the nation in both its domestic politics and its foreign relations, he can color the historical interpretation of his epoch for generations to come. His responsibility for the coloration that historical writing will take is enormous. . . .

History has a disconcerting way of confronting us when we are least ready to meet her. In the shadows behind every statesman addressing an international conference or affixing his signature to a treaty stands this enigmatic muse. She belongs to no party except the party of truth, and she stands watch serenely while heroes wax and wane.

The past is all we can know, for the future is concealed from us and the knife-edge of the present is too brief to be fully comprehended. The present is in any case unintelligible without the past. But, as the present is determined by the past, it can also be used to determine the past. As we seek to build a whole in the present, we sometimes undertake to work the past into that whole and use it to justify the whole, even though we must distort the past in order to accomplish this result. The only durably satisfactory present that we can fashion, however, must be constructed upon a frank appreciation of the realities of the past. This is to argue not for a canonization of the past but for such an understanding of the past as will illuminate and provide guidance in the present. If the present is made to rest upon only an officially approved past or an ideally conceived past, its foundations are shifting sand. And a future built upon such a present becomes increasingly shaky. An accurate reading of the past, therefore, is an essential precondition to every satisfying present and every successful future.

Past and Present: History and Contemporary Analysis

Allan J. Lichtman and Valerie French

Allan J. Lichtman is professor of history at the American University. He has written *Your Family History: How to Use Oral History, Family Archives, and Public Documents to Discover Your Roots* (1978) and *Prejudice and the Old Politics: The Presidential Election of 1928* (1979). Valerie French (b. 1941) received a Ph.D. in ancient history from the University of California at Los Angeles in 1971 and now teaches at the American University. She helped write a study on the child's influence in ancient Mediterranean civilization. The selection below is from *Historians and the Living Past: The Theory and Practice of Historical Study* (1978).

O ur understanding of the past informs and shapes our view of contemporary life on many levels. The past provides our only source of information for evaluating current affairs and making predictions about the future. Historical knowledge enables us to place our perceptions of the contemporary world into a meaningful context and to discern the cause-and-effect relationships between events that serve as the basis for future expectations. Without such knowledge we would be as bewildered as a quarterback entering the fourth quarter of a football game without knowing the score, the amount of elapsed time, or the successes and failures of plays and players.

More concretely, historical study helps us to understand and criticize decisions made in the realms of journalism, business, and government that critically affect our daily lives. These decisions are usually based, either explicitly or implicitly, upon "lessons of history" drawn from the decision makers' own conceptions of the past. An understanding of history is required either to recognize or to critique the historical analysis that underlies vital policy decisions.

We will illustrate our arguments about the relevance of history by examining a newspaper column on the Nixon pardon by George F. Will, published in the *Washington Post* on September 10, 1974, and a short book by George F. Kennan, *American Diplomacy, 1900–1950*, published in 1952.

Even "instant analysis," like the following article, is permeated with historical argument. Most journalists, especially editorial writers and commentators, constantly use historical arguments to persuade readers of their perspicacity and wisdom. Historical argument is but one of the elements in the skillful journalist's strategic design. He has an arsenal of weapons of persuasion. He can compel the readers' attention with sheer literary brilliance; he can use irony, humor, metaphor, analogy, and other rhetorical figures; he can anticipate his opposition's arguments and deflate them; and, finally, he can draw upon the past as he reconstructs it to buttress his own opinion of current affairs.

WHO HAS ERODED RESPECT FOR LAW
George F. Will

"Man," said Robert Louis Stevenson, "is a creature who lives not by bread alone but principally by catchwords." Americans will have to eat more bread now that President Ford has drained the nutritional value from the catchwords about "equal justice under law."

Those words are chiseled deep in stone over the portico of the Supreme Court building. Rather than try to erase them Mr. Ford should just chisel a big asterisk next to them. Then he should find a surface large enough and chisel on it all the exceptions to that rule.

It is an iron law of politics that when a politician intones support for a principle, he is about to make an exception to that principle for the benefit of a friend. ("I revere the free enterprise system, but the farmers in my district need this subsidy because. . . .") That is why an alert citizen listening to Mr. Ford's statement about pardoning Mr. Nixon knew what was coming when Mr. Ford sailed into the part about believing in "equal justice, for all Americans, whatever their station or former station."

That principle is not the only casualty of Mr. Ford's pardon for Mr. Nixon. The English Muffin Theory of History is now just another theory killed by a fact.

The theory was that a President who toasts his own English muffins for breakfast is somehow different from the general cut of politicians. The lethal fact is that Mr. Ford now has demonstrated that he is just one of the boys: he doesn't mean what he says.

Mr. Ford said he would let the judicial process work regarding Mr. Nixon. Two weeks later, when aborting the judicial process, Mr. Ford said, "I deeply believe in equal justice," etc. Mr. Nixon always said the people could not stand an impeachment process. Mr. Ford says the people could not stand a trial of a former President: it would shatter "domestic tranquility." Amazing, you think, how solicitous our leaders are about our peace of mind? But it is not really amazing when a politician decides that people cannot endure whatever he thinks is not in his interest to let happen.

In fact, Mr. Ford has done for Mr. Nixon what Mr. Nixon never quite mustered the gall to do for Lt. William Calley, the officer convicted on charges stemming from the My Lai massacre. By pardoning Mr. Nixon, Mr. Ford has ingratiated himself with an intense minority (Nixon bitter-enders) whom Mr. Ford evidently considers important to his political base.

We judge a politician, at least in part, by his political base, and by what he will do to curry favor with it. We also judge a politician by his ability to get something in exchange for something. Mr. Ford either did not seek or could not get Mr. Nixon to admit, in exchange for the pardon, that he was guilty of any of what Ford gingerly refers to as the "allegations and accusations" against him. All Mr. Nixon says is that he regrets not acting "more decisively" about Watergate and he has never admitted to and will never admit to anything worse than indecision. Of course, the June 23, 1972, tape shows that he acted decisively to obstruct justice.

Mr. Ford seems to think Mr. Nixon is a sociological not a legal problem. According to Mr. Ford a Nixon trial, like some social condition, might stir "ugly passions." Mr. Ford plunges through the looking glass to argue dizzily, that "the credibility of our free institutions" would be "challenged at home and abroad" if our free judicial institutions were allowed to work.

Mr. Ford may, as he says, have "the constitutional power to firmly shut and seal" the Watergate "book." But that does not mean that it was right for him to hastily slam the book shut before we could read it. That is what he did by rushing to prevent a judicial examination of Mr. Nixon's conduct, and by giving Mr. Nixon custody of the best evidence about Mr. Nixon's conduct.

Mr. Ford's motives no doubt included a desire to be compassionate, and a concern for Mr. Nixon's health. But in government effects and appearances can be as important as motives. And whether or not it was Mr. Ford's intention, the effect of his precipitate action appears rather like the effect of what used to be called, in less polite times, a cover-up.*

Even a cursory inspection of Will's article reveals that his analysis of President Ford's decision to pardon Richard Nixon rests on a series of historical assumptions and assertions. A closer scrutiny further discloses that many of the claims that Will puts forth so lightly actually involve interpretations of the past that are both complex and controversial. Some of these claims are obviously straw men, set up by Will merely to be knocked down. Others he presents as basic truths about the behavior and beliefs of the American people. Will's own interpretive judgments are sometimes identified, sometimes camouflaged with colorful language. Without clear distinctions, Will refers both to short-term historical trends and to the long run. Will's historical references form an essential component of his persuasive strategy; they enable him to criticize simultaneously the pardon decision, President Ford, the "general cut of politicians," and the American public.

The most notable historical argument included in Will's column is, of course, the "English Muffin Theory of History"—that "a President who toasts his own English muffins for breakfast is somehow different from the general cut of politicians." This homey theory of political life, Will argues, has been disproved by Ford's pardon, becoming "just another theory killed by a fact." Yet Will's message is not nearly as simple as it appears. Will uses the theory and its refutation to classify Ford as just another self-serving politician and to underscore the naiveté of public opinion. The "English Muffin Theory of History" rests on several important assumptions about American political life. First, the theory assumes that politicians generally require the services of others to avoid the mundane tasks that dominate the everyday lives of most of their constituents. Second, it assumes that a politician humble enough to perform such chores for himself is somehow different from most of his brethren. Third, the Muffin theory rests upon the premise that, prior to Ford's pardon of Nixon, most Americans believed in the first two assumptions.

---

*Editorial by George F. Will, *Washington Post*, copyright © 1974 by Washington Post Writers Group. Reprinted by permission.

Fourth, it assumes that, because of Ford's pardon, the second assumption is no longer held as valid. Fifth, the argument assumes that the pardon exemplifies the general conduct of politicians.

But, as already noted, Will's own assertions about the "English Muffin Theory" also rest upon dubious assumptions about the logic of historical inquiry. First, his own argument implies that a generalization about human behavior and belief can be disproved by a single contrary example—a rather odd reversal of the old adage that "the exception proves the rule." Second, Will suggests a fundamental distinction between a "theory" and a "fact." Facts, it appears, are what debunk theories. . . .

Will also sets up and then knocks down several other generally held beliefs about the nature of man. He begins his piece with Robert Louis Stevenson's wry observation that man "lives not by bread alone but principally by catch-words." Stevenson, of course, was playing on Jesus's saying that man cannot survive solely on physical nourishment but requires love and spirituality as well. Stevenson's parody suggests that the complement of mere existence is neither love nor spirit but empty slogans. By adding this ironic twist to his own argument, Will insinuates that long before Ford's pardon of Nixon, the concept of "equal justice under law"—the spiritual basis of the American legal system—had become more a slogan than a reality. He also suggests that Ford actually performed a public service by puncturing the soap bubble of our illusions.

The paragraph about bread and catchwords is followed by another "Willian" dictum: "It is an iron law of politics that when a politician intones support for a principle, he is about to make an exception to that principle for the benefit of a friend." Supposedly, this is another empirical statement, based on past experience, about the behavior of politicians. The "iron law" explicitly connects knowledge of the past to prediction of the future. Any "alert citizen" with an awareness of political history should easily have been able to predict President Ford's decision. Will's iron law also adds to the cynicism about human motivation that he first suggests by quoting Stevenson and then sustains throughout his article. For example, Will asserts that a politician generally "decides that people cannot endure whatever [the politician] thinks it is not in his interest to let happen." Thus he suggests that politicians have traditionally manipulated John Q. Citizen by misrepresenting attempts to promote their own selfish interests as selfless service for the public good.

Will employs one explicitly historical analogy, the Lieutenant Calley case, to buttress his argument about the pardon and puts it to particularly effective strategic use. By comparing the pardon granted Nixon to the aborted pardon for the convicted mass murderer, Will tars Ford with guilt by association. He also uses the Calley analogy to interpret the motivations not only of Nixon but of Ford as well. By implying that Nixon really wanted to pardon Calley but, in the face of political opposition, never mustered the courage (or gall) to do so, Will underscores the idea that Ford's decision to pardon Nixon rested upon political considerations, rather than on notions of justice or national interest.

Will further suggests that, in contrast to the Calley pardon, the Nixon pardon "drained the nutritional value from the catchwords about 'equal justice under law.' " This contention presupposes, however, that prior to the pardon, these catchwords truly reflected public sentiment about the American legal system. It further assumes that Ford's action (even though characteristic of the "general cut of politicians") so violated the popular view as to reorient fundamentally our thinking about "equal justice" in America.

Will concludes his article by linking Ford's action to an ongoing historical trend—a continuing cover-up of the Watergate scandals, a tendency of government officials to hide their actions from public scrutiny. However, Will's language here is cagey; perhaps he means to suggest that Ford knowingly aided the cover-up or perhaps that his actions simply created the appearance of complicity. Will's conclusion also heightens the tension that he has deliberately created between two seemingly contradictory ideas: first, that the Nixon pardon was a gross exception to the sacred principle of "equal justice," and second, that this pardon was consistent with the normal behavior of American political leaders.

Although Will's commentary clearly rests in part upon his understanding of the past, he rarely makes the premises of his historical arguments explicit. His conclusions often represent only the final step in a complex chain of implicitly historical reasoning that the reader must dig out on his own. On the other hand, Will does not pose as the impartial scholar interested only in "objective" truth. In his column, history is subservient to political commentary; he uses the past selectively as an instrument for criticizing Ford's decision to pardon Richard Nixon. It comes as no surprise, therefore, that Will the columnist, yet implicitly the historian, devotes little space to evidence that would lend credibility to his historical interpretations (except for a reference to the White House tape of June 23, 1972, the famous "smoking pistol" that decisively influenced the House Judiciary Committee's vote to recommend impeachment).

The reader who seeks to evaluate the use of history in contemporary journalism thus bears a heavy responsibility. He must be able to detect an author's historical propositions and their role in his strategic design. He must also reconstruct the implicit logic of arguments about the past and assess their empirical accuracy. Unless he is content to be snared by the commentator's skills, the reader must be prepared to deploy his own arsenal of analytic weaponry.

George F. Kennan's *American Diplomacy, 1900–1950*, although offered as a study in diplomatic history, is also a far-reaching commentary on the contemporary conduct of foreign affairs. Kennan views American diplomacy during the first half of the twentieth century as a series of well intended initiatives that failed. He attempts to isolate the factors responsible for American inability to cope with world affairs and to use these findings as the basis for proposed changes in both the ideology and institutions of foreign policy in the United States. Indeed, Kennan does not hesitate to discuss the past as it really was, the past as it might have been, and the future as it ought to be. For virtually every episode within the scope of his study, he details the policies followed by American diplomats, suggests the course they should have followed, and draws a moral for the guidance of policymakers in his own time.

Kennan locates the fatal flaw of American diplomacy in a characteristic which had been exalted as a virtue by most previous commentators. He indicts American statesmen, not for lack of intelligence, training, or integrity, but for a proclivity to conduct foreign policy on the basis of moral and legal principles. This proclivity, he claims, did not result from some peculiarity of the foreign policy establishment, but was "deeply rooted in the national consciousness." Unfortunately, the "moralistic-legalistic" approach to international relations contradicted the best interests of the nation and the goal of world harmony. Embedded within the structure of Kennan's historical arguments are several distinct criticisms of a diplomacy that rests on law and morality. The validity of these criticisms, however, depends upon the historical examples that are the focus of Kennan's narrative.

First, Kennan suggests that the application of law and morality to international affairs falsely assumes that nations within the world community behave like individuals within a single nation-state. Whereas individuals generally experience internal pressure to follow the laws and customs of a national culture, leaders feel no such compulsion to follow the rules of international politics. Statesmen do not subordinate the perceived interests of their nation to the requirements of international laws and compacts. Moral principles and codes of agreement are respected only insofar as they promote the already established goals of national policy. Moreover, international agreements, unlike those within a single nation, cannot be enforced with meaningful sanctions. For example, Kennan criticized America's Open Door policy in China, an attempt in 1899 and 1900 to gain international agreement on the principle that all nations should have access to trade and commerce in China, and that the political integrity of China should be respected. Kennan maintains that the Open Door policy had no practical effect on world affairs; foreign diplomats were willing to pay only lip service to a vague, moral principle that included no enforcement mechanisms. He further intimates that this policy was counterproductive, because rival nations suspected that it was merely a cloak for sinister motives on the part of the United States. Similarly, the Open Door policy contributed to the spread of anti-American sentiment since these nations also felt that American diplomats were asking them to sacrifice their vital interests without giving up or risking anything in return.

Second, Kennan believes that considerations of law and morality have genuine meaning only within cultures that share common legal systems and traditions. Moral precepts cannot be applied indiscriminately to diverse nations and peoples, and policymakers cannot assume that their own ethical systems are equally applicable to alien cultures. Indeed, the attempt to impose nationally conditioned standards of law and morality upon the international community leads to moral perversity, as lives, property, and goodwill are squandered in a futile attempt to alter national traditions and institutions. Kennan argues, for example, that American statesmen after World War I made the great mistake of indulging in "the colossal conceit of thinking that you could suddenly make international life into what you believed to be your own image." They ignored the realities "that a study of the past would suggest" and impudently sought to coerce the defeated Germans into restructuring their traditional institutions. This self-defeating policy served only to plunge Germany into social chaos and to leave her bitter, disillusioned, and thirsting for revenge.

Third, and most important, Kennan maintains that the attempt to conduct foreign affairs according to legal and moral principles leads to the disastrous policies of total war and unconditional surrender. If a nation resorts to force, not to secure a limited, well-defined political objective, but to rectify violations of law or morality, then warfare becomes a crusade, aimed at eradicating evil by any means available. Similarly, when a nation is aroused to undertake a great moral crusade, diplomats cannot easily bargain or compromise with the enemy—the goal of total war is unconditional surrender. Both World War I and World War II were total wars in which the victorious powers demanded the unconditional surrender of their enemies. In both cases, these misguided policies resulted in unnecessary death and destruction and jeopardized the prospects for lasting peace. Kennan emphasizes that Americans need to recognize the folly of using force to alter the nature of foreign regimes or to create a purified world order.

If American statesmen were preoccupied for a half century with legal and moral questions, Kennan suggests that they should have been preoccupied with determining the national interest of the United States. Only a foreign policy designed to preserve and protect America's vital interests would have avoided the contradictions of the moralistic-legalistic approach and responded to the realities of international affairs. Most important to the maintenance of America's security was the preservation of a balance of power among the industrialized nations of the world. By balance of power, Kennan means a situation in which no single nation or tightly aligned group of nations can dominate the rest of the civilized world. War is an almost inevitable result of serious breakdowns in the balance of power. Ironically, the result of both World War I and World War II was to disrupt the balance of power and sow the seeds of a new conflict. Kennan argues that, after World War I, Germany emerged as the strongest, most unified state in the middle of Europe. Germany was flanked on the East by Soviet Russia, whose interests were antithetical to those of the western democracies, and on the West by Britain and France, whose strength had been sapped by the exertions of world conflict. The effect of World War II was to eliminate any effective counter-force to the power of a resurgent Russia, either in Europe or the Far East.

According to Kennan, the failure of American diplomacy between 1900 and 1950 can be rectified only by fundamental changes in the future conduct of American foreign policy. Policymakers must never let moral and legal principles control decisions about war and peace. Warfare can be justified only by a hardheaded analysis of America's security interests. Similarly, American statesmen must recognize that warfare need not be total, and that surrender need not be unconditional. Rather, force can be used in a limited and controlled fashion to help maintain the international balance of power and protect the national interest.

Kennan further suggests that the United States should not blindly oscillate between periods of isolation and total involvement in world affairs. To a great extent, the rhythm of American foreign policy is determined by military strength. A decision to disarm and demobilize after the catharsis of total war would not only restrict America's ability to influence international events, but would also mean that the nation must be summoned to a new crusade before adequate rearmament could take place. Thus America must maintain her military strength even in time of peace and should promote her national interests through active participation in foreign affairs.

Kennan believes that American diplomats should be less responsive to the erratic swings of public opinion and more responsive to the balanced judgment of professionals. He maintains that subservience to popular whims has precluded a rational approach to foreign policy; he fears that ordinary citizens will never be able to transcend their "emotional" and "subjective" reaction to world events. Only an elite corps of professionals would have the knowledge, experience, and detachment to guide the foreign policy of the United States rationally and objectively.

In the final sections of his book, Kennan sketches the broad outlines of a realistic approach to Soviet-American relations, based upon the experience of both nations. The lesson that Kennan draws from Russian history is that the Communist regime will necessarily remain hostile to the United States and other western democracies. The destruction of all effective internal opposition has compelled Russian leaders to justify their dictatorship by stressing the menace of foreign opposition. But, despite their belief in the ultimate self-destruction of capitalism, the Soviets need not engage in dangerous military confrontations. Rather, they can afford to be patient, while relentless. Moreover, since Communist leaders are not bound by the fetters of public opinion, they are able to employ whichever tactical maneuvers appear most suitable at a particular time and to abandon them when circumstances change.

Faced with these grim facts, Kennan believes that the United States can no longer afford the luxury of amateur diplomacy based on fuzzy moral principles. He proposes the policy of containment as a realistic alternative to either war or capitulation. This policy can thwart the expansion of Communism without provoking the enemy into armed conflict. Expert diagnosticians of world affairs can contain "Soviet pressure against the free institutions of the western world . . . by the adroit and vigilant application of counterforce at a series of constantly shifting geographical and political points, corresponding to the shifts and maneuvers of Soviet policy." Under the direction of professionals, the policy of containment cannot "be charmed or talked out of existence," and in the long run, may lead to the internal destruction of the Soviet regime.

Kennan's book is especially important for contemporary minded students of American diplomacy, because the views that he expressed in 1952 were to a large extent adopted by American policymakers. National leaders have seen in the policy of containment as articulated by Kennan an acceptable middle ground between the extremes of appeasement and nuclear war. Indeed, the so-called domino theory—that a Communist takeover in one nation would lead to the toppling of neighboring governments—is but an extension of Kennan's ideas on containment. Similarly, the United States firmly embraced the notion that she could afford neither military demobilization nor isolation from the quarrels of foreign nations. Since 1950, the United States has maintained a vast military establishment and has actively defended its interests in far-flung corners of the globe. No conflict seemed too trivial for American involvement, no area of the world too remote or primitive. The United States has also followed Kennan's dictum regarding the use of force for the achievement of limited political objectives. The covert operations of the CIA, the American sponsored insurrections in Cuba and Guatemala, and the military interventions in the Dominican Republic and Vietnam, all exemplify the policy of limited war. Yet policymakers also seem to have heeded Kennan's warnings about the inability of the public rationally to evaluate foreign policy initiatives; America's military operations, both direct and indirect, are invariably justified to the American people on the basis of the very legal and moral principles scorned by hardheaded statesmen. The American foreign service has also become far more professionalized in the years following World War II. The professional staff of the State Department and other agencies involved in foreign affairs has increased at a fantastic rate; and expert analysts, using the best available information and technology, were intimately involved in the planning of such major enterprises as the Bay of Pigs invasion and the Vietnam War.

All of Kennan's prescriptions for the conduct of diplomacy evolve from his interpretations of past events. Kennan's plans for the future cannot be separated from his vision of the past. Therefore, to the extent that his historical arguments are misguided, his policy recommendations lose their rationale.

Many of Kennan's ideas about American diplomatic history have been disputed by other reputable scholars. While it is beyond the scope of this chapter either to describe competing interpretations in detail or to resolve any of the historical issues involved, we can set forth some of the more important objections to Kennan's views. Historians have challenged the fundamental thesis of *American Diplomacy*—that policymakers have been influenced primarily by moral and legal precepts. For example, a major school of thought, the "revisionists," has emphasized that American diplomats in the twentieth century have consistently sought to advance the economic interests of American business. In this view, the federal government has operated hand in glove with American corporations in an effort to extend the economic and political influence of the United States. "Revisionist" scholars have reinterpreted every one of the episodes discussed by Kennan and have attributed misguided policy to entirely different causes. American leaders do not emerge from the works of revisionist history as naive moralists, disdainful of power politics. Instead, they appear to be shrewd and calculating politicians, rationally pursuing a set of reasonably well-defined economic and political objectives. In contrast to Kennan's recommendations, the revisionist version of American diplomatic history would suggest that the United States should reduce its overseas commitments, slash defense spending, cease intervening in the affairs of foreign nations, seek mutual accommodations with Communist states, downgrade the role of foreign policy experts, and provide the American public the information necessary for an intelligent contribution to the policymaking process.

Kennan's historical analysis is also vulnerable to other substantive objections. Historians have questioned whether public opinion actually has restricted the flexibility of American foreign policy. They have suggested, for example, that leaders have been responsive only to the articulated opinions of a very small group of prominent citizens, and that the general public has been willing to endorse virtually any vigorous presidential initiative in the realm of international affairs. Scholars have also disputed Kennan's sanguine assessment of a diplomacy directed by professionally trained authorities. Researchers have found that experts have tended to become rigidly committed to particular viewpoints and disinclined to change policies in which they have vested personal interests. Professionals have not been responsive either to new ideas or to changing circumstances. Similarly, experts are often so preoccupied with their own areas of expertise that they ignore the broader context of policy decisions. Historians with a general grasp of world history have also suggested that it is extraordinarily difficult to wage a carefully controlled, limited war, and that armed conflict in pursuit of practical objectives is not necessarily more humane than conflict based on law or morality. They have further pointed out that, over the long-term, the maintenance of a balance of power among nations has not proved to be an effective means of avoiding war.

The logic as well as the substance of Kennan's work raises questions that must be considered by the serious reader. Kennan's analysis of diplomatic history rests on the assumption that it is possible to separate considerations of morality and national interest. Yet judgments of what is and is not in the national interest, no less than judgments of what is moral or immoral, depend upon the system of values being applied. These values determine the individual's view of what "ought to be," an essential component of any judgment about goals or objectives. For example, the different value systems of Barry Goldwater and George McGovern produce very different opinions about what constitutes the national interest. Moreover, Ken-

nan's own work is interlaced with moral judgments about international affairs. He morally condemns the ideologies of both Communism and Fascism as well as the specific regimes established by
Adolf Hitler in Germany and Joseph Stalin in Russia. He is morally
committed to the Judeo-Christian tradition and, despite some trep-
idations, to the institutions of American democracy.

Kennan's work also presupposes the existence of an "objective"
reality independent of the individual observer. Wise and knowledgeable statesmen should be able to discover this reality and guide their
policy decision accordingly. Yet most thinkers would agree that our
interpretation of the outside world is a function of both external
information and the preconceptions we bring to that information.
Individuals with different ways of looking at the world might draw
different conclusions from the same data; in other words, there are
no independent criteria for deciding which conclusions are right and
which are wrong. . . .

The works of Will and Kennan provide striking examples of present minded authors unabashedly using history to understand contemporary issues. Moreover, the disputes engendered by Kennan's
analysis particularly point to the desirability of having a firm basis
for evaluating historical arguments. Reputable scholars have contended that Kennan's description of how diplomats made decisions
on moral and legalistic grounds is not credible; that his view of the
influence of American public opinion on foreign policy decisions is
not sound; that his assessment of the abilities of specially trained
experts is overly optimistic; that a balance of power among nations
does not insure against war; and that it is not possible to distinguish
neatly between national interest and morality.

History and the Future

oes history allow us to predict or at least anticipate the future? Can it prepare us to build a better tomorrow? Students of the past have differing opinions on these questions, but most agree that a proper understanding of history is essential to constructing a sound future. The English historian Arthur Marwick believed history to be "a part of man's broad attack upon what is not yet known," and the American historian Charles Beard wrote that "all efforts . . . to guess the trends of the future . . . require some penetration into the depths of history."[1]

Many of the writers in this volume have expressed thoughts on the relationship between past and future. Nevins, for example, believed that the immediate future is illuminated by the past. Leff declared that history can make us better prepared to meet the unexpected and that it assists us to understand "what is indispensable to men." Gallie maintained that studying the past, like practicing games of skill, helps us to meet the problems of the future with increased confidence. On the surface Trevelyan appeared more pessimistic when he argued that "history cannot prophesy the future; it cannot supply a set of invariably applicable laws for the guidance of politicians; it cannot show, by the deductions of historical analogy, which side is the right in any quarrel of our own day." But, Trevelyan continued, the study of the past is important to the future because "it can mould the mind itself into the capability of understanding great affairs and sympathising with other men," and it can allow us to dimly perceive "the form of what we should be."

The writings in this section also suggest that history is important to our preparation for the future, but they tell us that accurate prediction based on the past is always difficult and frequently impossible. Barbara Tuchman is perhaps most pessimistic. She doubts that history will ever allow us to predict or even anticipate the future because of that "Unknowable Variable," human nature.

Even if Tuchman is correct, though, there can be little doubt that the past helps to shape the future. One cannot plan for the future without some reference to previous events. We are constantly influenced by what we perceive to be the lessons of the past, and often those "lessons" are put in the form of historical analogies which reflect superficial thinking.[2] We should remember the words of James Bryce, who wrote in *The American Commonwealth* (1888) that "the chief practical use of history is to deliver us from plausible historical analogies."

Some of the following essays examine analogies. George O. Kent shows how they intrude upon our lives, influence our plans, and perhaps determine what is yet to come. In this age of mass propaganda, we must guard against those who would misappropriate history. Arthur Schlesinger, Jr., also notes the uses and inadequacies of historical analogies, but he is more optimistic about predicting the future than Tuchman. He admits that Clio cannot answer questions at short range with confidence, but history does make long-term, large-scale prediction more likely.

We must not assume that there are no lessons to be learned from history. Rather, we should recognize, as Lester Stephens suggests, that most such lessons have limitations which are often misunderstood. This lack of understanding reduces the chances of accurate forecasting. Although history helps us to anticipate the future, Stephens likens prediction to "shooting an arrow at a distant target in a large field at twilight."

Perhaps this is but another way of reiterating a central point, namely, that there are few, if any, *simple* lessons to be learned from the past. It may be, as Nevins said, that "history is the sextant of states" without which we "would be lost in confusion."[3] Often, though, the past may be nothing more than a lantern on the stern of a ship, dimly lighting the route already traveled. Whatever Clio's nature, she is frequently the best, and sometimes the only, guide we have to chart our course for the future.

References

1. Arthur Marwick, *The Nature of History* (New York: Alfred A. Knopf, 1971), 10–11; and Charles Beard, *The Nature of the Social Sciences* (New York: Scribner's, 1934), 69.

2. Pardon E. Tillinghast writes that "there is . . . no way of looking at the future without using analogies from the past." See Tillinghast, *The Specious Past: Historians and Others* (Reading, Mass.: Addison-Wesley, 1972), 51.

3. See Nevins's essay in this volume.

Is History a Guide to the Future?

Barbara W. Tuchman

Barbara W. Tuchman (b. 1912) is a well-known writer whose books on history have had a wide audience. Her works include *Bible and Sword* (1956), *The Zimmermann Telegram* (1958), *The Guns of August* (1962), *The Proud Tower* (1966), *Stilwell and the American Experience in China* (1971), *Notes from China* (1972), and *A Distant Mirror: The Calamitous Fourteenth Century* (1978). The following selection was originally given as an address to the Chicago Historical Society in October 1966 and reprinted in Tuchman's *Practicing History* (1981).

*T*he commonest question asked of historians by laymen is whether history serves a purpose. Is it useful? Can we learn from the lessons of history?

When people want history to be utilitarian and teach us lessons, that means they also want to be sure that it meets scientific standards. This, in my opinion, it cannot do, for reasons which I will come to in a moment. . . .

If history were a science, we should be able to get a grip on her, learn her ways, establish her patterns, know what will happen tomorrow. Why is it that we cannot? The answer lies in what I call the Unknowable Variable—namely, man. Human beings are always and finally the subject of history. History is the record of human behavior, the most fascinating subject of all, but illogical and so crammed with an unlimited number of variables that it is not susceptible of the scientific method nor of systematizing.

I say this bravely, even in the midst of the electronic age when computers are already chewing at the skirts of history in the process called Quantification. Applied to history, quantification, I believe, has its limits. It depends on a method called "data manipulation," which means that the facts, or data, of the historical past—that is, of human behavior—are manipulated into named categories so that they can be programmed into computers. Out comes—hopefully—a pattern. I can only tell you that for history "data manipulation" is a built-in invalidator, because to the degree that you manipulate your data to suit some extraneous requirement, in this case the requirements of the machine, to that degree your results will be suspect—and run the risk of being invalid. Everything depends on the naming of the categories and the assigning of facts to them, and this depends on the quantifier's individual judgment at the very base of the process. The categories are not revealed doctrine nor are the results scientific truth.

The hope for quantification, presumably, is that by processing a vast quantity of material far beyond the capacity of the individual to encompass, it can bring to light and establish reliable patterns. That remains to be seen, but I am not optimistic. History has a way of escaping attempts to imprison it in patterns. Moreover, one of its basic data is the human soul. The conventional historian, at least the one concerned with truth, not propaganda, will try honestly to let his "data" speak for themselves, but data which are shut up in prearranged boxes are helpless. Their nuances have no voice. They must carry one fixed meaning or another and weight the result accordingly. For instance, in a quantification study of the origins of World War I which I have seen, the operators have divided all the diplomatic documents, messages, and utterances of the July crisis into categories labeled "hostility," "friendship," "frustration," "satisfaction," and so on, with each statement rated for intensity on a scale from one to nine, including fractions. But no pre-established categories could match all the private character traits and public pressures variously operating on the nervous monarchs and ministers who were involved. The massive effort that went into this study brought forth a mouse—the less than startling conclusion that the likelihood of war increased in proportion to the rise in hostility of the messages.

Quantification is really only a new approach to the old persistent effort to make history fit a pattern, but *reliable* patterns, or what are otherwise called the lessons of history, remain elusive.

For instance, suppose Woodrow Wilson had not been President of the United States in 1914 but instead Theodore Roosevelt, who had been his opponent in the election of 1912. Had that been the case, America might have entered the war much earlier, perhaps at the time of the *Lusitania* in 1915, with possible shortening of the war and incalculable effects on history. Well, it happens that among the Anarchists in my book *The Proud Tower* is an obscure Italian named Miguel Angiolillo, whom nobody remembers but who shot dead Premier Canovas of Spain in 1897. Canovas was a strong man who was just about to succeed in quelling the rebels in Cuba when he was assassinated. Had he lived, there might have been no extended Cuban insurrection for Americans to get excited about, no Spanish-American War, no San Juan Hill, no Rough Riders, no Vice-Presidency for Theodore Roosevelt to enable him to succeed when another accident, another Anarchist, another unpredictable human being, killed McKinley. If Theodore had never been President, there would have been no third party in 1912 to split the Republicans, and Woodrow Wilson would not have been elected. The speculations from that point on are limitless. To me it is comforting rather than otherwise to feel that history is determined by the illogical human record and not by large immutable scientific laws beyond our power to deflect.

I know very little (a euphemism for "nothing") about laboratory science, but I have the impression that conclusions are supposed to be logical; that is, from a given set of circumstances a predictable result should follow. The trouble is that in human behavior and history it is impossible to isolate or repeat a given set of circumstances. Complex human acts cannot be either reproduced or deliberately initiated—or counted upon like the phenomena of nature. The sun comes up every day. Tides are so obedient to schedule that a timetable for them can be printed like that for trains, though more reliable. In fact, tides and trains sharply illustrate my point: One depends on the moon and is certain; the other depends on man and is uncertain.

In the absence of dependable recurring circumstance, too much confidence cannot be placed on the lessons of history.

There *are* lessons, of course, and when people speak of learning from them, they have in mind, I think, two ways of applying past experience: One is to enable us to avoid past mistakes and to manage better in similar circumstances next time; the other is to enable us to anticipate a future course of events. . . . To manage better next time is within our means; to anticipate does not seem to be.

World War II, for example, with the experience of the previous war as an awful lesson, was certainly conducted, once we got into it, more intelligently than World War I. Getting into it was another matter. When it was important to anticipate the course of events, Americans somehow failed to apply the right lesson. Pearl Harbor is the classic example of failure to learn from history. From hindsight we now know that what we should have anticipated was a surprise attack by Japan in the midst of negotiations. Merely because this was dishonorable, did that make it unthinkable? Hardly. It was exactly the procedure Japan had adopted in 1904 when she opened the Russo-Japanese War by surprise attack on the Russian fleet at Port Arthur.

In addition we had every possible physical indication. We had broken the Japanese code, we had warnings on radar, we had a constant flow of accurate intelligence. What failed? Not information but *judgment*. We had all the evidence and refused to interpret it correctly, just as the Germans in 1944 refused to believe the evidence of a landing in Normandy. Men will not believe what does not fit in with their plans or suit their prearrangements. The flaw in all military intelligence, whether twenty or fifty or one hundred percent accurate, is that it is no better than the judgment of its interpreters, and this judgment is the product of a mass of individual, social, and political biases, prejudgments, and wishful thinkings; in short, it is human and therefore fallible. If man can break the Japanese code and yet not believe what it tells him, how can he be expected to learn from the lessons of history? . . .

Once long ago when the eternal verities seemed clear—that is, during the Spanish Civil War—I thought the lessons of history were unmistakable. It appeared obvious beyond dispute that if fascism under Franco won, Spain in the foreshadowed European war would become a base for Hitler and Mussolini, the Mediterranean would become an Italian lake, Britain would lose Gibraltar and be cut off from her empire east of Suez. The peril was plain, the logic of the thing implacable, every sensible person saw it, and I, just out of college, wrote a small book published in England to point it up, all drawn from the analogy of history. The book showed how, throughout the eighteenth and nineteenth centuries, Britain had consistently interposed herself against the gaining of undue influence over Spain by whatever power dominated the continent. The affair of the Spanish marriages, the campaigns of Wellington, the policies of Castlereagh, Canning, and Palmerston all were directed toward the same objective: The strongest continental power must be prevented from controlling Spain. My treatise was, I thought, very artful and very telling. It did not refer to the then current struggle, but let the past speak for itself and make the argument. It was an irrefutable one—until history refuted it. Franco, assisted by Hitler and Mussolini, *did* win, European war *did* follow, yet unaccountably Spain remained neutral—at least nominally. Gibraltar did not fall, the portals of the Mediterranean did *not* close. I, not to mention all the other "premature" anti-fascists, as we were called, while morally right about the general danger of fascism, had been wrong about a particular outcome. The lessons of history I had so carefully set forth simply did not operate. History misbehaved.

Pearl Harbor and Spain demonstrate two things: One, that man fails to profit from the lessons of history because his prejudgments prevent him from drawing the indicated conclusions; and, two, that history will often capriciously take a different direction from that in which her lessons point. Herein lies the flaw in systems of history. . . .

Theories of history go in vogues which, as is the nature of vogues, soon fade and give place to new ones. Yet this fails to discourage the systematizers. They believe as firmly in this year's as last year's, for, as Isaiah Berlin says, the "obstinate craving for unity and symmetry at the expense of experience" is always with us. When I grew up, the economic interpretation of history, as formulated with stunning impact by Charles Beard, was the new gospel—as incontrovertible as if it had been revealed to Beard in a burning bush. Even to question that financial interests motivated our Founding Fathers in the separation from Britain, or that equally mercenary considerations decided our entrance into the First World War, was to convict oneself of the utmost naïveté. Yet lately the fashionable—indeed, what appears to be the required—exercise among historians has been jumping on Beard with both feet. He and the considerable body of his followers who added to his system and built it up into a dogma capable of covering any historical situation have been knocked about, analyzed, dissected, and thoroughly disposed of. Presently the historical establishment has moved on to dispose of Frederick Jackson Turner and his theory of the Frontier. I do not know what the new explanation is, but I am sure there must be some thesis, for, as one academic historian recently ruled, the writing of history requires a "large organizing idea."

I visualize the "large organizing idea" as one of those iron chain mats pulled behind by a tractor to smooth over a plowed field. I see the professor climbing up on the tractor seat and away he goes, pulling behind his large organizing idea over the bumps and furrows of history until he has smoothed it out to a nice, neat, organized surface—in other words, into a system.

The human being—you, I, or Napoleon—is unreliable as a scientific factor. In combination of personality, circumstance, and historical moment, each man is a package of variables impossible to duplicate. His birth, his parents, his siblings, his food, his home, his school, his economic and social status, his first job, his first girl, and the variables inherent in all of these, make up that mysterious compendium, personality—which then combines with another set of variables: country, climate, time, and historical circumstance. Is it likely, then, that all these elements will meet again in their exact proportions to reproduce a Moses, or Hitler, or De Gaulle, or for that matter Lee Harvey Oswald, the man who killed Kennedy?

So long as man remains the Unknowable Variable—and I see no immediate prospect of his ever being pinned down in every facet of his infinite variety—I do not see how his actions can be usefully programmed and quantified. The eager electronic optimists will go on chopping up man's past behavior into the thousands of little definable segments which they call Input, and the machine will whirr and buzz and flash its lights and in no time at all give back Output. But will Output be dependable? I would lay ten to one that history will pay no more attention to Output than it did to Karl Marx. It will still need historians. Electronics will have its uses, but it will not, I am confident, transform historians into button-pushers or history into a system.

Clio the Tyrant:
Historical Analogies
and the Meaning of History

George O. Kent

George O. Kent (b. 1919) has been a historian for the United States Air
Force, the Department of State, and the Library of Congress, and a professor of history at the University of Maryland. His books include *Ar-
nim and Bismarck* (1968) and *Bismarck and His Times* (1978). The
following essay was written during the Vietnam War and shortly after
the Soviet invasion of Czechoslovakia in 1968. It was published in the
November 1969 issue of *The Historian*.

*L*ooking back from the vantage point of the middle of the twentieth century to his boyhood in western Ontario, James T.
Shotwell stated in his autobiography that the intervening
eighty years seemed to him like centuries rather than decades. His
experience, which is not uncommon, illustrates the necessity for
points of reference and association in one's life. To keep a sense of
proportion, to be able to judge and to give meaning to the present,
one has to compare it to the past. This process of comparison and
evaluation is going on all the time, consciously and subconsciously,
in private as well as in public affairs. Thus the past intrudes upon
the present and our attitude toward past events shapes the present as
well as the future.

"The present age is the most historical minded of all ages," E. H.
Carr, the noted British historian, wrote in *What Is History*. "Modern
man is to an unprecedented degree self-conscious," he said, "and
therefore conscious of history." This consciousness pervades all as-

pects of our life and none more so than politics. On the domestic scene the 1968 presidential campaign was often compared to that of 1948—Hubert Humphrey being compared to Harry Truman—while in foreign affairs our struggle in Vietnam is likened to the campaign as it should have been waged against Hitler in the 1930s, and the Soviet invasion of Czechoslovakia is being compared to Hitler's march into Prague twenty-nine years earlier.

The former comparison in particular is causing considerable discussion. President Johnson had very definite views on this subject and was acutely conscious of the position he had taken and of his role in history. As James Reston reported in the *New York Times* of October 1, 1967, the President carried with him "a piece of paper, which he recites, on the similarity between his problems and the problems of past war presidents," prominently among them Lincoln, Wilson, and Franklin Roosevelt. And the *Washington Post*, in a front-page story on December 5, 1967, informed its readers that "President Johnson compared Vietnam dissenters . . . to those who sought to appease Nazi Germany and Fascist Italy before World War II."

The argument that the world is experiencing a repetition of the issues of the 1930s—specifically that Hitler's aggression against Czechoslovakia is being re-enacted today by Hanoi against Saigon and by Moscow against Prague, and that the appeasement policy as exemplified by the Munich Conference of September 1938 is therefore morally and politically wrong—was the mainstay of the Johnson Administration's foreign policy in southeast Asia.

Not all the facts that led to the Munich Conference have been revealed, but enough are known to give a fairly reliable picture of the events that brought about the crisis thirty-one years ago and of the motives that influenced the major participants. It is generally accepted that Great Britain and France agreed to Germany's demands for the occupation of the Sudeten area of Czechoslovakia because of their fear of another major war and because of their unpreparedness to fight such a war. By making concessions to Hitler, certain British and French statesmen, and Neville Chamberlain, the British Prime Minister, especially, believed that they could satisfy Hitler's "just" grievances against the Versailles Peace Treaty and that in time Germany would become less aggressive. This "appeasement policy," as it became known, proved very shortly to be utterly fallacious

(Hitler's march into Prague on March 15, 1939, convinced almost everybody of his aggressive intent) and led directly, so it is generally believed, to Germany's invasion of Poland and the outbreak of World War II. Had the Western Powers stood up to Hitler at Munich, so the argument runs, World War II could have been avoided. The lesson: no appeasement!

How does this apply to present-day United States foreign policy? North Vietnam's (and indirectly China's) aggression against South Vietnam can be compared, Administration policy makers have said, to Germany's aggression against Czechoslovakia. The United States, however, unlike Britain and France, is fighting, not appeasing this aggression, and is thereby preventing World War III. This analogy seems mistaken on several counts. Britain and France were motivated by their fear of another world war and by the conviction of their own military inferiority. This, however, does not apply to the United States in the late 1960s. (If military weakness leads to appeasement, it would seem as Arnold Toynbee pointed out in *Life* magazine of December 8, 1967, that China is appeasing the United States to an unprecedented extent.) There is also the military-strategic factor. Germany in the 1930s was a highly industrialized state, actively rearming and pursuing a policy of thinly veiled aggression. (The re-occupation of the Rhineland and the annexation of Austria were the most obvious signs.) It seems, furthermore, that the strategic importance of the Sudeten areas to Britain and France in the 1930s was infinitely greater than that of South Vietnam to the United States today.

But if the Munich analogy is unsatisfactory, what in the past could be analogous to the present American predicament? In his paper "Uses and Abuses of Historical Analogies," read at the 82nd annual meeting of the American Historical Association in Toronto in December 1967 (of which a brief report appeared in the *New York Times* of February 5, 1968, p. 5), Professor Arno J. Mayer of Princeton paralleled United States intervention in Greece in 1947 and its current involvement in Vietnam. His arguments are perceptive and cogent and appear much more relevant than those put forth for Munich. Looking further into the past and with less sympathy for present day policy, one could compare American involvement in Vietnam to the intervention of the Japanese in Manchuria in the 1930s; to the Mexican adventure of Napoleon III in the 1860s; or to

Napoleon I's bloody intervention in Spain, the Peninsular War of 1808–9. None of these analogies is perfect; each has, on the other hand, enough similarities to the present situation to demand consideration.

At the first view, the similarity of the Soviet invasion of Czechoslovakia in August 1968 with the Nazi invasion of March 1939 is striking. On closer examination there are, however, important differences. In the case of the Soviet Union, it would seem that her rulers and those of East Germany, Poland, and Hungary, were much concerned about the changes that had occurred regarding ideological matters as well as about general internal developments in Czechoslovakia. The government of East Germany apparently felt, because of its precarious position, that this posed a serious threat to its own existence, and the Soviet Union, applying the domino theory to Central and Eastern Europe, may have considered that the Czech liberalization movement had to be stopped at all cost lest it corrupt and endanger its entire forward position in this area.

None of these considerations is applicable to German-Czech relations in 1938/39. Whether one takes the view that Hitler found in the post-Munich Czechoslovakia a ripe fruit ready to be plucked whenever the moment was right, or that his march into Prague was a logical and premeditated step on the road to the East, the fact is that the Czechs never posed a threat, ideological or otherwise, to the Germans in March 1939. Nor did Hitler ever make such a claim. The official justification was that "the Czechoslovak President declared that, in order to serve this object [the safeguarding of calm, order, and peace in this part of central Europe] and to achieve ultimate pacification, he confidently placed the fate of the Czech people and country in the hands of the Fuehrer of the German Reich."

Mistaken analogies are, of course, not unique. There are many examples of how political decisions and developments have been based on misinterpreting and misreading past events, and how historical myths have influenced statesmen and politicians. Of the many popular myths created in the nineteenth century, two, Pan-Germanism—the "mission" of the Germanic peoples to act as a bulwark against the Slavs—and the myth that the Italians are the successors of the Romans and their Empire, were revived in the twentieth century by German National Socialism and Italian Fascism. More to the point, perhaps, is the very real influence of the

French Revolution. It, together with the Revolution of 1848 and the Paris Commune of 1871, was forever in the minds of the Russian revolutionaries in 1917 and thereafter. According to Professor Carr, "the Bolsheviks knew that the French Revolution had ended in a Napoleon and feared that their own Revolution might end in the same way. They therefore mistrusted Trotsky, who among their leaders looked most like a Napoleon and trusted Stalin, who looked least like a Napoleon. . . ."

Our own time has been affected by other misconceptions. The myth of the monolithic structure of world communism and the continued refusal to recognize it as a myth, have contributed considerably to a lack of understanding of the current political scene in East Central Europe and southeast Asia. (The views of the late Senator Joseph McCarthy and his followers on the extreme Right, who believed in the "Great Conspiracy" and saw history in the simplistic terms of black and white, are the best known offshoots of this theory in the United States.) On the domestic scene, and with a long and honorable tradition, is the "agrarian myth," as Professor Henry Nash Smith has pointed out in his *Virgin Land: The American West as Symbol and Myth*, which, together with the frontier theory, has done much to "divert attention from the problems created by industrialization" and urbanization in nineteenth century America. One consequence of this diversion is the present urban crisis. The agrarian myth also contributed, according to Smith, to America's turning away from Europe and becoming increasingly isolationist in its attitude toward foreign affairs.

But not only in the United States do statesmen and politicians misread the past. Anthony Eden considered Nasser another Hitler when Nasser nationalized the Suez Canal in 1956 and, following the analogy of Hitler's re-occupation of the Rhineland in 1936, Britain and France (together with Israel) tried to stop Nasser by the invasion of Suez. This time they hoped to succeed in stopping a dictator where they had failed twenty years earlier.

The history of World War II is full of examples of misapplied historical parallels. Not only do generals fight existing wars according to old concepts, but civilians too, when in power, try to learn from history and apply this newly acquired knowledge to their area of competence. Thus, in World War II British reluctance to invade the Continent and open a second front in Europe can be explained to a large extent by Britain's failure to make a successful landing at Gallipoli in 1915/16 and her fear of suffering huge losses, similar to those she had suffered on the Western front in World War I. The French, for their part, were so obsessed with the Schlieffen plan of World War I that they and their allies penetrated deeply into Belgium in May 1940 and, in so doing, weakened their forces around Sedan where the German breakthrough occurred. The Germans, in turn, were no less immune to this type of historical interpretation and application. In their case it can be shown, however, that their disregard of historical parallels had disastrous consequences. In spite of repeated warnings and an accurate estimate of Russian military potential by some of his advisors, and with everyone mindful of the fate of Napoleon I, Hitler insisted on the invasion of Russia in June 1941. Nor did Germany's defeat in World War I deter Hitler from gambling on the outcome of a possible second world war in September 1939.

In this connection a little known episode from the days immediately prior to the beginning of World War II may serve to show the influence of history on diplomacy at a critical period. On August 23, 1939, the British Ambassador in Berlin had an interview with Hitler during which the Ambassador handed Hitler a letter from Neville Chamberlain. In it the British Prime Minister informed the German Chancellor that rumors had reached Britain that it was believed in Berlin that Great Britain would no longer come to Poland's assistance in time of need. This was a mistake, the Prime Minister wrote. And, recalling the diplomatic crisis over Germany's invasion of Belgium and Britain's attitude at the outbreak of World War I, he went on, "It is alleged that, if His Majesty's Government had made their position more clear in 1914, the great catastrophe would have been avoided. Whether or no there is any force in this allegation, His Majesty's Government are resolved that on this occasion there shall be no such tragic misunderstanding. . . ." The warning was ignored.

These random examples of the influence of historical analogies to current events pose a distressing problem. One can take to heart lessons of history and be wrong one time, and right another; or, disregard them and achieve similar results. It apparently is all a matter of proper interpretation. Unfortunately, the experts themselves do not agree on the correct interpretation of any series of events and so it seems that history fails to provide us with clear solutions or simple guidelines. Is the study of history therefore a vain waste of time and energy? Perhaps a further look into the nature and purpose of history is therefore necessary.

Writing history today is a very popular pastime and practically everyone tries his hand at it. With everyone his own historian and "instant historians" in the highest places of society, we are forever reminded that history will judge our actions. But how will history judge us, and what are its lessons? Santayana's famous dictum that "those who cannot remember the past are condemned to repeat it," is probably today's most popular quotation on the importance of history as a guide in the present. But which of the million events in our lifetime are we to remember?

History has been called many things. Gibbon thought it "the register of the follies and misfortunes of mankind"; Napoleon called it "lies agreed upon"; and Carlyle, "a great dustheap"; while Bolingbroke considered it "philosophy teaching by examples." This lack of consensus on the nature and purpose of history is by no means confined to the past. Present-day historians too are unable to agree on a universally acceptable definition. It follows that if there is no consensus on this among experts, neither can they be expected to agree on interpretation. History, then, is a very personal subject. The chronicler determines which events he considers important, colorful, or interesting enough to record. His judgment is influenced by his upbringing, his prejudices, and a score of other, minor factors— the weather, his state of mind, or his health at the time of his writing. (How, for instance, would Froissart's Chronicles have turned out, had he not been such a good drinking companion?) The historian, following the chronicler, is exposed to similar influences and many others. He is not just selecting the facts from the chronicles, documents, diaries, memoirs, eyewitness accounts, and other contemporary sources; he is putting these facts into some order, judging them, interpreting their meaning and significance, and constructing from them and from his own experience a narrative which reflects as much of himself and of his own time as it does of the period about which he is writing. Or, as E. H. Carr, referring to Mommsen's *History of Rome*, put it, "great history is written . . . when the historian's vision of the past is illuminated by insights into the problems of the present."

It is the historians (or in any case those who write history) who, in a very real sense, make history. Unless an action is recorded some-how, it is lost and, for all practical purposes, might never have hap-pened. That is probably why Christopher Columbus has prevailed over Leif Ericson. The latter, if he ever did discover the New World, lacked the publicity that Columbus had. For similar reasons govern-ments take great pains and are in a hurry to publish their version of events soon after the outbreak of a major war (the so-called colored books), hoping that public opinion will be influenced and morale strengthened on the home front. (On the other hand, scholarly ac-cess to and publication of material pertaining to a country's foreign policy are usually restricted and closely circumscribed.)

"Let the facts speak for themselves" is used many times as an appeal to reason and impartiality. But facts by themselves do not exist. A fact becomes a fact only after someone has recognized it, rescued it from oblivion, and recorded it. Facts assembled haphaz-ardly, lined up in chronological, or any other order, are largely mean-ingless. Facts have to be selected, arranged, and interpreted before they acquire meaning. And, as has been shown many times, the same facts, differently arranged and interpreted, can be used to arrive at different, even opposite conclusions. Illustrations abound; the Northern and Southern histories of the American Civil War, World War I as seen from Paris and Berlin, and the French Revolution as told by Mathiez and Madelin, to name but a few.

But what about "objective history," someone is bound to ask? If truth must be known, there is no such thing. At least not in the sense of history being detached, impersonal, or unprejudiced. The personal view of too many people intrudes into the process from the time a fact is recorded through its selection to the time the histor-ical narrative is written, printed, and reviewed. It is an exceedingly complicated process, as is history itself. Causes and effects cannot be explained merely in terms of good and bad. "To yearn for a single, and usually simple, explanation of the chaotic materials of the past, to search for a single thread in that most tangled of all skeins, is a sign of immaturity," Professor Commager wrote in *The Nature and Study of History.*

There is, furthermore, another aspect that complicates the search for historical truth and the writing of history. It has happened many times that people act on what they believe is true, even if what they believe to be true is contrary to the established facts. Skillful propaganda and the all too human desire to shift blame made millions of Germans believe that toward the end of World War I their armies had been "stabbed in the back" by civilians at home. The facts were quite different, but the consequences that followed this "stab in the back" myth were incalculable and helped to shape the history of Germany and of Europe for decades. "We must recognize frankly," Professor Dunning wrote in his essay "Truth in History," "that whatever a given age or people believe to be true, *is* true for that age and that people."

The understanding and writing of history clearly is not a simple task. It requires patience, tolerance, common sense, and a critical mind. Today the historian, and especially the historian of recent history, is exposed, as never before, to pressure groups, competing loyalties, and vacillating public opinion; all claiming his attention and contending for his approval. How is he to reconcile these conflicting pressures? How is he to do justice to his chosen field? A balanced and detached view and his conscience can serve as a guide and he should remember that his responsibility is not "to dogmas or creeds, but to truth and humanity."

In a world that is getting more interdependent and more complicated every day, both history and historians can be used and abused. With George Orwell we should recognize that "who controls the past, controls the future."

The Inscrutability
of History

Arthur M. Schlesinger, Jr.

Arthur M. Schlesinger, Jr. (b. 1917) is professor of history at the City University of New York. He formerly was special assistant to Presidents John F. Kennedy and Lyndon B. Johnson. His many works include *The Age of Jackson* (1945), which won a Pulitzer Prize for history; *The Vital Center: The Politics of Freedom* (1949); the multivolume *Age of Roosevelt* (1957–60); *A Thousand Days: John F. Kennedy in the White House* (1965); *The Imperial Presidency* (1973); and *Robert Kennedy and His Times* (1978). "The Inscrutability of History" was first published in *Encounter* (November 1966).

*A*s one who is by profession an historian and has been by occasion a government official, I have long been fascinated and perplexed by the interaction between history and public decision: fascinated because, by this process, past history becomes an active partner in the making of new history; perplexed because the role of history in this partnership remains both elusive and tricky.

It is elusive because, if one excludes charismatic politics—the politics of the prophet and the medicine man—one is bound to conclude that all thought which leads to decisions of public policy is in essence historical. Public decision in rational politics necessarily implies a guess about the future derived from the experience of the past. It implies an expectation, or at the very least a hope, that certain actions will produce tomorrow the same sort of results they produced yesterday. This guess about the future may be based on a comprehensive theory of historical change, as with the Marxists; or it may be based on specific analogies drawn from the past; or it may be based on an unstated and intuitive sense of the way things happen. But whatever it is based on, it involves, explicitly or implicitly, an historical judgment.

And the problem is tricky because, when explicit historical judgments intervene, one immediately encounters a question which is, in the abstract, insoluble: Is the history invoked really the source of policies, or is it the source of arguments designed to vindicate policies adopted for antecedent reasons? Moreover, even when history is in some sense the source of policies, the lessons of history are generally so ambiguous that the antecedent reasons often determine the choice between alternative historical interpretations. Thus, in France between the wars Reynaud and Mandel drew one set of conclusions from the First World War, Bonnet and Laval another. Yet one cannot, on the other hand, reduce the function of history in public policy to that of mere rationalization, for historical models acquire a life of their own. Once a statesman begins to identify the present with the past, he may in time be carried further than he intends by the bewitchment of analogy.

However hard it may be to define with precision the role of history in public policy, it is evident that this role must stand or fall on the success of history as a means of prediction—on the proposition that knowledge of yesterday provides guidance for tomorrow. This is a point, it should immediately be said, on which professional historians, on the whole, have few illusions among themselves. They privately regard history as its own reward; they study it for the intellectual and aesthetic fulfillment they find in the disciplined attempt to reconstruct the past and, perhaps, for the ironic aftertaste in the contemplation of man's heroism and folly, but for no more utilitarian reason. They understand better than outsiders that historical training confers no automatic wisdom in the realm of public affairs. Guizot, Bancroft, Macaulay, Thiers, Morley, Bryce, Theodore Roosevelt, Woodrow Wilson: one cannot say that their training as historians deeply influenced their practice as politicians; and the greatest of them—Roosevelt and Wilson—were harmed as politicians by exactly the moralism from which the study of history might have saved them. But then neither was a particularly good historian.[*]

---

[*] Churchill is a different matter; but he was a politician who turned to history, not an historian who turned to politics. So too was Kennedy.

Yet historians, in spite of their candor within the fellowship, sometimes invoke arguments of a statelier sort in justifying themselves to society. Thus Raleigh: "We may gather out of History a policy no less wise than eternal; by the comparison and application of other men's fore-passed miseries with our own errours and ill-deservings." Or Burke: "In history, a great volume is unrolled for our instruction, drawing the materials of future wisdom from the past errors and infirmities of mankind." In what sense is this true? Why should history help us foresee the future? Because presumably history repeats itself enough to make possible a range of historical generalization; and because generalization, sufficiently multiplied and interlaced, can generate insight into the shape of things to come.

Many professional historians—perhaps most—reject the idea that generalization is the goal of history. We all respond, in Marc Bloch's phrase, to "the thrill of learning singular things." Indeed, it is the commitment to concrete reconstruction as against abstract generalization—to life as against laws—which distinguishes history from sociology. Yet, on the other hand, as Crane Brinton once put it, "the doctrine of the absolute uniqueness of events in history seems nonsense." Even historians who are skeptical of attempts to discern a final and systematic order in history acknowledge the existence of a variety of uniformities and recurrences. There can be no question that generalizations about the past, defective as they may be, are possible—and that they can strengthen the capacity of statesmen to deal with the future.

So historians have long since identified a life-cycle of revolution which, if properly apprehended, might have spared us misconceptions about the Russian Revolution—first, about its goodwill and, later, when we abandoned belief in its goodwill, about the fixity and permanence of its fanatical purpose—and which, if consulted today, might save us from the notion that the Chinese Revolution will be forever cast in its present mold. Historical generalizations in a number of areas—the processes of economic development, for example, or the impact of industrialization and urbanization, or the effect of population growth, or the influence of climate or sea power or the frontier, or the circulation of political elites or entrepreneurial innovation—will enlarge the wisdom of the statesman, giving his responses to the crises of the moment perspective, depth and an instinct for the direction and flow of events. The consequences for

American society of the frustrations generated by limited war—the McCarthyism effect—is probably an example of permissible generalization. Sometimes this wisdom may even lead to what Bloch called "the paradox of prevision"—to the point when men, sufficiently warned by historical extrapolation of horrid eventualities, may take action to avert them, which means that prevision may be destroyed by prevision.

The result is historical insight: that is, a sense of what is possible and probable in human affairs, derived from a feeling for the continuities and discontinuities of existence. This sense is comparable not to the mathematical equations of the physicist but to the diagnostic judgments of the doctor. It is this form of historical insight which has led in recent years to Bertrand de Jouvenel's *L'Art de la Conjecture* and to the stimulating intellectual exercise involved in the search for *futuribles*. But *futuribles* are speculative constructions of possible long-range futures, useful perhaps to those who may be presidents and prime ministers in 2000, hardly to their predecessors in 1970.

Still every day around the planet great decisions are being made (or at least rationalized) in terms of short-run historical estimates. The whole Marxist world, of course, is sworn to a determinist view of the future, according to which fixed causes produce fixed effects and mankind is moving along a predestined path through predestined stages to a single predestined conclusion. For the Marxists, history has become a "positive model": it prescribes not only for the long but for the short run, not only strategy but tactics—the immediate policies to be favored, courses pursued, action taken. It is a tribute to the devotion of Marxists, if hardly to their intelligence, that they have remained so indefatigably loyal to their metaphysic in spite of the demonstrated limits of Marxism as a system of prediction.

For, if any thesis was central to the Marxist vision of history, it was that the process of modernization, of industrialization, of social and economic development, would infallibly carry every nation from feudalism through capitalism to communism: that the communist society was the inevitable culmination of the development process. Thus Marx contended that, the more developed a country was, the more prepared it was for communism, and that communism in consequence must come first to the most industrialized nations. In fact, communism has come only to nations in a relatively early stage of development, like Russia and China, and it has come to such nations precisely as a means to modernization, not as a consequence of it. Instead of being the climax of the development process, the end of the journey, communism is now revealed as a technique of social discipline which a few countries in early stages of development have adopted in the hope of speeding the pace of modernization. Instead of the ultimate destinations toward which all societies are ineluctably moving, communism now appears an epiphenomenon of the transition from stagnation to development. Modernization, as it proceeds, evidently carries nations not toward Marx but away from Marx—and this would appear true even of the Soviet Union itself.

History thus far has refuted the central proposition in Marx's system of prediction. It has also refuted important corollary theses—notably the idea that the free economic order could not possibly last. Far from obeying dogma and perishing of its own inner contradictions, free society in the developed world has rarely displayed more creativity and vitality. It is casting as powerful a spell on the intellectuals and the youth of the communist world as the communist would cast on us during the Depression thirty years ago.

Why did Marx go wrong here? His forecast of the inevitable disintegration of free society was plausibly based on the *laissez faire* capitalism of the mid-nineteenth century. This devil-take-the-hindmost economic order did very likely contain the seeds of its own destruction—especially in those tendencies, pronounced irreversibly by Marx, toward an ever widening gap between rich and poor (alleged to guarantee the ultimate impoverishment of the masses) and toward an ever increasing frequency and severity of structural economic crisis (alleged to guarantee the progressive instability of the system). This may indeed be a salient example of the "paradox of prevision"; for the Marxist forecast unquestionably stimulated progressive democrats to begin the reform of classical capitalism through the invention of the affirmative state. "The more we condemn unadulterated Marxian Socialism," Theodore Roosevelt used to say, "the stouter should be our insistence on thoroughgoing social reforms." The combination of the affirmative state with the extraordinary success of the free economic order as an engine of production—a success which, contrary to *laissez faire* dogma, government intervention increased rather than hampered—eventually thwarted the Marxist prophecy.

In the end, the Marxists were undone by Marxism. Ideology told them that those who owned the economy *must* own the state, and the state could therefore never act against their desires or interests. Yet fifteen years before the *Communist Manifesto* an American President, Andrew Jackson, had already suggested that the state in a democratic society, far from being the instrument of the possessors, could well become the means by which those whom Jackson called the "humble members of society" might begin to redress the balance of social power against those whom Hamilton had called the "rich and well-born." Thus, in the twentieth-century developed world, the economic machine drowned the revolution in consumers' goods, while the affirmative state, with its policies of piecemeal intervention in the economy, brought about both a relative redistribution of wealth (defeating Marx's prediction of the immiseration of the poor) and a relative stabilization of the economy (defeating Marx's prediction of ever deepening cyclical crisis). The last place to look for a Marxist victory is precisely the place where Marx said it would come first—i.e., in the most developed countries.

So the Marxist prophecy of a single obligatory destiny for mankind has missed in both its parts: in its prediction of the irresistible breakdown of the free economy, and in its prediction of the irresistible triumph of communism as the fulfillment of the development process. In spite of many subsidiary insights and successes, Marxism must surely stand in our time as the spectacular flop of history as prophecy. The failure, indeed, has been so complete that contemporary Marxists revile each other in seeking the true meaning of the most elementary doctrines; the more fanatical stand Marx on his head, rejecting his basic theory and arguing that communism will come "out of the countryside," not the city.

Yet the democratic world is hardly in a position to take too much satisfaction from the intellectual collapse of Marxism. It is true that our philosophical heritage—empirical, pragmatic, ironic, pluralistic, competitive—has happily inoculated us against rigid, all-encompassing, absolute systems of historical interpretation. But, though we may reject the view of history as metaphysically set and settled, we seem at times to embrace our own forms of historical fatalism, even if we invoke history less as theology than as analogy. This is only a marginal advantage. The argument by metaphor can generate a certitude almost as mischievous as the argument by determinism.

For democratic policymakers, history generally appears as a "negative" rather than a "positive" model. It instructs us, not like Marxism, in the things we must do, but in the things we must *not* do—unless we wish to repeat the mistakes of our ancestors. The traumatic experience of the First World War thus dominated the diplomacy of the Second World War, at least as far as the United States was concerned. So the American insistence on the doctrine of "unconditional surrender" in 1943 sprang from the belief that the failure to get unconditional surrender in 1918 had made possible the stab-in-the-back myth and guaranteed the revival of German nationalism. The American obsession with the United Nations came from the conviction that the failure to join the League of Nations had opened the way to the Second World War. The American readiness to make concessions to the Soviet Union (as Professor E. R. May has suggested) was based, in part, on an analogy with Clemenceau's France. The American President viewed the Soviet Union as a nation which, having lived in permanent insecurity, could be expected, like France twenty-five years earlier, to value security above almost anything else. "Roosevelt," Professor May has perceptively written, "was determined to see Stalin's point of view as Wilson had not seen Clemenceau's. He was determined that, in so far as possible, the Soviet Union should have the guarantees it wanted and should not be forced into the sullen self-preoccupation of the France of Poincaré."

The Second World War, then, provided a new traumatic experience. In the years since, the consciousness of policymakers has been haunted by the Munich and Yalta analogies—the generalization, drawn from attempts to accommodate Hitler in 1938, and Stalin in 1945, that appeasement always assures new aggression. Of these analogies, Munich, as the more lucid in its pattern and the more emphatic in its consequence, has been the more powerful; Yalta figures rather as a complicated special case. I trust that a graduate student some day will write a doctoral essay on the influence of the Munich analogy on the subsequent history of the twentieth century. Perhaps in the end he will conclude that the multitude of errors committed in the name of "Munich" may exceed the original error of 1938.

Certainly Munich was a tragic mistake, and its lesson was that the appeasement of a highly wound-up and heavily armed total-

itarian state in the context of a relatively firm and articulated continental equilibrium of power was likely to upset the balance and
make further aggression inevitable. But to conclude from this that
all attempts to avert war by negotiation must always be "Munichs"
goes beyond the evidence. No one understood this better than the
greatest contemporary critic of Munich. An historian himself,
Winston Churchill well understood the limits of historical analogy.
So he defined the issue in his chapter on Munich in *The Gathering
Storm:*

> It may be well here to set down some principles of morals and action
> which may be a guide in the future. No case of this kind can be judged
> apart from its circumstances. . . .
>
> Those who are prone by temperament and character to seek sharp
> and clear-cut solutions of difficult and obscure problems, who are ready
> to fight whenever some challenge comes from a foreign power, have not
> always been right. On the other hand, those whose inclination is to
> bow their heads, to seek patiently and faithfully for peaceful compro-
> mise, are not always wrong. On the contrary, in the majority of in-
> stances, they may be right, not only morally but from a practical
> standpoint. . . .
>
> How many wars have been precipitated by fire-brands! How many
> misunderstandings which led to war could have been removed by tem-
> porising! How often have countries fought cruel wars and then after a
> few years of peace found themselves not only friends but allies!

Sixteen years after Munich, when President Eisenhower invoked
the Munich analogy to persuade the British to join the Americans in
backing the French in Indochina, Churchill, as we have seen, was
unimpressed. He rejected Eisenhower's analogy, which did not, of
course, prevent Churchill's successor as prime minister two years
later from seeing Nasser and the Middle East in terms of 1938 and
committing his nation to the Suez adventure. This time it was
Eisenhower who rejected the Munich analogy. Such incidents illustrate the depressing persistence of the mentality which makes policy through stereotype, through historical generalization wrenched
illegitimately out of the past and imposed mechanically on the future. Santayana's aphorism must be reversed: too often it is those
who *can* remember the past who are condemned to repeat it. . . .

. . . The point is not terribly complicated. Burke long ago warned
against the practice of viewing an object "as it stands stripped of

every relation, in all the nakedness and solitude of metaphysical abstraction. Circumstances (which with some gentlemen pass for nothing) give in reality to every political principle its distinguishing color and discriminating effect." Even Toynbee, the magician of historical analogy, has remarked that historians are

> never in a position to guarantee that the entities which we are bringing into comparison are properly comparable for the purpose of our investigation. . . . However far we may succeed in going in our search for sets of identical examples on either side, we shall never be able to prove that there is not some non-identical factor that we have overlooked, and this non-identical factor is not the decisive factor that accounts for the different outcomes in different cases of what has looked to us like an identical situation but may not have been this in truth.

Or, as Mark Twain put it, somewhat more vividly, in *Following the Equator:* "We should be careful to get out of an experience only the wisdom that is in it—and stop there; lest we be like the cat that sits down on a hot stove lid. She will never sit down on a hot stove lid again—and that is well; but also she will never sit down on a cold one."

One cannot doubt that the study of history makes people wiser. But it is indispensable to understand the limits of historical analogy. Most useful historical generalizations are statements about massive social and intellectual movements over a considerable period of time. They make large-scale, long-term prediction possible. But they do not justify small-scale, short-term prediction. For short-run prediction is the prediction of detail and, given the complex structure of social events, the difficulty of anticipating the intersection or collision of different events and the irreducible mystery, if not invincible freedom, of individual decision, there are simply too many variables to warrant exact forecasts of the immediate future. History, in short, can answer questions, after a fashion, at long range. It cannot answer questions with confidence or certainty at short range. Alas, policymakers are rarely interested in the long run—"in the long run," as Keynes used to say, "we are all dead"—and the questions they put to history are thus most often the questions which history is least qualified to answer.

Far from offering a short cut to clairvoyance, history teaches us that the future is full of surprises and outwits all our certitudes. For the study of history issues not in scientific precision nor in moral finality but in irony. . . . The chastening fact is that many of the pivotal events of our age were unforeseen. . . .

. . . I have often thought that a futurist trying to forecast the next three American Presidents in early 1940 would hardly have named as the first President after Franklin D. Roosevelt an obscure back-bench senator from Missouri, anticipating defeat by the governor of his state in the Democratic primaries; as the second, an unknown lieutenant-colonel in the United States Army; and, as the third, a kid still at college. . . .

The salient fact about historical process, so far as the short run is concerned, is its inscrutability. . . .

History, in short, does not furnish the statesman with a detailed scenario of particular relationships or policies. Too often it equips his decisions with good rather than real reasons, holding out a mirror in which he fatuously sees his own face. This is not an argument against the knowledge of history: it is an argument against the superficial knowledge of history. The single analogy is never enough to penetrate a process so cunningly compounded not only of necessity but of contingency, fortuity, ignorance, stupidity and chance. The statesman who is surest that he can divine the future most urgently invites his own retribution. "The hardest strokes of heaven," Herbert Butterfield has written, "fall in history upon those who imagine that they can control things in a sovereign manner, playing providence not only for themselves but for the far future—reaching out into the future with the wrong kind of farsightedness, and gambling on a lot of risky calculations in which there must never be a single mistake."

The only antidote to a shallow knowledge of history is a deeper knowledge, the knowledge which produces not dogmatic certitude but diagnostic skill, not clairvoyance but insight. It offers the statesman a sense, at once, of short-run variables and long-run tendencies, and an instinct for the complexity of their intermingling, including the understanding that (as Rousseau once put it), "the ability to foresee that some things cannot be foreseen is a very necessary quality." Indeed, half the wisdom of statecraft, to borrow a phrase from Richard Goodwin, is "to leave as many options open as possible and decide as little as possible. . . . Since almost all important policy judgments are speculative, you must avoid risking too much on the conviction you are right."

Of course keeping too many options open too long may paralyze the lobe of decision and lose the game. There *does* come a time when accommodation turns into appeasement. This is the other half of the wisdom of statecraft: to accept the chronic obscurity of events without yielding, in Lincoln's words, firmness in the right as God gives us to see the right. In deciding when to decide, the criterion must be the human consequences—the results for people, not for doctrine.

Randolph Churchill's life of his father reproduces an extraordinary letter written seventy years ago by the young Winston Churchill to a New York politician of the time, Bourke Cockran. "The duty of government," Churchill said, "is to be first of all practical. I am for makeshifts and expediency. I would like to make the people who live on this world at the same time as I do better fed and happier generally. If incidentally I benefit posterity—so much the better—but I would not sacrifice my own generation to a principle however high or a truth however great."

Such an approach may seem too modest, even, perhaps, too cynical, for those theological statesmen whose self-righteousness has almost sunk our age. Most of these confident moralists have been high priests of one or another dogmatic faith (though some, alas, have been American Secretaries of State); but all have been prepared in the best conscience and in the name of history to sacrifice their generations on the altars of their own metaphors. It can only be said that, whether they see history as ideology or as analogy, they see it wrong. Far from unveiling the secret of things to come, history bestows a different gift: it makes us—or should make us— understand the extreme difficulty, the intellectual peril, the moral arrogance of supposing that the future will yield itself so easily to us.

"I returned," Ecclesiastes reminds us, "and saw under the sun that the race is not to the swift, nor the battle to the strong, neither yet bread to the wise nor riches to men of understanding, but time and chance happeneth to them all." The Old Testament carries the case against historical generalization to the extreme. But, without going so far, we can agree that history should lead statesmen to a profound and humbling sense of human frailty—to a recognition of the fact, so insistently demonstrated by experience and so tragically destructive of our most cherished certitudes, that the possibilities of history are far richer and more various than the human intellect is likely to conceive. This, and the final perception that while the tragedy of history implicates us all in the common plight of humanity, we are never relieved, despite the limits of our knowledge and the darkness of our understanding, from the necessity of meeting our obligations.

Lessons, Analogies, and Prediction

Lester D. Stephens

Lester D. Stephens (b. 1933) is head of the Department of History at the University of Georgia. He has written articles that deal with such topics as history and education, slavery, agriculture, and evolution. His books include *Developing Competency in Teaching Secondary Social Studies* (1974), *Historiography: A Bibliography* (1975), and *Joseph Le-Conte: Gentle Prophet of Evolution* (1982). "Lessons, Analogies, and Prediction" is from his book *Probing the Past: A Guide to the Study and Teaching of History* (1974).

"Those who cannot remember the past are condemned to repeat it," declared the philosopher George Santayana. Taking "history" as synonymous with "the past" in Santayana's statement, who can deny the value of historical study? The assumption underlying Santayana's dictum is, of course, that history does contain lessons. But we must raise the question of whether that is in fact the case.

How often have we heard the expressions "History has shown that . . ." or "History teaches us that . . ."! Implied in these facile statements is the belief that we know what the lessons of history are. That, unfortunately, too often expresses only our wishes and not reality. "The lessons of history," observes Carl G. Gustavson, "are not as easy to discern as some people would have us believe. Any statement in which the prefatory 'History teaches us that . . .' is used as a springboard should be very carefully scrutinized; the accompanying assertion may be quite valid and acceptable, but the odds are against it." A typical example of the belief that the lessons of history are clear may be found in the recent statement of a newspaper journalist. Indicting the Secretary of Defense for timidity in handling the seizure of the United States vessel *Pueblo* by the North Koreans in 1968, the writer asserts that

> The lesson of history is that victory goes to the bold and daring. If the free world fails to use its scientific and technological know-how to stop the armed hordes of communism, it may be bled to death by the modern guerrilla war version of the old oriental torture death of a thousand cuts.

How nice it would be if the lessons of history were so simple and clear-cut. Unhappily, the writer conveniently forgets that Hitler was bold and daring but hardly achieved any real victory; Japan boldly and daringly attacked a major power and instead of victory reaped disaster for its efforts—the story could go on with repeated examples refuting the writer's "lesson of history."

Although historians have been more reluctant than philosophers, prophets, and others to draw the lessons of history for us, even a few of them have endeavored to tell us what history teaches. Among them was Theodore Roosevelt, a historian in his own right and president of the American Historical Association in 1912. Speaking of the demise of Holland as an influential nation, Roosevelt pronounced that a lesson of history is: "To be opulent and unarmed is to secure ease in the present at the almost certain cost of disaster in the future." One cannot but wonder, though, to what extent Roosevelt's lesson of history was influenced by the events of the time in which he formulated it.

On the other hand, it may be foolish to argue that we cannot learn something from history. Whether or not we *do* is another matter, but that we *can* is something else. Certainly, the reflective historian is in a position to suggest some *possible* lessons in the form of generalizations about our past. Samuel Eliot Morison, the doyen of American historians, states that "the historian who knows, or thinks he knows, an unmistakable lesson of the past, has the right and the duty to point it out even though it counteract his own beliefs or social theories." It is indeed a risky business, but that is not an adequate reason to forego it altogether. If we understand the tentative quality of the lesson, then we are not in danger of reading more into it than is there. Hence we may profit from such a limited lesson or generalization as that drawn by Dexter Perkins from his long-time study of foreign affairs. In reference to communist revolutions Perkins believes he has discovered a useful lesson: "Not social discontent alone, but social discontent which has undermined the authority of the army and destroyed its morale, is the situation which brings about a Communist takeover."

What should now be obvious in our argument concerning lessons of history is that the lessons are circumscribed by time and the historian's own limited ability. The broader and more widely applicable the lesson reputes to be, the greater the danger that evidence will refute it. There is an added danger too. It is possible that a so-called lesson will be taken so much to heart by the people of a nation that they will become rigidly bound to their image of the past. In the 1890's Alfred T. Mahan, for example, drew what he felt were practical lessons about the influence of sea power upon the history of nations. Some national leaders took Mahan so seriously that his "lessons" played a critical role in the armaments race prior to World War I.

The past can in fact become onerous, Santayana notwithstanding. When man's image of his nation's past is not tempered by a critical view of history, it can lead to all kinds of unmitigated evil. As Herbert Butterfield so perceptively remarks, "Historical memories, especially in Eastern Europe—and also in Ireland—have engendered much of the national animosity of modern times. . . . One must wonder sometimes whether it would not have been better if men could have . . . thrown off the terrible burden of the past, so that they might face the future without encumbrances."

If historians are reluctant to point out lessons of history, they are less reserved about noting parallels, that is, about comparing events of a later period of time with those of an earlier era. Historical analogy is a legitimate use of history, though any analogy must not be extended beyond the limits which circumscribe it. Thus while it would be a mistake to assume too much applicability of historical analogies, we can at least expect them to provide us with insights about similarity of situations and perhaps some future *possibilities*.

Even though the historian is unlikely to believe in the inevitability of the outcomes of similar events, he is at least aware of the possibility that certain consequences will issue from events which are comparable to other events of the past. To explore and explain cause-effect relationships is part of his business, and these in turn necessitate some comparisons. Stringfellow Barr, for example, found some similarities between modern America and ancient Rome. The two states are alike, he concludes, in that each has a legend of beginning with a ship, the Aeneas and the Mayflower, and each ship bore an Elect, refugees who "founded a new City"; each became a young republic, "increased and multiplied, and its land hunger grew insatiably"; each "brought in slaves," from Africa in the case of America and as prisoners of war in the case of Rome; each developed a "desire for money"; and each moved to take vast "stretches of land," which invited the twin characteristics of "activism and voluntarism." Then, Barr further argues, while the two states are separated by "great and obvious differences," the "American Century" may lead to "where the Roman Century of Augustus led," with the development of a military-industrial complex and our swift rise to world power which may corrupt us with an unwonted "faith in the efficacy of power." Many questions leap to mind concerning Barr's comparison, such as "isolating just the one strain about the use of force"; but it is an analogy which deserves our consideration.

Analogies between past and present events need not be confined to comparisons of one nation or civilization with another, however. Similarities and parallels may be found between one era and another within the same country. Thus C. Vann Woodward observes the correspondence of conditions in the United States between circa 1930 and the mid-1950's and those of the South in the 1830's. Recognizing that the "dangers inherent in any such comparison between historical epochs are numerous and forbidding," Woodward proceeds with proper caution to "venture a comparison, not between the two institutions [of modern capitalism and slavery as a system of labor], but between the public attitudes toward them and the transformations that took place in those attitudes." The 1930's in the United States were a time of intense criticism of the capitalist system: "No corner nor aspect nor relationship of American capitalism was overlooked, and no shibboleth of free enterprise went unchallenged." This attitude was accepted on the whole as a salutary sign of the strength of the society. By the mid-forties, however, a transformation occurred, and the "floodstream of criticism dwindled to a trickle and very nearly ceased altogether." The nation was then beset with accusations, counteraccusations, charges of disloyalty, and Mc-

Carthyism or witch hunting of the first magnitude, and institutions which had been the object of criticism became the object of "rapturous praise."

This transformation, notes Woodward, was reminiscent of the events in the South in the 1830's, where, prior to that decade, "a vigorous school of antislavery" flourished. The critics of slavery, as with the critics of capitalism, "included men of influence and standing." But antislavery thought reached its apex in the debates over emancipation in the Virginia legislature of 1831–32, and from that point the movement "withered away to almost nothing in a very brief period during the middle thirties." In fact, by 1837 not a single antislavery society existed in the South, and as in the 1940's and 1950's, loyalty to institutions became a matter of conformity, with fervid attention given to scrutinizing the past records of men of public life. While several reasons explain the two transformations, Woodward observes that "both of these revolutions in public attitudes were reactions to contests for power in which the two societies found themselves involved." And what is the upshot of this comparison if not to draw some potential lessons? Woodward suggests that we may learn from this that

> economic systems, whatever their age, their respectability, or their apparent stability, are transitory and that any nation which elects to stand or fall upon one ephemeral institution has already determined its fate.

And in a broader sense this comparison implies that

> an overwhelming conviction in the righteousness of a cause is no guarantee of its ultimate triumph, and . . . the policy which takes into account the possibility of defeat is more realistic than one that assumes the inevitability of victory.

Perhaps the most popular analogy of the last decade has been that comparing North Vietnam's aggression against South Vietnam with Hitler's aggression against Czechoslovakia, or the Munich analogy. The analogy has been offered by officials of the United States government, including President Lyndon B. Johnson. The proponents of the analogy argue that the dissenters against United States involvement in Vietnam are like the appeasers of Nazi Germany at Munich in 1938. To have failed to stand against the aggression of North Vietnam would have been similar to the moral error committed at Munich, for appeasement only allows the aggressor to proceed with his policy of seizing more and more territory (often referred to as the Domino Theory). The validity of the analogy has been attacked by several historians. [See the essays by Schlesinger and Kent in this volume.] . . . The Munich analogy has for too many people become the guiding star for all future action in foreign affairs.

However limited the analogy, however short of being a law, fruitful comparisons are one use of history. Though pointing up analogies is not the sole function of the historian, perhaps many historians have overreacted to the work of metahistorians and consequently neglected to study, observe, and duly note analogies or parallels in history. Their comparisons will be stated as generalizations, but if we are not guided by valid historical generalizations, then we will be guided by myths.

The limitations of historical lessons and analogies necessarily reduce the possibility of forecasting future historical events. To predict the future on the basis of what happened in the past is somewhat like shooting an arrow at a distant target in a large field at twilight. Thus about the best the historian can do is locate the general direction of the target and aim in that direction. The target will at best be barely perceptible, and a number of factors may intervene so that the target moves or the arrow is thrown off course by a sudden gust of wind. Fortuitous circumstances are ever-present in the life of man, and man's reaction to events is never so constant that we can state with lawlike precision that he will behave in the same way at all times.

Anticipation of the possible outcome of a future event may be as close as history can ever bring us to the realm of prediction. "If, for instance, it is true that Prussia collapsed rapidly under military defeat in 1806 and 1918, one of the *possibilities* to anticipate should be the rapid collapse of Prussia after another military defeat." The argument here is, of course, not that the collapse of Prussia upon another military defeat is inevitable, only that it *may* be anticipated. The nature of history will never permit us to view the future with the certitude we often crave. "But," states Arthur Bestor,

> to expect that history will enable a man to arm himself with foresight
> is to cherish a rational hope. If foresight be defined as the ability to

make informed guesses about the characteristics of future situations and thus to encounter them forewarned, then history, by fostering foresight, is making no inconsiderable contribution to the intelligent conduct of human affairs.

To hope for more is to expect too much of history. But it is at least preferable to uninformed opinion and wild guess.

While historians are disinclined to peer into the future to guess at what may occur, they are not averse to glancing backward to speculate on how it could have been if certain things had happened differently. Some philosophers of history refer to this action as "retrodiction." At first consideration it may seem futile to speculate upon the "might-have-beens of the past," for the past is the past and therefore cannot be changed. "But the finality [of the past] means that historical events are irreversible, not that they are all necessary . . . ," Sidney Hook reminds us. Such conjectures are valid, of course, only as long as what is considered were actual possibilities at the time of the event. If they were possible, then the historian may contribute to our understanding by indicating the alternatives which were open at the time. In some instances mere luck or chance was the determining factor and therefore not under the control of men. In other cases, however, decisions were made by men, groups, or nations, and for that reason the "if . . . then" relationship points up what was a possible course of action that was either rejected or overlooked.

A few examples of "hypothetical history" should suffice to illustrate this point. Both of the following examples deal with World War II—a momentous event of our time and for that reason worthy of conjecture about alternative actions. In the first instance, William L. Shirer raises a "might-have-been" regarding the Munich crisis:

Germany was in no position to go to war on October 1, 1938, against Czechoslovakia and France and Britain, not to mention Russia. *Had* she done so, she would have been quickly and easily defeated, and that would have been the end of Hitler and the Third Reich. *If* a European war had been averted at the last moment by the intercession of the German Army, Hitler *might* have been overthrown by Halder and Witzleben and their confederates carrying out their plan to arrest him as soon as he had given the final order for the attack on Czechoslovakia.

The second example [from Robert J. C. Butow's *Japan's Decision to Surrender*] deals with the Potsdam Declaration and the surrender of Japan:

> The Allies thus had here, in late July 1945, the very document which Japan finally accepted in mid-August. Had Prince Konoye, as the fully empowered personal representative of the Emperor of Japan, been permitted to travel to Moscow (or anywhere else, for that matter) and had he there been handed the text of this proclamation prior to its release to the world at large, he conceivably could have resolved speedily the very issues which government leaders in Tokyo spent the next three weeks in debating without result. *Had* the Allies given the prince a week of grace in which to obtain his government's support for acceptance, the war *might* have ended toward the latter part of July or the very beginning of August without the atomic bomb and without Soviet participation in the conflict.

Surely, no one can assert positively that either of these events *would* have ended differently, but it is entirely possible that they *could* have. And such knowledge may afford us a better grasp of *why* events took the turn they did. At any rate, reflection about such alternative courses of action may help us to sharpen our mental processes and increase our ability to cope with decision-making situations.

History and Policymaking

*A*n important relation exists among decision making, the formulation of policy, and history, as previous selections by Kent, Schlesinger, and Stephens suggest. Policymakers can almost always be counted on to employ the past in some way. The question, therefore, is not whether history will be used in the decision-making process but whether it will be used judiciously. Unfortunately, it rarely is, as Ernest R. May established in *"Lessons" of the Past* (1973).[1]

The following essays show either how history has been put to good use in policymaking or how it might be better employed.[2] Colin B. Goodykoontz examines how the Founding Fathers drew on the past in creating the United States Constitution. History did not provide ready-made institutions or allow the Founding Fathers to predict the future. It did give these leaders a better understanding of the situation in which they worked. John Hope Franklin discusses how history and historians helped develop policies related to the struggle for civil rights in America. A better understanding of the origins of segregation, for example, strengthened the drive to bring about racial integration. David F. Trask explains that statesmen build "from a revealed past to a future not yet known." History is indispensable to policymaking and historians should be called upon to provide the best possible interpretation of the recent past.[3] In addition, Trask deals with a question raised in the previous section about anticipating the future. He believes that historians can sometimes be effective prophets.

Constructing "scenarios for the future" may be one of the most important contributions historians can make to policymaking, according to Otis L. Graham, Jr. In remarks originally addressed to other historians, Graham considers how history can be taught to people in government, business, and other walks of life. Although he is candid about history's limitations in decision making, he believes history can help us to see "matters whole" and to answer the question, "Where are we in the stream of time?"

References

1. Ernest R. May's study deals with history as it is applied to the formulation of foreign policy (*"Lessons" of the Past: The Use and Misuse of History in American Foreign Policy* [New York: Oxford University Press, 1973]). For an examination of how the past is appropriated by the judicial system in the United States, see Charles A. Miller, *The Supreme Court and the Uses of History* (Cambridge, Mass: Harvard University Press, Belknap Press, 1969). Also on history and decision making see Richard Neustadt, "Uses of History in Public Policy," *Humanities* (National Endowment for the Humanities) 2 (October 1981): 1–2.

2. For a discussion of history and military strategy see Michael Howard, "The Use and Abuse of Military History," *Parameters* 11 (March 1981): 9–14.

3. See Seymour Mandelbaum, "The Past in Service to the Future," *Journal of Social History* 11 (Winter 1977): 193–205.

The Founding Fathers and Clio

Colin B. Goodykoontz

Colin B. Goodykoontz (1885–1958) taught history for many years at the University of Colorado. His publications include *Home Missions on the American Frontier* (1939). He was president of the Pacific Coast Branch of the American Historical Association in 1953, and the following selection was his presidential address, published in the *Pacific Historical Review* (May 1954).

The men who framed the Constitution of the United States have been called the Founding Fathers of the nation. They stood at the culmination of a great movement in self-government, as evidenced in the writing of constitutions in the various states and for the country as a whole during and after the Revolutionary War. James Madison, who more than any other man deserves the title of "Father of the Constitution," declared in the Virginia ratifying convention that "nothing has excited more admiration in the world, than the manner in which free governments have been established in America. For it was the first instance from the creation of the world to the American Revolution, that free inhabitants have been seen deliberating on a form of government and selecting such of their citizens as possessed their confidence to determine upon, and give effect to it."

Although this claim to priority might be challenged on behalf of the Instrument of Government in Cromwellian England, Madison's statement does call attention to the contributions of the Americans to the development of the convention method of forming constitutions and giving reality to the compact theory. James Wilson of

Pennsylvania remarked that to form a good system of government for a single city or state required the strongest efforts of human genius. How much greater was the task of men who drafted a constitution which was intended for many states, some of them yet unformed, and for the "myriads of the human race, who will inhabit regions hitherto uncultivated." Faced with such responsibilities, men of conscience would naturally draw on all available resources of mind and spirit. Where should the Fathers turn for guidance?

At one stage in the Philadelphia deliberations old Ben Franklin called for daily prayers, saying, "I have lived, Sir, a long time, and the longer I live, the more convincing proofs I see of this truth—that God governs in the affairs of men. And if a sparrow cannot fall to the ground without His notice, is it probable that an empire can rise without His aid?" Although this suggestion was not accepted, partly perhaps because of Alexander Hamilton's alleged comment that the Convention was not in need of "foreign aid," there was a general willingness among the delegates to look to Clio, the Muse of History, for assistance; or, as they expressed it, to appeal to the experience of mankind. Pierce Butler of South Carolina said to his associates: "We have no way of judging of mankind but by experience." John Dickinson of Delaware warned them: "Experience must be our only guide. Reason may mislead us. It was not reason that discovered the singular & admirable mechanism of the English Constitution. It was not Reason that discovered . . . the odd & in the eye of those who are governed by reason, the absurd mode of trial by Jury. Accidents probably produced these discoveries, and experience has given a sanction to them. This is then our guide."

It was natural for the men who made the Constitution to turn to experience in order to supplement and check the dictates of reason. One of the oldest traditions in European culture was that history has a didactic value. Such common expressions as "the lessons of history," or "history tells us," testify to the wide acceptance of Edmund Burke's dictum that "experience is the school of mankind and they will learn at no other." To Dionysius of Halicarnassus was attributed the statement that history is philosophy teaching by examples. Cicero called history "the witness of the times, the torch of truth, the teacher of life." A knowledge of the past, said this orator and statesman, is essential to man's maturity, since he who knows not what happened before he was born remains always a child.

The historians, as might have been expected, have generally asserted that their art could and should serve some useful end. If time permitted, quotations from Herodotus, Thucydides, Polybius, Livy, Tacitus, the Venerable Bede, Machiavelli, and many others, could be read in support of such claims as these: history can instruct and inspire; it will aid in the interpretation of the future; it is the best of educations for practical affairs, and especially for political activities; it is the guide of statesmen; it is the judge of mankind; it reveals the moving of God's finger over the sands of time. These are pretty theories, but have men actually studied the lessons of history in time of crisis? Have statesmen gone to the record for guidance? Or, was Hegel right when he said that the only lesson of history is that mankind has never learned anything from history? Let us check this generalization by a brief inquiry into the use that was made of history by the men who drafted and ratified the Constitution of the United States. To what extent and with what results did the Founding Fathers appeal to Clio?

The debates in Philadelphia and in the several ratifying conventions were larded with historical allusions and arguments. History was one of the favorite forms of literature in the eighteenth century. Most of the delegates to the Federal Convention were educated men, and as such were well grounded in the classics; they had read the history of England; they were conversant with the writings of the various authorities on law and government. Francis Bacon once said that "histories make men wise." Here were men who had a considerable knowledge of political history. How wise were they?

In their appeal to experience the Fathers began with an appraisal of human nature and an assessment of the results of popular government. In the early days of the Convention there was a good deal of talk about the unfitness of the people as a whole to share actively in government. They were reported to be ignorant, passionate, impulsive, irrational: they fell easily under the control of demagogues. Democracy was a word with bad connotations: it signified instability, turbulence, "licentiousness." Elbridge Gerry of Massachusetts declared: "The evils we experience flow from the excess of democracy. The people do not want virtue: but are the dupes of pretended patriots." Gouverneur Morris of Pennsylvania said, "The framers of this Constitution had seen much, read much, and deeply reflected. They knew by experience the violence of popular bodies."

There were, however, farseeing statesmen among the delegates who had more faith in the political capacities of their countrymen and who pointed out that only a government that had the confidence of the great mass of the people could long endure: they warned against laying political foundations too narrow for stability. James Wilson, for example, said that he desired to raise "the federal pyramid to a considerable altitude, and for that reason wished to give it as broad a basis as possible."

But even if the masses had been excluded completely from a share in the government, there would have been other problems that resulted from certain common human characteristics. All men, rich and poor, learned and ignorant, were more or less selfish. What should be done about the self-interest and acquisitiveness of the upper classes? Morris had an answer. "History proves," he said, "that men of large fortune will uniformly endeavor to establish tyranny. How then shall we ward off the evil? Give them the second branch [of the legislature], and you will secure their weight for the *public good*. They become responsible for their conduct, and this lust for power will ever be checked by the democratic branch, and thus you form a stability in your government."

Another patriot of the period who stressed the necessity for balancing selfish interests was John Adams. He might well have been one of the framers of the Constitution if he had not been in 1787 our first minister at the Court of St. James. No American statesman of that generation had a wider stock of relevant historical information or had made better use of it in defense of the new republican constitutions. Adams, a realist, urged that men's natural inclinations, including their pride and vanity, be utilized for the public good. He asked, for what do men strive? For fame, attention, recognition. What rewards do they seek? A ribbon, a star, a garter. Frivolities though these be, said Adams, "yet experience teaches us, in every country of the world, they attract the attention of mankind more than parts or learning, virtue or religion." Hence, it was the part of statesmanship to give to men of merit, as Rome did, the outward marks of rank and achievement—a ring, the laticlave, an ivory chair, a crown of gold, a wreath of laurel—and thus encourage and reward distinguished service. Alas for the hopes of Mr. John Adams! When the time came to consider a fitting designation for the Chief Executive of the new nation, Congress would not so much as give him a title; and so that high functionary has remained plain Mr. President.

The solution of the political problems that grew out of the human limitations that so disturbed the Fathers was found, not in the general disfranchisement of the people, but rather in the attempt to balance conflicting interests and in the imposition of checks on hasty action. It was intended that the people should rule indirectly through their elected representatives. The temper of the times could be satisfied by nothing less than a republic. No other form of government, said Madison in *The Federalist*, "would be reconcilable with the genius of the people of America; with the fundamental principles of the Revolution; or with that honorable determination which animates every votary of freedom, to rest all our political experiments on the capacity of mankind for self-government." The Constitution was designed to suit "the genius of the people of America," but what that was could be understood only by men who knew the history of these people.

Of all systems of government the one to which the makers of the Constitution turned most frequently in their search for precedents was the British. In describing the procedure of the Convention, Pierce Butler said: "We had before us all the Ancient and modern Constitutions on record, but none of them was more influential on Our Judgements than the British in Its Original purity." However much a few men may have wished for a monarchy, the English pattern could not be followed with respect to king and nobility, and there were bound to be differences in details even where there was borrowing; but the essential safeguards of liberty that had been evolved in England were incorporated in or made the basis of the new Constitution. The most fundamental of these, with origins that went back at least as far as Magna Carta, was the supremacy of law over government. Moreover, the patriots of the American Revolution had reached back into the middle ages for the concept of a fundamental law that was above ordinary statute law. An act against the constitution is void, said James Otis in his attack on the writs of assistance. Sam Adams, voicing colonial protests against the Townshend Acts, insisted that Parliament had no right to pass such legislation. "There are," he said, "fundamental rules of the constitution which, it is humbly presumed, neither the supreme legislative, nor the supreme executive can alter. In all free states the constitution is fixed." The British authorities, in accordance with the prevailing theory of parliamentary supremacy, rejected this American contention; but the Fathers, when they were free to write a constitution, declared it to be the supreme law of the land. Likewise, mindful of the failure of the colonists in pre-Revolutionary days to make the point that the British empire was essentially federal and that a line of division could be drawn between the powers of Parliament and those of the colonial assemblies, the framers of the Constitution naturally provided for a federal union: they combined central authority and local autonomy. There was no great need to cite precedents for these more general features of the new system; they could be taken pretty much for granted. Instead, the specific references in the debates to English constitutional history had to do mainly with details of government: the veto power of the President, impeachment, the origin of money bills, the writ of habeas corpus, control of the army, the status of treaties, the length of term for members of Congress and their eligibility for appointment to other civil offices. So much attention was paid to English governmental principles and practices, including some venerable constitutional theories, that the Fathers would have discerned the truth of this statement by Professor George Burton Adams: "The history of the formation of the British constitution is a part of our own history. If it be asked where the history of our institutions is to be found previous to the middle of the seventeenth century, there is only one answer to the question which the historian can give. It is to be found in England." Indeed, there had been too much borrowing from the country whose rule had so recently been thrown off to please some of the more democratic members of the new republic. A disgruntled poetaster complained about the new Constitution:

> In five short years of freedom weary grown
> We quit our plain republics for a throne;
> *Congress* and *President* full proof shall bring,
> A mere disguise for Parliament and King.

For the Americans, this English heritage was closely related to their experiences as colonists and revolutionists; and nowhere were the lessons of history more vividly presented. They might have read about King John at Runnymede and about the Glorious Revolution, but they knew at first hand about the issues of the Stamp Act controversy and the alarm that spread through the land when the Old Bay State felt the shock of Shays's rebellion. From colonial days they knew the value of charters, of experience in self-government gained through disputes with royal and proprietary governors, of steps towards intercolonial union from the New England Confederation to the Continental Congresses. Uppermost in their minds and frequently a matter of comment were the weaknesses—or, as they liked to say, the "imbecilities"—of the government under the Articles of Confederation.

The citations of historical facts in the various conventions ranged from the immediate past to "the glory that was Greece and the grandeur that was Rome." There was at the time a lively interest in the classics, as shown not only by the curricula in school and college but also by place names and architecture. It was customary for pamphleteers and those who wrote for the press, especially if the subject were controversial, to sign names reminiscent of antiquity; a letter by Agrippa might provoke a reply from Brutus or Cassius. Furthermore, the ancient world furnished many of the models both for republics and confederations. Hence the oratory and political essays of the constitution-making period were replete with allusions to the Achaean League and the Amphictyonic Council, to tribunes and decemvirs, to patricians and plebians. In general, the references to ancient history by the advocates of constitutional change were intended to show that the early confederacies had often failed because of faulty organization; and that they had been in more danger from the insubordination of their own members than from the tyranny of rulers.

There were other appeals to experience and authority. The histories of three modern confederations, the United Netherlands, the German Confederation, and the Swiss Union, were frequently mentioned, often to emphasize the inadequacies of a weak central government and the dangers of foreign intrigues among the members of a loose union. The opinions of political philosophers and legal experts—Grotius, Vattel, Sidney, Harrington, Locke, Blackstone, Montesquieu—were often quoted. Locke's *Treatises on Government* presented an acceptable doctrine: the duty of government to protect the natural rights of life, liberty, and property. *The Spirit of the Laws* by Montesquieu, in its celebrated threefold division of powers, gave theoretical support to a check-and-balance system.

These remarks on the use of history by the Founding Fathers are not intended to minimize their originality and inventive genius in the realm of government. They developed a new form of union and made some remarkably effective new combinations of old political practices. Even as they looked back over the road by which man had advanced politically, they were aware that they were blazing a new path into the future. After the Federal Convention had been in session about two months, the North Carolina delegation reported to the governor of that state that it was not possible for them to determine how soon the business before them could be finished, since, as they put it, "a very large Field presents to our view without a single straight or eligible Road that has been trodden by the feet of Nations. A Union of Sovereign States, preserving their Civil Liberties and connected together by such Tyes as to Preserve permanent & effective Governments is a system not described, it is a Circumstance that has not Occurred in the History of men." James Madison, always alert to the admonitions of experience, noted the novelty of the undertaking before the Convention, saying that the history of earlier confederations served mainly as beacons which gave warning of a course to be shunned without pointing out that which ought to be pursued.

The men who drafted and passed on the Constitution were not historians; they had received no special training in historical criticism. In so far as their historical information came from books, it probably was based largely on general reading. As educated men they had read history for its literary and cultural values: now, as lawgivers, they turned it to practical ends. Among these men two different appeals to history can be distinguished: one, the search, presumably by men of open minds, for such information as would enable them to decide on a wise course of action; the other, the presentation of facts in support of opinions already formed. There is no clear line of demarcation between these two approaches, because it can always be claimed that an opinion now being defended had not been formed until after some earlier investigation which had been started without bias. However, the use of history for argumentative purposes calls attention to a danger that the Fathers did not entirely escape. When history is used to prove a point, however valid, it is open to this question: has all the relevant evidence been presented? A case in point was the contention by the advocates of constitutional change that the difficulties of the country after the Revolution were attributable mainly to the Articles of Confederation. So intent were these reformers on political defects that they overlooked to a large extent the economic and social causes of trouble that would have been operative irrespective of the framework of government.

Again, the strictures on democracy, as noted above, although bolstered by such expressions as "history proves," seem to have been frequently nothing more than assertions based on prejudices and impressions. The historical evidence presented on this point was drawn to a considerable extent from the ancient city states (where the record was admittedly inadequate) and from Rhode Island. Granted that the Islanders had gone to extremes in their paper money legislation and deserved some of the opprobrium that was cast upon them, little attention was paid by their critics to extenuating circumstances; and conclusions derogatory to the political competence of the people were drawn which might have been changed if there had been a fair examination of the actions of a larger number of popular bodies over a longer period of time.

Another weakness was an apparent belief among certain persons that there was something conclusive in old opinions and practices; some were inclined to rely too much on the past. This was illustrated in the discussion over the proper size of a republic. Montesquieu was quoted to the effect that a republican government was best suited to a small territory, while a large empire called for despotic authority. Opponents of the new Constitution seized on this opinion as an argument that the powers granted to the central government, and presumably necessary if it were to operate vigorously over a vast stretch of land, would endanger liberty. The obvious answer was made that Montesquieu's generalization had been based, in part at least, on the tiny Greek states where the principle of representation was either unknown or only slightly developed; his remarks, consequently, were inapplicable to the United States. True enough: but what neither side in this particular controversy fully realized was that the whole western world was on the eve of a revolution in transportation and communication that would soon bring the hitherto remote sections of a large territory nearer to one another in time than were the outlying parts of a small republic in the ancient world. At the very time the Federal Convention was in session John Fitch, "Crazy Johnny" he was called in derision, was experimenting with a steamboat on the Delaware River. On one occasion, we are told, a committee of delegates, having in mind possible powers of Congress over navigation, watched a trial run—a sign of the coming of a new day in transportation that would make obsolete old notions as to the optimum size of a republic.

Despite such limitations as have been noted with respect to the use of history by the Fathers, the net result of their labors was good and they clearly profited from their knowledge of the past. They had learned from the experience of earlier confederations that the use of force against the members of a union was either futile or a prelude to war. It was ineffective against the strong and a snare for the weak. They devised a union that was partly federal and partly national; they provided for a federal state that had direct compulsive power over individuals. Could they have done a better job if they had known more history? Perhaps, but it should be observed that the most serious weakness in the Constitution as tested by time—its failure to make clear the precise nature of the union and the exact location of sovereignty—could not have been avoided simply by the study of historical records, because history had little or nothing to report on this new form of federal union.

One great service that history rendered to the men who wrote the Constitution was in disclosing to them the long road over which they and their ancestors, spiritual as well as physical, had traveled to Independence Hall. Many cultural trails had come together. One ran back through colonial experience, with such landmarks along the way as the Fundamental Orders of Connecticut, the Mayflower Compact, and the first meeting of the Virginia House of Burgesses. Another had its origin in England where the Bill of Rights and the Petition of Right signalized struggles for liberty. Other trails could be traced back to Christian principles with respect to the worth of the individual; to Rome and its system of law; to Greece and the early attempts to find answers to questions that philosophers ask; to the Hebrew prophets who insisted that Jehovah desired from His people justice and mercy rather than sacrifices and burnt offerings. History did not enable the Fathers to reach back into the past and pick out some ready-made institutions for their own time. Much less did it make it possible for them to predict the future. It did help them understand the situation in which they found themselves; it did light some beacons; and it did record inspiring victories by men of indomitable spirit over "the slings and arrows of outrageous fortune."

Much has been written about the conservatism of the Founding

Fathers, and sometimes with such emphasis as to suggest that they were reactionaries. They were conservatives: they moved cautiously and with an ear tuned to the voice of experience. They were also men of the Enlightenment, and as such were rationalists; they had faith in the power of reason to provide solutions for human problems. But they knew that unless ratiocination was based on solid facts it was of little value. History was one source of these facts; experience tended to curb the exuberance of those who let reason ride off on the wings of imagination. Why did John Dickinson, as quoted above, warn his colleagues against reliance on reason? Was it because so many of the liberals of the time—the democrats, the humanitarians, the unorthodox, the devotees of the idea of progress, and those who professed faith in the goodness of man—all looked to reason as the guide of conduct? One of these freethinkers, Ethan Allen, had only recently issued a book entitled *Reason the Only Oracle of Man*. Within a few years another of that persuasion, Tom Paine, was to give the world his *Age of Reason.* Reason was the watchword of the radicals; conservatives put more stress on experience. The men who made the Constitution sought to find a compromise between these two points of view. If reason said the people must rule, experience added let it be through a republic but not a democracy; if reason said, the people can be trusted, experience warned that they should give heed to the counsels of men of sobriety and wisdom; if reason said, the will of the majority must prevail, experience cautioned that the rights of the minority should be protected.

The Fathers were conservative also in that they wished to conserve, to protect, their political inheritance. They knew that self-government had been won only after a long struggle. They did not want to endanger it by permitting or encouraging ill-advised actions that might discredit it and open the way for a tyrant or dictator. They may have been unnecessarily apprehensive; but if they had seen in a crystal ball the not-far-distant reign of terror in France and the rise of Napoleon, they would have regarded those developments as examples of the evils they feared if ever the mob came to power. History revealed how the institutions that seemed worthy of conservation had come into existence, why they had been passed on from one generation to the next, and how they acquired dignity with age. But history also showed that change has been a law of life, and that peoples and nations that failed to adjust themselves to changing conditions either became stagnant or died. This lesson was not lost on the Fathers. Great as was their concern for the preservation of their political legacy, they drafted a document in which was recognized the possibility, or even the necessity, of change. It was open to amendment, and it contained certain provisions so general that further movement in the direction of democracy, even without amendment, has been possible under it through usage and interpretation. . . .

. . . The Founding Fathers . . . saw that the best way to defend their political system was to improve it. It was not in vain that they sought the help of the Muse of History. History gave them perspective, enabled them better to balance the advantages of the old and the new, and provided them with the information on which they could decide more wisely as to the next step forward. These are among history's greatest services to mankind; they are still good answers to the old question: What is history good for? Among its many uses, history has the power, along with religion, philosophy, literature, and the arts, to lift the spirit of man as it were to a mountain top from which he can more clearly take his bearings in a time of change and confusion.

The Historian
and Public Policy

John Hope Franklin

John Hope Franklin (b. 1915) is professor of history at the University of
Chicago and a past president of the American Historical Association,
the Organization of American Historians, and the Southern Historical
Association. He is a specialist in black history, the South, and Reconstruction. His works include *From Slavery to Freedom* (1947), *Reconstruction After the Civil War* (1961), and *Racial Equality in America*
(1976). "The Historian and Public Policy" originally appeared in *The
History Teacher* (May 1978).

*M*any years ago the distinguished American historian Carl
Becker wrote an essay entitled "Everyman His Own Historian." From the title one might get the impression that
Professor Becker was offering to surrender the field that he had
mined so successfully to anyone who might come along and claim
it. That was not the case! What Professor Becker was actually con-
ceding was that every person had some notion—indeed, a rather
clear notion—of what history actually is. I tend to agree with him,
for the historian's experience is a confirmation of Becker's
assertion. . . .

The general public is not altogether responsible for developing
some rather clear and, at times, strong views on the role of history
and the historian in society. I am certain that each of us can make up
a rather long list of philosophers and statesmen who have summoned history to aid them in rallying the faithful to their banner.
That is what Pericles was doing in 430 B.C. when he told the Athenians that their forefathers had done much to strengthen the city
against the attacks of the Spartans. That is what the deputy in the

French National Assembly was doing in 1789 when he cried out: "The day of the Revelation has arrived, the bones of the victims found in the Bastille have risen at the call of French liberty. They testify against centuries of oppression and of death, prophesying the regeneration of human nature and of the life of the nations." And there is that all-too-familiar invocation of the past by Thomas Jefferson who said: "The history of the present king of Great Britain is a history of repeated injuries and usurpations, all having in direct object the establishment of an absolute tyranny over these States."

One hastens to add that some of the ablest and most successful practitioners of the craft have also contributed significantly to the development of such notions. In seeking to serve what they regard as a worthy public purpose, they have often used their historical materials and insights to serve some special interest or point of view. When the United States was young and needed a sense of unity and national destiny, it was the historian who stepped forward to serve that need. George Bancroft, one of the earliest historians of the new nation, took up where Jefferson left off in the Declaration of Independence. Describing the founding of the colonies in a very special way, he said: "Tyranny and injustice peopled America with men nutured in suffering and adversity. The history of our colonization is the history of the crimes of Europe." Just to make certain that the pages of his history would be a clarion call for the people to rally around the new republic's standard, he declared that the American Revolution was for "the advancement of the principles of everlasting peace and universal brotherhood. A new plebeian democracy took its place by the side of the proudest empires. Religion was disenthralled from civil institutions. . . . Industry was commissioned to follow the bent of its own genius." This is what may be called the pep-rally use of history in which any similarity of the characters in the drama, living or dead, is purely coincidental.

Likewise, when there was a need to promote the interests of a particular economic group or political party, the historian was available to promulgate the virtues of one party and to impugn the integrity of the other. As Pieter Geyl has observed, history has for ages been an effective weapon in party strife. In his book *Jefferson and Hamilton: The Struggle for Democracy in America*, published in 1925, Claude Bowers was not so much interested in democratic institutions as he was in the immaculate conception and virtuous history of the Democratic Party. In portraying Alexander Hamilton, the first Secretary of the Treasury, as a villain and in describing Jefferson, the first Secretary of State, as the able and selfless patriot who saved the nation from the treacherous Federalists, Bowers served the Democratic Party well. Then, performing above and beyond the call of duty, he virtually beatified the third president in his work *Jefferson in Power*, published in 1936. When one recalls that in 1939 the Democratic President, Franklin D. Roosevelt, appointed Bowers United States Ambassador to Chile, it can hardly be said that partisan history does not have its own rewards!

In virtually every area where evidence from the past is needed to support the validity of a given proposition, the historian can be found who will provide the evidence that is needed. This is as true in a discussion of whether democratic institutions had their origins in the German forests or on the American frontier as it is in the search for a valid historical explanation for the foibles and idiosyncrasies that characterize race relations in the United States. Two examples will suffice, one having to do with blacks, the other with Chinese.

Historians have usually been prepared to provide facile and quick explanations and justifications for the subordinate place of Negroes in American life. Some have assumed the role of physical anthropologists or biologists and have argued that blacks occupy a lowly place because of their tragically innate inferiority. Others have become, for the moment, sociologists and have argued that the structure of American society calls for homogeneity or complete assimilation, for which blacks could not, under any circumstances, qualify. Still others have been content with the explanation advanced by a noted historian of the South, Ulrich B. Phillips. In his essay "The Central Theme of Southern History," Phillips declared that the unifying principle of Southern history had been "the common resolve indomitably maintained" by the white man that the South "shall be and remain a white man's country. . . . The consciousness of a function in these premises, whether expressed with the frenzy of a demagogue or maintained with a patrician's quietude, is the cardinal test of a Southerner and the central theme of southern history." Apparently, the tragic fact of history was sufficient to justify the tragic fact of circumstance. One should add that by Southerner Phillips, of course, meant a white Southerner, ignoring the fact that more than one third of that region's population consisted of black Southerners.

Toward the end of the nineteenth century, when Americans began to agitate to bar East Asians from coming into the country, they summoned the so-called facts of history to support them. In 1902 the American Federation of Labor declared that "the free immigration of Chinese would be for all purposes an invasion by Asiatic barbarians, against whom civilization in Europe has been frequently defended, fortunately for us." The Federation did not bother to examine or acknowledge the indisputable fact that the Turks who had invaded Europe were *not* Chinese. Nor did the Federation concern itself with the crucial historical fact that the real Asian barbarians against whom they were *not* railing were assimilating quite well among their American hosts who, after all, had themselves been European barbarians! And the Federation ignored completely the indisputable historical fact that the Chinese had developed a high level of civilization centuries before European civilization reached a comparable level.

But one must attempt to distinguish between the historian's role, on the one hand, in supporting causes or offering explanations and justifications for the position to which they are already committed and, on the other, in trying to assist in the search for solutions to difficult problems in the area of public policy. It seems to me that one role is essentially partisan and defensive and is understandable even when it is indefensible. The other is essentially positive and affirmative and is more interested in how historical events can provide some basis for desirable change. It is a distinction that may not always seem clear to some or, indeed, may not even be regarded as defensible. It is one, however, that can provide a basis for a discussion of the historian and public policy.

The constructive role of the historian in public policy issues in the United States was suggested as early as 1908 in an important case that Louis D. Brandeis argued before the United States Supreme Court. Brandeis claimed that states had the power to prescribe maximum hours of employment of women in laundries. This imaginative student of law *and* history, who would later sit on the United States Supreme Court, presented an enormous brief that not only pointed out the conditions of work that led to excessive fatigue of women workers, but what the experience of women had been, over time, in many parts of the world. On the basis of his findings he concluded that laws regulating the hours of women's work and limiting their work day to ten hours were fully justified. . . . The Brandeis brief . . . had a profound effect on the justices of the Supreme Court in 1908. From that point on, as the Court decided for the women in this case, historical as well as sociological evidence was admissible in crucial legal and constitutional questions having to do with the human condition.

Almost fifty years after Brandeis made his presentation to the United States Supreme Court, that high judicial body directly influenced the emergence of the historian as an important participant in the determination of public policy. In seeking a basis for deciding the grave constitutional questions raised in the school desegregation cases in 1953 the Court asked several questions of legal counsel that historians were better prepared to answer than any other social scientists. In the 1952 October Term, counsel for the children who sought to break down segregation in the public schools had argued that racial segregation was a violation of the Fourteenth Amendment to the Constitution that provided equal protection of the laws for all persons, regardless of race. At the end of the term in 1953 the Court asked counsel on each side to assist it by answering the questions it propounded: "What evidence is there that the Congress which submitted and the State legislatures and conventions which ratified the Fourteenth Amendment [in 1868] contemplated or did not contemplate, understood or did not understand, that it would abolish [racial] segregation in public schools?" The Court also wanted to know from counsel that if neither the Congress nor the states understood that the Fourteenth Amendment required the immediate abolition of segregation in public schools, was it the understanding of the framers of the Amendment that future Congresses might have the power to abolish such segregation or that the Court could construe the Amendment as abolishing such segregation of its own force?

These searching and quite difficult questions sent legal counsel scurrying not to the history books but to the historians! The NAACP Legal Defense Fund provided the principal counsel for the plaintiffs. It recognized the crucial importance of the questions raised by the Court and consequently the Defense Fund assembled a dozen or so historians and other specialists to come up with the answers. It was the historians who then went scurrying to the sources, to read the minutes of the 1865–1866 Joint Committee on Reconstruction, the debates in Congress and in the legislatures that ratified the Fourteenth Amendment, the private correspondence of key figures of the Reconstruction period after the Civil War, and to survey public reaction and response to the events in Washington and the several states. The historians wrote at least a score of working papers for legal counsel, held innumerable conferences and seminars for the legal staff, and made themselves available for questions as well as additional assignments arising from the discussions. The test proved to be a test of the historians' physical stamina as well as their professional skill. Working week after week from September to December 1953, they became accustomed to the work habits of Thurgood Marshall, the Chief Counsel for the Legal Defense Fund, even if those work habits did not delight them. He could say as casually at midnight as he could say at high noon, "Suppose we take a ten minute break."

The historians and the lawyers were an unusually effective team. The historians provided data that traced the evolution of the concept of equality, with its culmination in the writing and ratification of the Fourteenth Amendment. They showed how the pre–Civil War views of the radical abolitionists dominated the egalitarian thinking of the framers of the Fourteenth Amendment. They were able to show, moreover, how the intent of the framers of the Amendment had been frustrated and vitiated by the separate but equal doctrine which, the lawyers contended, was conceived in error. (This doctrine had been set forth by the Supreme Court in 1896 when the justices said that there was no violation in segregating people by race as long as facilities were equal.) The lawyers were then able to take the materials provided by the historians, place them in a legal framework, and by tracing legal precedents as well as changes in the political and social climate, argue quite convincingly that the original intent of the Fourteenth Amendment had indeed been nullified by the actions of its enemies, who were racial segregationists.

Using the findings of the historians, the lawyers argued that the "history of segregation laws reveals that their main purpose was to organize the community upon the basis of a superior white and an inferior Negro caste." The lawyers sounded very much like historians when they said: "history buttresses and gives particular content to the recent admonition of this Court that 'whatever else the framers [of the Fourteenth Amendment] sought to achieve, it is clear that the matter of primary concern was the establishment of equality in the enjoyment of basic civil and political rights and the preservation of those rights from discriminatory action on the part of the States based on considerations of race and color.' " The historians had found the lawyers to be apt, even adroit, students of history!

It is not possible, of course, to assess the influence of the historians' findings on the Court's decision which outlawed segregation in the public schools. Perhaps its influence was great, perhaps not. But the Court had asked questions that only historians could answer; and deciding in favor of the plaintiffs, the Court also decided in favor of the historians. Under the circumstances the temptation is great indeed to argue that the historians played an important part in deciding the issue of segregation in the public schools. In any event, they had answered the call to participate in an important public policy question; and it would seem that their participation had been effective. In any case, the more ardent historians who participated in the case were not at all modest in the claims they made that they contributed substantially to the decision that ended racial segregation in the nation's public schools.

The dispute over segregation in the late 1940's and early 1950's brought forth another quite unique use of historical evidence in the effort to break both the law and the custom of segregation. As some Americans began to inveigh against racial segregation and to fight it in public discussion as well as in the courts, other Americans contended that racial segregation was so *deeply imbedded* in American ethos and practice that it was virtually ineradicable. They assumed that things had always been that way. "Or if not always, then 'since slavery times,' or 'since the War,' or 'since Reconstruction.' " Some even thought of the system of racial segregation as existing along with African slavery. It was the distinguished historian of the South, C. Vann Woodward, who, recognizing the distortions and inaccuracies that arose from such assumptions, decided to try to set the record straight. If he could show that much of the legal segregation of the races was as recent as it was vagarious, then those who defended it could not fall back on the specious argument that things had always been that way.

Woodward decided to do what no proponents of segregation had ever bothered to do, or, for that matter, what no opponents of segregation had done. He went back to the historical record and examined the origins of some of the segregationist laws and practices. He did not attempt to show that there had been *no* legal segregation until late in the nineteenth century. The time-honored practice of racial segregation in schools, churches, and the army clearly indicated that a considerable amount of racial segregation had existed much earlier. Nor was he interested, in this instance, in writing a definitive history of racial segregation. Much more research than he had done would be required for such an undertaking. (I once wrote an article under the impressive and comprehensive title "A History of Racial Segregation in the United States." But in those nine pages I could not have even covered the subject of the segregation of dogs and cats of black and white owners in the cemeteries of the United States.) Woodward was content to make a modest contribution to the current debate by suggesting that segregation was neither as universal in origin nor as venerable in age as many on both sides of the argument assumed that it was. Because of the lack of basic research in the field, he believed that he would make mistakes; and he welcomed corrections on the part of his readers.

Woodward's book, *The Strange Career of Jim Crow,* is a notable example of the historian's participation in a public policy discussion. As brief as it is, it has much to say about the uneven hand with which the South meted out its laws to disfranchise, segregate, and create a permanently subordinate Negro caste. Those who argued that blacks had not voted in any elections since Reconstruction ended in 1877 seemed quite unaware of the fact that several blacks were elected to the United States Congress in the 1890's and that literally hundreds of them held local elective offices in many parts of the South as late as 1900. Those who claimed that the Democratic Party had always been the exclusive domain of the white man did not know that some blacks, at the urging of whites, voted the Democratic ticket until the end of the nineteenth century and that the Democratic white primary is in fact a twentieth-century phenomenon, or aberration or, if you will, monstrosity. Those who said that the races had always been separated did not understand that some states did not adopt laws to segregate the races on railroad trains and in waiting rooms until the end of the century and that the bulk of the segregation statutes date from the 1890's or later.

Woodward did not deny the existence of widespread anti-Negro feeling, better known as Negrophobia, or long-held views of Negro inferiority. These were indisputable facts which no amount of research or arguing could eradicate; and he did not desire to do so. As a matter of fact, he *did* see an increase in racism, or Negrophobia, brought on by uncertainties and anxieties in the political and economic spheres. He *did* see that the belief in Negro inferiority had been bolstered by those who subscribed to Social Darwinism and by those who practiced social and political demagoguery. But what he saw most clearly—and what he wanted his contemporaries to see— was that the arguments favoring the sanctity and veneration of segregation could not prevail because they were not grounded in fact and that segregation was merely another gambit in the South's determination to have its own way in the crucial matter of race relations. The South, moreover, was ambivalent, uncertain, shifty, and unclear. Today, there was no segregation; tomorrow there would be. What was true in one county was not necessarily true in another. The laws in one state were quite different from the laws in another state. In the face of all this, it was difficult to argue that pervasive and comprehensive segregation had always been and always would be. Racists would have to find some other argument, one that had some shred of validity and credibility in their desperate attempt to hold on to segregation. Woodward believed that they would not be able to find it.

Indeed, as Woodward expected, there were those who criticized him, primarily for not doing what he did not undertake to do, namely, to prove that there had been no segregation until the 1890's. Others gleefully called attention to some early segregation statute that he had overlooked or that he did not know existed. . . . Such findings detracted little from Woodward's argument that segregation statutes and practices were uneven and that most of the laws came much later.

There is no way of knowing what effect Woodward's book had on the dispute that was raging when he wrote it. One doubts that it converted many segregationists or that it persuaded many legislators to believe that they could safely vote to repeal laws that separated the races. But it was an eloquent affirmation of the point that in a public policy question such as racial segregation it was possible to distort and exploit the past for the wildest and most pernicious purposes. It was, moreover, a significant contribution to the discussion and, perhaps, may even have helped prepare the ground when the segregation statutes themselves slipped largely into disuse after the passage of the Civil Rights Act of 1964. Whenever a Negro American traveled in the South after 1964 and noticed the range of services available to him in hotels, restaurants, and other places of public accommodation, he would perhaps be inclined to challenge William Graham Sumner's 1907 dictum that "stateways cannot change folkways." He might also be inclined to agree with C. Vann Woodward, who had argued in 1955 that since segregation statutes were neither very old nor very sacred, it made no sense to argue that they could never be changed.

The area in which the historian participates in public policy issues has grown enormously in recent years, thanks to the increasing use made of historians by the several levels of government. Today virtually every department in the executive branch of the United States government has its staff of historians, ranging from the highly esteemed branch of historical policy research in the U.S. Department of State to the rather modest historical section in the National Park Service in the U.S. Department of the Interior. These persons, many of whom are very talented and highly trained, perform yeoman service in their roles as participants in policy formulation and decision-making in their respective departments.

It is, of course, important that the Department of State have experts who can provide the historical background of United States foreign policy in, say, Southeast Asia or Western Europe or South America. Surely, the need for historians and other students of Southeast Asia became obvious when the United States found itself deep in the morass of the internal affairs of Indo-China without an adequate understanding of the historical background on which to base a sound public policy. It is likewise important that the National Park Service know something of, say, the land conservation policies and the way they were administered before the Park Service came into formal existence in 1916. These, however, are essentially service functions; and the historians who perform them have a relationship to their departments that is understandably supportive of the team to which they belong. It is no reflection on the ability or even the integrity of official historians if one should assert that their independence in speaking out on controversial public policy issues is quite limited, especially if their views do not coincide with those of their departments.

When he was President of the United States, Theodore Roosevelt was his own historian in formulating the historical basis for matters of public policy. A close student of history and a future President of the American Historical Association, the aggressive-minded President believed that armed force and military rule were fully justifiable methods of dealing with "backward peoples." The Chinese, he insisted, lacked the qualities that to him spelled civilization. If the United States fell into the hands of "the futile sentimentalists of the international arbitration type," he warned, then it would be reduced to the "timidity and inefficiency" of the Chinese. This dim view of the Chinese did not stem from his ignorance of the rich culture of the Chinese, but from his racial intolerance and his lack of respect for a people who failed to use their own culture and civilization to fight for a more important place in the family of nations. It was this view of the past and the present that not only influenced U.S. policy toward China for a full generation but that set the tone of U.S. foreign policy in general.

One cannot be certain that official historians, whether holding elective office or merely civil servants, will always serve the best interests of the public. For, as Herbert Butterfield has reminded us, when historians are in the service of the government and the public policy of that government rests on a certain set of historical precedents, it is difficult for men to place truth above public advantage when public advantage might mean the winning of a war, the circumvention of a diplomatic crisis, the covering of a reputation, or even an improvement in general welfare. Their commitment is to a policy that, having been determined and agreed upon, does not seek alternatives to the same or a similar end and rejects differences or challenges as inimical to its objectives.

It would seem highly important, therefore, that historians with *no* governmental connections should participate in the discussion of public policy with that independence of mind and spirit that their private position affords. Indeed, from their relatively detached position, they could engage, challenge, debate, and criticize their governmental colleagues who are a part of the apparatus where public policy is determined. Historians on the outside could raise questions about the operation of a given policy that is defended on the ground that it is in line with historical public policy in that area. Indeed, and by the same token, the outsiders could challenge the traditional public policy if on the basis of their examination of the record they find it to be out of line with historical facts as well as current interests and needs. They, most of all, could challenge the sanctity and validity of a traditional policy that might not even be the tradition but that is followed for the sake of a so-called tradition and not necessarily for the sake of the public interest.

In 1935, for example, the manual of the Federal Housing Administration stated that in order to maintain community stability, real estate properties should continue to be occupied by the same racial and social classes as in the past. On the basis of this stated public policy, segregated public housing was erected with the support of the federal government all over the United States. It is lamentable that some outside historian had not challenged the policy and stated then and there that since the Civil War, blacks and whites lived next door to each other—and were still doing so in 1935—in Richmond, Raleigh, Charleston, Mobile, New Orleans, and dozens of other places. In the absence of such a challenge the policy stood and, in the words of one housing authority, it did more to entrench housing bias in the American neighborhoods than any court could undo by a ruling. . . .

As a nation views its history and the various positions that it has taken, it is not difficult to conclude that its postures have been mixed and exist on several levels of morality. At times, in the case of the United States, at least, its public policy has been humane, healthy, and worthy; it has helped earthquake victims, fed starving peoples, and fought the Nazi barbarians. At other times, it has been bereft of many or any praiseworthy objectives. It has upheld corrupt regimes abroad, interfered in the internal affairs of sovereign nations, and taken territories belonging to others. It is the function of the historian to keep before the people, with as much clarity as possible, the different lines of action that have been taken, the several, often complicated reasons for such action, and to point to the conflicts and inconsistencies, the contradictions and illogicalities, and the defects and deficiencies when they exist. One might argue that the historian is the conscience of his nation, if honesty and consistency are factors that nurture the conscience. Perhaps that is too much to claim for the historian who, after all, is not in the business of protecting the morals of a people.

It would be enough if in our time the historian were to look at our many public policies that we claim to be firmly based in the hallowed past and see if that is in fact the case. As we celebrate the bicentennial of our national independence and as we pursue many of our public policies in the name of the founding fathers . . . the historian and, indeed, all of us should take a hard look at what we ascribe to the founding fathers. But the time is at hand for us to recognize the fact that deep veneration is one thing and uncritical approbation is quite another. If we cannot celebrate their achievements and, at the same time, recognize their human frailties which led them to make numerous mistakes, we are unworthy of the legacy we claim to celebrate.

The people, yes, the people, shall judge; but they require a sound basis for making judgments. They will have that basis if and when they know what has happened, why it has happened and, consequently, how the public policies growing out of historical events or shaping those events can serve the common good. If, then, the people prefer to ignore their past mistakes and prefer to live in a world of fantasy and make-believe, they will deserve to suffer the fate of repeating the grave errors that they could easily have avoided.

A Reflection on Historians and Policymakers

David F. Trask

David F. Trask (b. 1929) has taught history at Boston University, Wesleyan University, the University of Nebraska, and the State University of New York at Stony Brook. His books include *Captains and Cabinets: Anglo-American Naval Relations 1917–1918* (1972) and *The War with Spain in 1898* (1981). When the following essay appeared (in the February 1978 issue of *The History Teacher*), Trask was director of the Office of the Historian in the United States Department of State, which edits and publishes the documentary series *Foreign Relations of the United States.*

Do history and historians have a legitimate role to play in the task of making policy? Obviously, if policymakers feel no need for history or if historians fail to identify a usable past, we are wasting our time discussing the lessons of experience. What, then, is the rationale for history as an aid to policymakers? Is historical thought an indispensable aspect of policymaking?

Surely the behavior of our public men constitutes a presumptive case for the high utility of history in policymaking. Statesmen inveterately dwell on historical developments and their lessons. A former Secretary of State is no exception; Dr. Henry Kissinger spoke forthrightly in this vein:

> The American people have learned the lessons of history. They are committed to a permanent, active, and responsible American role in the world. They are dedicated to standing by our friends and allies; they are determined to resist aggression; they deeply believe in the moral necessity of building a more stable peace; they are prepared to cooperate in the dialogue between industrial and developing countries for promoting human progress.

In advancing this interpretation Secretary Kissinger proved faithful to a judgment rendered in his book of 1957 entitled *A World Restored:*

> No significant conclusions are possible in the study of foreign affairs—the study of states acting as units—without an awareness of the historical context. For societies exist in time rather than in space. . . . [A state] achieves identity only through the consciousness of a common history. This is the only "experience" nations have, their only possibility of learning from themselves. History is the memory of states.

Just because leaders so frequently appeal to history we might expect to find a considerable number of professional historians serving as advisors to people in power, but surely such isn't the case. Leaders do not turn regularly to trained historians for advice, and trained historians rarely put themselves forward as counselors.

What are some of the reasons for this state of affairs? To begin with, the prestige of history is now in temporary decline, a casualty of revolutionary changes during our times. It is often argued, however tendentiously, that history is either irrelevant or dangerous, because the future before us bears no relation to past times, because bad examples crowd the pages of history—knaves, fools, and criminals—and because historians distort reality. The French poet Paul Valéry, surely one of the most effusive cliophobes in memory, summarized this case:

> History is the most dangerous product ever concocted by the chemistry of the intellect. . . . It causes dreams, inebriates the nations, saddles them with false memories, exaggerates their reflexes, keeps their old sores running, torments them when they are at rest, and induces in them megalomania and the mania of persecution. It makes them bitter, arrogant, unbearable, and full of vanity.

All too often untrained or incompetent historians produce history of the sort that Valéry decried. The pseudohistorian, filling the vacuum left by the professional, snips out of the historical pattern only what suits his particular passion. His tortured view violates sound canons of historical scholarship but gains transient approbation because it provides simplistic explanations of complex events. Small wonder that such efforts eventually serve only to muddy the waters and to discredit legitimate practitioners.

But difficulties of this nature pale into insignificance when we consider how often respectable scholars themselves deny that history and historians can provide anything of use to policymakers. Usually historians achieve this end by committing the sin of omission; few make known their opinions on important public questions. What accounts for this stillness?

Surely the very act of historical study often induces quietism in its votaries because, in the grandest perspective, the contemplation of transient human affairs inbues many historians with a sense that in the long run existence is inescapably tragic. Some even decide that life has no larger meaning, a conclusion drawn from recognition that even the greatest leaders and the strongest institutions eventually come to grief. Given this truism, that in the fullness of time degradation and destruction lie at the end of every path, it is hardly surprising that historians commonly attribute less importance to the day-to-day activities of governments than scholars engaged in other disciplines.

Another circumstance, albeit less cosmic, tends to inhibit the public activism of historians. Many of them harbor serious doubts concerning the legitimacy of what is called "recent history" or "contemporary history"—that form of historical analysis usually associated with policymaking. Good numbers among them ask probing questions. "Is reliable evidence available so soon after the fact to warrant defensible historical conclusions?" "Do sufficient perspective and adequate objectivity exist to permit sound evaluation of events just past?" Often historians answer these queries with a resounding "No" and then dismiss recent history as a trivial exercise in "current events." One consequence is that all too many people are encouraged in the delusion—for delusion it is—that history and historians have nothing to offer policymakers.

Let us turn, then, to the question of whether historical thought constitutes a mere frill in the making of policy or whether it is an indispensable element. To facilitate this inquiry let me offer some simple definitions.

When I speak of "history" I have in mind *the study of past processes.* I refer to the analysis of developments in some specified location across a given span of time. It is often said that history is the study of the past, but this definition is too broad. A moment's thought reveals that many scholars besides historians study the past; for example, political scientists, geographers, archaeologists, and demographers. The unique enterprise that separates the historian from other students of the past is that he thinks *processionally*, that is, in terms of time passing. The alternative possibility—the approach used by others who study the past—is to think *structurally*, that is, to eliminate the time factor. A simple analogy helps draw this distinction: consider that historians make motion pictures of the past whereas others make still photographs. A study of the structure of politics at some given moment in the past—for example during the reign of George III—serves many useful purposes, but it is a study in political science, not history. If such a work is really history, a processional study, it ought to be entitled "The Process of Politics in the Age of George III." The purpose I have in mind is to demonstrate that we have available two ways of viewing the past. There is virtue aplenty in both of these ways—the processional way and the structural way. I note the difference to pin down the specific service of the historian. He makes processional studies.

Analysis of past processes concentrates attention on two kinds of developments. Historians search for continuity—those elements which do not alter over time—and they search for change—those elements which do, indeed, differ over time. Students of process can identify continuity and change effectively. Social scientists such as economists, sociologists, and other equally constructive scholars cannot generalize about continuity and change with the authority of the historian simply because they do not study processes.

But I have pursued this idea—that history is properly defined as the study not simply of the past but of past processes—to a sufficient extent. Let me turn to a second definition. What do we mean by the word "policy"? The term refers to a plan by which leaders hope to influence the outcome of one or another process in the future. Policy by definition constitutes a strategy, that is, a comprehensive design to bring about certain future outcomes as against other possible outcomes. Policy is a calculated course of action intended to shape future history, a scheme by which we hope to achieve desirable continuities and changes at some future time.

Ordinarily we decide what policy is desirable by measuring conceivable options against two standards. One standard is pragmatic in nature: "How workable are the various options?" Another standard is ethical in nature: "How do various options comport with concepts of good as against evil?"

This observation brings us to the policymaker. What does he do?

He might, to be sure, decide that the proper policy is to make no change, that is, to accept ongoing continuities and changes. If, however, the policymaker decides on some new course, he plans one or more of three interrelated designs. He plans ways of modifying processes or he plans ways of ending processes or he plans ways of inaugurating processes. If the policymaker concentrates so extensively on processes, why shouldn't we call him a historymaker? He specializes in planning the manufacture of the future as process, that is, the creation of the future as history.

The policymaker has no alternative but to make use of historical information and historical thought simply because he is specifically concerned with processes, the bread and butter of historians. Policymakers consider plans for influencing future processes by reference to comprehension of past processes. History provides much of the data and ways of thinking available to those interested in shaping the future as process.

We now have a common-sense explanation of the reasons why the statesman so frequently refers to "the lessons of history." The statesman builds from a revealed past to a future not yet known. He is compelled to consult history for assistance in making policy, that is, for help in planning future processes. Historical information and historical thought constitute inherent and indispensable aspects of policymaking.

There remains, then, only one consideration. To whom do policymakers go for their history? I noted earlier that they don't seem anxious to enlist professional historians. All too often, I fear, they depend on their own historical resources, often insufficiently developed, or on those of dedicated but ill-informed advisers. I cite this circumstance as a reason for advocating the use of professional, as well as amateur, historians in the vital arena of advice to decisionmakers. I take as my guideline the assumption that we should speak truth to power.

What, then, can we reasonably expect from historians? Let me discuss briefly two broad contributions to policymaking that can issue from professionals in the field.

One of these contributions obviously must be to provide the best possible version of recent history. Earlier I mentioned the tendency of professional historians to derogate the study of relatively contemporary processes. This bias reflects itself in the academic preparation of historians. Few institutions stress this specialty, ignoring the plaint of so distinguished an historian as the late Herbert Feis, who wrote not long ago: "The historian of the recent past should not be regarded as low man on the totem pole. His service to the life of the nation, all nations, is too important." In this same spirit Ernest R. May has summarized the rationale for recent history, arguing that historians

> must somehow become better able to study those events most likely to influence people in public life—that is, events of the relatively recent past. Even though many of these events seem as much experience as history, they are susceptible of being better understood if carefully re-constructed—above all if reconstructed by historians of varying approaches who examine the same evidence and dispute about its meaning.

I want to endorse this view and call for full-blown programs of historical study designed to train specialists in the opportunities and challenges of recent history. Otherwise, we leave the arena to non-specialists, whose contributions are not always sufficient unto the day.

A common contemporary conceit is that anyone can be as good at history as anyone else, but is it not the part of wisdom to seek historical advise from those trained specifically to offer such counsel? By no means am I suggesting that amateurs should not feel free to advise on historical matters. I am simply arguing that professional historians should not concede the historical turf entirely to them. When we need plumbing repairs, we may consult a helpful neighbor, but we also call in a plumber. It follows that when we need advice on future historical processes we should call in among others those with special expertise on processes in general.

Let me turn now to a second aspect of the historian's service to policymakers, much more recondite and controversial than the question of recent history. I want to evaluate the historian's qualifications as a prophet, that is, to decide whether he has special insights into the future. Professor May succinctly summarizes a point of view on this question. He writes, "It may be that historians come closer than most scholars to engaging systematically in prophecy. For they predict backward. They construct hypotheses about the forces that produce change or continuity in some past period. In the process, they may develop some skill at least in identifying questions to be asked by those ahead." I agree with this argument and hope to extend it, although first I want to quibble with it in one respect. May uses the terms "prediction" and "prophecy" as though they were synonyms. I would like to distinguish between them, because that distinction makes a great deal of difference. It should be clear that the prophet does not predict the future in flat terms. Unlike the predicter the prophet deals in that wonderful word "if." He does not simply say that something will happen and let it go at that. The prophet claims that something will happen *if* certain things are done as against other things. For this reason prophecy is contingent, whereas prediction is immutable. The ancient prophet Jeremiah, for example, informed the wayward people of Judah that they could dwell happily in their ancient homeland "if you truly amend your ways and your doings, if you truly execute justice one with another, if you do not oppress the alien," and so on. Otherwise Jehovah would have punished the people and the land; all would have burned unquenchably.

Now that we have a working definition of prophecy, let us consider its relevance to our discussion. My contention is a simple one—that the act of policymaking entails continual exercises in prophecy. The policymaker concerns himself above all with the different outcomes that might follow from various courses of action. He weighs available options and their consequences as the means of discriminating between them and reaching a decision. This is another way of saying that the policymaker is a secular prophet.

Most historians manifest considerable skepticism about their ability to make recommendations concerning the future. This modesty becomes them, but I contend that it is misplaced. I side with May in believing that the very nature of historical thought, concentrating as it does on the analysis of continuity and change, confers upon historians not only unique perspectives on the future but special prophetic abilities. Therefore, as a second aspect of his service to power, I urge that the historian advance his views on options available to statesmen and his vision of their consequences. He might even go further by specifying his preference among those options, the result of weighing them against pragmatic and ethical standards.

Having said so much, let me issue certain caveats. I, of course, do not claim for the historian any monopoly on prophetic counsel, just as I would not deny him an appropriate piece of that action. Second, I hasten to add that the eventual decision must remain with the statesman, just as I would not withhold from men and women in power the benefit of informed prophetic advice from professional historians.

My answer to the question posed at the outset—Do historians have a legitimate role to play in the task of making policy?—is that they have an indispensable part. In advising statesmen they should not only analyze appropriate past processes but also weigh policy options by means of a prophetic exercise.

Those who study the past often concur in Arthur Schlesinger, Jr.'s judgment, "Man generally is entangled in insoluble problems; history is consequently a tragedy in which we are all involved, whose keynote is anxiety and frustration, not progress and fulfillment," but historians must also consider Schlesinger's further injunction, that nevertheless "a sense of the great and intricate stream of historical experience is exceedingly helpful in making intelligent judgments about current policy." During the latter part of the nineteenth century one of the greatest of historians, the pessimistic Jacob Burckhardt, insisted that only "Barbarians and modern American men of culture live without consciousness of history." I hope that today and tomorrow we so comport ourselves as to refute this sour judgment. Contemporary pessimists, overwhelmed by the pace of change in our times, all too often advise us either to ignore past processes or to concede that we cannot draw sustenance from analyzing them. To the contrary, I would insist on the proposition that historical insight is never so useful as during revolutionary times, even if, in such conditions, we have to reexamine the nature and meaning of the intellectual enterprise we call history. This reality explains why the great philosophers of history often flower in times of unrest, a thought that Georg Wilhelm Friedrich Hegel sought to convey in his famous aphorism, "The owl of Minerva takes flight when the shadows of night are falling."

Historians are expert at conjuring up all manner of reasons for not taking action. Just for a moment, I urge them to consider the opportunities as well as the dangers in the present setting. We ought now to act with energy and dedication comparable to the high standards of scholarship and responsibility which actuated distinguished forebears from George Bancroft to Charles A. Beard to Samuel Eliot Morison. Those historians never doubted that the past as process, including the recent past, could be mobilized to assist policymakers. We who carry on possess sound models; all that we need add is dedication.

Uses and Misuses
of History:
Roles in Policymaking

Otis L. Graham

Otis L. Graham (b. 1935) has taught history at the University of California, Santa Barbara, and the University of North Carolina at Chapel Hill. He has written about the United States in the twentieth century and has been especially interested in reform and national planning. Among his books are *An Encore for Reform: Old Progressives and the New Deal* (1967); *The Great Campaigns: Reform and War in America, 1900–1928* (1971); and *Toward a Planned Society: From Roosevelt to Nixon* (1976). The following selection appeared in the *The Public Historian* (Spring 1983).

*M*uch is novel these days in the study of the past. This is manifestly true in the realms of method and topic, and if that were not enough to shift the ground beneath our feet, there is the novelty of new applications and audiences. The public or applied history movement has come to flourishing life in less than a decade, altering, through augmentation, both the graduate education and the roles of some older historians and many more of the young. My topic, history in the policymaking process, may imply that I intend to join those proposing even more novel applications of history in the nonacademic world. To my mind it is too late to recommend such applications; rather I see myself attempting to catch up with and appraise them, for they have been for some time in full swing. I am reminded of the French revolutionary leader whose amorous interlude was interrupted by the sounds of a mob in the street. He rushed to the balcony and cried: "There go my followers. I am their leader. I must follow them." It is said that he did not quite get his trousers on. Historians who ply their trade in the conventional ways and settings must feel some resonance with his situation.

Note that my topic is more focussed than the question of history's usefulness outside the classroom. It is narrower even than the utility of historical skills to nonacademic institutions such as governments and corporations. That utility appears to have an impressive potential range, extending at least to records management, institutional biography, and other internal services that present the institutional past to the public. All of these uses are presently flourishing on a small but growing scale within American corporations. . . . But neither in business nor in government do we find much evidence that the extra-academic expansion of the social role of historical studies has penetrated the policy process directly, or that it should. Past policies, of course, have always been historians' terrain, shared with political scientists and others. But policy analysis has been done on campuses or at research centers, not within policymaking institutions. In fact, it is unclear how much policymakers are influenced by policy analysis, historical or otherwise, though governments pay for a good bit of it. The industry of analyzing past policies lies outside my main concern. Instead, I will explore the engagement of historical thinking and research with the policymaking process itself, and reflect upon the past as it affects the present and the future.

The first step may be taken quickly. Selling our product to busy policymakers is not necessary. We in the academy did not have the monopoly we expected. Our product—respect for and study of the past—is marketed and consumed by millions of citizens off-campus. Policymakers in private and public sectors are devoted to history, and are well supplied with it, on the black market as it were, without coming to us. Amateurs have long dabbled in history, as the professional knows well, but few notice how important these amateurs have become. The past, along with its "lessons" and insights, is deeply involved in policymaking, but it has gotten away from us: there are no royalties, no permissions forms, little consultative shepherding, not even a thank you. Carl Becker told us that Everyman was his own historian, which we must accept, but Everyman turns out to be presidents, legislators, judges, chief executive officers and their staffs—Everymen of real power. And not only are they historians, they appear to be quite poor ones, using the past mostly to reinforce bias and strengthen advocacy positions derived from other perspectives.

Passing acquaintance with the history of decisions in public and private organizations uncovers this reality. No one to my knowledge has exposed this so well, for the public sector at the federal level at least, as Ernest May in *Lessons of the Past*. His examples of federal policymaking in the twentieth century reveal the powerful influence of the past upon a series of major policy decisions stretching from the 1940s to the 1960s. May finds that influence pernicious, in retrospect. His examples—the most powerful of them to my mind being the case of Harry Truman and his advisors in dealing with the Korean conflict—are well known. They lay bare the omnipresent power of assumptions about "what history teaches." These assumptions were exceedingly amateurish, implicit rather than explicit and thus unexamined. They took the form of a remarkably simplistic analogizing from some remembered catastrophe—principally what "Munich" was thought to have taught about the necessity to meet "aggression" with resistance. Truman and his men, like FDR before him and his successors later on, looked at present issues through lenses of memory every time. In all cases offered by Professor May, this was not a happy influence for policy or for the future. Policymakers were not good at utilizing history, but they were hopelessly addicted to doing so.

May's instructive book drew upon case studies of his own choosing. Had his colleague Bernard Bailyn written it, surely the findings would be the same but drawn from late eighteenth-century policy. Had his other colleague Al Chandler written it, surely the twentieth-century business executive would have been found to think and decide in similar ways.

. . . President Reagan is a devout student of history. One learns from an early book on his presidency that he has established precise goals in his counterrevolution: to return the nation to 1955 in its foreign policy situation, and to 1925 in its domestic political economy. But the past for him and his advisors has a stronger hold than merely to offer tempting visions of the ideal. Why, he was asked, would his tax cut, main tool of supply-side economics, work in 1982? He responded as follows: " 'Cause it always has. It did when Kennedy did it. It did in the time of Coolidge. Andrew Mellon has written about the tax cuts, and they worked. So I just—I take my personal experience in pictures. I was in that excessively high tax bracket after WWII and I know what I did. . . . Once I had reached that bracket, I just turned 'em down."

Thus it is much too late to debate whether history should serve power. Power answered that question a long time ago, and we who have a special relation to the past have not fully recognized its extent and meaning. It seems odd that our many accounts of policy decisions do not expose the historical assumptions at work with the relish and care one would have expected from historians discovering the past as a steady companion of the great and the busy. What decisions do *not* flow to some extent from assumptions about what the past appears to teach? History is useful, and utilized. It pervades the decisionmaking process of individuals and groups. And familiarity with that influence, almost invariably covert and unexamined, suggests that the past is not serving policymakers well. We know where the blame should rest. The past is inert. It is policymakers who manipulate it toward error and confusion. For every case of a policy decision guided by historical assumptions toward desired ends, there must be five or ten bent toward miscalculation. Ernest May found miscalculation every time. Let such studies flourish, and establish a better sense of how the amateurs are doing as they reach back for authority and guidance. We may safely assume, I think, that the mob is in motion but not toward desired or desirable ends. The misreading of the past may be a more significant source of policy error than is generally appreciated.

This is the starting point for an NEH-sponsored course entitled History for Decision Makers which four colleagues and I are offering, now in the second year, at the University of North Carolina (UNC) Business School. We do not try to convince the young executives and entrepreneurs that they should "use" history. We demonstrate that they *will*, inevitably, that their predecessors did so, that decisionmaking is inextricably bound up in past events and their analysis, and that the assessment of the past is very poorly done as compared with the assessment of present and future circumstances. We have little difficulty with this point, utilizing case studies from both public and private sectors. The students expected an invitation, perhaps a supplication, to join us as devotees of history. Instead, we welcome them to a guild broader than any of us thought; it includes us all.

How, then, to do it right? Can "the professionals" sharpen the skills of the amateurs? Here the path becomes more steep. What are trained historians to say to busy decisionmakers with little education in history and (usually) no interest in it? How can their uses of the past, which all now concede to be both inevitable and uninformed, be improved?

The MBA students at once grasped the meaning and appreciated the importance of case after case of decisionmaking in which presumed and usually misleading "lessons of the past" had been powerful factors in shaping decisions. They then expected that we would teach them to select the *proper* analogies and lessons. We surprised them. For it was analogies themselves that we intended to question, implanting a deep suspicion of the deathless human assumption that if a thing worked once it will work again, that if it brought disaster before it will always bring disaster. We tried also to undercut the faith in simple projections of past trends, another way that historic data are misused in selecting policy. "You cannot step in the same river twice," we kept repeating, though of course we did not go so far as to urge historical nihilism, the *forgetting* of past episodes. Analogies, in which past experience bears some resemblance to the present, have their uses in thinking about present and future, but we have decided not to take that road. We read the history of decisionmaking to reveal that analogies have too strong a hold, and we attempted to instill in the students' minds a suspicion of that mode of reasoning so deep as to verge upon a refusal to see history as teaching by example.[1]

We had insufficient time to develop in the students a sophisticated grasp of the limited gains to be had simply by studying episodes in search of examples of past failures and successes in business, or anywhere else. We took them another way, arguing that the chief benefit of thinking historically lay not in skill at ransacking the past for formulas or models, but rather in the characteristic modes of thought among historians when they are at their best. These, we argued, in what is surely only one formulation of the matter, constituted a special sensitivity and skill in two dimensions of human life—the dimension of time and of context, dimensions which might also be called the diachronic and the synchronic after Robert Berkhofer's usage, or sequence and setting, or even the vertical and the horizontal. Utilizing multiple case studies of policymaking in both public and private sectors, we elucidated during a semester of study the complementary axes of analysis which are always employed by the historical mind in its fullest exercise.

The first idea holds that an executive or executive group making policy, public or private, will benefit from a trained sensitivity to our profession's central preoccupation: change and continuity over time. As Lawrence Veysey put it recently, "An overriding concern for temporality distinguishes the historian from academics of all other persuasions—except astronomers, earth scientists, and some biologists, who might be called the historians of nature." Where are we in the stream of time? Historians push that question to the front of discussion, and then proceed to disaggregate the confluence of flowing matter which constitutes any present. If we develop skill at anything, it is in the ability to discern which parts of the received heritage of any contemporary moment retain or even gain in force and momentum, and which tend toward debility. Every moment, and of course the future, is composed of stands from the past, but these are never of equal vitality. Reasoning by simple analogy confers on every part of the inherited past—all institutions, practices, ideas, organizations, memories—the same force and effect they possessed when last they meshed. Historical nihilism regards them all as depleted, the world as made new. Historians do not agree on many things, but we all know that time enervates *and* initiates as it moves, that it undermines many a fighting faith before that is fully known, and launches new forces of unsuspected power. The trick, it might be said, is to know when the hand of heritage is heavy or light, and where. This assists us in accounting for uneven rates of change, perceiving when situations are open for movement and innovation, or jelled and stalemated against change.

The second idea restates history's credentials as an integrative discipline, and stresses the insistence of the historical imagination upon seeing matters whole. Sister disciplines would not readily concede such a claim, but which of the social sciences possesses the inclination to blend economic, political, intellectual, cultural, climatic, geographic, demographic, scientific, technological, organizational, and psychological factors and concepts? Most, in fact, confine their energies within the boxes of ideas, organizations, marketplace, or politics. Historians have of course been so confined, as every year's crop of monographs attests. But at its best the historian's grasp is eclectic. We thirst for the social whole, the relevant if not the entire context.

Policymakers who develop such an appetite for the impinging variables of social context will have reaped a second sort of benefit from the craft of historical reconstruction. Whether this be called synchronic analysis, or attention to setting or context or the horizontal dimension, its neglect is the primary occupational hazard of each social science in its turn, and also of each trade, each corporation marketing a product, each segmented part of complex institutions. Policy error comes often in the form of a surprise from some impinging factor or factors whose bearing upon one's own narrower plans, indeed whose very existence, was often screened out of the analysis. "Exogeny forever!" suggested Arthur Schlesinger, Jr., when asked for the historians' motto. We honor our assignment at contextual reconstruction most often in the breach, perhaps, but our discipline is inherently holistic and better nurtures that contextual perspective which is so often defeated by the training of the economist or psychologist, by the organizational confines of the bureaucrat or executive.

I have attempted to sketch one version of an intellectual interface between policymakers and the discipline of history. Some think this engagement should be embodied chiefly in undergraduate and graduate training for those headed for policy careers, along with a steady flow of policy-oriented histories. Others wish to go beyond this cautious, campus-based contact, and to implant historical skills—which presumably means trained historians—within corporations and governments. And what are they to do? Some will manage records, some will write institutional histories. But are some to breach the policy process itself? The May group at Harvard might answer that historians touch that process as helpfully as they can when they instruct the decisionmakers, as we do in Chapel Hill. Teach them that they *will* draw upon history, that they will do it badly on the whole, that they must be wary of analogies and turn to them with skill and care, that they do not know an issue until they know its history, that organizations and individuals are captives of their own history and must seek a larger context for their thinking. Teach them the suffocating power of the "lessons" they carry in their heads. Teach them the meaning of time, and how to recognize where change holds sway and where continuity. Teach them a desire for context and the skills to frame holistic understandings. So might go the mission, in classrooms and research centers, of training people so that they would not have to say, as did T. S. Eliot in "Dry Salvages" from *Four Quartets*, "We had the experience but missed the meaning."

In my view we cannot stop there, but must and will go on to join the policy process itself, in forms we have yet to devise. Robert Kelley once launched an idea that led to a formal letter from a group of leading American historians asking that President Jimmy Carter establish in the White House an Office of Historical Studies, to be at work exploring the historical dimension of policy issues. There we would be, down the hall, more numerous and better staffed than Schlesinger when he served Kennedy or Goldman when he helped LBJ. Like the economists, we would have our council of advisors.

. . . A more promising route of infiltration leads through planning.

Institutionalized planning is important within large corporations and governments at all levels but that of the national state, where it is currently assumed that God will look after the future. People who perform this planning function in more enlightened institutions are called planners, with their own special training and sadness. But there is reason to believe that historians should be there. The purpose of planning, one might interject, is to make the *future* turn out differently, to produce forecasts and optional scenarios for decision-makers. True enough. But historians should begin to recognize that the future is or can be their second special terrain. Forecasting, after all, is not merely projection: it involves judgment. I like the summary statement of an English geographer, Peter Hall, who writes in his splendid book *Great Planning Disasters*:

> The heart of the problem [of reducing uncertainty and error] is to produce scenarios to suggest how events—technological, economic, social, cultural, political—will unfold and interrelate in the future. . . . This kind of activity is the stuff of history, and it needs a good historian to capture it, so as to write history in reverse.

I am persuaded that he is right, though historians may not quite yet be ready to be of such high service. Certainly Hall's conviction of our usefulness is not very widely shared by those who make policy. But the process has started, as I learned in conversation with the head of the history department at West Point. Several of his commissioned instructors, with Ph.D.'s in history, must occasionally be re-assigned from teaching to other parts of the Army. He finds that they take best to the work of the planning offices of the large Army groups, where their skills at research, literary exposition, and above all the construction of plausible social paths and combinations make them uniquely suited to the planning task. Army planning, unlike city planning, has no ready cadre of credentialed people, and thus reaches eagerly for more historians. Businesses and other large institutions might do some or more of the same, particularly if our public history graduate curricula begin to break down the walls between past and future.

Let me attempt a summary of the prospect so far sketched out. All "historians," however defined, practice history for clients (or, if inherited wealth eliminates all need of income, at least for an audience). The public historian accepts a more direct client relationship than the campus-based practitioners who have been the core of the profession since the expansion of the modern university. How might we summarize for the new clients the historical services to policymaking? At the margins of policy, historical research and analysis could provide orderly institutional records, a memory for internal issues and organization, shelves of studies of past decision-making. And, bolder if more problematical, specialists in social change from a discrete historical office or historians involved in the planning process might provide history-informed commentary upon institutional choices and scenarios for the future.

Historians in the latter role will not offer up tested, guaranteed models and formulas. They want to be more than memory banks. They offer a mode of analysis for future events, sharpened in the study of the human past. They offer an inhouse or consultative critique of the uses to which decisionmakers already put the past, to make those assumptions visible, then more sophisticated and perceptive. Their services should not be seen as "something of a luxury if not a distraction," in the words of one possible complaint, for they would provide not a new line of information so much as a critique and enlargement of an established one. And while tending to make complicated and vulnerable many of the simplistic institutional assumptions, historians need not be seen as our business students often initially saw them—as counselling delay or caution. Historians often see complexity and dampen the enthusiasm for striking démarches, but as often they enlarge the awareness of executive choice. In Rothman and Wheeler's words, the historian's perspective often leads to "a sharp and vital sense of options, opportunities, and abilities to maneuver."[2]

Having said so much in a positive vein about this new frontier for applied history, let me now work the other side of the street for a bit. As a historian speaking to historians, I am not surprised to discover a high degree of complexity about this matter, and confess that much that I see runs in cautionary directions. I am reminded of a comment Rex Tugwell made to me years ago when he learned that I had embarked upon a history of national planning: "You are getting into a swamp." I would only amend this to say that history, as the memory of the past, is already in a swamp of daily decisionmaking, and historians are trying to decide whether and in what formations to join her there.

Our hesitation is not attached to the idea of producing case studies of policy, public and private. We have been doing this quite happily for some time, though not, I think, with the sensitivity to the influence of institutional, cohort, and individual memories that one would have expected. Surely no one has major qualms about the archival function, or about providing institutional biographies and internal studies. It is the engagement with policy directly, and thus necessarily with the art of forecasting, that contributes the uneasiness. The threat to the scholar's objectivity mounts, most of us would concede, with the distance we move from Widener Library or a graduate seminar at Stanford toward the executive offices of governments or corporations. To become embroiled directly, or even in the somewhat consultative mode of the planner offering options, is to share responsibility for huge stakes.

This is not only new, but after the first wipeout, the first conspicuously bad historical advice, historians will have to deal with an unpleasant and quite warping memory of their own and the pressure it exerts upon objectivity. If we bring bad news, we will learn that, unlike students, grown people often shoot the messenger. Historians in such situations will be expected "to get on the team," experiencing a more intense organizational pressure than that normally felt in acedemic settings. They will feel Irving Janis's "groupthink" more intensely than in faculty meetings, it might be anticipated, since private sector organizations tend to have more focussed goals. Faculty meetings, sometimes stifling, do not produce much organizational discipline. Historians working for off-campus clients will be expected to hurry, to simplify, and to condense, when all their instincts as historians will lead them toward the complex, toward reconsidering and stretching out nets of qualification. They will hear their employers, like Harry Truman, plead for one-handed historian advisors. "When I have a problem," said one executive, "I want it addressed. Historians bleed too much." Historians may enjoy such work, with its opportunities for challenge and influence and earning a living at their trade. But they will be eternally reminded of the airline stewardess who noticed the enormous diamond on the hand of a female traveller, whose admiring remark was met with: "It is the Plotkin Diamond, third largest in the world." "How marvelous!" "Not really; it comes with a curse." "What curse?" "Plotkin!"

And these will be the most straightforward of our problems, those external to our craft, deriving from the institutional setting within which policy-oriented "applied historians" might work. More vexing, I suspect, will be our unreadiness as a profession for this new assignment. Like the weatherman, a historian cannot predict the future. Some of us do not believe in the effort, and the rest have little experience in trying. Those of us ready for the attempt may be armed with the strong belief that we would make fewer errors than those economists or sociologists or futurologists who have preceded us in guessing about the future, but we must admit to having little track record and some chastening professional handicaps.

These must be confronted by anyone touting the historian's advisory potential for policymakers. The analytical virtues of the historians' method, as I have asserted them, may be an abstraction, selectively derived from our collective performance over time, and especially from the great histories written in the era when synthesis seemed possible. Can today's historians offer that blend of sequence and setting, time and context that I sketched earlier? Perhaps the academic reverence for the monograph is so widespread that few of us are tuned up to offer the historian's largest perspective, to recreate whole situations. We are devoted to synthesis as individuals, but in an average year we are not required to do much of it. There may be among us more atrophied muscles for synthesis than we know. Certainly the historians' passion for blending time and context, sequence and setting is not always evident in our individual publications, nor adequately realized in our graduate training. The annual bibliographies reveal us, one sometimes thinks, as a race of monographers who honor synthesis but have left it to textbook writers or practice it only in unrecorded classroom exertions.

Our profession may not yet be fully ready to serve policymakers in other respects. For work on the contemporary era—the only interest of policymakers—we must possess that broad social knowledge to which the master historians of nineteenth-century America aspired, but which today eludes most of us: knowledge of the natural as well as the social sciences, commerce and technology, as well as politics, ideas, and culture. To assist in policymaking in small and closed systems we need not be Encyclopedists. But large organizations venturing to act in, influence, and even control broad patterns of social behavior require historian-advisors (as well as policymakers) with broad educations. The narrow training of today's business executives is often acknowledged as a painful fact. It may be doubted that we historians are fully ready for our own part in guiding large decisions, should this role materialize.

Finally, our clients will discover that, even more than doctors, car mechanics, and bridge engineers, perhaps even more than the confident psychologists and economists whose services have long been used by corporations and government, historians don't agree. We are invigorated by reasonable levels of controversy, like all other professionals. Yet recently we have been even less in agreement than before about what are the answers, indeed the questions themselves, as well as the methods for making headway toward understanding. We have lost such consensus as we had concerning the principles upon which the narrative synthesis could be constructed. We are in an era of fragmentation, reductionism, intense digging in isolated areas for insights which are hard to connect in a unified whole. Gene Wise, among others, suggests that the history profession is in a "paradigm shift" similar to that described in science by Thomas Kuhn. However one describes the intellectual ferment and questioning among those writing history, the question, "Where are we in the stream of time?" must be directed not only toward public historians' clients but also toward the scholars themselves.

Historians are further split by our usual biases toward ideas or social structure, toward economic, psychological, or political motivations. We do not agree on the role of social theory. Some of us are avid to use and improve theory. Others see chance and contingency, and agree with Tawney that "Life is a Swallow, but theory is a snail," or with Eric Lampard, who hopes that historians will begin "holding up 'scientific' findings and rhetoric, especially when they contain generalizations about the past, to broader standards of historical experience. . . . The more historical experience we can persuade policy science to include in the parameters of its models, the more likely its predictions would end up as tentative and confused as the exogenous world it presumes to straighten out."

We must acknowledge that historians are not even agreed upon time. How much of it does the historian analyze, in order to see what man could and could not do? The European historians tend to use one end of the telescope, discerning broad and long cultural patterns, and disdaining "events." The Americanists more typically are convinced that in any short run, men may break away from established patterns, that short pieces of time are workable analytic units. Thus on several levels clients may find us, in the 1980s, less unified in outlook than other professionals for hire (though a glance toward economists brings relative reassurance).

But no more of this survey of our imperfections. One is never fully prepared when opportunity opens. Let us advance along the learning curve! People are going to continue to believe that history teaches this or that and apply these lessons to present and future. It is an error to underestimate the importance of this sort of reasoning in the world at large, and futility to admonish the amateurs to refrain. As Woodrow Wilson said of the British maritime violations during our neutrality period in World War I: "We are face to face with something they are going to do, and they are going to do it no matter what representations we make." In our case, policymakers public and private will continue to use and misuse history in deploying fateful power.

If a thing is to be done, it ought to be done well. Mindful of the shortcomings of our profession even in traditional roles, which of us would cede the uses of the past to untutored persons successful in other lines of work? Who would hold historians back, almost alone among social scientists, from answering the need for advice and counsel? What other discipline or profession or hobby reaches out to embrace the entire human past, while not unmindful of the non-human environment which shapes human life? Who else will come equipped as both social scientists, with the commitment to theory as well as exactitude, and as humanists, who know that not everything that can be measured is really important?

In light of these reflections, at once sobering and emboldening, I suggest that we catch up to our runaway followers, even if they have run into unsavory neighborhoods on dubious errands, and do a little leading toward the wiser uses of the past.

References

1. For a more positive view of the use of analogy, see Peter Stearns and Joel Tarr, "Applied History: New/Old Frontier for the Historical Discipline," *Institute News* 1 (October 1982): 6–9. More skeptical is Seymour Mandelbaum, "The Past in Service to the Future," *Journal of Social History* 11 (Winter 1977): 193–204.

2. David Rothman and Stanton Wheeler, eds., *Social History and Social Policy* (New York: Academic Press, 1981), 1–7.

CONCLUSION

In many ways we live in an antihistorical age, antihistorical in the sense that significant numbers of people doubt the past's ability to speak meaningfully to the present. Such attitudes seem especially evident in the second half of the twentieth century. Perhaps they should not be surprising in societies drastically transformed by science and technology, where attachments to place and family have been severely ruptured.

But are such attitudes wise? We remain immersed in the past, our lives inextricably bound up with what went before. History impinges upon us in innumerable ways and at many different levels of consciousness. As Becker reminded us, our memory of often mundane past events influences our daily behavior. Perkin noted that "the very fields and footpaths, streets and houses, pubs and churches, shops and public buildings have been placed where they are in relation to each other by men in the past, and for better or worse we still have to live with their decisions." Consider the mass media and notice the multitude of images portraying the past to be found there. When you watch a motion picture or a television program, be it a fictional account or a documentary, observe the uses of history and the number of references made deliberately or otherwise to the past. Turn to a best-seller list and note how many books offer fictional reconstructions of the past.

Much of our orientation in the present and our plans for the future rest with our understanding of history. Frequently memories of a strictly personal nature or of previous happenings from our local environment strongly influence our actions. Sometimes our interpretations of why major historical events occurred dictate important decisions about political, social, economic, and religious issues. How often in our generation, for example, does our understanding of World War II or Vietnam affect the way we think of politics? One recalls the words of the novelist William Faulkner: "The past isn't dead; it isn't even past."

We return to the original question posed in this book: How valuable is history for our generation? Is it possible to make sense out of the world around us or to function intelligently without an understanding of history? In the final selection in this book, David Hackett Fischer rejects a number of arguments sometimes given for studying history and offers several others of his own. The most important function of history, he believes, is to teach people "how to think historically." The fact that we live in a new age, one of nuclear, biological, and chemical weapons, makes this task not less urgent but more so. "If men continue to make the *historical* error of conceptualizing the problems of a nuclear world in prenuclear terms, there will not be a postnuclear world," he warns. Reason as developed through the study of history may be "a pathetically frail weapon in the face of such a threat. But it is the *only* weapon we have."

The Importance
of Thinking Historically

David Hackett Fischer

David Hackett Fischer (b. 1935) has spent most of his professional career teaching at Brandeis University in addition to visiting appoint-
ments at Harvard and the University of Washington. He has a special
interest in historiography. In addition to *Historians' Fallacies* (1970),
from which the following selection is taken, he has also written *Growing Old in America* (1977).

*A*ny serious attempt to answer the question "What is good
history?" leads quickly to another—namely, "What is it good
for?" To raise this problem in the presence of a working historian is to risk a violent reaction. For it requires him to justify his
own existence, which is particularly difficult for a historian to do—
not because his existence is particularly unjustifiable, but because a
historian is not trained to justify existences. Indeed, he is trained not
to justify them. It is usually enough for him that he exists, and
history, too. He is apt to be impatient with people who doggedly
insist upon confronting the question.

Nevertheless, the question must be confronted, because the answer is in doubt. In our own time, there is a powerful current of
popular thought which is not merely unhistorical but actively anti-
historical as well. Novelists and playwrights, natural scientists and
social scientists, poets, prophets, pundits, and philosophers of many
persuasions have manifested an intense hostility to historical
thought. Many of our contemporaries are extraordinarily reluctant
to acknowledge the reality of past time and prior events, and stubbornly resistant to all arguments for the possibility or utility of historical knowledge.

The doctrine of historical relativism was no sooner developed by historians than it was seized by their critics and proclaimed to the world as proof that history-as-actuality is a contradiction in terms, and that history-as-record is a dangerous delusion which is, at best, an irrelevance to the predicament of modern man, and at worst a serious menace to his freedom and even to his humanity. . . .

These prejudices have become a major theme of modern literature. Many a fictional protagonist has struggled frantically through six hundred pages to free himself from the past, searching for a sanctuary in what Sartre called "a moment of eternity," and often finding it in a sexual embrace.

In Aldous Huxley's *After Many a Summer Dies the Swan*, Mr. Propter is made to say, "After all, history isn't the real thing. Past time is only evil at a distance; and of course, the study of past time is itself a process in time. Cataloguing bits of fossil evil can never be more than an ersatz for eternity." In the same author's *The Genius and the Goddess*, John Rivers compares history to a "dangerous drug" and dismisses it as a productive discipline of knowledge:

> God isn't the son of memory: He's the son of Immediate Experience. You can't worship a spirit in spirit, unless you do it now. Wallowing in the past may be good literature. As wisdom, it's hopeless. Time Regained is Paradise Lost, and Time Lost is Paradise Regained. Let the dead bury their dead. If you want to live at every moment as it presents itself, you've got to die at every other moment. That's the most important thing I learned.

Some entertaining errors of the same sort appear in John Barth's splendid picaresque novel *The Sot-Weed Factor*, where, in sixty-five chapters, Clio is ravished as regularly as most of the major characters. In an epilogue, the author writes,

> Lest it be objected by a certain stodgy variety of squint-minded antiquarians that he has in this lengthy history played more fast and loose with Clio, the chronicler's muse, than ever Captain John Smith dared, the Author here points in advance, by way of surety, three blue-chip replies arranged in order of decreasing relevancy. In the first place be it remembered, as Burlingame himself observed, that we all invent our pasts, more or less, as we go along, at the dictates of Whim and Interest. . . . Moreover, this Clio was already a scarred and crafty trollop when the Author found her; it wants a nice-honed casuist, with her

sort, to separate seducer from the seduced. But if, despite all, he is convicted at the Public Bar of having forced what slender virtue the strumpet may make claim to, then the Author joins with pleasure the most engaging company imaginable, his fellow fornicators, whose ranks include the noblest in poetry, prose and politics; condemnation at such a bar, in short, on such a charge, does honor to artist and artifact alike.

Other literati have set their sights on historians, rather than history. Virginia Woolf asserted, "It is always a misfortune to have to call in the services of any historian. A writer should give us direct certainty; explanations are so much water poured with the wine. As it is, we can only feel that these counsels are addressed to ladies in hoops and gentlemen in wigs—a vanished audience which has learnt its lesson and gone its way and the preacher with it. We can only smile and admire the clothes." Similar sentiments are cast as characterizations of historians in Sartre's *Nausea*, Kingsley Amis's *Lucky Jim*, George Orwell's *1984*, Aldous Huxley's *Antic Hay*, Wyndham Lewis's *Self-Condemned*, Anatole France's *Le Crime de Silvestre Bonnard*, Edward Albee's *Who's Afraid of Virginia Woolf?*, Stanley Elkin's *Boswell*, and Angus Wilson's *Anglo-Saxon Attitudes*. "It's so seldom that Clio can aid the other muses," says one character in the latter work. "Bloody fools, these historians," growls another.

The antihistorical arguments of our own time have infected historians themselves, with serious results. . . . I have heard five different apologies for history from academic colleagues—five justifications which are functional in the sense that they permit a historian to preserve some rudimentary sense of historicity, but only at the cost of all ideas of utility.

First, there are those who claim that history is worth writing and teaching because, in the words of one scholar, "It is such fun!"[1] But this . . . argument . . . is scarcely sufficient to satisfy a student who is struggling to master strange masses of facts and interpretations which are suddenly dumped on him in History I. It is unlikely to gratify a graduate student, who discovers in the toil and loneliness of his apprenticeship the indispensable importance of a quality which the Germans graphically call *Sitzfleisch*. It will not be persuasive to a social scientist who is pondering the pros and cons of a distant journey to dusty archives. It cannot carry weight with a general reader, who is plodding manfully through a pedantic monograph which his conscience tells him he really ought to finish. Nor will it reach a public servant who is faced with the problem of distributing the pathetically limited pecuniary resources which are presently available for social research. And I doubt that it has even persuaded those historiographical hedonists who invoke it in defense of their profession.

For most rational individuals, the joys of history are tempered by the heavy labor which research and writing necessarily entail, and by the pain and suffering which suffuses so much of our past. Psychologists have demonstrated that pleasure comes to different people in different ways, including some which are utterly loathesome to the majority of mankind. If the doing of history is to be defended by the fact that some historians are happy in their work, then its mass appeal is likely to be as broad as flagellation. . . .

Another common way in which historians justify historical scholarship is comparable to the way in which a mountain-climbing fanatic explained his obsession with Everest—"because it is there." By this line of thinking, history-as-actuality becomes a Himalayan mass of masterless crags and peaks, and the historian is a dauntless discoverer, who has no transcendent purpose beyond the triumphant act itself. If the object is remote from the dismal routine of daily affairs, if the air is thin and the slopes are slippery, if the mountain is inhabited merely by an abominable snowman or two, then all the better! If the explorer deliberately chooses the most difficult route to his destination, if he decides to advance by walking on his hands, or by crawling on his belly, then better still! By this convenient theory, remoteness is a kind of relevance, and the degree of difficulty is itself a defense.

This way of thinking is a tribute to the tenacity of man's will but not to the power of his intellect. If a task is worth doing merely because it is difficult, then one might wish with Dr. Johnson that it were impossible. And if historical inquiry is merely to be a moral equivalent to mountaineering for the diversion of chairborne adventurers, then historiography itself becomes merely a hobbyhorse for the amusement of overeducated unemployables.

A third common justification for history is the argument that there are certain discrete facts which every educated person needs to know. This view has been explicitly invoked to defend the teaching of required history courses to college freshmen, and to defend much research as well. But it is taxonomic in its idea of facts and tautological in its conception of education. What it calls facts are merely the conventional categories of historians' thought which are reified into history itself. And what it calls education is merely the mindless mastery of facts—a notion not far removed from the rote learning which has always flourished in the educational underworld but which no serious educational thinker has ever countenanced.

There are *no* facts which *everyone* needs to know—not even facts of the first historiographical magnitude. What real difference can knowledge of the fact of the fall of Babylon or Byzantium make in the daily life of anyone except a professional historian? Facts, discrete facts, will not in themselves make a man happy or wealthy or wise. They will not help him to deal intelligently with any modern problem which he faces, as man or citizen. Facts of this sort, taught in this way, are merely empty emblems of erudition which certify that certain formal pedagogical requirements have been duly met. If this method is mistaken for the marrow of education, serious damage can result.

Fourth, it is sometimes suggested that history is worth doing because it is "an outlet for the creative urge."[2] Undoubtedly, it is such a thing. But there are many outlets for creativity. Few are thought sufficient to justify the employment of thousands of highly specialized individuals at a considerable expense to society.

Tombstone rubbing is a creative act. So is the telling of tall stories. If history is to be justified on grounds of its creative aspect, then it must be shown to be a constructive, good, useful, or beautiful creative act. . . .

A fifth justification for history is cast in terms of the promise of future utility. I have heard historians suggest that their random investigations are a kind of pure research, which somebody, someday, will convert to constructive use, though they have no idea who, when, how, or why. The important thing, they insist, is not to be distracted by the dangerous principle of utility but to get on with the job. It is thought sufficient for an authority on Anglo-Saxon England to publish "important conclusions that all Anglo-Saxonists will have to consider." If enough historians write enough histories, then something—the great thing itself—is sure to turn up. In the meantime we are asked to cultivate patience, humility, and pure research.

This argument calls to mind the monkeys who were set to typing the works of Shakespeare in the British Museum. So vast is the field of past events, and so various are the possible methods and interpretations, that the probability is exceedingly small that any single project will prove useful to some great social engineer in the future. And the probability that a series of random researches will become a coherent science of history is still smaller.

A comparable problem was studied by John Venn some years ago. He calculated the probability of drawing the text of *Paradise Lost* letter by letter from a bag containing all twenty-six signs of the alphabet—each letter to be replaced after it is drawn, and the bag thoroughly shaken. Assuming that there were 350,000 letters in the poem, Venn figured the odds at 1 in $26^{350,000}$, which if it were written out, would be half again as long as the poem itself. . . .

A series of researches can be expected to yield a coherent result only if they are *not* random. If a historian hopes that his work will promote some future purpose, then he must have some idea of what that purpose might be. The question cannot be postponed to another day. It must be faced now. . . .

All five of these justifications for history are functional to historical scholarship, but only in the sense that they serve to sustain a rough and rudimentary historicity in the work of scholars who have lost their conceptual bearings. But these attitudes are seriously dysfunctional in two other ways. First, they operate at the expense of all sound ideas of social utility. Secondly, they stand in the way of a refinement of historicity, beyond the crude level of contemporary practice.

ACADEMIC HISTORIANS have been coming in for a good deal of abuse lately, and with a great deal of justification. There is a rising chorus of criticism which is directed principally against the sterility and social irrelevance of their scholarship. Only a few professional pollyannas would assert that these complaints are without cause.

But the reform proposals that accompany these protests are worse than the deficiencies they are designed to correct. Historians of many ideological persuasions are increasingly outspoken in their determination to reform historical scholarship, and often exceedingly bitter about the willful blindness of an alleged academic establishment which supposedly stands in their way. But these reformers are running to an opposite error.

Historians are increasingly urged to produce scholarship of a kind which amounts to propaganda. There is, of course, nothing new in this idea. It appeared full-blown in the work of James Harvey Robinson and other so-called New Historians more than fifty years ago. There was much of it after the Second World War, in the manifestoes of conservative anti-Communist scholars such as Conyers Read, and in the monographs of liberal activists during the 1950s. There is still a great deal of it today in Eastern Europe, where more than a few historians imagine that they are "scholar-fighters," in the service of world socialism. Today, in America and Western Europe, this idea is being adopted with increasing fervor by young radical historians, who regard all aspirations to objectivity as a sham and a humbug, and stubbornly insist that the real question is not whether historians can be objective, but which cause they will be subjective to.

These scholars are in quest of something which they call a "usable past." But the result is neither usable nor past. It ends merely in polemical pedantry, which is equally unreadable and inaccurate.

There have always been many historians who were more concerned that truth should be on their side than that they should be on the side of truth. This attitude is no monopoly of any sect or generation. But wherever it appears in historical scholarship, it is hateful in its substance and horrible in its results. To make historiography into a vehicle for propaganda is simply to destroy it. The problem of the utility of history is not solved but subverted, for what is produced by this method is not history at all. The fact that earlier generations and other ideological groups have committed the same wrong does not convert it into a right. . . .

IF HISTORY IS WORTH DOING TODAY, then it must *not* be understood either in terms of historicity without utility, or of utility without historicity. Instead, both qualities must be combined. . . .

History can be useful, as history, in several substantive ways. It can serve to clarify contexts in which contemporary problems exist—not by a presentist method of projecting our own ideas into the past but rather as a genuinely empirical discipline, which is conducted with as much objectivity and historicity as is humanly possible. Consider one quick and obvious example—the problem of Negro-white relations in America. It is surely self-evident that this subject cannot be intelligently comprehended without an extended sense of how it has developed through time. Negro Americans carry their history on their backs, and they are bent and twisted and even crippled by its weight. The same is true, but less apparent, of white Americans, too. And precisely the same thing applies to every major problem which the world faces today. Historians can help to solve them, but only if they go about their business in a better way—only if they become more historical, more empirical, and more centrally committed to the logic of a problem-solving discipline.

Historical inquiry can also be useful not merely for what it contributes to present understanding but also for what it suggests about the future. A quasi-historical method is increasingly used, in many disciplines, for the purpose of forecasting—for establishing trends and directions and prospects. Historians themselves have had nothing to do with such efforts, which many of them would probably put in a class with phrenology. Maybe they should bear a hand, for they have acquired by long experience a kind of tacit temporal sophistication which other disciplines conspicuously lack—a sophistication which is specially theirs to contribute.

Third, history can be useful in the refinement of theoretical knowledge, of an "if, then" sort. Econometric historians have already seized upon this possibility, and political historians are not far behind. What, for example, are the historical conditions in which social stability, social freedom, and social equality have tended to be *maximally* coexistent? No question is more urgent today, when tyranny, inequality, and instability are not merely disagreeable but dangerous to humanity itself. This is work which a few historians are beginning to do. Maybe it is time that more of them addressed such problems, more directly.

Fourth, historical scholarship can usefully serve to help us find out who we are. It helps people to learn something of themselves, perhaps in the way that a psychoanalyst seeks to help a patient. Nothing could be more productive of sanity and reason in this irrational world. Historians, in the same way, can also help people to learn about other selves. And nothing is more necessary to the peace of the world. Let us have no romantic humbug about brotherhood and humanity. What is at stake is not goodness but survival. Men must learn to live in peace with other men if they are to live at all. The difficulties which humanity has experienced in this respect flow *partly* from failures of intellect and understanding. Historical knowledge may help as a remedy—not a panacea, but a partial remedy.

And if this is to happen, professional historians must hold something more than a private conversation with themselves. They must reach millions of men, and they will never do so through monographs, lectures, and learned journals. I doubt that they can hope to accomplish this object by literary history or by the present forms of popular history. Instead, they must begin to exploit the most effective media of mass communication—television, radio, motion pictures, newspapers, etc. They cannot assign this task to middlemen. If the message is left to communications specialists, it is sure to be garbled in transmission. All of these uses of history, as history, require the development of new strategies, new skills, and new scholarly projects.

In addition to these four substantive services which historians can hope to provide, there is another one which I regard as even more important. Historians have a heavy responsibility not merely to teach people substantive historical truths but also to teach them how to think historically. There is no limit to the number of ways in which normative human thinking is historical. Nobody thinks historically all the time. But everybody thinks historically much of the time. Each day, every rational being on this planet asks questions about things that actually happened—questions which directly involve the logic of inquiry, explanation, and argument which is discussed in this book.

These operations rarely involve the specific substantive issues that now engage the professional thoughts of most historians. They do not touch upon the cause of the First World War, or the anatomy of revolutions, or the motives of Louis XIV, or the events of the industrial revolution. Instead, this common everyday form of historical thought consists of specific inquiries into small events, for particular present and future purposes to which all the academic monographs in the world are utterly irrelevant.

Historical thought ordinarily happens in a thousand humble forms—when a newspaper writer reports an event and a newspaper reader peruses it; when a jury weighs a fact in dispute, and a judge looks for a likely precedent; when a diplomat compiles an *aide-memoire* and a doctor constructs a case history; when a soldier analyzes the last campaign, and a statesman examines the record; when a householder tries to remember if he paid the rent, and when a house builder studies the trend of the market. Historical thinking happens even to sociologists, economists, and political scientists in nearly all of their major projects. Each of these operations is in some respects (not all respects) historical. If historians have something to learn from other disciplines, they have something to teach as well.

The vital purpose of refining and extending a logic of historical thought is not merely some pristine goal of scholarly perfection. It involves the issue of survival. Let us make no mistake about priorities. If men continue to make the *historical* error of conceptualizing the problems of a nuclear world in prenuclear terms, there will not be a postnuclear world. If people persist in the *historical* error of applying yesterday's programs to today's problems, we may suddenly run short of tomorrow's possibilities. If we continue to pursue the ideological objectives of the nineteenth century in the middle of the twentieth, the prospects for a twenty-first are increasingly dim. . . .

Responsible and informed observers have estimated that by the 1990s as many as forty-eight nations may possess nuclear weapons. As the number of these arsenals increases arithmetically, the probability of their use grows in geometric ratio. Biological and chemical weapons of equal destructive power and even greater horror are already within the reach of most sovereign powers, and many private groups as well.

Natural scientists have helped to create this deadly peril; now it is the business of social scientists to keep it in bounds. Here is work for historians to do—work that is largely educational in nature— work that consists in teaching men somehow to think reasonably about their condition. Reason is indeed a pathetically frail weapon in the face of such a threat. But it is the *only* weapon we have.

References

1. Fritz Stern, ed., *Varieties of History: From Voltaire to the Present* (New York: Meridian Books, 1957), 30.

2. Norman Cantor and Richard I. Schneider, *How to Study History* (New York: Crowell, 1967), 3. For a more extended argument, see Emery Neff, *The Poetry of History* (New York: Columbia University Press, 1947).

INDEX